T0339995

e-Research

Routledge Advances in Research Methods

1. e-Research
Transformation in Scholarly Practice
Edited by Nicholas W. Jankowski

e-Research
Transformation in Scholarly Practice

Edited by
Nicholas W. Jankowski

Routledge
Taylor & Francis Group
New York   London

First published 2009
by Routledge
711 Third Avenue, New York, NY 10017

Simultaneously published in the UK
by Routledge
2 Park Square, Milton Park, Abingdon, Oxon OX14 4RN

Routledge is an imprint of the Taylor & Francis Group, an informa business
First published in paperback 2012

© 2009 Taylor & Francis

All rights reserved. No part of this book may be reprinted or reproduced or utilised in any form or by any electronic, mechanical, or other means, now known or hereafter invented, including photocopying and recording, or in any information storage or retrieval system, without permission in writing from the publishers.

Trademark Notice: Product or corporate names may be trademarks or registered trademarks, and are used only for identification and explanation without intent to infringe.

Library of Congress Cataloging-in-Publication Data

E-research : transformation in scholarly practice / edited by Nicholas W. Jankowski.
    p. cm.—(Routledge advances in research methods ; 1)
    Includes bibliographical references and index.
    1. Social sciences—Computer network resources.   2. Social sciences—
Research.   3. Social sciences—Methodology.   4. Internet research.   I. Jankowski, Nick.
    H61.95.E22 2009
    300.285'4678—dc22
    2009003903

Book Web site: http://www.virtualknowledgestudio.nl/scholarly-transformation/

ISBN13: 978-0-415-99028-8 (hbk)
ISBN13: 978-0-203-87504-9 (ebk)
ISBN13: 978-0-415-64753-3 (pbk)

Contents

List of Figures   ix
List of Tables   xi
Acknowledgments   xiii

PART I
Introduction

1   The Contours and Challenges of e-Research   3
NICHOLAS W. JANKOWSKI

PART II
Conceptualization

2   Towards a Sociology of e-Research:
Shaping Practice and Advancing Knowledge   35
JENNY FRY AND RALPH SCHROEDER

3   e-Research as Intervention   54
ANNE BEAULIEU AND PAUL WOUTERS

PART III
Development

4   Developing the UK-based e-Social Science Research Program   73
PETER HALFPENNY, ROB PROCTER, YU-WEI LIN AND ALEX VOSS

5   e-Research and Scholarly Community in the Humanities   91
PAUL GENONI, HELEN MERRICK AND MICHELE WILLSON

6   The Rise of e-Science in Asia. Dreams and Realities for Social
Science Research: Case Studies of Singapore and South Korea   109
CAROL SOON AND HAN WOO PARK

PART IV
Collaboration

7 Creating Shared Understanding across Distance: Distance
Collaboration across Cultures In R&D 129
PETRA SONDEREGGER

8 Moving from Small Science to Big Science: Social and
Organizational Impediments to Large Scale Data Sharing 147
ERIC T. MEYER

PART V
Visualization

9 Visualization in e-Social Science 163
MIKE THELWALL

10 A Picture is Worth a Thousand Questions: Visualization
Techniques for Social Science Discovery in Computational Spaces 182
HOWARD T. WELSER, THOMAS M. LENTO, MARC A. SMITH, ERIC GLEAVE
AND ITAI HIMELBOIM

PART VI
Data Preservation and Reuse

11 Web Archiving as e-Research 205
STEVEN M. SCHNEIDER, KIRSTEN A. FOOT AND PAUL WOUTERS

12 The Promise of Data in e-Research: Many Challenges,
Multiple Solutions, Diverse Outcomes 222
ANN ZIMMERMAN, NATHAN BOS, JUDITH S. OLSON AND GARY M. OLSON

13 Naming, Documenting and Contributing to e-Science 240
SAMUELLE CARLSON AND BEN ANDERSON

PART VII
Access and Intellectual Property

14 Open Access to e-Research 259
ROBERT LUCAS AND JOHN WILLINSKY

15 Intellectual Property in the Context of e-Science 273
DAN L. BURK

PART VIII: Case Studies

16 Situated Innovations in e-Social Science   291
    BRIDGETTE WESSELS AND MAX CRAGLIA

17 Wikipedia as Distributed Knowledge Laboratory:
    The Case of Neoliberalism   310
    CLIFFORD TATUM AND MICHELLE LAFRANCE

Contributors   329
Index   339

Figures

1.1	e-Research as interrelated clusters of scholarly tasks.	8
6.1	Organization structure of the national Grid.	112
9.1	Basic visualization choices for researchers.	168
9.2	A history flow visualization of the Wikipedia chocolate page.	170
9.3	A screen-shot of an Evolino simulation.	171
9.4	Blog posts alluding to visualization during 2007–2008.	173
9.5	A Google TouchGraph of 'Cyberinfrastructure'	174
9.6	The MySpace friends of one person, illustrated by a mashup.	176
9.7	The Figure 9.6 mashup after zooming in with four mouse clicks.	176
10.1	Treemap of posts to Microsoft public hierarchy, circa 2001.	192
10.2	Treemap and hyperbolic graph of invitation and language group.	192
10.3	Detail tree map of 528111's descendents and Highlight of 528111's lineage.	193
10.4	Community size compared to number of posts across classes of discussion groups.	194
10.5	Days active compared to posts per thread within different support newsgroups.	195

10.6   Graphs of a thread and the larger group context.   197

10.7   Egocentric neighborhood visualizations of social
         network participants.   198

10.8   Combining types of visualizations to identify roles.   199

16.1   The White Rose Grid portal architecture.   299

16.2   Modeled distribution of offenders, England at 5 km.   303

16.3   Scheduling the job from the White Rose Grid portal.   303

16.4   OGC-compliant Web Map Service allowing overlay
         and query of distributed data.   305

17.1   Wikipedia page layout.   316

17.2   Neoliberalism article: Edit activity and word count.   319

17.3   Neutral point of view (NPOV) placard.   320

Tables

2.1	Approaches to e-Research as an Object of Research	39
2.2	Approaches to e-Research as an Object of Development	39
4.1	Node Research Themes 2004–2007	77
6.1	Expenditure of National e-Science Budget	115
6.2	Web site Sizes of Korean Politician Homepages	120
9.1	Classification of Visualizations	165
10.1	Dimensions of Social Spaces that Alter Social Action	186
17.1	Edit Distribution among Contributors to the Neoliberalism Article & Talk Page	318

Acknowledgments

So many people contributed so much to this project, an undertaking stretching across four years, that it is difficult knowing how to formulate an adequate expression of appreciation. The project was conceived during a half-year fellowship in the spring of 2004 at the Oxford Internet Institute (OII). I was invited to join OII while helping coordinate another project on the uptake of the Internet by a range of political actors during national elections. Without knowing it at the time, that Internet & Elections (I&E) Project reflected many of the core features of what was labeled elsewhere e-science: international collaboration, Internet-based data collection and analysis, use of large datasets, research management performed primarily through mediated forms of communication. OII provided a diverse and stimulating intellectual environment within which to undertake that project. Conversations with Bill Dutton, Stephen Coleman, Ted Nelson, Alexandre Caldas, Miriam Lips, and John Taylor were particularly refreshing and provoking. I had the exceptionally good fortune to secure temporary housing in the same student-style brick house in Oxford's Jericho neighborhood where OII staff member Ralph Schroeder was then lodging. This chance arrangement facilitated opportunity for frequent collective walks to the office, and end-of-the-day drinks and meals. During the course of this project, Ralph and I collaborated on several events including preparation of a day-long workshop at a conference of the National Centre of e-Social Science (NCeSS) in Manchester and of a panel that was part of the Association of Internet Researchers (AoIR) conference in Vancouver.

Near the end of my stint at OII I had come to realize that 'something was a brew', often going by the name 'e-science'. My experiences with the I&E Project, a quick scan of the then limited literature, and my own basic instincts convinced me of its potential importance. About that time I approached Susan Herring, then editor of the *Journal of Computer-Mediated Communication* (JCMC) whether she would be interested in a theme issue. Her response was positive, and her editorial guidance throughout the trajectory of announcing the issue, selecting submissions, and preparing manuscripts for publication was exemplary of quality editorship. I am grateful for her guidance in preparing that issue, released in January 2007.

Arrangements with JCMC and Susan were such that some of the material prepared for that theme issue might constitute the basis for an edited volume. Many people contributed to the refinement of the proposal for that book, particularly staff members of the Virtual Knowledge Studio for the Social Sciences and Humanities (VKS) in Amsterdam, an initiative of the Royal Netherlands Academy of the Arts and Sciences. I became a Visiting Fellow of VKS in mid-2006, mainly with a mandate to complete the e-science book project, subsequently renamed 'e-research' for reasons provided in Chapter 1. During the two years at VKS I have enjoyed exposure to the broad range of intellectual interests reflected by its staff, past and present: Paul Wouters, Anne Beaulieu, Sally Wyatt, Charles van den Heuvel, Ernst Thoutenhoofd, Jan Kok, Andrea Scharnhorst, Iina Hellsten, Katie Vann, and Matt Ratto. The weekly VKS research meetings have been high points in my association with this group of colleagues, generous with their ideas and constructive criticisms. In addition, Andrea and I quite recently co-organized a double-billed panel on e-collaboration at the 2008 Oxford e-science conference.

Of course, the authors of the chapters to this book deserve special acknowledgement because of their intellectual labor, and their perseverance and commitment to this project. It has been a genuine pleasure working with this large, diverse, and talented group of scholars, and particularly pleasurable when that collaboration would transpire in face-to-face venues. Many of us have met at conferences, like at the NCeSS workshop, the AoIR panel, and the e-collaboration panel that was part of the Oxford eResearch Conference 2008. Several of us also took part in a special meeting at the Department of Media and Communications at Goldsmiths, University of London. The Goldsmiths event was notable for several reasons, including exposure to the healthy skepticism that several department staff expressed towards aspects of e-science. I am grateful to Natalie Fenton for initially arranging this event and to Guinevere Narraway and Tamara Witschge for arranging the logistics. Other presentations of material related to this project were made under the auspices of the European COST A30 Action research program 'East of West: Setting a New Central Eastern European Media Research Agenda' in Budapest, Milan, and Sarajevo. Those discussions were rich, enlightening, and illustrative of the large differences evident in the thinking about e-research across Europe.

Many others have contributed along the way, including students at a University of Ljubljana graduate seminar who engaged me in extended discussion about early versions of the introductory chapter. VKS colleagues also provided comment on that chapter—particularly Paul, Anne, Charles, Sally, and Ernst—as did several chapter authors, especially Eric Gleave and Ann Zimmerman. Loet Leydesdorft reminded me of the communication 'turn' and the need for discussion of research directions; Maja Turnšek Hančič made valuable suggestions on a range of issues, including the political economy of e-research initiatives; Steve Jones frequently shared materials on publishing innovations and tribulations, some of which found their way into the chapter section on scholarly communication. I am surely forgetting some persons and for this I apologize; such omission is unintentional and should not be construed as any more than fading memory—one of the human foibles e-research probably never will be able to repair.

In sum, once again, my thanks to all for their contributions to this project and I hope many more research initiatives related to e-research follow in its path.

Nick Jankowski, December 2008

Part I
Introduction

1 The Contours and Challenges of e-Research

Nicholas W. Jankowski

INTRODUCTION

Every so often major shifts emerge in the way society is imagined. Historical periods have acquired labels, albeit debated and disputed, that reflect such shifts: Reformation, Enlightenment, Industrial Revolution, Information Age. The scholarly enterprise has been integral to the formulation of these shifts and that enterprise itself has been the subject of transformation. Introduction of the experimental method is associated with such a shift, as is evolutionary theory; the switch from Newtonian physics to general acceptance of Einstein's theory of relativity also reflects such transformation. During the past few years, discussions in policy and academic circles suggest yet another move is underway, some claim revolutionary in scope, impacting the full breadth of the scholarly enterprise. This latest shift is attributed to the widespread availability and incorporation of high-speed computers and electronic networks, particularly the Internet, into the research enterprise, making very large volumes of data available that provide opportunity for addressing new questions in new ways. Reflection on this transformation of scholarship, particularly within the social sciences and humanities, is the concern of this book.

The signals suggesting such transformation are many: blue-ribbon committees have been mandated to explore changes and to recommend policy initiatives; national offices have been established to fund research and development; reports, proceedings, papers, and journal articles are appearing, as well as a handful of edited volumes such as this one. These signals span the spectrum of scholarly disciplines and are evident around the globe: in North America, Europe, Asia and Australasia. The signals are, understandably, stronger for some disciplines and countries than for others. Still, the overall strength of the indicators is substantial and reinforces need for a considered examination of the transformation.

This introductory chapter sketches the development of this transformation and begins with examination of competing terms currently in vogue that are meant to describe the change. The issues and challenges associated with these transformations constitute the substance of the contributions to this book but one issue, scholarly communication, is of overriding

importance and is sketched in this chapter. Next, the organizational structure of the book is elaborated with short introductions to the chapters in
each section of the book. Finally, a few remarks on further research directions are made in a concluding note.

CONCEPTUALIZING SCHOLARLY TRANSFORMATION

A small coterie of terms reflects current changes in the conduct of science and, more generally, of scholarship. The most prevalent of these are:
'e-science', 'cyberinfrastructure', and 'e-research'. These terms have historical antecedents and competitors for prominence. Beginning with the past,
one alternative conceptualization is 'Big Science' which initially described
weapons-related research during World War II, particularly the Manhat-
tan Project mandated to construct an atomic bomb. Big Science continued
through the Cold War and reflected government-sponsored research generally oriented towards weapons development and national security.[1] Subsequently, non-military projects, such as those associated with high-energy
physics laboratories like CERN in Geneva and initiatives to unravel DNA
like the Human Genome Project, took on the characteristics of Big Science.
All of these projects require a need for large-scale instrumentation, budgets running in the billions, and personnel numbering in the thousands. In
some cases, as with experiments involving particle accelerators like those
at CERN, distant collaboration among scientists is commonplace, often
crossing national borders. The transformation of science as reflected in
these features was identified relatively early by Alvin Weinberg (1961) in a
Science article eulogizing the passing of small-scale, solo scholarship.[2]

A more recent conceptualization is *cyberscience*, elaborated by Michael
Nentwich (2003) who provides a comprehensive overview of the transformations of science and scholarship, reflected in the subtitle of the volume:
'Research in the Age of the Internet'. Nentwich's definition of cyberscience
is broad: " . . . all scholarly and scientific research activities in the virtual
space generated by the networked computers and by advanced information and communication technologies in general" (Nentwich, 2003: 22).
Tracing the genealogy of the term, Nentwich (2003: 22, note 41) suggests
that it originated in an article by Paul Wouters (1996) and subsequently
surfaced in various papers and conference panels.[3] Use of the term has since
been mainly limited to publications and projects emerging from Nentwich's
institutional home, the Austrian Institute of Technology Assessment. In
addition, it appears in the title of a recent study by Christine Hine (2008),
Systematics as Cyberscience. Otherwise, the term seems to have faded into
disuse. Of more durability, however, has been the fundamental feature
present in both Nentwich's study, as in Wouters' initial formulation: an all-
encompassing approach that acknowledges the importance of computers
and electronic networks, but that is grounded in a broad vision of the scholarly enterprise. The inclusion of scholarly communication and publishing

within that approach resonates with the formulation of another conceptualization, e-research, which is outlined shortly.

The term *e-science* is basically a European version of the American term 'cyberinfrastructure'. Rooted in British initiatives, John Taylor, then Director General of the Office of Science and Technology in the U.K., is credited for coining it at the launch of a major funding initiative in 1999. The focus of e-science then, as now, was on the natural and biological sciences and was designed to facilitate the processing of very large volumes of data with the aid of Grid computer networks. Euphoric statements about transformation of the scientific enterprise marked the launch and subsequent promotion of e-science.[4] Shortly thereafter, in 2001, the National e-Science Centre (NeSC) was established, which has since become the main governmental body for coordinating and allocating funding for e-science projects in the U.K. One of the pages on the NeSC Web site sketches the anticipated trajectory of science:

> In the future, e-Science will refer to the large scale science that will increasingly be carried out through distributed global collaborations enabled by the Internet. Typically, a feature of such collaborative scientific enterprises is that they will require access to very large data collections, very large scale computing resources and high performance visualization back to the individual user scientists. (NeSC, n.d.)

In this description, as elsewhere, e-science is closely associated with Grid computer network architecture that enables the global collaboration considered basic to e-science.[5] These features are expected, in turn, to spurn development of new, specialized Internet-based tools for conducting research.

One of the spin-offs of the e-science development in the U.K. involved initiation of a government-sponsored office to stimulate and coordinate e-science in the social sciences (Jankowski & Caldas, 2004). Called the National Centre for e-Social Science (NCeSS) and launched in December 2004, it involves a decentralized structure of 'nodes' engaging universities across the U.K. Most of the projects emphasize incorporation of Grid computer architecture into the infrastructure of social science. An exception to this accentuation is the Oxford University node of the NCeSS, which takes a social-shaping approach (OeSS Project, n.d.). Although an exception, this node is embedded in the Computing Laboratory of Oxford University and, in that respect, reflects the original core concerns with e-science on computation and computer networks.

Another conceptualization, *cyberinfrastructure* is primarily rooted in initiatives based in the U.S. and was initially promoted in a commission report funded by the National Science Foundation (NSF) in 2003, subsequently known as the Atkins Report (2003): 'Revolutionizing Science and Engineering Through Cyberinfrastructure'. This title reflects the promotional and visionary language present throughout the document: "A new age has dawned," (p. 31), "The time is ripe," (p. 12), "a once-in-a-generation opportunity to lead the revolution" (p. 32). Basically, the term cyberinfrastructure refers to an infrastructure of distributed computer, information, and communication technologies. The development is seen as parallel to the infrastructures already integral to modern societies: roads and railways for transportation; water, gas, and power networks for basic services and resources.[6] In the words of the Atkins Report, "If infrastructure is required for an industrial economy, then . . . cyberinfrastructure is required for a knowledge economy" (Atkins, 2003: 5).

Not unsurprisingly, the first waves of cyberinfrastructure initiatives were situated in the natural and biological sciences where large volumes of data are involved in research endeavors requiring high-speed computer processing: particle physics, astronomy, meteorology, and DNA research. These initiatives typically involve collaboration with staff at supercomputing research centers.[7] Christine Borgman, (2007: 23), among others, argues that there has always been space within initial conceptualizations of cyberinfrastructure for the entire breadth of scholarly endeavor. And in a keynote NCeSS conference presentation, Noshir Contractor (2007) suggests that the components of cyberinfrastructure can be seen as spanning the gambit of university services: from high-performance computing, libraries, referral services, through training, outreach and mentoring services. Little is left out in the cold from such formulations of cyberinfrastructure, but they misconstrue where emphasis has been historically and is currently: in the fields of science and engineering that are engaged in processing large volumes of data with the aid of Grid computer networks and related software.

The Atkins Report, it should be stressed, is not so much a scientific publication, but a manifesto and, as such, is less concerned with conventional scholarly concerns such as qualification, criticism and evidence. The report can be easily dismissed for lacking such features, but Hine (2003: 2) reminds us that such perfunctory discarding of visionary statements misses opportunity for a potentially valuable scholarly enquiry into how these statements are translated into initiatives and, possibly, how some changes in the scientific enterprise may be impacted by the ideas and funding related to such visions. Although perhaps premature to assess the definitive contribution of the Atkins Report, it is fair to note that the concerns expressed in the document have found considerable institutional and disciplinary resonance. The NSF has established an Office of Cyberinfrastructure, suggesting a serious form of institutionalization. Various disciplines have established their own committees producing reports and initiatives to investigate ways to consciously take advantage of both the features and the funding being made available for cyberinfrastructure initiatives.[8]

These initiatives have not remained restricted to the natural and biological sciences. The American Council of Learned Societies (ACLS, 2006), for example, issued a report on cyberinfrastructures for the humanities and social sciences. Other efforts to integrate the social sciences are reflected in the introduction of social network analysis as a tool with which to study science communities (SNAC, 2005) and in many of the initiatives introducing Internet research and digital studies into university curricula and research programs (see, e.g., Nissenbaum & Price, 2004).

Elsewhere, a different approach has been taken where the term *e-research* is seen as more reflective of the work of both social scientists and scholars in the humanities, a terminological development also observed by Borgman (2007: 20). The contribution by Anne Beaulieu and Paul Wouters in this volume sketches this approach, as developed in the Netherlands, formally initiated in October 2006 and called the Virtual Knowledge Studio for the Humanities and Social Sciences (VKS). It can, in fact, be seen as successor to Wouters' earlier notion cyberscience, and as one more amenable to the conceptualization of scholarship in the social sciences and humanities. Moreover, the term e-research acknowledges forms of scholarship that do not primarily emphasize use of high-speed computers for processing large datasets, but that place weight on incorporation of a wide variety of new media and electronic networks in the research process; see Chapter 3.

Terminology in a terrain as dynamic as this one is difficult to pin down with precision. Undoubtedly, much more energy will be expended in the coming years on refining the ideas underlying the various conceptualizations. For the purposes of this volume, however, a broad pluralistic approach is more suitable than one narrowly formulated. Such an approach is better able to accommodate the diversity of disciplines and approaches under consideration, particularly given interest in a perspective inclusionary of both the social sciences and humanities. The following list can be construed as the seeds for a Web 2.0 'cloud' of e-research features, and concurrently reflects the concerns addressed by the contributors to this volume. Taken as a whole, these features suggest that e-research is a form of scholarship conducted in a network environment utilizing Internet-based tools and involving collaboration among scholars separated by distance, often on a global scale. Although the 'weight' and priority of these features varies by context and discipline, they nevertheless suggest areas where scholarship is undergoing transition:

- Increasing *computerization* of the research process, often involving high-speed, large capacity machines configures in a *networked environment*;
- Reliance on network-based *virtual organizational structures* for conducting research increasingly involving *distant collaboration* among researchers, often international in scope;
- Development of *Internet-based tools* facilitating many phases of the research process including communication, research management, data collection and analysis, and publication;
- Experimentation with new forms of data *visualization*, such as social network and hyperlink analysis, and multimedia and dynamic representations;
- *Publication, distribution and preservation* of scholarship via the Internet, utilizing traditional and formal avenues (e.g., publishing houses, digital libraries) as well as those less formal and less institutionalized (e.g., social networking sites, personal Web sites).

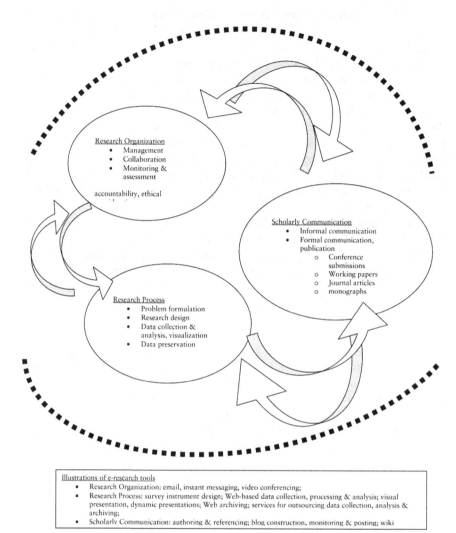

Figure 1.1   e-Research as interrelated clusters of scholarly tasks.

Figure 1.1 illustrates the interrelatedness of these features of e-research, situated within three clusters of activities associated with many forms of scholarship.[9] The context of these clusters is the networked environment mentioned above, typically the Internet, and may involve high-speed computers linked together via Grid construction. In the figure this environment is suggested by the unconnected dashed lines at the top and bottom. The broken features of the lines suggest the porous nature of the network: not everyone and everything is connected to and operating within a networked environment all of the time; research activities occur both within and outside this environment. The network infrastructure is very often (as in employment of email) taken-for-granted; in other cases, as when Grid computer architecture is used, involvement of specialists (e.g., computer scientists) may be required; see Chapter 16 for an illustration of such cross-disciplinary engagement.

The cluster situated in the upper-left of Figure 1.1, Research Organization, consists of the various divisions and tasks associated with managing an academic research project, often involving a principle investigator, senior academic participants, post-docs and PhD candidates, administrative and technical staff. In an e-research environment a 'virtual organization' is established to coordinate the tasks associated with these divisions, employing a variety of communicative tools that supplement face-to-face exchange for conducting business: email, instant messaging, video conferencing, wikis. Perhaps the key component of such a virtual organization is collaboration at a distance among project participants. Several contributions to this book examine collaboration, notably Chapters 7 and 8. Some of the activities of the Research Organization may relate to externally oriented concerns such as accountability exercises required by a funding body or for ethical issues as formulated by an Institutional Review Board. Ethical concerns in an e-research environment, however, are different from those of more conventional studies and require particular attention (see, e.g., Ess & AoIR Ethics Working Group, 2002; Jankowski & Van Selm, 2007).

The cluster located in the lower section of the figure, Research Process, reflects the tasks most often associated with the 'research act': problem formulation with a context of theoretical relevancy; construction of a research design with attention to data collection and analysis; and data preservation. In the e-research environment Internet-based tools are utilized for: instrument design and deployment (e.g., Web survey tools, Web site annotation tools); data analysis, qualitative and quantitative; and data preservation, often termed archiving, usually in a form suitable for long-term retention and access by other researchers. See especially Chapters 9 and 10 on data visualization and Chapters 11, 12 and 13 on archiving and data reuse.

The third and final cluster of research activities in the figure is termed Scholarly Communication and has similarities with the activities often associated with science communication (see e.g., Garvey, Lin, Nelson, & Tomita, 1972). Like constructions of science communication, scholarly communication in an e-research environment involves two overlapping forms of communication, both directed at parties external to the research project: informal and formal. Informal scholarly communication is reflected in blog postings, contributions to discussion lists maintained by individuals, institutions, disciplines, and scholarly associations; and specialized wikis. Formal scholarly communication, often considered synonymous with academic publishing, may involve preparation and distribution of conference papers, institutional working papers, journal articles, chapters in edited books and single-authored monographs. All of these forms of external, formal scholarly publication can transpire in a networked environment through the posting of manuscripts on personal Web homepages, to placement on pre-print and post-print article repositories, through publication of manuscripts in on-line journals and on the sites of Web-based book publishers. These forms of scholarly publishing are illustrated in more detail in the next section; see also Chapters 14 and 15 for discussion of access and intellectual property.

At the bottom of the figure are indications of the e-research tools related to each of the activity clusters. This indication of tools is incomplete, as are other features of the figure. For example, the figure suggests a relational form between the three clusters of research activities by the two-directional arrows. The exact nature of that relation—at what points in time with what intensity and regarding which specific facets of the clusters—is not specified. Important as such concerns are, they go beyond the general purpose of this figure within the context of this anthology, which is to suggest a place for the topics addressed in the book chapters. In addition, the figure is meant to suggest a framework for the previously specified characteristics of e-research: computerization, networked environment, virtual organization, collaboration, tools, visualization, and issues related to publication. This last characteristic is part of the cluster Scholarly Communication. Although attended to in the book, particularly in Chapter 14, the cluster merits further elaboration, which is provided in the following section.

SCHOLARLY COMMUNICATION

A thread running through e-research—any form of research, for that matter—is communication. This thread has come to be termed the 'communication turn' in some circles (Leydesdorff, 2002).[10] The centrality of communication is perhaps so self-evident that it is taken for granted, considered an unconscious and natural given. Scholarly communication, a subunit of this communication turn, is very broad and can be delineated differently.[11] Microsoft External Research (2008), for example, suggests the 'Scholarly Communication Life Cycle' consisting of four cyclic phases of knowledge production: data collection and analysis; authoring; publication and distribution; and archiving and preservation. In some of these areas, like authoring, much development has already taken place and the resulting tools are well integrated into scholarly work: word processing software, sometimes in a networked environment (e.g., Google Docs) and referencing and annotation tools (e.g., EndNote, Citeulike, and Zotero). In this chapter, however, scholarly communication is viewed as the presentation of research findings to an audience external to the research project, home department or institution of the researcher, for the purpose of sharing and contributing to knowledge. As noted in the previous section, such communication may be informal or formal in character. Traditionally, emphasis rested with, and importance was attributed to, formal communication as reflected in journal and book publications. Such tradition is still prominent across the social sciences and humanities, but changes are appearing with the emergence of e-research.

Change there is, but determination of intensity, duration, and extensiveness are difficult tasks, and these aspects are not the objectives of this modest introduction. Instead, the purpose is to present a range of illustrations related to ongoing concerns in scholarly communication. Using the previously suggested division, the illustrations are framed according to informal and formal types of scholarly communication, a division adopted in other studies, particularly in the field of science communication (e.g., Garvey et al., 1972; Hurd, 2000).

Informal scholarly communication

Depending on the academic environment in question, use of informal Web-based communication seems to be exploding: wikis; Web sites for sharing photos, videos and slides; blogs; social network sites; Web meeting tools and platforms allowing variants of instant messaging. Precursors of contemporary social media are email lists, newsgroups and electronic bulletin board systems that became prominent in the 1980s. These early systems have since been refined and now it is commonplace for many scholars to subscribe, and occasionally contribute, to a range of discussion and mailing lists focusing on specific disciplines and themes. Blogs are also regularly maintained by scholars in particular fields; research centers and less formally organized research groups often maintain group blogs designed to perform a similar function: provision of a virtual outlet for sharing information and reflections on topics of interest.[12] Wikis have become standard venues for projects and research groups. Some social networking sites like Facebook offer group pages and organizations such as the Association of Internet Researchers maintain a space on this site; others like LinkedIn are designed to cultivate professional networks, and SlideShare is illustrative of a venue where Powerpoint presentations, optionally including an audio overlay, can be stored and shared; YouTube is the repository for some academics wishing to share videos of their own presentations, occasionally achieving thousands of viewings.[13] Perhaps the pinnacle of such informal scholarly communication venues is the rapid growth of research and educational institutions with a presence in Second Life, 'places' supporting instruction and research projects (e.g., Shepherd, 2007).[14]

Although there is clearly much development in the area of informal scholarly communication, little is known beyond anecdotal information; quite basically, it is not known which scholars in which disciplines use which social media for what purposes, with what assessment. Without such information, there may be a tendency to extrapolate from unrepresentative personal knowledge and assume more interest and use than are actually present.

One of the few studies designed to systematically explore informal scholarly communication is, at the time of this writing, on-going, with an interim report released in August 2008. This report suggests much less interest and use of social media for scholarship than implied by the large number of media initiatives noted above (Harley, Earl-Novell, Acord, Lawrence, & King, 2008). The study is based on exploratory interviews with faculty at different stages of career development, mainly located at the University of California Berkeley and distributed across seven disciplines: archaeology, astrophysics, biology, economics, history, music, and political science. Perhaps the overall—and very tentative—observation by the authors of this report is a reserved and discipline-differentiated view: the general enthusiasm for new media "should not be conflated with the hard reality of tenure and promotion requirements . . . in highly competitive professional environments" Harley et al., 2008: 1).

Although understandably cautious in drawing conclusions at such an early stage in the project, Harley and colleagues (2008: 6) stress the importance of disciplinary culture and tradition, and that these factors may "override the perceived 'opportunities' afforded by new technologies, including those falling into the Web 2.0 category". In fact, innovative scholarship may not necessarily relate to the use of cutting-edge technologies: "More than a few scholars have suggested that technology used indiscriminately and for its own sake can limit the scope of questions asked and therefore lead to detrimental effects on the quality of scholarship" (Harley et al., 2008: 6). Some of the disciplinary differences noted in the report suggest that astrophysicists, political scientists, and economists are more predisposed to sharing scholarship through pre-print repositories and personal Web sites than are scholars in biology, history and archaeology. Nevertheless, there is "universal enthusiastic embrace" (Harley et al., 2008: 12) of Internet-based scholarly materials such as electronic journals, e-books, datasets, and governmental archives.

One factor that may influence future use of social media in informal scholarly communication not specifically addressed in this report is the increasing utilization of these media in the university classroom. Web sites, wikis, and blogs are becoming prominent, and initiatives are being undertaken to incorporate student familiarity and acceptance of social network sites in classroom activities (see, e.g., Salaway & Caruso, 2008).[15] Considerable and substantive change, in other words, may be forthcoming in the arena of informal scholarly communication as the education setting adopts social media (Maron & Smith, 2008).[16]

Formal scholarly communication

Formal scholarly communication, sometimes termed traditional academic publishing, is undergoing intense debate among the core groups involved— authors, editors, publishers, librarians—and much of this debate relates to the convergence of four factors:

- Escalating costs of periodicals, particularly in the fields of science, technology and medicine;
- Decreasing university resources for library acquisitions and for publication of scholarly monographs by university presses;
- Mounting revolt by coalitions of research librarians, journal editors, board members, and authors against the pricing practices of commercial publishers;
- Expanding opportunities for publishing through digitalization, especially through tools for authoring, processing, and distributing scholarship via the Internet.

The fusion of these factors has resulted in an explosion of initiatives on almost all fronts of formal scholarly communication. The amount and rate of change is great and on-going, making reflection difficult and prediction impossible. This section provides, then, a mere snapshot of innovations for journal and book publishing.

Regarding the first three points, various observers have charted the escalating costs of periodicals. Townsend (2003) calculates that science, technology and medicine (STM) journals increased by 600% in the period 1982–2002. Simultaneously, funds for acquisition by research libraries decreased along with the number of subscriptions.[17] Buckholtz (2001) compiles stories of academics that have taken a public stand against the escalating prices of journals that essentially confine access to those scholars affiliated with well-endowed research institutions; these academics have refused to write, edit or otherwise serve such titles.[18] In some cases like an Elsevier title on computer programming, entire editorial boards have resigned in protest to rising costs. In this case, some of the editors established a new title with Oxford University Press, reducing the subscription price substantially.[19]

Regarding the fourth point, digitalization, since the early days of electronic publishing in the late 1980s there has been a generally optimistic proclamation as to how the publishing industry would be affected. John Thompson (2005) devotes a series of chapters in his definitive work *Books in the Digital Age* to critically examining this 'digital revolution'. Many experiments have been initiated across the past two decades with forms of electronic publishing, a number of which are detailed by Thompson. Here, only a small selection of recent reports and innovations are noted.

To begin, the potential of this 'digital revolution' is described in the Ithaka Report 'University Publishing in a Digital Age', using an upbeat style strikingly similar to that used to describe e-science and cyberinfrastructure:

> We believe the next stage will be in the creation of new formats made possible by digital technologies, ultimately allowing scholars to work in deeply integrated electronic research and publishing environments

that will enable real-time dissemination, collaboration, dynamically-updated content, and usage of new media. (Brown, Griffiths, & Rascoff, 2007: 4)

In fairness to the authors, the remainder of the report describes the considerable challenges facing university publishing houses within such an environment, particularly the need to address the central mandate of these houses—contributing to the public availability of scholarship—in a financially constrained setting.

One of the developments related to digitalization is the multitude of initiatives to create digitalized copies of the holdings of national and research libraries worldwide. Most major national libraries have such projects or have joined alliances with third-parties, notably Google. The Google initiative, initially proposed in 2006, has been both roundly lauded and equally criticized. The praise basically relates to making knowledge accessible beyond the holdings of individual libraries; in the words of one reflection composed immediately after legal agreement was reached on 28 October 2008, "this agreement is likely to change forever the way that we find and browse for books, particularly out-of-print books" (Von Lohmann, 2008). The reservations relate to protection of intellectual property, commercial interests, and bias towards scholarship published in English from American institutions.[20]

Digitalization of books is not only an activity involving libraries and their collections, but also publishers and their interest in securing a sustainable market for academic-oriented publications. The scholarly monograph has been an endangered species in the world of publishing for decades and university presses have tried a large variety of rescue operations, none particularly successful (see, e.g., Thompson, 2005; Townsend, 2003). Some of the more recent rescue efforts include offering for free digital versions of monographs, gambling that such 'give-aways' may stimulate purchase of the printed version by libraries.[21] Commercial publishers have experimented in a more limited manner with this same strategy, as have government bodies (e.g., The National Academies Press, http://www.nap.edu/).

Journals

Although much in the world of journal publishing has changed since 1665 when Henry Oldenburg launched *Philosophical Transactions*, the first scholarly periodical, the four functions of journals have remained central: registration, dissemination, peer review, and archival record (Armbruster, 1989). What has changed, sometimes radically, is how journal publishing attends to these functions, particularly since digitalization and the Internet. To begin, scholarly journals have been proliferating at an astounding rate. Such multiplication of titles has been the order of the day for several decades, coupled to a profitable commercial strategy (Townsend, 2003).

Digitalization and the Internet have accelerated this already established trend. Other contributions to change regarding the functions are less visible, but equally significant, such as software installation automating back office procedures for processing manuscripts, contributing to more efficient processing. Online manuscript management has become standard practice among most titles. Two other developments, still on-going and highly relevant to e-research, are peer review procedures, and online access to and repositories for articles.

Peer review

Formal scholarly communication, at the most fundamental and general level, is about contributing new knowledge and subjecting contributions to peer review and public debate. Various mechanisms have been established to assess the quality of contributions, of which peer review is the most prevalent. Peer review takes many forms, from the kind of collegial reactions provided during a departmental staff meeting about a draft manuscript to formalized double-blind reviewing procedures of submissions to publishers and funding agencies.

With regard to academic journals, peer review involves agreement by authors to allow their work to be assessed by other scholars prior to publication. When the procedure works well, extended substantive comment is received from two or more anonymous experts. These reviews are considered by a journal editor who comes to a decision regarding publication, sometimes after several rounds of review and manuscript revision. Although this process has been made more efficient and rapid since widespread use of email and software for journal management, the review process can still take several months to complete, which is one of the enduring criticism authors have of peer review.[22]

Other criticisms of peer review have been voiced (e.g., Godlee & Jefferson, 1999) and poignantly summarized:

> It is unreliable, unfair and fails to validate or authenticate; it is unstandardized and open to bias; blinded peer review invites malice, either from ad hominem attacks on the author or by facilitating plagiarism; it stifles innovation; it lends spurious authority to reviewers; reviewers knowledgeable enough to review a study are often competitors, and therefore have a conflict of interest; and it causes unnecessary delays in publication. (Huston, 2001)

Despite such critique, peer review of journal articles is almost universally accepted as the necessary procedure for scholarly work to be admitted to the formal record of scientifically-based knowledge. Double-blind peer review is considered, in fact, the 'gold standard' for quality journal publishing across the spectrum of scholarship. In an international study of peer review, commissioned by the Publishing Research Consortium (Ware & Monkman, 2008), academics strongly support the principles of peer review. Based on responses from 3101 journal authors, reviewers, and editors, the study reflects the opinions of scholars in the sciences, humanities, and social sciences.[23]

Experiments abound to improve or even to dispense with conventional double-blind peer review. A few exceptionally innovative titles, like the *British Medical Journal* (BMJ), have a long history with open access and open peer review procedures.[24] One recent experiment, resulting in a different assessment of open peer review, was conducted by *Nature* in 2006. The editors were interested whether a venue for open, signed comment might contribute to manuscript improvement; readers were polled and there seemed to be much interest in this form of review. During the four-month period of the trial, authors of submissions, nearly 1400, were asked whether they wished to have their work placed on the server established for the experiment; a small fraction (5%, 71 papers) agreed to take part. Of these papers about half received comments; the majority were technical in nature. The largest number of comments received by any one paper was ten. By the end of the trial period, only a small number of authors had decided to take part and an even smaller group had received comments of a substantive nature. In these respects the degree of participation resembles that of discussion lists: a handful of participants within a population of thousands (Schneider, 1997; Hagemann, 2002). In contrast, as suggested by the BMJ experience, other titles involving other scholars operating in other disciplinary cultures may come to different assessments of open peer review.

Some opportunities for online commentary fall short of the intentions of journal article peer review, but nevertheless merit mention here because they contribute to collective debate of manuscripts, albeit less formal. *Scientific American*, for example, placed an initial version of an article-in-development on its Web site and invited commentary from readers (Waldrop, 2008). During the course of five weeks, some 130 comments were posted, a large number of which were extended and substantive. The initiative *MediaCommons* does essentially the same, using software that permits paragraph-by-paragraph commentary.[25]

Online access & repositories

Another prominent area of change in journal publishing is the relatively rapid development and embracement of an online environment by scholars and publishers. Most major journal publishers now offer institutional subscribers a variety of packages that may include a set of titles made available in print and also accessible from a Web site maintained by the publisher. Other Web-based initiatives in this area are taken by scholarly associations and special interest groups. These initiatives, however, are little more than mirror-images of print journals; very few titles are exploring multimedia publishing formats with inclusion of dynamic visualizations and access to datasets.[26]

The most significant issue related to online journal publishing is the kind and degree of open access provided to journal titles and articles. Commercial publishers have been reticent to take a lead in this area; as a consequence, the primary initiatives have been developed by scholarly associations, sometimes in collaboration with universities. The Public Library of Science (PLoS) journals are the prototype of this kind of publishing. At present there are seven PLoS journals in the biology, medicine, and genetics (see http://www.plos.org/). One of the reservations voiced regarding some open access journals is that a fee is charged for publication. The PLoS journals, for example, request such a fee, although payment is not required. A few commercial publishers have adapted the author fee model and offer free and immediate access to an author's article providing the author pays for such. Some authors publishing under the auspices of funded projects can arrange for payment, but many other scholars do not have such financial freedom. In 2008 the University of California at Berkeley, following initiatives at other institutions, announced the Berkeley Research Impact Initiative (BRII) that is designed to help support open access to scholarship by establishing a fund to assist scholars in paying any necessary fees (BRII, 2008).

Perhaps the greatest incentive encouraging access to scholarship has occurred outside the domain of publishing: funding agencies, universities and associations of scholars have contributed to development of digital repositories for scholarship. Scholarly associations frequently maintain repositories of papers accepted for presentation at conferences, but submission of material is often voluntary and authors are sometimes concerned that availability, even in those cases where these repositories are restricted to members of the associations, may be construed as a form of publication and prohibit subsequent submission to academic journals. Some of the natural sciences have established repositories for papers, including texts not yet accepted for journal publication. The pioneering initiative of this kind, arXiv, was launched a decade ago and has archived more than a half-million documents in the fields of physics, computer science, quantitative biology, and statistics; see http://arxiv.org/. Depending on the procedures, pre-print repositories may resemble variants of self-publishing with no external quality control, but for some disciplines immediate public release of an idea is more important than the patience required for peer review certification.

Some funding agencies, such as the National Institutes of Health (NIH) in the U.S., require that publications, and in some cases data, be deposited in publically available repositories. Universities are also establishing institutionally-based repositories of papers published or accepted for publication; participation is sometimes mandatory, particularly when institutions are concerned about research assessment exercises as in some European countries (Borgman, 2007: 195). The number of repositories across disciplines, countries, and institutions is multiplying rapidly; the Directory of

Open Access Repositories, OpenDOAR, notes more than 1200 at the time of this writing; see http://www.opendoar.org/.

ORGANIZATION OF BOOK

As previously mentioned, the chapters in this volume provide a panoramic portrayal of issues related to e-research. Although several organizational structures for the collection could be suitably employed, preference is given here to seven clusters of concerns reflected in Figure 1.1: conceptualization of e-research, policy developments, collaboration among researchers, visualization of findings, data preservation and reuse, access and intellectual property, and case studies of projects illustrating features of e-research. Many of the chapters address several of these concerns and almost all are concerned with conceptualizing e-research, but there is accentuation as reflected in these categories. The final category, case studies, is the exception and here presentations are made of full e-research projects.

Conceptualization

Two chapters concentrate on issues directly related to the conceptualization of e-research. In *Chapter 2*, Ralph Schroeder and Jennifer Fry construct a map of social science approaches and e-research. This map provides an overview of different disciplines involved in e-science research, specifically those disciplines closely affiliated with e-science. The authors discuss the relations identified and illustrate them through attention to a range of projects in the U.K. The overview suggests the considerable diversity in disciplinary approaches to e-research, and this insight can be valuable in understanding its co-constructed character, involving both the technologies and the specific transformations of these by scholars in a diversity of disciplines. One of the concluding concerns Schroeder and Fry raise is the degree to which e-research will contribute to a longer term understanding within the sociology of science.

In *Chapter 3*, Anne Beaulieu and Paul Wouters approach the conceptualization of e-research from a perspective emphasizing intervention, and they take as their starting point the Virtual Knowledge Studio for the Humanities and Social Sciences (VKS) in the Netherlands. The authors discuss the tensions involved in combining reflexive analysis with the practical design of scholarly practices. These dual objectives entail that the VKS is both a research program and an infrastructural facility for scholars, a combination that can be problematic: design and analysis are different types of scientific and scholarly work, with different temporal horizons and different coalitions of interests. How this duality plays out and how the Internet can be used as an arena for research is the challenge addressed.

Development

The next section, development, consists of three chapters, each addressing aspects of policy and its implementation as related to the emergence of e-science and e-research in different geographic regions. *Chapter 4*, prepared by Peter Halfpenny, Rob Procter, Yu-Wei Lin and Alex Voss, focuses on developments in the U.K. related to what has come to be known as e-social science. The authors reflect on the development of the research program of the National Centre for e-Social Science (NCeSS) and delineate its achievements and the challenges faced. Attention focuses on engagement and interaction with users, facilitating communication between social scientists and computer scientists, outreach towards the wider social science research community, and collaboration with the e-science community at an international level. To provide an account of the current state of e-social science in the U.K., a wide range of sources is reviewed, tracing the origin and development of the Centre. In the process, the authors map the British 'e-social science community', identifying its stakeholders, the state-of-the-art technologies, how these technologies are deployed, and the strategies emerging that facilitate uptake.

Chapter 5 focuses on e-research as a reflection of the scholarly community in the humanities in Australia. The chapter authors, Paul Genoni, Helen Merrick, and Michele Willson, describe e-research practices in the humanities, based on a survey exploring how scholars use the Internet for teaching and research purposes. Of particular interest are the informal, behind-the-scenes, communicative and collaborative practices that instigate, manage, and produce e-research outcomes. The authors examine communication processes facilitated by computer-mediated communication, drawing upon specific case studies of new and existing e-research groups and distributed collaborative projects. One of their conclusions notes the importance of institutional, social and economic factors in the adoption and use of e-research technologies.

Chapter 6, prepared by Carol Soon and Han Woo Park, explores the emergence of e-social science policy in South Korea and Singapore. This chapter contributes to re-addressing a Western bias by focusing primarily on issues related to scholarly practice in e-research within the context of two Asian countries. The high level of Internet and broadband penetration in Singapore is a result of that government's initiatives to create an e-inclusive society within the nation-state. In the case of South Korea, the country is currently an important node in advanced research networks. One of the challenges to e-science development in these Asian countries is the need for a change among social scientists and humanities scholars regarding the value of e-research. An increase in education and training programs may, according to the authors, positively contribute to further development.

Collaboration

The third section is concerned with collaboration among researchers, often at a distance, and includes two chapters. *Chapter 7*, prepared by Petra Sonderegger, addresses the planning and management of globally distributed research teams. It is unclear to what extent the discovery and interpretation of new research problems necessitate the co-presence of researchers. And, as projects become more complex and are distributed over greater distances, in-person meetings are often not feasible or practical. While new communication technologies allow more frequent communications between distant collaborators, they also reduce the richness of that communication; facial expressions, body language, and tone of voice may be lost. However, successful collaboration relies to a large extent on intense interaction to create a shared language, a common understanding of problems, and the trust required for members of a group to suggest original and untried solutions. Sonderegger, drawing on an ethnographic study conducted in Bangalore, India, explores how corporations and researchers deal with the challenge of collaborating across geographic distance and organizational boundaries using technology-mediated communication.

In *Chapter 8*, Eric Meyer discusses issues that arise when small scientific projects become part of larger scientific collaborations, seen from a social informatics perspective. Data from two distinct areas of scholarship are presented: a study of humpback whale research involving federating data related to the population and movements of these mammals in the Pacific Ocean and a study of collaboration among scholars in the field of psychiatric genetics contributing to a large, shared data repository. While these two cases represent very different scientific domains, they share a number of characteristics including decentralized decision-making, limited data management expertise, and long-term collections of data—all of which have contributed to difficulties in moving into an e-science environment. One of the issues Meyer raises is the tension between flexibility and innovation in scientific practice, counter-balanced by need for compatible data standards in large-scale data infrastructures.

Visualization

Chapter 9, authored by Mike Thelwall, draws upon experiences in the field of Webometrics to describe the problems and techniques involved when collecting and visualizing data about the Internet. Social science research, drawing upon raw data from search engines, is in the unprecedented position of being granted free access to a huge heterogeneous corpus of information, but requiring technical computing knowledge to understand the data and extract it efficiently. Thelwall provides examples of visualizations used in a variety of disciplines in the social sciences and humanities, and examines some of the software available for preparation of such illustrations.

Three detailed cases of visualizations are presented: the visualization of Wikipedia edits, charted in the History Flow project of IBM; a dynamic display of group interactions that is part of the research project Evolino; and a treemap of Usenet postings generated within the Microsoft Netscan project. Thelwall concludes with suggestions for further exploration, the first of which involves documentation of the emergence of visualizations across disciplines and across time.

Chapter 10, by Howard Welser, Thomas Lento, Marc Smith, Eric Gleave, and Itai Himelboim, presents initiatives to enhance data visualization developed at Microsoft Research. Researchers and technologists increasingly apply information visualization techniques to the data generated by social media on the Internet in an effort to gain insights that may have been far more difficult to grasp with qualitative methods alone. In recent work, the authors have explored for representations of data structures, such as hierarchies and network structures. The authors present examples of visualizations that highlight the range of behaviour performed in computational social media. They illustrate work around Usenet, one of the oldest institutions and infrastructures of social interaction on the Internet, and describe the scales, structures and maps created and containing elements from these spaces, some of which may be relevant to more recent developments with social media.

Data preservation & reuse

Chapter 11, prepared by Steven Schneider, Kirsten Foot, and Paul Wouters, is concerned with one of the enigmas of e-research: preserving Web sites in a manner allowing scientific study. As the Web has become an object of research, Web archiving has emerged as a form of inquiry enabling developmental and retrospective analyses of many kinds of online phenomena. Web archiving has become a component of e-research practiced by scholars concerned with phenomena mediated via digital, networked technologies. The authors analyze current and potential uses of Web archiving and the challenges this imposes on research practice. The analyses facilitated by Web archiving utilize both quantitative and qualitative methods employed on a large scale, over time, and by distributed research teams. The chapter concludes by identifying the challenges social researchers encounter in archiving Web-based material.

Chapter 12, by Ann Zimmerman, Nathan Bos, Judy Olson, and Gary Olson, provides a panorama of the problems encountered in sharing data. The need to share data and to exchange knowledge about data is a primary driver behind many visions of e-science. Yet, efforts to share data face considerable social, organizational, legal, scientific, and technical challenges. This chapter reports findings from an analysis of the data sharing approaches used by large collaborations in several scientific disciplines. The findings are based on a five-year study of distributed collaborations across many domains. The results suggest that different types of data sharing solutions place different demands on those who produce data, and on those who are responsible for collecting, managing and making data available for use by others.

In *Chapter 13* Samuelle Carlson and Ben Anderson present four case studies: SkyProject, SurveyProject, CurationProject, and AnthroProject. These projects provide the empirical basis through which the authors consider the extent data can be extracted from its original context and made available for other researchers operating in other contexts. Considerable difference was found regarding data sharing among these four projects, generally following the disciplinary lines of the projects: the astronomers associated with SkyProject, for example, differed radically from the anthropologists of AnthroProject regarding the suitability of providing access to data beyond the original team of researchers and regarding the possibility of preserving the data outside the initial research context. These four case studies contribute to an ongoing discussion of the potential benefits and drawbacks of embedding e-(social) science in everyday practice and the incentives required to do so. They suggest that the future of e-social science depends heavily on the existing practices of disciplines and on whether data are 'born digital'.

Access & intellectual property

Robert Lucas and John Willinsky, the authors of *Chapter 14*, consider the idea of open access as related to e-research. They present an ethical and epistemological argument for open access to scholarly publications and review recent developments in access to data and published work. They propose that, in addition to strengthening scholarly practice, open access enables scientific findings to better inform public debate and promote the ideal of free inquiry in the broader culture. The field of medicine is presented as an example of how greater public access to research has contributed to the democratic quality of people's lives, and it is suggested that this societal benefit can be extended across the spectrum of scholarship.

Chapter 15, by Dan Burk, is concerned with intellectual property in the arena of e-science. Intellectual property regimes are generally problematic in the practice of science: scientific research typically assumes practices of openness that may be hampered or obstructed by intellectual property rights. Much attention has been paid to documenting and analyzing the impact of patents on research in the biomedical area, and the history of recent major scientific initiatives, such as the Human Genome Project, have been punctuated by clashes over the propriety and provision of patent rights in the accumulated data. These developments are examined in this chapter and are related to innovative proposals such as the open source 'copyleft' model. This model may be a valuable mechanism for preserving similar values in e-science. Burk argues for awareness not only of the technical structure, but also of the social and communicative structures of e-science in order to adapt licensing solutions to scholarly practice.

Case studies

The final section of the book presents two case studies that include a broad range of the features of e-research, which could not easily be included in one of the earlier sections. *Chapter 16*, prepared by Bridgette Wessels and Max Craglia, discusses a co-construction project involving social scientists and computer scientists. Participants in the project explore the opportunities offered by Grid computer architecture in addressing the relationship between socio-economic characteristics, neighborhoods, and crime—a relationship at the forefront of criminology for decades. The authors consider the significance of change in relation to the character- istics of the social sciences and the ways scholars may wish to shape the practice of e-social science.

Chapter 17, by Clifford Tatum and Michele LaFrance, explores the collaborative processes used in the development of Wikipedia content. Through examining the construction of Wikipedia articles via the lens of established knowledge constructs, the authors aim to gain insight into prac- tices of collaborative e-science. Specifically, Tatum and LaFrance examine the consensus model of knowledge production and conflict resolution of Wikipedia articles. Using a theoretical framework developed by Latour and Woolgar (1979), three components emerge as valuable in the analysis of the articles: construction, agonistic field, and reification. These components are elaborated and the authors speculate on transformations of scholarly communication illustrated by Wikipedia and other forms of Web-based social media.

CONCLUDING NOTE

Ending where this chapter began, there seems to be much change afoot across the social sciences and humanities, but how much, where exactly, and how lasting these changes may be are unknowns. The contributions to this book set out to clarify much of this uncertainty in the disciplines and topics addressed. The authors also begin to identify areas for further empir- ical work, designed to understand the transformations related to e-research seemingly underway. This is not the place to repeat the suggestions for further investigation the authors provide, but it is opportunity to mention a few overarching issues.

First, two kinds of chronicling seem to be required to understand pos- sible transformations in scholarship. In the first place, the kind of in-depth qualitative study Christine Hine (2008) provides for a single discipline, the division of biology called systematics, is needed for many other disciplines.

The insightful richness provided by such ethnographies is hard to surpass and her work follows in a tradition emphasizing this kind of investigation (e.g., Latour & Woolgar, 1979). At the same time and in almost the same breadth, broad surveys are required that monitor adoption, adaption, and assessment of specific components of e-research. The empirical work of the group at the U. C. Berkeley Center for Studies in Higher Education (Harley et al., 2008) is illustrative of such cross-disciplinary, focused investigation. Of course, such surveys should be extended beyond elite universities in the U.S., and include research institutions situated in other geographic regions.

Second, much insight is to be gained from exploring the non-adopters and 'laggards'—an observation frequently made about the introduction of new media more generally (e.g., Wyatt, 2008: 9). Understanding why members of some disciplines reject distant collaboration, data sharing, and currently fashionable Web 2.0 tools may help realize the limitations of the 'revolution in science' frequently prophesized.

Third, and last, it is important to emphasize the contextualization of change reflected in scholarly cultures, disciplines, and associations as situated in broader social, economic, and political factors at work in crafting the course of science and, more generally, of scholarship. Of course, globalization is a prominent factor in developments, but so are less international visions of nation-states and their governmental administrations with agendas designed to achieve the competitive and economic benefits attributed to e-science, cyberinfrastructure, and e-research.

Christine Borgman (2007: xix) concludes the preface to *Scholarship in the Digital Age* with an enticing invitation: "Let the conversation begin." She and others have, indeed, contributed much to that conversation. The chapters in this book may be considered additions to such discourse, but also to a growing array of studies spanning the social sciences and humanities regarding the emergence of e-research and the ongoing transformations of scholarly practice. Rephrasing Borgman, let the exploration continue.[27]

NOTES

1. Illustrative of Big Science institutions is the Lawrence Livermore National Laboratory that was established at the height of the Cold War for weapons research and run by the University of California for the U.S. government. This facility has since been reorganized as a "national security laboratory . . . responsible for ensuring that the nation's nuclear weapons remain safe, secure, and reliable . . ." (LLNL, 2008).
2. An alternative conceptualization of Big Science, formulated later by de Solla Price (1993), places emphasis on the maturity of the scientific field rather than on the largeness of its instrumentation, budget and wealth of data; see Borgman (2007: 28).
3. Christine Hine (2008: 25–27) accentuates the prescient nature of Wouters' contribution, reproducing in entirety the call for papers he prepared for a

1996 conference session of the European Association for Studies of Science and Technology. The most striking feature of this call is the wide range of topics, 23 in total, suggested as suitable contributions for the proposed session on cyberscience.

4. Some of these early visionary statements remain available on the Web site of the British National e-Science Centre (NeSC), including Taylor's claim that "e-Science will change the dynamic of the way science is undertaken" (quoted at NeSC, n.d.).

5. A technically-oriented literature on Grid computer architecture is available, but the basic description of this Grid relates the development to other systems of services, like the electrical Grid that provides electricity to homes and industries. Foster (2003) and Buyya and Venugopal (2005) provide accessible introductions for non-specialists.

6. This metaphor belies the complexity of the notion 'infrastructure', which is critically addressed in the workshop report 'Understanding Infrastructure: Dynamics, Tensions, and Design' (Edwards, Jackson, Bowker, & Knobel, 2007). One of the ideas Edwards and his colleagues criticize is that infrastructure somehow reflects a "planned, orderly and mechanical act" (Edwards et al., 2007: i).

7. A relatively recent formulation of cyberinfrastructure from the University of Indiana suggests essentially the same ingredients: "Cyberinfrastructure consists of computing systems, data storage systems, advanced instruments and data repositories, visualization environments, and people, all linked together by software and high performance networks to improve research productivity and enable breakthroughs not otherwise possible" (Indiana University, 2007).

8. One of these initiatives is CTWatch, 'Cyberinfrastructure Technology Watch', which strives to "engage the science and engineering research community in the news, ideas, and information surrounding the emergence of cyberinfrastructure as the essential foundation for advanced scientific inquiry" (CTWatch Quarterly, 2005). Another initiative is CI Outreach, 'Empowering People to use Cyberinstrastructure Resources', and is concerned with soliciting and supporting the education, training, and outreach needs of the scientific research projects within the cyberinfrastructure community, targeting underrepresented groups such as women, minorities and the disabled; see http://www.ci-outreach.org/index.php.

9. Daniel Atkins, former director of the NSF Office of Cyberinfrastructure, has constructed a large number of figures illustrating the features of cyberinfrastructure, sometimes in relation to the other terms noted in this chapter—e-science, e-research, e-infrastructure, cyberscience; see, e.g., http://www.nsf.gov/od/oci/TeraGrid6–06.pdf. Seldom, however, is indication provided in these figures of the respective contexts, histories, components, and relations among the terms. These relations were also left largely unaddressed in a recent presentation by Atkins during the 2008 Oxford eResearch Conference (http://www.oii.ox.ac.uk/microsites/eresearch08/index.cfm), suggesting that additional comparative analysis is still awaiting attention.

10. This 'turn' leans on the previously suggested turn to linguistics in philosophy (Rorty, 1967 / 1992). The metaphor has also been used to suggest a 'cultural turn' describing the emergence of cultural studies and a 'qualitative turn' reflecting increased interest in interpretative research (Jensen, 1991).

11. The amount of research conducted on scholarly communication is daunting. One of the most complete bibliographies of this work (Bailey, 2002) contains some 230 pages and thousands of entries.

12. For an illustration of an institutional blog see the one maintained at the Oxford Internet Institute site: http://people.oii.ox.ac.uk/. In a similar fashion,

the Association of Literary Scholars and Critics sponsors a group blog called The Valve: http://www.thevalve.org/go.

13. Some institutions, such as the Berkman Center for Internet & Society (http://cyber.law.harvard.edu/interactive), have their own YouTube channels at which presentations hosted by the institutions are archived. Individual scholars similarly make use of YouTube to document presentations; see, e.g., the presentation by Michael Wesch, University of Kansas, at the Library of Congress, 23 June 2008, 'An anthropological introduction to YouTube': http://uk.youtube.com/watch?v=TPAO-lZ4_hU&feature=related.

14. The number of university-level institutions that have 'taken up shop' in Second Life is not known precisely and is difficult to determine; see http://secondliferesearch.blogspot.com/2007/07/current-list-of-universities-in-second.html. A report released in May 2008 suggests three-quarters of all U.K. institutions for higher education are represented in Second Life (Kirriemuir, 2008).

15. A recent thread on the AoIR discussion list (November 2008) considered ways to use Wikipedia for classroom assignments. Blogging as a pedagogical tool has been discussed extensively (e.g., http://www.det.wa.edu.au/education/cmis/eval/curriculum/ict/weblogs/). Platforms for educational use of blogs were experimented with as early as 2003 (http://incsub.org/2005/edublogs-are-go); two years later Edublogs (http://edublogs.org/) was established and in 2008 this platform hosted nearly 250,000 educationally-oriented blogs.

16. One example of such adoption is the place being given to YouTube in the classroom; see the George Lucas Educational Foundation group blog Edutopic for a series of postings: http://www.edutopia.org/search/node/youtube. See also initiatives by Michael Wesch in using YouTube and other new media in cultural anthropology courses at Kansas State University: http://www.ksu.edu/sasw/anthro/wesch.htm.

17. Presentation of such figures is frequently found on the Web sites of associations of libraries and librarians; see the Stanford University library site on scholarly communication for a recent overview, including a graph illustrating rising costs across time: http://www-sul.stanford.edu/scholarly_com/. A large number of universities maintain sections of their web sites describing these and other aspects of scholarly communication (e.g., copyright, repositories, policies from funding bodies regarding access to publications). About a dozen such sites are listed at the UC Berkeley Library site: http://www.lib.berkeley.edu/scholarlycommunication/beyond_berkeley.html

18. Such 'tales' are multiplying across disciplines, albeit most notably in the natural sciences. See Birman (2000) for an account of similar concern in mathematics. For an example outside the sciences, see danah boyd blog entry (6 February 2008) announcing a personal boycott of "locked-down academic journals" related to communication and Internet studies: http://www.zephoria.org/thoughts/archives/2008/02/06/openaccess_is_t.html

19. Some commercial publishers have reacted defensively to these developments, notably Elsevier (2004). Thompson (2005: 100–101) suggests that Elsevier's pricing of periodicals is in line with industry-wide increases. Other commercial publishers have sought alliance with initiatives favorable to open access, like HighWire Press; see http://highwire.stanford.edu/.

20. Jean-Nöel Jeanneney (2007), president of the *Bibliothèque nationale de France*, has penned perhaps the most compelling foreign dissenting opinion to the alliance with Google by research libraries, entitled *Google and the myth of universal knowledge*. A number of research libraries in the U.S. initiated a collective lawsuit against Google in 2005, which was resolved

in October 2008 and involves among other things, payment of 45 million U.S. dollars to copyright holders of documents scanned and digitalized. Overall, initial reactions were very positive about this settlement; one contributor to the Balkinization blog termed it a "win-win-win-win" situation for Google, copyholders, libraries and the public (Netanel, 2008). For an overview, commissioned by the Association of Research Libraries and the American Library Association, see Band (2008).

21. In 2007 the University of Michigan Press established 'digitalculturebooks' as "an experimental publishing strategy" and has made titles available in both for free electronic and conventional for sale print versions (see, e.g., Turow & Tsui, 2008). MIT Press also offers some titles free on its Web site (e.g., Willinski, 2005) as part of its Open Access program. This program was preceded by the first initiative of this sort when, in 1994, MIT Press decided to release *City of Bits* in this dual fashion—at some measure of financial success, according to Thompson (2005: 330–331).

22. Although such criticism is understandable, journal editors are experiencing increasing difficulty in securing quality reviews of submissions, requiring issuance of multiple requests for assessments and resulting in delayed reports to authors. This is one of the many issues addressed by a range of journal editors at a publishing workshop held at the 2008 annual conference of the Association of Internet Researchers (IR 9.0, Copenhagen, 15–18 Oct., http://conferences.aoir.org/).

23. Although this survey is perhaps the 'best there is' regarding assessment of peer review by scholars, the findings are based on a return rate of less than 7.7% of the more than 40,000 persons approached. It would be prudent to note that specific disciplinary findings are only indications rather than statistically representative reflections. Still, when aggregated, the respondents overwhelming feel peer review is necessary (93%), improves published papers (90%), provides a system of control (83%), and double-blind review is preferred (56%) as the most effective assessment procedure (Ware, 2008: 4).

24. On October 28, 2008, BMJ became an official open access journal, after a decade-long period with open access to research articles and a short-lived reversal to restricted access; for details see Open Access News: http://www.earlham.edu/~peters/fos/2008/10/bmj-converts-to-gratis-oa.html

25. The editors of *MediaCommons* describe this initiative, launched in 2007, as an all-electronic scholarly publishing network rather than as a conventional journal that "will not simply shift the locus of publishing from print to screen, but will actually transform what it means to 'publish,' allowing the author, the publisher, and the reader all to make the process of such discourse just as visible as its product." See further: http://mediacommons. futureofthebook.org/. Various blog posts by Kathleen Fitzpatrick, instrumental in launching this initiative, deal with the basic principles involved; see especially 'On the Future of Academic Publishing, Peer Review and Tenure Requirements', 6 January 2006: http://www.thevalve.org/go/valve/article/on_the_future_of_academic_publishing_peer_review_and_tenure_requirements_or.

26. In contrast, *Vectors, Journal of Culture and Technology in a Dynamic Vernacular*, places emphasis on publication of multimedia contributions; the *International Journal of Communication* (IJOC) notes such publishing possibilities in its mission statement. *Vectors* is design oriented, IJOC reflects a relatively conventional approach to scholarship. See http://www.vectorsjournal.org/; http://ijoc.org/.

27. The exploration also continues on the Web site for this book: http://www.virtualknowledgestudio.nl/scholarly-transformation/

REFERENCES

ACLS (2006). *Our cultural commonwealth: The report of the American Council of Learned Societies Commission on cyberinfrastructure for the humanities & social sciences. American Council of Learned Societies (ACLS).* Retrieved November 15, 2008, from http://www.acls.org/uploadedFiles/Publications/Programs/Our_Cultural_Commonwealth.pdf

Armbruster, C. *(2001).* Moving out of Oldenburg's long shadow: What is the future for society publishing? *Learned Publishing,* 20, 259–266. Retrieved November 15, 2008, from http://64.233.183.132/search?q=cache:DCrtm9_H1eYJ:eprints.rclis.org/archive/0001316/01/Society_Oldenburg.pdf+registration,+dissemination,+peer+review,+and+archival+record&hl=nl&ct=clnk&cd=2&gl=nl

Atkins Report (2003). Revolutionizing science and engineering through cyberinfrastructure. Report of the National Science Foundation Blue-Ribbon Advisory Panel on Cyberinfrastructure. Retrieved November 15, 2008, from http://www.nsf.gov/od/oci/reports/toc.jsp

Bailey, C. W. (2002).Scholarly electronic publishing bibliography. Version 43, 21 June. University of Houston Libraries. Retrieved November 15, 2008, from http://epress.lib.uh.edu/sepb/archive/43/sepb.pdf

Band, J. (2008). A guide for the perplexed: Libraries & the Google Library Project settlement. Report, Association of Research Libraries and American Library Association, 13 Nov. Retrieved Nov. 15, 2008, from http://www.arl.org/pp/ppcopyright/google/

Birman, J. S. (2000). Scientific publishing: A mathematician's viewpoint. *Notices of AMS,* 47(7): 770–774.

Borgman, C. L. (2007). *Scholarship in the digital age; Information, infrastructure and the Internet.* Cambridge, MA: MIT Press.

BRII (2008). Berkeley Research Impact Initiative: Advancing the Impact of UC Berkeley Research. Web site. Program description, 21 January. Retrieved Nov. 15, 2008, from http://www.lib.berkeley.edu/brii/index.html

Brown, L., Griffiths, R., & Rascoff, M. (2007). University publishing in a Digital Age. Ithaka Report. 26 July. Retrieved Nov. 15, 2008, from http://www.ithaka.org/strategic-services/Ithaka%20University%20Publishing%20Report.pdf

Buckholtz, A. (2001). Declaring independence: Returning scientific publishing to scientists. *Journal of Electronic Publishing, 7(1).* Retrieved Nov. 15, 2008, from http://dx.doi.org/10.3998/3336451.0007.101

Buyya, R., & Venugopal, S. (2005). A gentle introduction to Grid computing and technologies. *CSI Communications,* 29 (1), 9–19.

Contractor, N. (2007). From disasters to WoW—enabling communities with cyberinfrastructure. Kenote presentation, National Centre for e-Social Science, 29 June. Retrieved Nov. 15, 2008, from http://www.ncess.ac.uk/events/conference/2006/keynotes/presentations/KeynoteNoshirContractor.pdf

CTWatch Quarterly (2005). Cyberinfrastructure Technology Watch, press release. *CTWatchQuarterly,* 17 Feb. Retrieved Nov. 15, 2008, from http://www.ctwatch.org/

Hagemann, C. (2002). Participation in and content of two Dutch political party discussion lists on the Internet. *Javnost-The Public,* 9(2): 61–76.

Edwards, P. N., Jackson, S. J., Bowker, G. C., & Knobel, C. P. (2007). Understanding infrastructure: Dynamics, tensions, and design. Report of the workshop 'History and Theory of Infrastructure: Lessons for New Scientific Cyberinfrastructures'. Retrieved Nov. 15, 2008, from http://hdl.handle.net/2027.42/49353

Foster, I. (2003). The Grid: Computing without bounds. *Scientific American,* *288*(4): 78–87.

Elsevier (2004). Elsevier's comments on evolutions in scientific, technical and medical publishing and reflections on possible implications of Open Access journals for the UK. Report. February. Retrieved Nov. 15, 2008, from http://www.elsevier.com/authored_news/corporate/images/UKST1Elsevier_position_paper_on_stm_in_UK.pdf

Ess, C., & AoIR Ethics Working Group (2002). *Ethical decision-making and Internet research: Recommendations from the aoir ethics working committee.* Report, Association of Internet Research, 27 Nov. Retrieved Nov. 15, 2008, from www.aoir.org/reports/ethics.pdf

Garvey, W. D., Lin, N., Nelson, C. E., & Tomita, K. (1972). Research studies in patterns of scientific communication: I. General description of research program. *Information Storage and Retrieval, 8*(3): 111–122.

Godlee, F., & Jefferson, T. (Eds.) (1999). *Peer review in Health Sciences.* London: BMJ Publishing Group.

Harley, D. (2008). The university as publisher: Summary of a meeting held at UC Berkeley on Nov. 1, 2007. *Journal of Electronic Publishing, 11(2)*. Retrieved Nov. 15, 2008, from http://dx.doi.org/10.3998/3336451.0011.208

Harley, D., Earl-Novell, S., Acord, S.K., Lawrence, S., & C. Judson King, C. J. (2008). Assessing the future landscape of scholarly communication. Interim report. Center for Studies in Higher Education, University of California, Berkeley. Retrieved Nov. 15, 2008, from http://cshe.berkeley.edu/publications/publications.php?id=300

King, C. J., Harley, D., Earl-Novell, S., Arter, J., Lawrence, S., & Perciali, I. (2006). Scholarly communication: Academic values and sustainable models. Report. Center for Studies in Higher Education, University of California, Berkeley. 27July. Retrieved Nov. 15, 2008, from http://cshe.berkeley.edu/publications/publications.php?id=23

Hine, C. (2003). Systematics as cyberscience: The role of ICTs in the working practices of taxonomy. Paper presented at Oxford Internet Institute. *Information, Communication & Society* Symposium, 17–20 September, University of Oxford, UK. Retrieved Nov. 15, 2008, from http://www.soc.surrey.ac.uk/pdfs/hine_oii.pdf

Hine, C. M. (ed.) (2006). *New infrastructures for knowledge production; Understanding e-Science.* Hershey, PA: Information Science Publishing.

Hine, C. (2008). *Systematics as cyberscience; Computers, change, and continuity in science.* Cambridge, MA: MIT Press.

Hurd, J. M. (2000). The transformation of scientific communication: A model for 2020. *Journal of the American Society for Information Science, 51*(14): 1279–1283.

Huston, P. (2001). Book review: *Peer review in Health Sciences. Chronic Diseases in Canada.* 22(2). Retrieved Nov. 15, 2008, from http://www.phac-aspc.gc.ca/publicat/cdic-mcc/22-2/e_e.html

Indiana University (2007). Indiana University Cyberinfrastructure Newsletter, March. Retrieved Nov. 15, 2008, from http://racinfo.indiana.edu/newsletter/archives/2007-03.shtml

Jankowski, N., & Caldas, A. (2004). e-Science: Principles, projects and possibilities for communication and Internet studies. Paper presented at *Etmaal van de Communicatiewetenschap* (Day of Communication Science), Nov., University of Twente, the Netherlands.

Jankowski, N. W., & Van Selm, M. (2007). Research ethics in a virtual world: Guidelines and illustrations. In N. Carpentier, P. Pruulmann-Vengerfeldt, K. Nordenstreng, M. Hartmann, P. Vihalemm, B. Cammaerts, & H. Nieminen

(Eds.), *Media technologies and democracy in an enlarged Europe*, pp. 275–284. Tartu: Tartu University Press. Retrieved Nov. 15, 2008, from http://www.researchingcommunication.eu/reco_book3.pdf

Jeanneney, J.-N. (2007). *Google and the myth of universal knowledge*. Chicago: University of Chicago Press.

Jensen, K. B. (1991). Introduction: The qualitative turn. In Jensen, K. B., & Jankowski, N. W. (Eds.), *A handbook of qualitative methodologies for mass communication research*, pp. 1–11. London: Routledge.

Kirriemuir, J. (2008). A spring 2008 'snapshot' of U.K. higher and further education developments in Second Life. Report, October 2008. Eduserv Foundation. Retrieved Nov. 15, 2008, from http://www.eduserv.org.uk/~/media/foundation/sl/uksnapshot052008/final%20pdf.ashx

Latour, B., & Woolgar, S. (1979). *Laboratory life: The social construction of scientific facts*. Beverly Hills: Sage Publications.

Leydesdorff, L. (2002). The communication turn in the theory of social systems. *Systems Research and Behavioral Science*, 19: 129–136.

LLNL (2008). Lawrence Livermore National Laboratory, About LLNL. Web site, 13 February. Retrieved Nov. 15, 2008, from https://www.llnl.gov/llnl/about/ (consulted 11 Nov. 2008).

Maron, N. L., & Smith, K. K. (2008). Current models of digital scholarly communication. Results of an investigation conducted by Ithaka for the Association of Research Libraries. Report, Nov. Washington, DC: Association of Research Libraries. Retrieved Nov. 15, 2008, from http://www.arl.org/bm~doc/current-models-report.pdf

Microsoft External Research (2008). Scholarly communication. Web site. Retrieved Nov. 15, 2008, from http://www.microsoft.com/mscorp/tc/scholarly_communication.mspx.

Nature (2006). Overview: *Nature*'s peer review trial. *Nature*. doi: 10.1038/nature05535. Retrieved Nov. 15, 2008, from http://www.nature.com/nature/peerreview/debate/nature05535.html

Nentwich, M. *Cyberscience: Research in the age of the Internet*. Vienna: Austrian Academy of Sciences Press. Retrieved Nov. 15, 2008, from http://hw.oeaw.ac.at/3188-7

NeSC, (n.d.). Defining e-science. National e-Science Centre. Retrieved Nov. 15, 2008, from http://www.nesc.ac.uk/nesc/define.html

Netanel, N. (2008). Google Book search settlement. 28 Oct., Posting to Balkinization blog, Retrieved Nov. 15, 2008, from http://balkin.blogspot.com/2008/10/google-book-search-settlement.html

Nissenbaum, H., & Price, M. E. (Eds.) (2004). *Academy & the Internet*. New York: Peter Lang.

OeSS Project (n.d.). Oxford e-Social Science Project. Ethical, legal and institutional dynamics of Grid-enabled e-sciences. Retrieved Nov. 15, 2008, from http://www.oii.ox.ac.uk/microsites/oess/index.cfm

Pochoda, P. (2008). Scholarly publication at the digital tipping point. *Journal of Electronic Publishing*, 11(2). Retrieved Nov. 15, 2008, from http://dx.doi.org/10.3998/3336451.0011.202

Rorty, R. M. (ed.) (1967 / 1992). *The linguistic turn. Essays in philosophical method*. Chicago: University of Chicago Press.

Schwartz, M. (2008). The trolls among us. *New York Times Magazine*, 3 Aug. Retrieved Nov. 15, 2008, from http://www.nytimes.com/2008/08/03/magazine/03trolls-t.html?pagewanted=1&_r=1

Shepherd, J. (2007). It's a world of possibilities; Virtual campuses are springing up in Second Life, as universities discover the advantages of cyberspace. *Guardian*, online edition. Retrieved Nov. 15, 2008, from http://www.guardian.co.uk/education/2007/may/08/students.elearning/print

SNAC (2005). Social networks and cyberinfrastructure. Workshop 'The role of social network research in enabling cyberinfrastructure and the role of cyberinfrastructure in enabling social network research'. 3–5 Nov. Retrieved Nov. 15, 2008, from http://www.ncsa.uiuc.edu/Conferences/SNAC/

Salaway, G. & Caruso, J. B., with Nelson. M. R. (2008). *The ECAR study of undergraduate students and information technology, 2008.* Research study, vol. 8. Boulder, CO: EDUCAUSE Center for Applied Research. Retrieved Nov. 15, 2008, from http://www.educause.edu/ecar

Schneider, S. M. (1997). *Expanding the public sphere through computer-mediated communication: Political discussion about abortion in a Usenet newsgroup.* Unpublished Doctoral, Massachusetts Institute of Technology, Cambridge, Massachusetts.

de Solla Price, D. (1993). *Little science, big science.* New York: Columbia Univ. Press.

Steele, C. (2008). Scholarly monograph publishing in the 21st Century: The future more than ever should be an open book. *Journal of Electronic Publishing, 11*(2). Retrieved Nov. 15, 2008, from http://dx.doi.org/10.3998/3336451.0011.201

Suber, P. (2008). Open access in 2007. *Journal of Electronic Publishing, 11*(1). Retrieved Nov. 15, 2008, from http://dx.doi.org/10.3998/3336451.0011.110

Thompson, J. B. (2005). *Books in the Digital Age: The transformation of academic and higher education publishing in Britain and the United States.* Cambridge, UK: Polity.

Townsend, R. B. (2003). History and future of scholarly publishing. *Perspectives,* American Historical Association, October.

Turow, J., & Tsui, L. (Eds.) (2008). *The hyperlinked society; Questioning connections in the Digital Age.* Ann Arbor: University of Michigan Press. Retrieved Nov. 15, 2008, from http://www.digitalculture.org/hyperlinked.html

Von Lohmann, F. (2008). Google book search settlement: A reader's guide. Retrieved Nov. 15, 2008, from http://www.eff.org/deeplinks/2008/10/google-books-settlement-readers-guide

Waldrop, M. M. (2008). Science 2.0—Is open access science the future? *Scientific American.* April. Retrieved Nov. 15, 2008, from http://www.sciam.com/article.cfm?id=science-2-point-0

Ware, M. (2008). Peer review: Benefits, perceptions and alternatives. PRC Summary Papers 4. Publishing Research Consortium. London. Retrieved Nov. 15, 2008, from http://www.publishingresearch.net/documents/PRCsummary4Warefinal.pdf

Ware, M., & Monkman, M. (2008). Peer review in scholarly journals: Perspective of the scholarly community—an international study. Report. Publishing Research Consortium. Retrieved Nov. 15, 2008, from http://www.publishingresearch.net/documents/PeerReviewFullPRCReport-final.pdf

Weinberg, A. M. (1961). Impact of large-scale science on the United States: Big science is here to stay, but we have yet to make the hard financial and educational choices it imposes. *Science, 134*(3473): 161–164.

Willinsky, J. (2005). *The access principle: The case for open access to research and scholarship.* Cambridge, MA: MIT Press. Retrieved Nov. 15, 2008, from https://mitpress.mit.edu/books/willinsky/TheAccessPrinciple_TheMITPress_0262232421.pdf

Wouters, P. (1996). Cyberscience. *Kennis en Methode, 20*(2): 155–186.

Wyatt, S. (2008). Challenging the digital imperative. Inaugural lecture. Maastricht University, the Netherlands, 28 March. Retrieved Nov. 15, 2008, from http://www.unimaas.nl/bestand.asp?id=10221

Part II

Conceptualization

2 Towards a Sociology of e-Research
Shaping Practice and Advancing Knowledge

Jenny Fry and Ralph Schroeder

INTRODUCTION

The availability and appropriation of advanced computing tools in the sciences, social sciences, and humanities have accelerated in recent years. Although technology-driven research is not new to some intellectual fields, such as traditional big science, e.g. particle physics, or the emergent biosciences, e.g. genomics and bioinformatics, the Internet and high-performance computing have given a new impetus to the application and direction of computing in science and scholarship more generally. Several national funding programs have been initiated that can be broadly described as e-research, such as the U.K. e-Science Program funded by the EPSRC (Economic and Physical Science Research Council) and the Cyberinfrastructure Program funded by the NSF (National Science Foundation) in the U.S. These initiatives have been accompanied by large-scale funding and the development of projects across a range of application areas, from combinatorial chemistry to the interpretive social sciences. The vision underpinning these programs is that the new tools and resources being developed will greatly enhance research and enable new forms of global collaboration.

Although these novel large-scale research efforts have been driven, to a certain extent, by technological developments, they have already raised a number of non-technological issues, including legal, ethical, institutional, and disciplinary ones. Indeed, it is increasingly argued that the obstacles to the effectiveness of e-research are not so much technical, as social. In the social sciences, however, there is a variety of approaches that address the shaping of new forms of research, governance, communication, and collaboration, such as the sociology of science, the economics of innovation, and research policy.

In this chapter, we categorize these different social science approaches in the context of e-research and provide illustrations of how they have been deployed. The aim is to highlight the diversity of these approaches, show complementarities among them, and point to how they might shape the e-research enterprise. We take those scholars who are interested in studying or shaping e-research as an object of social research as the primary focus of this chapter. We also include, however, e-researchers who are concerned with the technical development of e-research technologies and infrastructure and categorize their approaches to development. Our categorization of approaches is based on a combination of examining the related literature and our own engagement with e-research communities in the U.K. from the perspective of the sociology of science, and we use examples of these to illustrate our argument. The conclusion weighs the different approaches and assesses their potential influence on the development of e-research and the future role of the social sciences in e-research.

The background to e-research, how it has emerged both programmatically, which is the focus of this chapter, and as a collection of small-scale independent efforts, has been explained in more detail elsewhere.[1] In order to provide context for the categories of social science approaches to e-research and the implications that we identify, we would like to highlight two points in particular. Firstly, that programmatic e-research, at least in the U.K. and U.S., was initially developed within the physical and life sciences and subsequently extended to the social sciences and humanities. The report by Berman and Brady (2005) was pivotal in marking the shift to the social sciences, citing issues such as attacks on the security of electronic computer networks and online identity theft as urgent issues that the social sciences could address through the adoption of e-research tools and resources. Berman and Brady also placed emphasis on new techniques for analyzing social behavior as well as the study of the implications of using the array of techniques, tools and resources afforded by e-research. Secondly, the U.K. initiative in science and engineering is already winding down as a distinct initiative that is separate from mainstream programs of research funding, as evidenced by the fact that dedicated e-science funding programs have ceased. Policy makers and funding agencies do not intend this to result in the end of e-research in the U.K., but rather to lead to the integration of e-research within other initiatives, either embedded within the disciplines or on a national infrastructural level. This U.K. funding strategy also means, however, that unless there are new national programs, the development of e-research as a distinct research initiative will likely take on a different guise. In the U.S., there is likewise increasing concern about how to extend and ensure the future uptake of the cyberinfrastructure initiatives. In both the U.S. and U.K., therefore, much of the emphasis is thus turning to developing a sustainable e-research infrastructure.

DISCIPLINES AND BOUNDARIES

Apart from describing e-research in terms of national efforts, it is important to take into account the disciplines involved and the extent to which they themselves are being transformed. The first feature to notice is that, as with many other technology-led initiatives, there is an imbalance that has meant technologies have been developed without taking social aspects into account. Overlooking the social side is typical of the early phase of large-scale and complex science and engineering projects (Hughes, 1998). Thus, David (2004: 3) has pointed out that "engineering breakthroughs alone will not be enough to achieve the outcomes envisaged for these undertakings. Success in realizing the potential of e-science, in the case of the U.K., and 'cyberinfrastructure', in the U.S., will more likely be the resultant of a nexus of interrelated social, legal *and* technical transformations." The social issues to emerge from e-research are now moving to the policy and funding foreground, but they also relate to wider changes in scientific and scholarly communication and collaboration such as electronic publishing, open science, distributed interdisciplinary collaboration, and the availability of networked digital resources. Nonetheless, on the whole, the discipline of computer science and its development of new technologies have dominated the early phase of e-research.

e-Research does not just consist of research apparatuses for manipulating data and the physical environment; e-research tools can also be a means for scientific communication.[2] With e-research, the scope and scale of collaboration have generally increased, which means that communication itself poses formidable organizational problems and yet extends the technological infrastructure of research. Put differently, e-research faces new challenges involving the coordination and control of research (Fry, 2006). Collaboration-at-a-distance could thus arguably also be seen as a way of underpinning consensus and replicability by using research instruments or research technologies.[3] The balance between the two—research instruments for manipulating the objects of research and instruments for communication and collaboration—is not yet clear. In the latter case, it might be asked whether two different intellectual fields in the social sciences—library and information science in the case of scholarly communication, and the sociology of science in the case of research instruments—are best equipped to focus on the topic from within their domain, or whether there is common ground between them.

Another point to note is that it is not necessarily the case that the natural sciences are 'earlier adopters' of Internet-related tools more than the social sciences and humanities. In fact, Nentwich argues (e.g., 2003: 107–9) that there are some disciplines *within* these broad disciplinary groupings that are 'ahead' of others. Nevertheless, as we highlighted earlier, national programs have broadly followed the pattern of initiating programs in the natural sciences and then following up with initiatives in the social sciences and humanities. Thus, in the U.K., the e-science Program was followed by an e-Social Science Program and various other initiatives in the U.K. at a much later stage. Similarly in the U.S., the Berman and Brady report (2005) was published two years after the Atkins report (2003). In any case, the initiatives have rippled outward across more and more disciplinary boundaries, although perhaps the argument that Kling and McKim (2000: 1306) have made for "electronic media supporting scientific communication," that field differences are likely to persist, also applies to e-research.

If we consider the scale of funding for the different projects and disciplines involved, clearly funding in the natural sciences outweighs funding in the social sciences. For example, in the U.K. it is estimated that £250 million has been spent on natural science (Jeffreys, 2005), whereas the social sciences have committed far less and the humanities are on a smaller scale again. This must be put in the context of the historical competition between the social and natural sciences for resources, whereby the social sciences and humanities have traditionally been funded on a much smaller scale.

SOCIAL SCIENCE APPROACHES TO E-RESEARCH

We might expect that the newness of developments in e-research should constitute a core concern for any social science approach, critically informing them even if they are not centrally concerned with it. The reason for this is that the newness has the potential to pinpoint, in a neutral way, the elements of e-research that sets it apart from other kinds of research. The social implications of science and technology in-the-making, however, fall most closely within the social sciences into the subdiscipline of the sociology of science. One question that can therefore be addressed by examining how the social sciences are involved in shaping e-research efforts is the extent to which this subdiscipline informs other approaches, and how it is placed within the social sciences to contribute to the understanding and shaping of e-research.

In an earlier article (Schroeder & Fry, 2007) upon which this chapter is based we restricted our categorization of social science approaches to those studies concerned with e-research as an object of research, rather than practical efforts towards the technical development of e-research. Here we extend the categorization to also include the latter based on two dimensions:

- The degree to which approaches are pragmatic (focusing on the practical aspects of development and use of e-research tools and resources) or are research oriented (concerned with problematizing or theorizing specific aspects of e-research);
- The degree to which approaches attempt to engage with e-research on a proactive level or, in contrast, take a detached stance.

Plotting the approaches we identified along these two dimensions (that should be conceived as continua rather than binary fixed points) results in a taxonomy consisting of four main categories: proactive-engagement/pragmatic; proactive-engagement/research; detachment/pragmatic; detachment/research. This taxonomy yields eight approaches; see Tables 2.1 and 2.2 below.

Table 2.1 Approaches to e-Research as an Object of Research

	Pragmatic	*Research*
Proactive-Engagement	**Usability/practical** e.g. How appropriation can be enhanced through refining understanding of practice, user representations, and human computer interaction	**Value free/attempted neutrality** e.g. Measuring dimensions of distributed communication and collaboration
Detachment	**Advocacy/steering and aligning structures** e.g. Fostering institutional, economic, and legal structures that enable distributed communication and collaboration. Promoting a particular type of open and accessible e-research	**Critique/reflexive or prospective** e.g. Social implications of e-research; ability to deliver on claims; policy

Table 2.2 Approaches to e-Research as an Object of Development

	Pragmatic	*Research*
Proactive-Engagement	**Agenda Neutral/Supporting Paradigms** e.g. Concern with tools being user-led; development efforts addressing user-needs in a specific research paradigm, e.g. discourse analysis, gene ontologies, text-corpora in linguistics. Social factors perceived as technology and policy re-engineering problem	**Embedded in the Disciplines/ Sustainability as Adoption** e.g. Emerging from a positivistic tradition. Addressing computational and processing issues for domain-specific problems; uptake and use perceived as a result of overcoming technical problems
Detachment	**Agenda Aligned/Supporting Generic Infrastructure** e.g. Concern with development of services across disciplinary boundaries; social factors perceived as a social re-engineering problem	**Skepticism/Non-use from within the Disciplines/ Sustainability as Project/** e.g. Possibly leading to resistance; uptake and use related to perceived relevance of e-research

A limitation of taxonomies is that they tend to present stereotypes and suggest that the objects of categorization fit neatly into mutually exclusive categories, but as we know social phenomena rarely behave in this way. Our intention in developing the taxonomy represented in Tables 2.1 and 2.2 is nevertheless to understand current approaches, how they relate to one another, and the ways in which they are shaping the role of the social sciences in e-research. Despite the analytical distinction into eight main types of approach, there are synergies at the intersection of the pragmatic/ research continuum and the proactive-engagement/detachment continuum. We shall return to discuss these synergies after presenting a brief illustration of the eight approaches.

Proactive-Engagement/Pragmatic

Perspectives that fall within this quadrant of the taxonomy, shown in Tables 2.1 and 2.2, are concerned with how the effectiveness and uptake of e-research can be enhanced through, for example, refining understanding of practice, user representations, and human computer interfaces. Research councils developing e-research programs are increasingly acknowledging that usability issues are a key barrier to the uptake and use of advanced digital technologies. Funding mechanisms to support usability research have been implemented in programs such as the EPSRC call for "Research into the Usability Challenges to Emerge From e-Science." This focus is also reflected in the emergence of communication fora such as the "Designing for Usability in e-Science" Workshop sponsored by EPSRC and NeSC (http://www.nesc.ac.uk/action/esi/contribution.cfm?Title=613).

Usability/Practical

An illustration of this approach is the eDiaMoND project (Jirotka et al., 2005), which was a flagship U.K. e-science project. The aim of this project was to create a federated database of digitized mammograms. This would enable x-rays for breast cancer screening (mammograms), which are currently done on film, to be stored and annotated digitally. This digitization would also allow the images and expertise, which are now located at individual breast cancer screening units and 'double-read', to be shared across a network.

In this case, many usability issues were found by means of ethnographic and quasi-naturalistic evaluations of work practices in the creation of prototype systems. One of the most important was 'trust', both in the new technology, and between radiologists. Interpersonal trust is developed in particular ways in the 100 or so Breast Care Units across the U.K. The co-location of technicians, radiologists, and other experts in traditional Breast Care Units allows personal histories to be developed, such as where a person trained, who they trained with, how they calibrate the machinery, their particular competencies, and knowledge gaps. The introduction of a distributed system for reading mammograms reconfigured the ways in which trust could be built, and new practices were necessary in order to know the other's capabilities and to come to rely on the other in new ways. Another set of issues concerned the sharing of data, whereby it was deemed generally unethical to share mammograms between clinics and outside of the clinicians and readers who had had direct involvement with the patient and with each other.

The usability findings in this case could be used to try to address these issues by technical means, such as developing interfaces that afford the communication of contextual information, or by social means, such as reconfiguring practice. In fact, the two were difficult to separate into distinct issues. An important outcome of the usability research on the eDiaMoND project has been to highlight the immense obstacles that would be faced in translating the 'proof of concept' into a workable system that could be adopted on a large scale across the U.K. National Health Service, as originally envisioned (http://www.ediamond.ox.ac.uk/whatis.html). In this respect, the usability aspect of this project was typical of usability research: identifying practical obstacles on the ground that then can potentially be overcome by taking into account the needs of diverse sets of users and social settings. Seen from a greater distance, such case-bound usability research is typically and increasingly a tool for making laboratory or prototype technologies robust enough to withstand the vagaries of real world settings.

Agenda Neutral/Supporting Paradigms

This approach is exemplified by development projects that are concerned with research practice on a fine-grained level; how individuals handle and process data, how collaborative groups work together, and the like. These projects typically involve truly multidisciplinary teams. These teams differ from those described under 'Practical/usability' in that rather than having an intermediary between developer and potential user, such as a user requirements engineer, these teams involve developers, domain experts and practitioners. Two of the research nodes of the U.K.-based National Centre for e-Social Science (NCeSS, http://www.ncess.ac.uk/), Mixed Media Grid (MiMeG, http://www.ncess.ac.uk/research/video/mimeg/) and Digital Record (Understanding new forms of digital record http://www.ncess.ac.uk/research/digital_records/) are examples of this type of development approach.

Approaches in this quadrant tend to be agenda neutral because they are case or paradigm bound and are focused on developing tools for a clearly delineated set of practices, such as collaborative video analysis (see Mixed Media Grid, MiMeG, above). They thus tend to be concerned with extending methods and supporting research distributed across multiple people, disciplines, locations and resources. This means that individual practices and task-specific applications are prioritized over generic infrastructure, standardization and interoperability. Consequently, development efforts are more engaged with the use and adoption of e-research tools, but tend to be distanced from directly advocating overarching e-research agendas.

Also included in this category are localized small-scale development efforts that are not part of any national e-research program and therefore tend to be agenda neutral at least in terms of explicit institutional policies towards e-research. Of course, the scope and penetration of these efforts are subject to other forms of governance. Tools currently being developed that form part of the social science community engaged in e-research include VOSON (Virtual Observatory for the Study of Online Social Networks), the SocScibot and LexiURL suite of tools and Issue Crawler. These tend to be decentralized tools, utilizing an infrastructure not institutionalized and tools that are also available as freeware. We have excluded the Internet Archive, which is becoming an important e-research resource within the social sciences, from this category because it is centralized on an institutional level with collaborating institutions such as the Library of Congress and the Smithsonian, and although it is freely available, it is not being developed on open source principles unlike some of the other examples that allow for some co-development between creators and users.

Proactive-Engagement/Research

This quadrant represents approaches that are research, as opposed to practice-oriented, and that engage with the object of research, whether it is to evaluate the impact of technologies or to develop indicators of changes in practices. This quadrant is therefore of more relevance to approaches that are concerned with e-research as an object of research than those that are concerned with e-research as an object of development. Nonetheless, it is applicable to both instances when we take the broader social sciences into account as potential users of e-research technologies and infrastructure.

Value Free/Attempted Neutrality

There are of course debates in the social sciences about whether value-free research and neutrality are possible. At the same time, many researchers aspire to such a goal, even when they are aware of its potential limits. One area of the study of e-research where this approach is often in evidence is in the study of communication and collaboration. Research that falls into this category includes, for example, the analysis and evaluation of collaboratories (Finholt, 2002; http://www.scienceofcollaboratories.org/). Further examples of work in this area include identifying patterns of new modes of scientific communication and collaboration using methods and measures such as social network analysis, co-citation practices, co-authorship, and hyperlink networks. This work is sometimes policy related and often involves large-scale analysis or comparison of many cases, for example, when measuring scientific productivity or incentives among scientists for collaboration. However, one of the aims is typically an objective assessment of the inter-organizational relations in science.

One illustration of this approach is a study by Cummings and Kiesler (2005) of collaborative scientific projects in the U.S. They examined 62 collaborative projects that were funded by the National Science Foundation, most with partners distributed across a number of locations, and most of which were multi-disciplinary. One of their findings was that collaborative research across institutions is more difficult than collaborative research across disciplines in terms of project coordination and project outcomes. They also noticed that communication in distributed projects tended to drop off over time. In conclusion, they argue that there may be a 'trade-off' in the advantages that these projects can bring between "innovation opportunities versus coordination costs" (2005: 720). These findings, even if they did not arise directly from e-research projects, are clearly relevant to e-research. Many e-research projects are still at too early a stage of developing the capabilities for collaboration-at-a-distance for one to be able to tell if they are effective and able to bridge distances in collaboration. It is clear, however, that coordination problems of the type identified by Cummings and Kiesler (2005), which are almost always multi-disciplinary and distributed, will also affect e-research. Sonnenwald (2006), for example, who studied one e-research multi-institutional collaboration (although with limited multi-disciplinarity) over the course of several months, noticed a host of problems of coordination across distributed institutions.

Embedded in the Disciplines/Sustainability as Adoption

Development efforts in this category place an emphasis on computational and data processing needs for specific research problems. The focus is on sustainability, ensuring a steady flow of human and financial resources in order to maintain tools and resources and support communities of users, rather than generic infrastructure. In the U.K., social science projects that fall under this category tend to be in areas of quantitative social science, such as the NCeSS funded MoSeS (Modelling and Simulation for e-Social Science, http://www.geog.leeds.ac.uk/projects/moses.html) research node which aims to develop tools and resources for simulating populations, based on national statistical datasets such as Census UK. The added value that projects such as MoSeS claim to contribute to the social sciences through e-research is the potential contribution to evidence-based policy making in critical areas such as health and transport. Policy Grid (http://www.csd.abdn.ac.uk/research/policygrid/) is another research node funded by the NCeSS that falls within this approach as its aims are to develop semantic Grid technologies to support mixed data and mixed methods within rural development and policy making. In this quadrant we can also place research aimed at gauging the adoption of e-research tools without being prejudicial to the success of e-research as a project, such as the research carried out as part the e-Infrastructure of NCeSS (http://www.ncess.ac.uk/services/research/) which is aimed at surveying users, including about non-use and about tools that are not part of the NCeSS effort.

Detachment/Pragmatic

Approaches in this quadrant attempt to create a new momentum beyond individual projects; here the emphasis is on setting and implementing a new agenda for research. This effort will entail enrolling new actors, in addition to researchers and users, because new institutions must be created or existing ones aligned in order to allow this new type of research, with its novel values and benefits, to flourish.

Advocacy/Steering and Aligning Structures

Advocacy is mainly aimed at general issues affecting e-research, rather than specific e-research projects or e-research agendas, although it engages with agendas in pursuance of its goals. These include fostering structures that enable communication and collaboration across disciplinary, institutional, and geographic frontiers. For example, in his evaluation of the legal and economic dynamics of scholarly publishing, Nentwich (2006) seeks a socio-technical solution to current quality control mechanisms that are seen as a threat to open science. He argues that "what is needed is hardly more technology, but organization, management procedures and legal as well as economic knowledge at the interface of technology and the social environment" (Nentwich, 2006: 201).

There are parallels between Nentwich's (2006) discussion of digital publishing and Hine's (2005) case study of systematics in biology (see discussion of the critique/reflexive or prospective approach below). It may be, for example, that the drive for open digital access to information about species will undermine processes whereby cataloguing was traditionally peer reviewed, just as Nentwich's advocacy of open access may undermine the traditional peer review structure of journals. The de-commodification of information that Nentwich advocates also raises issues (again, echoing Hine's work) of how archives and collections will be maintained and disseminated effectively in an open-access system and who will fund such resources.

Such general issues of resources and organizational frameworks are typically at the forefront of the 'advocacy' social science approach. This approach is illustrated by the work of David and Spence (2003), in their account of the institutional infrastructures for e-science. They seek out the economic advantages and pitfalls of the Internet's open architecture and culture. In the process, they discuss, among other issues, the question of how such an infrastructure could be funded, including whether the traditional models of journal publisher revenues can be maintained in open publishing, and how intellectual property rights can be implemented when data are made openly accessible or shared. From the point of view of the structural/advocacy position of David and Spence, it is primarily the legal, political, and administrative structures that have been experienced as constraints to Grid-based collaboration by the first generations of Internet and Grid users.

A specific policy-related example of David and Spence's work that they touch on is the movement towards open access publishing (cf. Schroeder,

2007). This movement aims to make research publications that are currently available only in the form of expensive journal subscriptions freely available. Regardless of the outcome of open access debates, however, in this case social science can point to the advantages (and disadvantages) of policy recommendations accordingly, and promote putting these into practice.

Agenda Aligned/Supporting Generic Infrastructure

It is in this category that we place national publicly accessible resources, such as the Internet Archive, given their institutional alliance and primary concern with developing a generic service that is not embedded in any specific discipline or research paradigm. Other social science initiatives that constitute a wider agenda, such as those that are part of the ESRFRI (European Strategy Forum on Research Infrastructures) effort to create pan-European infrastructures (for example, in the social sciences, CESSDA, which promotes integration of social science data; see http://www.nsd.uib.no/cessda/newsarchive.html#2007_5), also fall into this quadrant.

Detachment/Research

Approaches in this quadrant are concerned with the interrelationship between micro-level research practices, on the one hand, and macro-level policy and technology implementation, on the other. Whether from the perspective of critiquing e-research in the context of social and institutional factors, or from the perspective of potential social science users with concerns regarding the social implications (e.g., recognition and reward). Sustainability viewed from this approach is concerned with social barriers and perceived relevance of e-research.

Critical/Reflexive or prospective

The critical/reflexive approach is concerned with the social implications of e-research and tends to highlight the discrepancy between visions and practice. The focus is often on the analysis of high-level discourses around e-research, such as policy documents or future visions. The discussion typically revolves around the 'values' and 'expectations' embedded in technologies as well the evolving meaning of terminology, definitions, and boundaries. This perspective tends to couple its argument with the need for researcher immersion in ethnographic case studies (Vann & Bowker, 2006; Woolgar & Coopmans, 2006).[4]

Vann and Bowker (2006), for example, explore 'prospective texts' around e-research and argue that in order to understand the impact of e-research on knowledge-producing practices, social scientists need to "consider decisions that get made about how the skill, commitment, performance, and product demand of scientists can be coordinated and stabilized" (2006: 71). In other words, visions lock in particular trajectories of the way in which the work of the research is done. This approach thus looks to concrete instantiations of local scientific practices—such as how the 'labor' of research of different forms of research is talked about (Hine, 2005; Vann & Bowker, 2006)—or at new disciplinary identities (Hine, 2006) and forms of accountability in scientific practice.

Hine's work (2005) is a good illustration of this approach. She explores the relationship between the visions for global online cataloguing and digitization of species and the cultural specificity of the systematics field in biology. To do this, she examines the discourse of the House of Lords Select Committee on Science and Technology review of the state of systematics in Britain, combining this with ethnographic observation of the problems encountered in practice. In the process, she challenges the inevitability of the digital solutions perspective: 'if you build it they will come'.

Systematics is also an interesting case study for exploring what Hine (2005: 4) describes as the 'political geography' of a discipline, whereby the geopolitical history of a discipline shapes collective notions of social justice in the present. For example, human geographers try to distance themselves from the colonial geographies of the 18th century, and anthropologists are also keen to rectify and distance themselves from the cultural imperialism of the same period. In the case of systematics, access to the world's most critical taxonomic collections has historically been held by national institutions of developed countries, often with a history of colonization. This centralization of resources and exclusion of developing countries in the past (which are typically the source of the data held in national repositories of specimens) make the rhetoric of open access and data sharing compelling to a sense of social justice within the disciplinary community. The 'political geography' of systematics also converges with the "archaic image of systematic biology" (Select Committee on Science and Technology, 2002, in Hine 2005: 6) to ensure that digital technologies are perceived within systematics to hold both 'practical purchase' and 'symbolic qualities'. Indeed, Hine argues that "particular sets of expectations around digital technologies have played an important part in shaping the discipline's response to the Internet, playing out both on a level of individual practices and in high level policy forums where the discipline's activities are evaluated" (2005: 5).

Researchers who adopt the critical/reflexive perspective argue that the compelling rhetoric around the transformative nature of digital technologies will preclude appropriate discussions about the real needs for digitizing resources and for evaluating the needs of users.

Skepticism/Non-use from within the disciplines/Sustainability as Project

A skeptical approach may lead to non-use or resistance to e-research. The U.K. National Centre for e-Social Science (NCeSS) perceives that potential users of e-social science will fall into three main categories (Halfpenny,

2006): early adopters (current award holders under the e-Social Science program); enthusiasts (who will need practical demonstration of the potential benefit of tools in their research area and for whom the new technology fits with existing work practices); and the unengaged (for whom the complexity of e-science infrastructure would be a disincentive and tools would need to be black-boxed and easily usable). In this quadrant the perceived development and uptake will be viewed with skepticism, with resources perhaps better allocated to an agenda that is less technology-driven and that sees the extension of tools to the 'unengaged' as being of doubtful value.

DISCUSSION

In this chapter we have used a limited number of examples to illustrate each of the eight types of social science approaches to e-research that we have identified. Although we have categorized these approaches into four discrete categories, the taxonomy presented in Tables 2.1 and 2.2 represents potential tensions and synergies. In order to understand the working of a particular aspect or component of e-research practice or policy, it may be beneficial if a combination of approaches were applied. For example, a project concerned with the sustainability of e-research may feasibly employ a 'usability/practical' approach as a complement to a 'value free/attempted neutrality' approach. However, the various approaches—whether practical in contrast to critical, or neutral rather than advocacy—are likely to shape both our understanding and the outcomes of e-research in different ways.

Potential Impact

The 'critical/reflexive' stance, for example, is likely to have an indirect effect on e-research, seeking to shift the debate about its overall aims and opening up a space for a wider debate about the role of science in society that includes more than just researchers. Advocacy may also contribute to steering e-research, and may do so in a direct way, but one question mark is bound to be the strength of the influence of social science on policymaking. In this case, it is important to consider the fora—policy organizations, scientific advisory boards, academic conferences, and the like—in which these policy debates take place.

The examples illustrate that the line between the social, technical, legal, and economic aspects of e-research are becoming blurred. In usability approaches, the line between technical and social improvements may be hardest to draw, even if, as in the eDiaMoND case described earlier, there were many researchers with a social science background involved. In a value-free/attempted neutrality approach, social science can learn much about how science works in the case of these large technological systems.

For the projects developing e-research tools and resources (Agenda Aligned/Supporting Generic Infrastructure), on the other hand, the question is whether those projects that are mainly being developed as part of a larger concerted e-research agenda are more likely to succeed than those which are agenda neutral or embed themselves within disciplines. A key factor here must be whether the larger, agenda-driven funding programs will continue, or if e-research tools and resources will be absorbed into existing disciplines or scientific (and social scientific) advances.

Potential Synergies

It will be obvious that, despite our efforts to separate the four social science approaches, there is much overlap between them. This applies not only to the thin line between critical and neutral approaches, but also between critical approaches and usability: For example, the usability issues that were described in the eDiaMoND study led the researchers to say that their findings aimed to "respecify" (Jirotka et al., 2005: 395) the original "visions" of the project, just as Hine's (2005) work wants to re-size the visions of systematics. Note, however, that in the eDiaMoND case, this respecification of visions was done in order to "make their accomplishment more achievable in the long run" (Jirotka et al., 2005: 395), whereas Hine's (2006) conclusions throw into doubt the very achievability of the visions.

There is also an age-old tension between theory and practice[5] or, in this case, between becoming so involved in constructive engagement (the policy and usability approaches) that all the necessary distance of the critical or neutral approaches is forsaken, with the result that little of value is gained for social science understanding of the implications of new research technologies. Or the opposite: that the distance between the neutral or critical perspectives and practice is so large that no lessons can be derived for guiding the development of new research technologies. It will only be possible to gauge these tensions—and how they pull in one or other direction in the case of the e-research—once e-research projects and infrastructures have matured.

Another point is that different social science approaches may influence e-research at different stages. Thus, for example, critics of the visions may dominate in the early phases of the e-research enterprise and may fade as the visions—in whatever form—become translated into mundane practices or when they have faded into practical realities.

The push to develop and use different e-research tools and resources would no doubt benefit from the application of complimentary perspectives, but in practice these are bound to be pulled in different directions, not least to the same intellectual and social considerations that e-research itself is subject to.

CONCLUSIONS

Coming back to the question of common ground and diversity among the eight social science approaches we have identified, it would seem that despite the complementarities that we highlight above, an integration of goals has not yet transpired. It may be the case that over time, the eight distinct approaches will mature into an intellectual field of its own right or become embedded in a broader adoption of e-research practices. In terms of our hypothesis about the 'newness' of e-research being a force for common ground among the approaches, we conclude that such newness or novelty shifts in and out of focus depending on whether an approach is proactively engaged on a research level, or detached from a pragmatic perspective.

The newness of e-research is perhaps least relevant to 'usability/practical' approaches, because here the main concern is a pragmatic one: making tools work. By employing sociology of science concepts—such as trust, incentives and interdependence between researchers—'usability/practical' approaches can, however, locate the focus of where bottlenecks may lie. A 'critical/reflexive or prospective' approach will also not be primarily concerned with novelty, but rather with the extent to which the vision lives up to or reifies the realities of the sciences. Nevertheless, a useful way of gauging whether e-research becomes translated into effective scientific practice is how e-researchers cope, for example, with the challenges of uncertainty that accompany novelty (Whitley, 2000). 'Advocacy/steering and aligning structures' approaches are concerned with whether e-research is enhancing research efforts more broadly, and so will focus on whether e-research is providing a basis for more powerful ways of organizing research. A 'value free/attempted neutrality' approach, on the other hand, will need to establish which sociological concepts are adequate to the task of describing this new form of science and how well they fit different e-research developments.

In development and use, there is also a programmatic element, apart from an instrumental one, at play: how, via pushing tools and resources across disciplines 'from above', or providing a raft of these tools and resources as part of a sustained platform, there is an aim to actively overcome systemic bottlenecks and creating novel supporting institutions. A skeptical approach will regard these efforts as overbearing and ultimately headed towards limited success, if any. For agenda-neutral approaches and those embedded within disciplines, on the other hand, this will depend on how research technologies and the resources they deploy can cross disciplinary boundaries or be successful within them interstitially; that is, whether the institutional momentum can simultaneously reshape the landscape of research.

A final set of ideas that can be taken from the sociology of science is that across all e-research projects, one effect which seems mostly unintended is that e-research projects make visible or explicit many processes that were previously invisible or implicit.[6] Examples abound, and include workflow organization, intellectual property issues, and inter-institutional commitments. e-Research projects do this partly because computerization necessitates, for example, that data are put into a certain format or stored in a certain way or made accessible across a network. These e-research developments all require standardization of rules and procedures that may previously have been unstated or unformalized or do not apply to non-digital material. At the same time, e-research may also hide or marginalize other research efforts that are not amenable to the process of rendering research into digital formats.

Earlier we posed the question of the potential influence of the sociology of science, as a disciplinary foundation across these approaches. Perhaps a more prudent question would be: what is the likely impact of these approaches and of e-research itself upon the sociology of science? Is the focus within the subdiscipline of sociology of science coupled to its object such that it promotes the advance within this subdiscipline, or is the subdiscipline promoted by means of engaging pragmatically in helping to reshape the new technologies?

Taking the social science approaches identified above more broadly, are the diversity of perspectives (we have identified four) beneficial, contributing essential, yet distinct, inputs to different levels of research policy and practice, do they merely reflect fragmentary characteristics of the social sciences? Are we witnessing, on the other hand, a concerted shift in research organization towards a shared set of approaches and goals?

These questions must be posed with the understanding that the shift of resources and collaboration within online networks represents an entwining of an emerging large technological system for online research with the social environment of research institutions and settings. Can such a socio-technical system be reshaped by social scientists who analyze research in diverse ways, or will the social sciences themselves rather become engulfed by the new system of tools that are reconfiguring research across different arenas and institutions of knowledge production? In short, how is the object of research (e-research) coupled to the different social science perspectives that have been discussed? The question of how the social sciences relate to e-research as e-research transforms the nature of knowledge cuts across all four social science approaches as we have distinguished them here and will continue to evolve. Categorizing the different social science perspectives in terms of their potential relation to the object of research is a useful start and provides a better grasp on e-research, as e-research, in turn, re-shapes the sciences and advances knowledge.

ACKNOWLEDGMENTS

This chapter is an updated and revised version of an earlier journal article (Schroeder & Fry, 2007). We would like to thank Nick Jankowski, two anonymous referees, and the participants at the "Social Science Perspective on e-Sciences" workshop at the Second International Conference on e-Social Science, Manchester, June 28–30, 2006, for helpful comments and suggestions. The work for this chapter has been supported by ESRC grant RES-149–25–1022 and is part of the Oxford e-Social Science (OeSS) project.

NOTES

1. See the introductory chapter to this volume and also an earlier version of this essay (Schroeder & Fry, 2007). It can be difficult to define e-science or e-research independently of the funding programs that have fostered it. Schroeder (2008: 133) defines it as "the use of computing tools for networking in order to share distributed digital resources in scientific or academic research."
2. Koku, Nazer, and Wellman (2000) argued some time ago that electronic communication does not do away with face-to-face communication among researchers; here, as elsewhere, the two are complementary. Nevertheless, Koku et al. also noted that communication among researchers in a variety of different modalities has become denser—that is, more frequent and more multi-channel. e-Research contributes to this trend, complementing rather than displacing existing ways of doing research.
3. Schroeder (2007, 2008), drawing on Collins (1994), argues that because e-research consists of research technologies, these technologies play a unique role in promoting the advance of knowledge since they are generic devices which operate across knowledge domains, have a more global scope, and allow research materials to be more powerfully malleable. This argument can be applied to research technologies in the social sciences as well as the natural sciences, though with the proviso that research technologies are coupled differently to their research domains depending on the knowledge domain. Further, research technologies operate on different levels, sometimes as part of research infrastructures, sometimes as part of the science communication system, and in other cases as individual tools or resources—though for e-research, these are also networked and distributed.
4. Woolgar and Coopmans (2006) use the term "virtual witnessing."
5. Max Weber's "Objectivity" essay (1949) remains a key starting point in this debate; see also Rule (1997) for a recent overview.
6. This has been discussed by Fuchs (1992) outside of the context of e-research, whereby researchers make their findings presentable to their peers, or they standardize and make their instruments more robust, contributing to a process of enhancing visibility and explicitness in scientific practices. In the context of e-research, the argument is made by Schroeder (2007, 2008).

REFERENCES

Atkins, D. E., et al. (2003). *Revolutionizing science and engineering through cyberinfrastructure.* Report of the National Science Foundation Blue-Ribbon Advisory Panel on Cyberinfrastructure. Arlington, VA: Directorate for Computer and Information Science and Engineering, National Science Foundation.

Berman, F., & Brady, H. (2005). *Final report: NSF SBE-CISE workshop on cyberinfrastructure and the social sciences.* Retrieved December 7, 2006 from http://vis.sdsc.edu/sbe/reports/SBE-CISE-FINAL.pdf

Collins, R. (1994). Why the social sciences won't become high-consensus, rapid-discovery science. *Sociological Forum, 9*(2): 155–77.

Cummings, J., & Kiesler, S. (2005). Collaborative research across disciplinary and institutional boundaries. *Social Studies of Science, 35*(5): 703–22.

David, P. A. (2004). Towards a cyberinfrastructure for enhanced scientific collaboration. *OII Research Report No. 4*. Oxford: Oxford Internet Institute, University of Oxford. Retrieved September 28, 2006 from http://www.oii.ox.ac.uk/
resources/publications/RR4.pdf

David, P. A., & Spence, M. (2003). Towards institutional infrastructures for e-science: The scope of the challenge. *OII Research Report No. 2*. Retrieved December 5, 2006 from http://www.oii.ox.ac.uk/resources/publications/RR2.pdfm

Finholt, T. A. (2002). Collaboratories: Science over the Internet. In S. J. Lita, S. D.
Nelson, & A. H. Teich (Eds.), *AAAS science and technology policy yearbook*,
pp. 339–344. Washington, DC: American Association for the Advancement of
Science.

Fry, J. (2006). Coordination and control of research practice across scientific fields:
Implications for a differentiated e-science. In C. Hine (Ed.), *New infrastructures
for knowledge production: Understanding e-science*, pp. 167–187. Hershey, PA:
Information Science Publishing.

Fuchs, S. (1992). *The professional quest for truth*. Albany: State University of New
York Press.

Hine, C. (2005, November). The politics and practice of accessibility in systematics. *Past, present and future of research in the Information Society*. An official
side event preceding Phase II of the World Summit on the Information Society
(WSIS), Tunis.

Hine, C. (2006). Computerization movements and scientific disciplines: The reflexive potential of new technologies. In C. Hine (Ed.), *New infrastructures for
knowledge production: Understanding e-science*, pp. 26–47. Hershey, PA:
Information Science Publishing.

Hughes, T. (1998). *Rescuing Prometheus*. New York: Pantheon Books.

Jeffreys, P. (2005). Presentation at Oxford Internet Institute workshop. December 2.

Jirotka, M., Procter, R., Rodden, T., & Bowker, G. C. (2005). Collaboration and
trust in healthcare innovation: The eDiaMoND case study. *Computer Supported Cooperative Work, 14*(4): 369–398.

Klein, J. T. (1996). *Crossing boundaries: Knowledge, disciplinarities, and interdis-
ciplinarities*. Charlottesville, VA: University Press of Virginia.

Kling, R., & McKim, G. (2000). Not just a matter of time: Field differences and the
shaping of electronic media in supporting scientific communication. *Journal of
the American Association for Information Science, 51*(14): 1306–1320.

Koku, E., Nazer, N., & Wellman, B. (2000). Netting scholars: Online and offline.
American Behavioral Scientist, 43(10): 1752–1774.

Nentwich, M. (2003). *Cyberscience: Research in the age of the Internet*. Vienna:
Austrian Academy of Sciences Press.

Nentwich, M. (2006). Cyberinfrastructure for next generation scholarly publishing. In C. Hine (Ed.), *New infrastructures for knowledge production: Understanding e-science*, pp. 189–205. Hershey, PA: Information Science Publishing.

Rule, J. (1997). *Theory and progress in social science*. Cambridge, UK: Cambridge
University Press.

Schroeder, R. (2007). e-Research infrastructures and open science: Towards a new
system of knowledge production? *Prometheus, 25*(1): 1–17.

Schroeder, R., & Fry, J. 2007. Social science perspectives on e-sciences. *Journal
of Computer-Mediated Communication, 12*(2). Retrieved 20 June, 2008 from
http://jcmc.indiana.edu/vol12/issue2/schroeder.html

Schroeder, R. (2008). e-Sciences as research technologies: Reconfiguring disciplines, globalizing knowledge. *Social Science Information, 47*(2): 131–157.

Select Committee on Science and Technology. (2002). *What on earth? The threat
to the science underpinning conservation*. London: House of Lords.

Sonnenwald, D. (2006). Collaborative virtual environments for scientific collaboration: Technical and organizational design frameworks. In R. Schroeder R. & A.-S. Axelsson (Eds.), *Avatars at work and play: Collaboration and interaction in shared virtual environments*, pp. 63–96. Dordrecht, Netherlands: Springer.

Vann, K., & Bowker, G. (2006). Interest in production: On the configuration of technology-bearing labours for epistemic IT. In C. Hine (Ed.), *New infrastructures for knowledge production: Understanding e-Science,* pp. 71–97. Hershey, PA: Information Science Publishing.

Weber, M. (1949). "Objectivity" in social science and social policy. In M. Weber, *The methodology of the social sciences,* pp. 49–112. New York: Free Press.

Whitley, R., (2000). *The intellectual and social organization of the sciences* (2nd ed.). Oxford: Oxford University Press.

Woolgar, S., & Coopmans, C. (2006). Virtual witnessing in a virtual age: A prospectus for social studies of e-science. In C. Hine (Ed.), *New infrastructures for knowledge production: Understanding e-science*, pp. 1–25. Hershey, PA: Information Science Publishing.

Wouters, P., & Beaulieu, A. (2006). Imagining e-science beyond computation. In C. Hine (Ed.), *New infrastructures for knowledge production: Understanding e-science*, pp. 48–70. Hershey, PA: Information Science Publishing.

3   e-Research as Intervention

Anne Beaulieu and Paul Wouters

INTRODUCTION

New research tools, be they digital libraries or digital work environments, are usually seen as means to support and further develop research. This also holds for the relatively recent investments in cyberinfrastructures for research in the U.S. and the e-science program in the U.K. (Atkins et al., 2003; Berman, Fox, & Hey, 2003; Hey & Trefethen, 2002). The hope is that it will be possible to create powerful "Virtual Research Environments", "consisting of a set of sophisticated tools and technologies that will ease the extraction of information from data, and of knowledge from information" (Hey, 2006: vii). By working in these new information environments, researchers should become more productive and better able to cope with interdisciplinary problems. Physics, astronomy, and the life sciences have been at the forefront of e-science, but e-science is increasingly seen by some actors as relevant to the social sciences and humanities as well. The series of conferences on *e*-social science that started in 2005 in Manchester, within the framework of the UK e-science program, is an interesting example of this development.[1]

In this chapter, we focus on this new development by discussing an initiative to analyze and support e-research in the humanities and social sciences in the Netherlands, which officially started on 1 January 2006: the Virtual Knowledge Studio for the Humanities and Social Sciences, funded by the Royal Netherlands Academy of Arts and Sciences.[2] We are ourselves involved in this project and our discussion can be read as an exercise in prospective reflexivity: an attempt to analyze the tensions we are experiencing and expect for the next few years.

We also hope to contribute to the discourse in social science about the different ways to cope productively with the tension between engagement and distance as attitudes and practices in research. This is a long-running debate, and in itself the development of e-research practices does not immediately change the parameters of the debate. It does raise, however, new forms in which this tension materializes and is being played out. We will discuss some of the most salient of these novel forms and indicate how we wish to deal with them in the framework of the Virtual Knowledge Studio (VKS).

In short, the chapter has a double goal. First, we wish to contribute to e-research by seeing e-research as a specific, historically situated, set of interventions in existing practices in the social sciences and humanities. Second, we wish to contribute to the methodological, political and epistemological debate in the social sciences, by drawing the implications of e-research for the old tension between being engaged as social researcher or alternatively remaining at a distance from one's object of study and from the implications of studying it.

E-SCIENCE VERSUS E-RESEARCH

We would like to begin with a distinction between e-science and e-research. Terminology is not innocent and the differences in the integration of cyberinfrastructures and tools in scholarly dominant use of the term e-science in discussions of new information infrastructures for the humanities and social sciences carries with it an emphasis on data-oriented, computational, or quantitative analysis (Wouters & Beaulieu 2006). We propose to use the term e-research instead. This term is more inclusive of a variety of research modes, and thereby acknowledges disciplinary practices (Fry, 2006; Kling & McKim, 2000).

e-Science, termed cyberinfrastructure in the US,[3] is generally defined as the combination of three different developments: the sharing of computational resources, distributed access to massive datasets, and the use of digital platforms for collaboration and communication. The core idea of e-science is that knowledge production will be enhanced by the combination of pooled human expertise, data and sources, and computational and visualization tools. e-Science has become a buzzword for funding large-scale facilities in research fields driven large-scale data processing. It claims to be no less than a revolution in the way knowledge can be created (CSTB, 1999). This development started in the US at the end of the 1990s in the framework of supercomputer centers (Vann & Bowker, 2006). It was picked up in the UK in 2001, when an 'e-science' research program was launched, with funding of 250 million pounds for a period of 5 years (Hey, 2006). The Grid technology developed by computer scientists working in particle physics settings played an important role for e-science. In the framework of their research, it was important to go from sharing information (via the Internet) to sharing computation (via the Grid), turning "the global network of computers into one vast computational resource" (Grid Café, no year). The idea then took the shape of a generic computational infrastructure for scientific research. The domains that are supposed to be affected by this revolution vary according to the national variety of e-science. But, so the claim goes, almost all disciplines will be transformed in some way or other.

We have discussed elsewhere the tension this has created between e-science as a generic novel paradigm of research and its practice as a local infrastructure in a limited set of fields (Wouters & Beaulieu, 2006). This led us to a plea for forms of non-computational e-science, and for the use of e-research as the more inclusive term. e-Research acknowledges forms of research that are not reliant on high-performance computing, as well as other ways of making use of new media and digital networks. Email and Web sites, used by hundreds of thousands of scholars may have more import than a Grid application used by a few hundred.

As far as we know, the term e-research in a methodological sense was used first by Terry Anderson and Heather Kanuka in 2002 (Anderson & Kanuka, 2002). In their research manual addressed to researchers in the field of education, they define e-research basically as 'Net research'. It includes online surveys and interviews, log file analysis, analysis of social behavior in virtual reality environments and online evaluation of knowledge. Their use of the term e-research is very close to Christine Hine's use of the term virtual methods (Hine, 2005) or the term Internet Research by a growing group of social and humanities scholars, in particular the group organized in the Association of Internet Researchers AoIR (www.air.org) (Jankowski, Jones, Lievrouw, & Hampton, 2004).

Since 2004, we have used e-research differently,[4] as a critique of the notion of e-science rather than as a generic word for Internet research or virtual methods (Wouters, 2004). Our critique addresses three different aspects of e-science: the underlying philosophy of science, assumptions about diffusion of e-science across academia, and expectations about the technological infrastructure needed.

First of all, in contrast to the implied philosophy of science in most e-science writing, we wish to celebrate rather than diminish the pluriformity that exists in academia. We do not expect that making clever use of ICT will in itself make the social sciences or humanities 'harder' or more like experimental science. Nor should it: our use of e-research is both descriptive and performative. Our second point of critique addresses the assumption that e-science is supposed to diffuse across academia. With respect to the diffusion model, we emphasize that if more fields make use of ICT, this will not be a simple wholesale adoption. Rather, we foresee an active transformation, in which the models of research prevalent in the relevant field shape the way ICT is conceptualized and used. Rather than a *diffusion* of e-science, we propose to think along the lines of *translation* of e-research. The implication is that it is not a matter of simply setting up a proper Grid infrastructure, and then expecting that users will flock to it and become e-scientists. A translation model of e-research posits a different dynamic between tools and users, where mutual shaping and adaptation takes place, and where what 'e-science' can mean as a practice is also subject to transformation.

This leads to the third element of our critique: which technologies are actually needed by scholars in a variety of fields? Or perhaps more precisely, which technologies could support and enhance research practices in a given field? Very often, researchers will not need a Grid—nor whatever paradigm comes next in computer science. They may will be more interested in some rather 'low-level' technology like better email applications—robust and portable rather than cutting edge—which may not be very exciting for computer scientists, but may be far more helpful to advance the field in question.

Our critique implies a particular stance, and this too has implications for the kind of work supported. This user-oriented perspective may lead to conservatism, since it emphasizes a business-as-usual focus. By making the user so central, we run the risk of undermining the dynamic of innovation that can be coupled to initiatives like e-science. In this respect we are on the side of some of the champions of e-science, in that we also feel that it should be possible to play more creatively with both concepts and technologies in many fields in the social sciences and humanities than is currently the case. We think this type of innovation of epistemic cultures (Knorr-Cetina, 1999) will always need to start from the position of a group of researchers in a particular field and the creation of room and support for activities that explicitly involve exploration and experimentation,[5] however, rather than with a technology looking for users. This forces us to play a rather complicated game in which we both promote innovation in academia and are suspicious of the innovation talk that comes with it. We expand on how we are dealing with these tensions later in this chapter.

On this issue of e-research, let us finally note that the term seems to have become far more widespread recently. This is partly due to discussions at the series of international conferences on e-social science, and partly due to the creative activities in 'digital humanities'. The Oxford e-research Centre has also taken up the term, and shifted from the use of e-science to e-research to designate their new research program. This development reached a high point in 2007 at the Third International Conference of e-Social Science in Ann Arbor, where the former director of the UK e-science program Tony Hey explicitly noted the restrictive character of the label e-science, and affirmed that in the social sciences, e-research would be a much better term instead (Hey, 2007).

E-RESEARCH AS INTERVENTION

We conceptualize the development of e-research in the humanities and social sciences as an intervention in the practice of knowledge creation. The drive to create new modes of knowledge generation that is dependent on, and mediated by, high-performance computing networks has usually not been the result of the autonomous development of the field in question, but rather of interactions. For example, cell biologists did not accidentally hit upon the idea of simulating a living cell in a three-dimensional graphical immersive environment. Rather, this resulted from interaction with computer scientists involved in the creation of virtual reality environments and of visualizations (Lenoir, 1998), initially mainly funded by DARPA (Sutherland, 1968), leading to projects such as the Virtual Cell.[6]

Coalitions are therefore created around advanced research instrumentation. Funding schemes, tools, researchers, institutional frameworks and research agendas interact to form these coalitions. Presently, we are witnessing the emergence of this type of interaction in the social sciences and humanities. The result of these interactions can perhaps best be characterized as a parade of prototypes, applications developed within the framework of a particular project but aimed at broader area of scholarly communities. For example, papers presented at the First International Conference of e-Social Science in 2005 in Manchester showed ways to put social science applications on the Grid (Crouchley et al., 2005), a spatial decision support system (Birkin & McFarland, 2005), tools for distributed data analysis (Fraser et al., 2005), modeling and simulation environments (Birkin & MacFarland, 2005) and a prototype for networking social science resources on the Web (Schumann et al., 2005). It is not yet clear to what extent these prototypes will survive their initial period of funding and contribute substantively to social science research. If other researchers do not use them, this may simply be because they are not sufficiently relevant to the field, or even invisible to the core group of experts in the field. It may also be that certain kinds of actors, such as large firms and professional software developers need to be involved in these coalitions, because of their ability to shape availability and usability of tools.[7]

In all these cases, it may be fruitful to conceptualize e-research as an intervention in current practices, potentially upsetting these practices and disrupting the existing fabric of social relationships that carry knowledge creation. This conceptualization also emphasizes the recognition of theoretical and methodological pluriformity we attach to the term e-research. By seeing e-research as intervention, we not only underline that translation work is needed if e-research is to be adopted in new fields, but also that this has a cost. It is not only a matter of spreading the wealth around; it is also a matter of redirecting and thereby upsetting research agendas.

Conceptualizing e-research as intervention, we make visible the complexities of the work involved and the difficulties in prospective evaluation of its possible outcomes. It is not enough to weigh the costs and benefits of one research agenda over the other. It is also relevant to acknowledge the fact that e-research as intervention needs to be understood in sociological as well as epistemological terms. We need to step back from involvement in the culture of a particular field to be able to see these intricacies. This is why we find the expertise developed in the field of science and technology studies especially useful. Because our primary accountability as scholars is not in the particular field being investigated, this provides a relative distance from its dominant paradigms. We thereby have a degree of freedom to engage in experiment and play with new forms of research that may be enabled in e-research, and to reflect on the consequences. This leads, of course, to an immediate new involvement in that field, opening a virtuous cycle of engagement and disengagement. This cycle can only be sustained on the basis of a theory about innovation in a particular field that is partly independent of the state of affairs in that field. For example, in one of our projects at the VKS, we work together with economic historians to create a collaboratory for their research. In order to understand the problems historians may encounter in switching to mediated and large-scale forms of collaboration, we can draw on experiences in other fields. We therefore need to draw upon knowledge such as developed in the "science of collaboratories"[8], while maintaining an analytic standpoint that remains aware of the particularities of economic history. In other words, having a conceptual framework to understand the dynamics of knowledge production enables a different appreciation of new practices around new tools. The field of science and technology studies has not only developed well-honed theories and methodologies to understand these dynamics, but has also thought hard about the balance between engagement and distance.

INTERVENTION AS CONCERN FOR SOCIAL SCIENCE

In order to reflect on intervention, we draw on the body of work on intervention in STS and on the STS scholarship on the "dynamics of expectations" (Brown, 2003; Brown & Michael, 2003). We are especially interested in how it is possible to combine critical analysis with design-oriented research in the context of analyzing and creating e-research practices and infrastructures (Hine, 2006a). This is not a new question, and earlier generations of researchers in science and technology studies have dealt with it. More recently, in the U.K. and the U.S., STS has partly moved to new academic environments in such innovative directions as business schools (Coopmans, Neyland, & Woolgar, 2004), where intervention seems a given of the institutional context.

According to Gibbons and colleagues (Gibbons, Limoges, & Nowotny, 1994), a new mode of knowledge production has emerged in the past decades in which basic research has become intimately intertwined with contexts of application. The mode 2 thesis has been criticized because it tends to lump unrelated phenomena together, underestimates the extent to which mode 2 science was dominant in the past (for example in chemistry), and tends to present the emergence of new accountability regimes as inevitable and politically neutral (Rip, 2002a, 2002b; Shinn, 2002). This critique is even more relevant if we study the shifting contexts of STS research itself. But, as Coopmans and colleagues note, a key question remains for whom is engagement a form of progress (Coopmans et al., 2004: 6).

In a recent issue of *Science as Culture* (Zuiderent-Jerak & Jensen, 2007) and in other publications, the problem of interventionist science and technology studies has been explored in relation to the tradition of action research and to the normative implications of social research (Callon & Rabeharisoa, 2008; Chilvers, 2008; Lengwiler, 2008; Stirling, 2008).

To sum up these brief reflections (which are expanded on the Web site accompanying this book), our starting point is that intervention oriented STS may present many issues that may feel 'new', especially if one is newly dependent on research funding—where many schemes demand that attention be paid to added value, to social relevance and other forms of intervention—but that can also be constituted as an opportunity for reflection and better interventions. We think these problems are relevant along three dimensions: theoretical, methodological, and political. We wish to explore these dimensions on the basis of the Virtual Knowledge Studio for the Humanities and Social Sciences (Wouters, 2004).

HOPE AND INTERVENTION AROUND THE VIRTUAL KNOWLEDGE STUDIO

The promise of the new and the promise of intervention are closely entwined in the case of the Studio, and in this section we attempt to show the mutual shaping of particular hopes regarding new technologies and changing research practices. New technologies, in this case, information and communication technologies carry a particular set of hopes about increased efficiency, relevance or novelty (Hine, 2006b). Funding bodies also foster particular hopes about doing something for a particular constituency. Indeed, by the time funding is on offer, what this 'something' should be is already partly shaped. Expectations are constitutive, and like hype, they "mobilize the future into the present" (Brown, 2003: 6).

In May 2004, the KNAW issued an international call for a program leader in the area of e-science for the humanities. This call was based on the notion that it should be possible both to support 'e-science initiatives' in the humanities and social sciences and to critically analyze them. This can be seen as the result of a debate of a few years in which scholarly insights from STS were mobilized in the framework of Academy research policy (Bijker et al., 2003). However, the idea that technology may drive new scholarly developments is also prominent in the call: "Potentially e-science can have a profound influence on research, the questions researchers ask and the way research is carried out" (KNAW, 2004: 2). A particular kind of hope for what ICT could do for the humanities was therefore embedded in the call, using the language of impact, of newness, of overcoming difficulties via technology. At the same time, the call maintained that both analytic and contributory work should happen under the auspices of the program.

The successful proposal in this procedure was written by one of us (Wouters, 2004) and forms the basis for a new KNAW program, The Virtual Knowledge Studio for the Humanities and Social Sciences. It aims to support researchers in the humanities and social sciences in the Netherlands in the creation of new scholarly practices, as well as in their reflection on e-research in relation to the development of their fields. A core feature of the VKS is the integration of design and analysis in a close cooperation between social scientists, humanities researchers, information technology experts and information scientists. This integrated approach provides insight in the way e-research can contribute to new research questions and methods in the humanities and social sciences. Importantly, the program entails a subtly different formulation of the "problem of e-science in the humanities and social sciences". It thereby effects a shift that can be seen as a first concrete intervention, not only at both institutional and organizational levels at which the future of the program is being decided, but also in the way the Studio presents itself to the researchers in the fields where it is mandated to intervene.

The program shifts the notion of e-science, as electronic science, towards the notion of *e* for 'enhanced', and towards a more general (though still normative) notion of 'e-research' rather than e-science. These shifts create a space for interventions, where 'e' is decoupled from a particular type of technology (which is evoked by the e for electronic). Second, the shift from 'science' to 'research' establishes the Studio as recognizing the particularities and specificities of the humanities and social sciences (Bijker & Peperkamp, 2002; Boonstra, Breure, & Doorn, 2004; Kircz 2004). As discussed above, this formulation aims to turn threat into promise, and aligns the proposal with social sciences and humanities, in the face of the e-science movement.

By showing awareness of the limitations of particular e-science promises, and sensitivity to the ways in which the humanities are particular, we hope the program can become a solid basis for humanities researchers. The promise is one of support in reaping the benefits of ICT, without having to conform to what is articulated in e-science dreams of physicists. In this way, identifying the hype may perhaps help develop other hopes. The moral valence of the Studio's intervention may seem grounded in contrast to inflated promises, and to provide more localized, context-sensitive stories of potential benefit, thereby profiting from what might be seen as 'the hype' in other areas. The VKS program becomes one of the sites where actors come to share a belief in the promise of interventions. If this is successful, they share not only expectations, but also obligations. These relations between funders, researchers and those who believe they will benefit from the interventions promised can be thought of as a network (Van Lente, 2000).

Finally, the VKS program specifically maintains an analytic stance with regards not only to current practices, but also to current technological paradigms. It argues that important fields in the humanities and social sciences are characterized by a huge epistemic diversity; by specific, sometimes person-bound, roles of the researcher; by the lack of consensus about the research agenda in a host of specialties; by a relatively low-tech research environment (often aggravated by the scarcity of university fund-ing); by the specificity of writing and reading as features of knowledge cre-ation; and by a historically grounded and relatively large share of solitary research practices (Becher, 1989; Whitley, 2000). In all these dimensions, many fields seem ill-suited to become enthusiastic adopters of the e-science paradigm as it now stands. Therefore, if e-research is to make sense to a variety of specialties in the humanities and social sciences, new non-computational and computational paradigms of e-research may need to be developed (Wouters & Beaulieu, 2006). The Studio therefore promises to be a clearing house of expertise, partner in the development of new prac-tices, and provider of insight into new dynamics of knowledge creation in ways relevant to STS research.

At the time of writing this chapter, the Studio has been intervening for two years. Fighting our tendency to look ahead to what we would still like to accomplish, we reflect briefly on the shape of our interventions so far. As part of our research activities, the VKS has been able to pursue the issue of intervention in the shape of a project that specifically examines how dif-ferent scholars have juggled that issue in their careers,[9] while this chapter considers intervention as a more programmatic and institutional activity.

We have also been able to develop a number of projects where inter-vention is part of the expected process or outcome of the projects. With regards to kinds of interventions, we have been relieved to see that an early fear has not materialized. We were wary of being perceived as a 'helpdesk', and that researchers in the various fields we see as our constituency would mainly seek us to intervene as technology experts. This has not happened much so far. Indeed, our own work practices, while experimental and innovative in some respects, tend to be relatively low-tech, as the research-ers currently developing a web-based collaborative workspace for the VKS have commented.

While it is still early in our research program, specific kinds of inter-ventions do seem to have been dominant so far. In particular, our role as 'broker' among groups and as 'host' to particular practices seems to have gained most support and recognition so far. Several of our successes with funding rely on our ability to function as brokers between groups. In these projects, our activities are represented as the creation of interfaces between disciplines and research practices, as supporting hubs between sub-fields or as having a networking role.[10] Yet another set of projects emphasizes the element of mediation. In these projects, the role of the VKS members is to reflect upon and shape the insertion of particular tools (web-based applica-tions, simulations, mediated communication) or the coordination of new kinds of sources (web archives, mailing lists, other kinds of digital data).[11] These emerging metaphors of *interface* and *mediation* would appear to be rather rich descriptions of our potential—at least they evoke more complex processes than if our interventions were to be characterized as 'implemen-tation' or 'digitization'.

We should note that constraints are also becoming apparent. These interventions are part of our work, but given our primary identity as a research group, they are performed 'on top' of the expectations one has of a research institute. This is a pressure that comes not only from the need to justify ourselves to our funders, but also from the need to remain visible as scholars for the fields in which we hope to keep intervening. Having the status of scholars linked to a given field seems to work as an important prerequisite. A second issue has been our encounter with conventions about intervention. We have received several variations of the following comment in reviews of our interventionist work: who are you exactly in this process? Being both subject and object, part of a change and its agent, seems to be something that is difficult to articulate (for us as writers) and to evaluate (for reviewers and editors). Certainly, the convention of anonymisation is difficult to implement when writing about our initiatives, where we are both authors and participants in the material discussed. It may be that reviewers have to get used to listening to a different kind of interventionist voice. Perhaps interventions are not to be written about in research articles. Perhaps there is a way to do it, but we have not yet found it.

We also seem to have been able to develop a particular kind of internal interface with members of the Studio. While different members surely experience this in a variety of ways, there is a general feeling, in our own discussions and in the perception of the Studio, that we have set up a way of working in which intervention is possible. VKS researchers work with a degree of openness and an intensity of interaction that is somewhat unusual for a humanities or interpretative social science research setting and that seems to be gradually developing into a hybrid between a scholarly and a designer style of working. Practicing what we preach may also be contributing to building up our skills to intervene with colleagues outside the Studio.

CONCLUSIONS: MANAGING EXPECTATIONS

As will be clear by now, the expectations that underlie the funding and support of the Virtual Knowledge Studio are related to 'modernization' or 'rationalization' of humanities and qualitative social science research. The expectation is for improved ('enhanced') research, through the mobilization of technology. This is not something the Studio explicitly embraces, but this element is present in its discourse, if only as a straw man / bogeyman. In approaching possible constituents, the VKS is able to leverage STS sensibilities to disciplinary differences as a way of differentiating the Studio from those who would unilaterally impose natural science processes on the humanities. This discourse also posits the Studio as an obligatory passage point, through which particular segments of social scientists and humanities scholars might get access to some of the funds associated with ICT, while also maintaining their distinct identities through our 'validation' of the particularities of their practices. Concretely, this means speaking a language of experiment and new experiences, rather than of overhaul and revolution.

It bears repeating, at this point, that the interface with actors in the field is a fruitful site, not only of funding, but also of important insights for STS. For example, the definition of e-science is not strictly a technical issue. It also raises important questions for STS itself, regarding the dynamics of innovation, processes of academic agenda setting, and the role of 'promises' in the development of new tools and practices (Fry, 2006). These questions are addressed by researchers in STS in a scholarly manner (in contrast to our discussion here about the pragmatics of the initiative). Yet, the scholarly and pragmatic dimensions intersect in this kind of work.

The problem as formulated in our work is strongly shaped by the STS tradition, and a constructivist approach to technology that seeks to open up black boxes and questions the ways they come to be closed. It emphasizes practices rather than technologies, to prevent a tool-push approach. Nevertheless, the existence of particular promises associated with e-science has been very important in giving the means to realize and conceptualize the VKS. Shaping hopes as a kind of intervention is furthermore present in some of the earliest work in the Studio, in writings about the kinds of hopes that fields such as women's studies might like to see taken up in the way e-science develops its promise (Wouters & Beaulieu, 2006). Hope therefore enables this work and forms a site of intervention. In the same way, our developing track record may also be shaping future possibilities.

The double role of STS research in the management of expectations is our answer to the question whether it is possible to combine critical analysis with design. The Studio therefore plays a complicated game in which it alternates positions in order to enable a critique of *both* the present scholarly practices in the humanities and social sciences and of the modernist critique of these practices. This may be enabled by the fact that the Royal Netherlands Academy for Arts and Sciences (KNAW) itself is an organization in which intellectual excellence is highly valued and in which a variety of philosophical positions about the value of knowledge can be found. We propose a sharpened analytic framework for understanding the relationship between STS and intervention. It is an approach that is prospective, reflexive and strategic, and in which STS has been so aware of the power of promises and hope in science that it also becomes aware of the power of promises and hope for its own goals. This chapter is an occasion to further develop this aspect of our work. Following Brown, we believe that 'situatedness of expectations' is an important goal to diminish the costs of hype/unfulfilled promises: "we need to reflect upon the actual contexts and conditions in which expectations, hype and future imaginings are embedded" (Brown, 2003: 10). But also, in our view, this is a way to produce better STS research. Again, it is important to note that we are not trying to do away with hype/hope, because it is constitutive of present and near future activities, as has been argued by Brown (2003). Intervention also implies power to change situations.

Our first preliminary conclusion is the importance of developing a critical stance with respect to the underlying motivations of research funding in interventionist contexts. These motivations (whether they be constellations of more or less distributed ambitions, drives, or needs) should first of all be taken seriously. At the same time, these motivations can be approached critically and this critique can form an integral part of the research project. As our research develops, we also come to realize that this question is also relevant to smaller gestures (collaborations, co-authorship, etc) and to other kinds of large ones besides funding—such as infrastructural or institutional decisions. Interests, big or small, remain important elements in shaping what kinds of research are possible.

Our second conclusion is that it might be a fruitful strategy to open up the research process to a variety of actors and conflicting influences. In the case of the Studio, the research program is under discussion with the funder (the KNAW) and the scholarly communities involved (STS community, humanities communities, social science communities). This strategy might also be useful in other contexts, such as society and genomics or the social impact of nanotechnology, since it prevents a monopoly position of the funding agency.

Our third conclusion is that it becomes more urgent to work pro-actively on the criteria of one's own assessment—a stance we increasingly see in other research institutions and universities. The traditional indicators of academic quality (publications in high-reputation journals and publishers) are perhaps not enough, since they cannot capture the relevant dimensions of the role of intervention in present scholarly practices. Other criteria may become important in this respect: participation of scholars in the Studio, invitations, new software tools, accessibility of datasets and digital resources, in-links to our Web sites and, not least, success in acquiring additional funding. This signals the need for theories that can be mobilized to develop assessment indicators and approaches, knowing that not every important dimension can be measured quantitatively, and that various criteria must be coordinated rather than added-on.

Developing these three strategies will perhaps also make clear what can be learnt from e-research in methodological terms. The discussion about the merits of action research versus more distanced analytical work has mostly focused on the value of a particular research project with only a few researchers involved. In e-research, however, we are dealing with an infrastructure as intervention. To what extent does this difference in mode of intervention matter? Does it make it more difficult for researchers to 'speak back' to the intervention, unless the infrastructure is explicitly made a topic for conversation and dispute? A second dimension might be the technological. In our research we are explicitly using technology as a probe to analyze and disturb existing scholarly practices. In most discussions about interventionist research, technology does play an important role, but the intervention is usually located in the persona of the researcher herself. In our practices this may be the case to a lesser extent, although we acknowledge that this is also a matter of framing. Perhaps we will have more leeway in dealing with the tensions between being involved in e-research and being critical about it, because we are not seen as the primary source of intervention. On the other hand, our role as interface, broker or mediator seems to be our fastest growing concern.

Finally, and perhaps most importantly, e-research may enable the actors themselves to become the prime interventionists. In other words, e-research may help create an invitation to scholars in the humanities and social sciences to intervene themselves in their own practices, or at least to be more reflexive about these changes. At least one chapter in this collection points in this direction, where the probing of researchers about the role of a new application led to reflection and articulation by researchers of their own changing expectations of the technological support (See Chapter 5 in this volume by Genoni, Wilson and Merrick). We have tried to draw out the ways in which the requirement for intervention, in its precise formulation and counter-formulation (or reformulation), have shaped the approaches, structures and recent developments of the Studio. By opening up this area of expectations, our article is not only a reflection upon and critical analysis of the management of expectations, but also an invitation to participate in it and thereby shape the Studio into what it may become.

ACKNOWLEDGMENTS

This chapter builds on reflections begun in an article for a special issue of JCMC, and has benefited from the comments made by the editor and reviewers. The role of debates with past and present members of Nerdi and the VKS and with all participants to the procedures leading up to the current initiative is also gratefully acknowledged. This chapter conveys our personal interpretations of recent activities of the Studio, and other accounts of the VKS by participants or observers will inevitably differ.

NOTES

1. See the Web site of the conferences, http://www.ncess.ac.uk/events/conference/ (accessed 9 April 2008).
2. For more information about the VKS, see http://www.virtualknowledgestudio.nl/en/ (accessed 9 April 2008) and about the Academy, see http://www.knaw.nl (accessed 9 April 2008).
3. In our view, the interchangeable use of these terms threatens to collapse distinctions between tool, practice and knowledge. These are of course interrelated concepts, but an indiscriminate use of cyberinfrastructure to refer to research practices elides what might be needed beyond the hardware.

4. At the time, we were not aware of the work of Anderson and Kanuka, and wish to thank Nick Jankowski for bringing this reference and other use of the term to our attention.
5. By this we mean financial space, less pressure to have only traditional output, access to expertise, space for new tools, etc.
6. See for example http://www.nrcam.uchc.edu/login/login.html (accessed 9 April 2008).
7. Whether this is a desirable and unavoidable condition is beyond the scope of this chapter but it is a crucial issue, given the current dependence of researchers and universities on contracts with firms.
8. See for a sustained research program in the science of collaboratories: www.scienceofcollaboratories.org (accessed 9 April 2008).
9. See the project undertaken by Ernst Thoutenhoofd and Teun Zuiderent, http://www.virtualknowledgestudio.nl/staff/ernst-thoutenhoofd/intervention_technology.php (accessed 9 April 2008).
10. See www.virtualknowledgestudio.nl for descriptions of current and completed projects.
11. See the projects developed by Jan Kok and the resulting work of Stefan Dormans and Jan Kok in setting up and analysing collaboratories: http://www.virtualknowledgestudio.nl/projects/socio.php (accessed 9 June 2008).

REFERENCES

Anderson, T., & Kanuka, H. (2002). *e-Research: Methods, strategies, and issues* (1st ed.) Boston: Allyn & Bacon.
Atkins, D., Droegemeier, K., Feldman, S., Garcia-Molina, H., Klein, M., Messerschmidt, D., Messina, P., Ostriker, P. P., & Wright, M. H. (2003). *Revolutionizing science and engineering through cyberinfrastructure: Report of the National Science Foundation Blue-Ribbon Advisory Panel on Cyberinfrastructure.* Washington DC: National Science Foundation. Available at: http://www.nsf.gov/od/oci/reports/atkins.pdf
Becher, T. (1989). *Academic tribes and territories: Intellectual inquiry and the culture of disciplines.* Buckingham: SHRE & Open University Press.
Berman, F., Fox, G., & Hey, T. (2003). The Grid: Past, present, future. In F. Berman, G. Fox & T. Hey (Eds.), *Grid computing. Making the global infrastructure a reality,* pp. 9–50. Somerset, NJ: John Wiley.
Bijker, W., & Peperkamp, B. (2002). *Geëngageerde geesteswetenschappen. Perspectieven op cultuurveranderingen in een digitaliserend tijdperk* (No. Achtergrondstudie nr. 27). Den Haag: Adviesraad voor het Wetenschaps- en Technologiebeleid.
Bijker, W., Schurer, K., Stronks, E., Uszkoreit, H. Wittenburg, P., & Woolgar, S. (2003). *Building the KNAW international research institute on e-science studies in the humanities and social sciences (IRISS).* Amsterdam: Royal Netherlands Academy of Arts and Sciences. Available at: http://www.knaw.nl/publicaties/pdf/90000111.pdf
Birkin, M., & McFarland, O. (2005). HYDRA: A prototype Grid-enabled spatial decision support system. Paper presented at First International Conference of e-Social Science, Manchester, UK, 22–24 June. http://www.ncess.ac.uk/events/conference/2005/papers/papers/ncess2005_paper_Birkin.pdf
Boonstra, O., Breure, L., & Doorn, P. (2004). *Past, present and future of historical information science.* Amsterdam: Netherlands Institute for Scientific Information Services, Royal Netherlands Academy of Arts and Sciences.

Brown, N. (2003). Hope against hype: Accountability in biopasts, presents and futures. *Science Studies, 16*(2): 3–21.

Brown, N., & Michael, M. (2003). A sociology of expectations: Retrospecting prospects and prospecting retrospects. *Technology Analysis & Strategic Management, 15*(1): 3–18.

Callon, M., & Rabeharisoa, V. (2008). The growing engagement of emergent concerned groups in political and economic life: Lessons from the French association of neuromuscular disease patients. *Science, Technology & Human Values, 33*(2): 230–261.

Chilvers, J. (2008). Deliberating competence: Theoretical and practitioner perspectives on effective participatory appraisal practice. *Science, Technology & Human Values, 33*(2): 155–185.

Coopmans, C., Neyland, D., & Woolgar, S. (2004). Does STS mean business? Some issues and questions. Provocation piece for the workshop "Does STS mean business?" Saïd Business School, University of Oxford, 30th June 2004.

Crouchley, R., van Ark, T., Pritchard, J., Kewley, J., Allan, R., Hayes, M. & Morris, L. (2005). Putting social science applications on the Grid. Paper presented at the First International Conference of e-Social Science, Manchester, UK, 22–24 June. http://www.ncess.ac.uk/events/conference/2005/papers/papers/ncess2005_paper_Crouchley.pdf

CSTB (Computer Science and Telecommunications Board). (1999). *Funding a revolution: Computer support for computing research.* Washington, DC: National Academy Press.

Fraser, M., Biegel, G., Best, K., Hindmarsh, J., Heath, C., Greenhalgh, C., & Reeves, S. (2005). Distributing data sessions: Supporting remote collaboration with video data. Paper presented at the First International Conference of e-Social Science, Manchester, UK, 22–24 June 2005. http://www.ncess.ac.uk/events/conference/2005/papers/papers/ncess2005_paper_Fraser.pdf

Fry, J. (2006). Coordination and control of research practices across scientific fields: Implications for a differentiated e-science. In C. Hine (Ed.), *New infrastructure for knowledge production: Understanding e-science*, pp. 167–188. London: IDEA Group.

Gibbons, M., Limoges, C., & Nowotny, H. (1994). *The new production of knowledge: The dynamics of science and research in contemporary societies.* London: Sage.

GridCafé (n. d.). *What is the Grid?* Retrieved March 26, 2008, from http://gridcafe.web.cern.ch/gridcafe/whatisgrid/whatis.html

Hey, T. (2007). Relationship between traditional and e-social science. Presentation at Fourth E-social Science Conference, Ann Arbor, MI, 7–9 October.

Hey, T. (2006). Foreword. In C. Hine (Ed.), *New infrastructures for knowledge production*, pp. vi-vii. Hershey, PA: Information Science Publishing.

Hey, T., & Trefethen, A. E. (2002). The UK e-science core program and the Grid. *Future Generation Computer Systems, 18*(8): 1017–1031.

Hine, C. (Ed.). (2005). *Virtual methods: Issues in social research on the internet.* Oxford: Berg.

Hine, C. (Ed.). (2006a). *New infrastructures for knowledge production. Understanding e-science.* Hershey, PA: Information Science Publishing.

Hine, C. (2006b). Computerization movements and scientific disciplines: The reflexive potential of new technologies. In C. Hine (Ed.), *New infrastructure for knowledge production: Understanding e-science*, pp. 26–47. Hershey, PA: Information Science Publishing.

Jankowski, N. W., Jones, S., Lievrouw, L. A., & Hampton, K. (2004). Editorial. *New Media & Society, 6*(1): 5–7.

Kircz, J. (2004). *E-based humanities and e-humanities on a SURF platform.* Amsterdam: KRA Publishing Research.

Kling, R., & McKim, G. (2000). Not just a matter of time: Field differences and the shaping of electronic media in supporting scientific communication. *Journal of the American Society for Information Science, 51*(14): 1306–1320.

KNAW (2004). Call for program leader: Developing e-science in the social sciences and humanities. KNAW, Amsterdam, April 2004.

Knorr-Cetina, K. (1999). *Epistemic cultures: How the sciences make knowledge.* Cambridge, MA: Harvard University Press.

Lengwiler, M. (2008). Participatory approaches in science and technology: Historical origins and current practices in critical perspective. *Science, Technology & Human Values, 33*(2): 186–200.

Lenoir, T. (1998). Shaping biomedicine as an information science. In M.E. Bowden, T. Bellardo Hahan, & R.V. Williams (Eds.), *Proceedings of the 1998 conference on the history and heritage of science information systems.* ASIS Monograph Series. pp. 27–45. Medford, NJ: Information Today.

Rip, A. (2002a). Reflections on the transformation of science. *Metascience, 11*(3): 317–323.

Rip, A. (2002b). Regional innovation systems and the advent of strategic science. *Journal of Technology Transfer, 27*: 123–131.

Schumann, N., Meier, W., & Schmiede, R. (2005), Networking social science resources on the Web: SozioNet. Paper presented at First International Conference of e-Social Science, Manchester, UK, 22–24 June. http://www.ncess.ac.uk/events/conference/2005/papers/papers/ncess2005_paper_Schumann.pdf

Shinn, T. (2002). The triple helix and new production of knowledge: Prepackaged thinking on science and technology. *Social Studies of Science, 32*(4): 599–614.

Stirling, A. (2008). "Opening up" and "closing down": Power, participation, and pluralism in the social appraisal of technology. *Science, Technology & Human Values, 33*(2): 262–294.

Sutherland, I. (1968). A head-mounted three dimensional display. In *Proceedings FJCC*, pp. 757–764. Washington, DC: Thompson Books.

Vann, K., & Bowker, G.C. (2006) Interest in production—on the configuration of technology-bearing labours for epistemic-IT. In C. Hine (Ed.), *New infrastructures for knowledge production: Understanding E-science*, pp. 71–97. Hershey, PA: Information Science Publishing.

Van Lente, H. (2000). Forceful Futures: From Promise to Requirement. In N. Brown, B. Rappert, & A. Webster (Eds.), *Contested futures. A sociology of prospective techno-science*, pp. 43–64. London: Ashgate Publishing Company.

Whitley, R. (2000). *The intellectual and social organization of the sciences.* Oxford: Oxford University Press.

Wouters, P. (2004). The Virtual Knowledge Studio for the Humanities and Social Sciences @ The Royal Netherlands Academy of Arts and Sciences. Program proposal. Amsterdam.

Wouters, P., & Beaulieu, A. (2006). Imagining e-science beyond computation. In C. Hine (Ed.), *New infrastructures for knowledge production: Understanding e-science*, pp. 46–70. Hershey, PA: Information Science Publishing.

Zuiderent-Jerak, T., & Jensen, C. B. (2007). Editorial introduction: Unpacking 'Intervention' in science and technology studies. *Science as Culture, 16*(3): 227.

Part III
Development

4   Developing the UK-based e-Social Science Research Program

Peter Halfpenny, Rob Procter, Yu-Wei Lin and Alex Voss

INTRODUCTION

The National Centre for e-Social Science (NCeSS) was established by the U.K. Economic and Social Research Council (ESRC) in 2004 as its contribution to the U.K. e-science program. NCeSS's mission is to enable social scientists to exploit innovations in digital infrastructure so that they are able to address key challenges in their substantive research fields in new ways. This infrastructure, known as the 'Grid' or increasingly commonly as 'e-Infrastructure' (or 'Cyberinfrastructure' in the U.S.), comprises networked, interoperable, service-oriented, scalable computational tools and services.

The Centre forms part of the ESRC's strategy to develop leading-edge methodological tools and techniques to enhance the U.K. social science research community's capacity to collect, discover, access, manipulate, link, share, analyze and visualize both quantitative and qualitative data.[1] To achieve its aims, NCeSS coordinates a program of e-social science research and makes available information, training, advice and support. The Centre is leading the development of an e-infrastructure for the social sciences and is also responsible for providing advice to the ESRC on the future strategic direction of e-social science.

NCeSS has a distributed structure, with a coordinating Hub at the University of Manchester, and a set of major three-year research Nodes and smaller one-year projects distributed across the U.K. The Hub acts as the central resource base for e-social science issues and activities in the U.K., integrating them with ESRC research methods initiatives and the U.K. e-science core program.

In this chapter, we review the progress of the NCeSS program, report on its current impact on social science research, reflect on the development of the research roadmap and, taking into account factors likely to influence future adoption, consider its trajectory over the next five years.

First steps in U.K. e-Social Science

In late 2000, the U.K. government announced funding for a research initiative in e-science (Hey and Trefethen, 2004). This comprised a so-called 'core program' of research into e-science technologies and applications through a series of demonstrator projects, together with the commitment of the six individual research councils to fund programs specific to their disciplines and communities.[2] The ESRC launched its contribution to the program by commissioning four scoping studies:

- Grid-enabling quantitative social science datasets (Cole, Schurer, Beedham, & Hewitt, 2003).
- Qualitative research and e-social science (Fielding, 2003).
- Human-centred design and Grid technologies (Anderson, 2003).
- Social shaping perspectives on e-science and e-social science (Woolgar, 2003).

The focus for these studies reflected core social science research orientations which were likely to raise quite different requirements for applications; the existence of an already well-established and mature infrastructure for the curation of research data through the Economic and Social Data Service;[3] and the understanding that social scientists had a distinctive contribution to make to the U.K. e-science program by applying social science research methods to investigate barriers to the adoption of e-science.

Following the recommendations of the scoping studies, the ESRC allocated £500k to fund Pilot Demonstrator Projects (PDPs): small scale projects to explore how e-infrastructure could be used to generate exemplars to showcase the potential to the wider social science research community, and test the level of interest in e-social science. This approach acknowledged that the number of social science researchers ready at this early stage to grasp the potential of e-social science was likely to be small. A phased approach was seen as essential to facilitate a bootstrapping process where the success of 'innovators' or 'early adopters' would trigger interest and, eventually, lead to adoption by the wider community.

Eleven PDPs were funded, four with a main focus on aspects of data infrastructure and integration, six on statistical analysis and modeling (see, e.g., Peters, Clark, Ekin, Le Blanc, & Pickles, 2007) and one on collaborative qualitative video data analysis. Two PDPs also explored how e-social science might break down the divide between quantitative and qualitative research methods. Social shaping issues, as represented by, for example, the usability of new technologies, figured in many of these projects.

The limited funding per PDP meant that deployment of usable research tools and services was unlikely. This would require resources on a scale that only a significantly bigger program could provide. Accordingly, in 2004, the ESRC announced the next step in its e-social science strategy: the formation of the National Centre for e-Social Science (NCeSS) with funding of £6M for a first phase over the period 2004–2007 and funding for a second phase contingent on the outcome of a review. The Centre was to be structured around a coordinating Hub, a small number of large

(£500K) projects or 'Nodes' and a larger number of smaller (£50K) projects. It was designed to ensure sufficient resources were available in the Nodes to developed innovative tools and services, at least to the stage of delivering demonstrators or, better, usable prototypes to the wider community, while the smaller projects maintained the program's capacity to explore more speculative ideas.

The National Centre for e-Social Science 2004–2007

Building on the pattern established by the scoping studies, the specification for the NCeSS research program in its 2004–2007 phase identified two principal strands of research.

The *applications strand* aimed, through substantive problem-driven research projects, to explore the use of e-infrastructure to make advances in quantitative, qualitative and mixed-methods economic and social research. Its long term aim was to build an e-infrastructure providing new and more powerful research resources to the wider social science research community. Such resources would include datasets, analysis tools and services, and virtual research environments providing integrated access to them.

The *social shaping strand* aimed to understand how e-infrastructure is being developed, how it is being used across the research community, and what its implications are for scientific practices and research. 'Social shaping' was defined broadly to include all social, economic and other influences on the genesis, implementation, use, usability, immediate effects and longer-term impacts of the new technologies.

This first phase of the NCeSS program began with a call for Hub applications. The University of Manchester's proposal was selected from a shortlist of three and began work in May 2004. At the same time, the second-ranked Hub proposal was awarded a Node grant. There followed two calls for Node applications. The first was issued in May 2004 and resulted in three nodes being commissioned. The second was issued in November 2004 and resulted in a further three Nodes being commissioned. Significantly, four of the original eleven PDPs were successful in graduating to Node scale funding. The research objectives of the seven Nodes were as follows.

- The Collaboratory for Quantitative e-Social Science Node (CQeSS: Lancaster University and Daresbury Laboratory) aimed to develop tools and services to advance the state of the art in quantitative methods. It focused on developing middleware that would allow users to exploit distributed research resources such as datasets and more powerful computational facilities while continuing to be able to employ their favorite desktop analysis tools (Crouchley et al., 2005; Grose et al., 2006).
- The Mixed Media Grid Node (MiMeG: Bristol University and King's College, London) focused on developing tools to support distributed, collaborative video analysis (Fraser et al., 2006; Tutt, Hindmarsh,

Shaukat, Fraser, & McCarthy, 2007; Shaukat and Fraser, 2007). Digital video has become an invaluable tool for social scientists to capture and analyze a wide range of social action and interactions. Video-based research is increasingly undertaken by research teams distributed across institutions in the UK, Europe and worldwide but there was little existing technology to support collaborative analysis.

- The Modeling and Simulation for e-Social Science Node (MoSeS: Leeds University) aimed to develop a suite of modeling and simulation tools for application in policy making (Birkin et al, 2005; Birkin, Townhend, Turner, Wu, & Xu, 2007; Townend, Xu, Birkin, Turner, & Wu, 2007). The chosen policy applications drivers were healthcare, transport planning and public finance. Social science problems of this type are characterized by a requirement for extensive data integration and multiple iterations of computationally intensive scenarios.

- The Digital Records for e-Social Science Node (DReSS: Nottingham University) sought to develop new tools for capturing, replaying, and analyzing multi-modal digital records of people's activities (Crabtree, French, Greenhalgh, Rodden, & Benford, 2006; Crabtree et al., 2006; Greenhalgh et al., 2007; Knight et al., 2006). Social scientists worked in close partnership with computer scientists on three substantive research driver projects in order to explore the salience of new forms of digital record for research and to determine requirements for tools.

- The Geographic Virtual Urban Environments Node (GeoVUE: University College, London) focused on developing geographical information systems (GIS) tools and research environments to enable users easily to map and visually explore spatially-coded socio-economic data (Batty, Steadman, & Xie, 2006; Milton and Steed, 2007). Driver applications included urban planning and design.

- The Semantic Grid Tools for Rural Policy Development and Appraisal Node (PolicyGrid: Aberdeen University) brought together social scientists with interests in rural policy development and appraisal with computer scientists with experience in Grid and Semantic Web technologies. The objective was to explore how Semantic Grid tools (Chorley, Edwards, & Preece, 2007; Heilkema, Edwards, Mellish, & Farrington, 2007; Pignotti, Edwards, & Preece, 2007) could be used to support social scientists and policy makers using mixed-methods research techniques (e.g., surveys and interviews, ethnographies, case studies, simulations).

- The Oxford e-Social Science Node (OeSS: Oxford University) addressed the inter-related social, institutional, ethical, legal and other issues surrounding e-infrastructures and research practices. The focus was on confidentiality, privacy, data protection, intellectual property rights, accountability, trust and risk in distributed collaborations (Axelson and Schroeder, 2007; Carusi and Jirotka, 2007; Dutton, 2007).

Under this first tranche of research funding, twelve small grant projects were also commissioned.

Node research themes and synergies

The Node awards can be broken down into six applications strand Nodes and one social shaping strand Node, although it is worth remarking that all applications strand Nodes addressed social shaping issues (e.g., usability) in their work plans. Of the applications strand Nodes, the majority (MoSeS, PolicyGrid, MiMeG and CQeSS) had data analysis tools as their main focus and one (DReSS) had data collection and management as its main focus. A more detailed analysis of Node research themes (as defined in the call for Node submissions) is shown in Table 4.1. Unsurprisingly, because of their established use of computing, quantitative methods (i.e., statistical analysis, simulation and high performance computing) figure quite prominently in the Node themes whereas qualitative methods figure less prominently. Table 4.1 also reveals an interesting gap in this first phase of the NCeSS program with the absence of any contribution to the text/data mining theme.

Table 4.1   Node Research Themes 2004–2007

	Data infrastructure			Data analysis								Collaboration		Social shaping				
	Datasets from multiple sources	Data description/discovery/management/re-use	New sources of social data	Quantitative methods	Simulation	High performance computing	Tools integration, user portals	Visualization	Text/data mining	Qualitative methods	Mixed methods	Collaboration tools	Inter-disciplinary collaborations	Usability	Confidentiality	Sustainability	Social, economic and other determinants	Implications for nature and practice of science
CQeSS	+			++			++	+						+				
MiMeG											++	++		+				+
DReSS	++	++	++	+		+	+			++	++	+	++	+				+
Policy-Grid		++		+	+		++			+	++	++	++	+				+
MoSeS	+			++	++	++	+						+	+	+			
GeoVuE							++					+		+				
OeSS			+									+	+		++	+	+	++

Table 4.1 suggests a significant number of potential synergies between the Nodes. For example, DReSS and PolicyGrid form a cluster around data description / discovery / management / re-use; CQeSS, DReSS, PolicyGrid and MoSeS form a cluster around quantitative methods and, within this cluster, CQeSS and MoSeS form a mini-cluster around high performance computing and MoSeS and PolicyGrid form a mini-cluster around simulation. Similarly, a cluster (MiMeG, DReSS, PolicyGrid, GeoVUE, OeSS) exists around the theme of collaboration.

Supporting emergence of program synergies and outreach

Theme clusters are important to the NCeSS program for strategic reasons. NCeSS is a managed program where the objective is not only to ensure that research projects individually achieve their potential but that they work effectively together, that collaborations and synergies flourish and that, collectively, the program is able to establish partnerships with the wider e-science community in the UK and internationally. A problem of research programs is that individual projects often find it hard to release the effort to take on the additional burden of collaboration. As we will consider later, communication appears to be a key issue for the success of interdisciplinary projects, but this has to be complemented with resources if collaborations between program members are to work in practice.

In NCeSS, alongside administrative arrangements introduced to foster synergies and cooperation between the Nodes, the most effective measure has been to initiate a joint project that provides motivation and a focus for collaborative activities by the Hub and Nodes and, most importantly, funding for them. This is the e-infrastructure for the Social Sciences Project (Daw et al., 2007). Its main objective is to deploy research resources and demonstrators selected from those being developed within the Nodes, Small Grant Projects and PDPs. In this way, the project aims to:

- provide a platform for disseminating the benefits of e-social science to the wider social science research community;
- enhance understanding of issues around resource discovery, data access, security and usability by providing a test bed for the development of metadata and service registries, tools for user authorization and authentication, and user portals;
- lay foundations for an integrated strategy for the future development, support and sustainability of e-social science infrastructure and services.

However, by providing the Nodes with the motivation and resources to work together, the e-infrastructure project has also proved an effective response to the challenges of promoting synergies across NCeSS and other ESRC investments, coordinating activities and identifying areas in which to promote the benefits of common policies and technology standards.

International collaboration

A key objective for e-science is to foster and further scientific research by collaboration across disciplinary and geographical boundaries. e-Social science requires international collaboration in order to integrate an expanded range of data and computing resources. Development of a comprehensive e-infrastructure supporting social science research in a wide range of contexts can only be achieved through the establishment of globally recognized standards and through exchange of experience on implementation and use.

NCeSS has devoted substantial effort to establishing these international links. Members of the Hub have been actively involved in ICEAGE (The International Collaboration to Extend and Advance Grid Education[4]) whose major objective is to establish a worldwide initiative to inspire innovative and effective Grid education. The Hub also participated in the recently completed E.U.-funded AVROSS project studying the adoption and sustainability of e-infrastructures (Barjak et al., 2007).

The Hub has established a series of annual International Conferences on e-social science.[5] The 1st and 2nd conferences were held in Manchester in 2005 and 2006 respectively. With the support of the U.S. National Science Foundation (NSF), the 3rd international conference was co-organized with Michigan University in 2007. The conferences bring together international representatives of the social science and e-infrastructure research communities in order to create better mutual awareness, harmonize understanding, and instigate coordinated activities to accelerate research, development, and deployment of e-infrastructure to support the social science research community. NCeSS also hosts a program of visiting research fellowships welcoming scholars from outside the U.K. to make extended visits to the Hub and Nodes. The EUAsiaGrid project[6] in which NCeSS is a partner enables the Centre to extend these activities significantly by establishing strong links with key players within the E.U. and beyond. The partners in this project share experiences of building and using e-infrastructure in the social sciences and pursue a program of studies about the development of these technologies across the international e-science community.

Despite or perhaps because of this encouraging start, much remains to be done to foster international collaborations in e-social science. The way forward is to begin with commonality of more established e-science at a global level, build upon the NCeSS experience of studying how e-infrastructures and research practices are mutually shaped and then engage other interested partners in e-social science.

Developing the Research Roadmap

Since the launch of NCeSS, the Hub has been working to develop the research roadmap and to extend its engagement with the social science research community. A variety of specific activities have been used to facilitate this.

First, NCeSS has organized a rolling program of Agenda Setting Workshops (ASWs) to which social scientists are invited to hear about opportunities for using e-infrastructure and to reflect on how these technologies might address the obstacles they face in pursuing their research objectives. A total of thirteen ASWs have been held since November 2004. Topics have included: development and use of ontologies; combining and enhancing data; applications of simulation and modeling in policy making; trust and ethics; visualization techniques; using text mining to bridge quantitative and qualitative methods; collaboration in e-science; confidentiality issues and clinical data; quantitative methods; qualitative methods; and recording human activities.

The ASWs have helped to identify new areas for the application of e-infrastructure in the social sciences. For example, a theme emerging from several of the Workshops is that Grid-enabled datasets, services and tools are key enablers for the wider take-up of e-social science. The ASWs have also enabled NCeSS to begin to profile the social science research constituency in terms of its awareness and readiness to adopt new technologies and begin to map the membership of the 'interested' community, that is, those prepared to take up new tools and services if properly supported.

Second, as the outcomes of the ESRC's own strategic deliberations crystallized in mid 2007, these were fed into the roadmap. The ESRC National Data Strategy[7] identified the provision of a world class social science *data infrastructure* as essential to improving the re-use of existing data collections and to meeting the challenges of the 'data deluge' arising from a profusion of new, 'naturally occurring' sources of digital data. The ESRC Key Research Challenges[8] identified *succeeding in the global economy; international relations and security; understanding and shaping individual decisions; education and life chances; religion, ethnicity and society; population change;* and *environmental change* as its strategic research priorities for 2007–2010.

Providing a world class data infrastructure will require implementation of a technology strategy that will make available to researchers better tools for describing, locating and accessing data, cleaning it, maintaining its confidentiality, combining datasets, and facilitating secondary analysis. Meeting the ESRC's strategic research priorities will require more collaborative and inter-disciplinary approaches, and the infrastructure and tools to support them.

Third, there have been two external reviews of NCeSS, one focusing on the Hub and the second on the ESRC's e-social science strategy as a whole. The latter concluded that the ESRC had made an extremely promising start in its e-social science investments. As a result of these external reviews, the NCeSS Hub was refunded in 2007 for an additional five years and the NCeSS research program received a new round of funding in mid 2007. A new phase of Node commissioning was initiated in late 2007, based on the evolving research roadmap, with the aim of funding eight three-year Nodes from 2008.

Research Roadmap 2007–2012

The 2007–2012 research roadmap retains the twin tracks of an applications strand and a social shaping strand. A key difference, however, is that the 2007–2012 roadmap has not only to identify new avenues for the application of e-social science but also to identify the best ways of building on the achievements of the first phase. Three major themes were identified in the applications strand: data infrastructure, data analysis and collaboration. Within these, several more specific issues were highlighted in the second phase Node call:

- Many of the new sources of social data are distinctive in that they are 'born digital' and continuously updated by people's everyday activities. Research is needed to explore how to realize a 'population observatory' in which social scientists can discover, access and use these new forms of data, while remaining sensitive to ethical issues relating to privacy, confidentiality and access.
- As sources of social data grow and proliferate, the problem of resource description becomes ever more acute and yet remains critical to data discovery and use. Mechanisms are needed to automate the adding of metadata to datasets. Ways of harnessing community generated contributions (tagging or 'folksonomies') and combining them with more formal representations (ontologies) are also required.
- Secure procedures for accessing confidential data are an overarching requirement for increasing the research value of existing and new sources of social data. Current provision, based on physically secure locations, represents a major barrier to the effective exploitation of such data.
- Multi-scale modeling, including that which combines physical, biological and socio-economic phenomena, is becoming an increasingly important tool for exploring complex, inter-connected systems such as climate change and disease. Real-time modeling driven by data from sensor Grids and from population observatories is increasingly possible.
- The extension of text mining techniques to social and economic data will be critical in exploiting new large-scale data resources, with a wide range of potential applications. For example, the capacity to gather qualitative data now vastly outstrips the capability to analyze it. The related technique of data mining has also yet to find wide application in academic social science research.
- Solving complex problems often involves multiple steps where the output of one step is used as the input in the next. Tools are needed to assist in the management of research processes that involve the synthesis of complex, multi-stage analyses.
- Virtual research environments, that is, persistent digital spaces where researchers can share data and tools, are vital for distributed

collaboration. Examples are rapidly emerging, including a growing number taking inspiration from social networking sites,[9] but work remains to be done to improve the usability and interoperability of tools and to extend support to cover the overall research 'lifecycle'.

- Inter-disciplinary collaborations involving the social, medical and natural sciences will be essential for success in tackling many ESRC research priorities. New collaborative resources, such as 'population laboratories' providing secure access to medical and social data, and new powerful tools for data linking and analysis will be essential in order to support such collaborations.

Further social shaping research is critically important as e-science moves beyond its initial phase in the U.K. and elsewhere. e-Science is beginning to take shape in ways that need to be understood as both applications and technologies co-evolve. Studying patterns of adoption will help to reveal factors which enable or inhibit the diffusion of e-infrastructure-supported research methods and will facilitate interventions that can enhance the e-infrastructure's effectiveness. The social shaping agenda addressed four themes:

- Genesis of e-infrastructure, including historical comparisons with the development of other communications technologies and a consideration of broader institutional and political contexts;
- Social, economic and other determinants of the design, uptake, use and sustainability of e-infrastructures;
- Implications for the nature and practice of science, including social science, and for the character and direction of knowledge production, validation and use;
- International comparisons, examining how different national science policies and legal frameworks influence the funding and organizations of these developments.

Measuring the impact of investment is vital both for the effective management of research programs and the shaping of future science policy. It is very challenging, however, to capture the full range of impacts, especially within short timescales.

Challenges

The NCeSS program is 'work in progress' and e-social science is far from being a routine undertaking. It carries significant risk arising from such factors as the uncertain path of technological innovation; the lack of experience among potential users of the technologies involved; issues arising from the social organization of research including embedded research practices and the established reward structure; and the management of processes of change. We have outlined various initiatives that NCeSS has undertaken to counter these risks in the pursuit of its core aims, notably the Agenda Setting Workshop series and the e-infrastructure for the Social Sciences Project. In this section, we reflect on some of the most significant challenges that need to be tackled as NCeSS seeks to build upon its achievements to date.

Widening adoption

The target audience for NCeSS dissemination and capacity-building activities can be segmented by academic discipline, methodological approach and career stage but the most useful profile is in terms of knowledge and skill. It is on this basis that the Hub's strategic planning is organized around the tri-part division between the 'early adopters', the 'interested' and the 'unengaged'.

The *early adopters* are largely already part of NCeSS (Hub, Nodes, Small Grant Projects, Pilot Demonstrator Projects, and Visiting Fellows) and are keen to push to the limit what e-social science makes possible. The Hub supports early adopters by facilitating networking and encouraging the sharing of technical expertise. The e-Infrastructure Project is playing an important role in this.

The *interested* form the test-bed for e-social science applications. In return for their assistance in helping to identify requirements, NCeSS offers them demonstrators of how e-infrastructure might aid their research. NCeSS also supports their adoption of new tools and services (produced by early adopters) and monitors their experiences to feed back into the development process. The Hub has used an action-oriented ethnographic approach in a series of small-scale case studies to understand the needs that arise in the everyday research practices of the interested and, in parallel, promoted e-infrastructure developments to address their needs.

Not all of the *unengaged* have the same view of e-infrastructure. Some simply do not know what is available (Lin, Procter, Halfpenny, Voss, & Baird, 2007), and they are the target of NCeSS's awareness-raising efforts that again employ demonstrators to illustrate the potential of new tools and services. Others are aware but do not have the time or inclination to invest in new ways of working. Yet others are epistemological skeptics, believing that any use of information and computer technologies taints the resultant social science. These will be the hardest to win over.

Even the more tractable of the unengaged will adopt new tools and services only when these are 'hardened' to production level (that is, become easy to use, stable, documented and supported); when they offer immediate benefits that quickly outweigh the costs of learning to use them; and when they complement existing research practices. Only when NCeSS has moved beyond proofs of concept, demonstrators and prototypes to near production level tools and services can it begin to engage them. It is the ease-of-use and utility of e-infrastructure, and its contribution to advancing social scientists' substantive research, that will persuade them to adopt new ways of working, not the provenance of the technology. In this respect, the major breakthrough in wider adoption of e-infrastructure will be when its e-science origins become invisible, just part of the normal landscape of research methods. In this way, even the epistemological skeptics can be enticed into the fold.

Understanding and tackling barriers to adoption

Complementing its small-scale, focused studies, the Hub has also been involved in mapping the adoption of e-infrastructure across disciplines at the U.K. and European levels. This mapping provides the groundwork to develop mechanisms to tackle barriers to adoption and improve outreach (Barjak et al., 2007; Voss et al., 2007b). The e-Infrastructure Use Cases and Service Usage Models (eIUS)[10] project aims to gather and document evidence of how e-infrastructure is currently being used to facilitate research processes. The Enabling Uptake of e-Infrastructure Services project (e-Uptake)[11] aims to develop strategies for widening adoption of e-infrastructure. Both projects are funded under the Community Engagement strand of the U.K. Joint Information Services Committee's e-infrastructure program.

What this work confirms is that, as with any innovation, barriers that potential users of e-infrastructure face are numerous and, singly or in combination, they can delay or even prevent adoption (Rogers, 1995; Molina, 1997). For e-infrastructure to be widely adopted, costs as perceived by users must be outweighed by the benefits. Potential users must be aware of e-infrastructure, must understand the advantages it can bring to their research, must be willing to invest in new skills, and must have access to the facilities and support they need for successful adoption. At the same time, e-infrastructure services must be reliable, robust and easily usable if researchers are to be persuaded to trust their mission critical work to them. Moreover, users must be confident that services will not only continue to be available but also improve in response to their needs so that the benefits increase over time.

Having mapped the adoption of e-infrastructure and identified how users respond to barriers, strategies then need to be devised that enable uptake, for example, by providing clear and well-supported migration routes. These routes are likely to be different for late adopters drawn from among the unengaged and early adopters at the forefront of e-social science. Late adopters, for example, may require direct and personalized support in the form of staff development courses (both face-to-face and self-paced on-line learning); specific consultancy to develop new applications to utilize services in novel ways; and a single well-curated source of information about technical components and services, along with exemplars of their use.

As users' requirements mature, their support needs may also change. Moreover, different user communities will be at different phases of the adoption cycle at any one time and so support has to be provided for all phases simultaneously. Explicitly or implicitly, e-infrastructure users will go through cycles of evaluating their requirements and assessing the appropriateness of services while providers will similarly go through cycles of improving services and developing new ones to meet emerging needs. Accordingly, potential user communities—and their experiences of barriers and responses to them—are likely to be highly diverse. Extensive, flexible and varied resources will be needed to promote e-social science to them effectively. Furthermore, technical and social issues cannot be separated given the dynamic between them—which is the focus of NCeSS's social shaping research agenda. Accordingly, e-infrastructure adoption will only reach full maturity when social, organizational, cultural, ethical and legal issues are resolved in tandem with the creation of technology-based tools and services. This is the main message of studies of previous efforts to develop large-scale infrastructures: success depends on aligning technical components and stakeholder interests (Edwards, Jackson, Bowker, & Knobel, 2007).

Collaboration

e-Social science is underpinned by a vision of the transformation of research practice into collaborative activity that combines the abilities and resources of distributed groups of researchers in order to achieve research goals that individual researchers or local groups could not hope to accomplish (Voss, Procter, Budweg, & Prinz, 2007a). Also, e-social science is inherently cross-disciplinary, given that its development is dependent on close collaboration between social scientists and computer scientists. Beyond this, its full potential will be realized only when it spans further disciplines, including medical and environmental sciences, thereby enabling the investigation of the full complexity of determinants of individual action and social behavior.

Yet there are numerous institutional constraints on collaboration, most notably the academic reward system in which career advancement and scientific reputation depend heavily on individual achievements. The reality of individual competition over discovery claims, grants, promotion and space in top-ranking journals is far removed from the ideal of openness and sharing of data and other resources promoted by the e-science vision. While the current rapid spread of 'Science 2.0' (Waldrop, 2008) provides grounds for optimism that research cultures are indeed changing, continuing investigation of barriers to real-world interdisciplinary collaboration, and mechanisms to overcome them remains a critical element of the NCeSS social shaping research program.

Sustainability

A variety of factors conspire to make issues about the sustainability of e-infrastructure impossible to ignore. First, U.K. e-science has reached that point in the innovation lifecycle where it must seek engagement with users beyond the early adopters and it is important that the pace of adoption does not falter. To progress, the interested must be supplied with tools and services that meet their needs and they must be supported as they seek to embrace innovative practices, or their enthusiasm will wane. Second, the existence of competing technical solutions can be a disincentive to the adoption of innovations, and recent divergent developments are a cause of confusion within the e-infrastructure community. Five years ago, the e-infrastructure technical roadmap was indistinguishable from that of the 'Grid'. Now, however, the rise of Web 2.0 has caused many to consider alternative, more lightweight approaches where sophisticated Grid-based solutions are not required. While this may have the effect of promoting adoption in some quarters, it also carries the risk of deterring others from engaging, at least until a clear technical winner has emerged. Third, if the accumulation, sharing and re-use of resources called for by the e-research vision generates a substantial increase in both the numbers and the types of research resources available, then priorities will have to be established to determine which will receive continued support, given that funding is unlikely to keep pace.

This brings us to a fundamental question for sustainability, which is how research resources originating in time-limited projects can be re-built to production level quality, then curated, maintained and managed so that they remain viable for use by the whole research community in the long term. In particular, where, in a landscape of multiplying, diverse and distributed resources, will the necessary effort and expertise come from, and what funding models are most appropriate to pay for it (Voss et al., 2007b)? Funding bodies are concerned that sustaining the burgeoning body of research resources will consume an ever increasing proportion of their budgets.[12] The existing institutional infrastructure as represented by current service providers and the funding models that support them is in tension with the opportunities that the new technical infrastructure affords. It is time to consider whether a blueprint for a new institutional infrastructure, possibly with a greater number and diversity of service providers, is necessary, but there are few signs as yet that the relevant stakeholders (existing or potential) are ready or able to explore and agree how to best exploit—and fund—the options available to them.

Impact and its measurement

Measuring the impact of the e-social science program is vital for planning its future strategic direction. However, evaluating the impact of innovation is notoriously difficult, especially in the short term since results take time to disseminate and their significance may only become clear after a considerable delay. Moreover, impacts do not flow solely from technical advances; these are mediated by a wide range of social, institutional, cultural and economic factors. Impact can manifest itself as improvements in research performance, for example, efficiencies in data integration, or in novel research outputs, such as new findings that could not have been achieved without innovative technologies. In addition, impact in terms of added value obtained from innovations can be economic, social, personal or more diffusely realized. For these reasons, conventional uni-dimensional impact measures (such as peer reviews, citation analyses and other bibliometric approaches) have severe limitations. Other approaches, such as impact modeling, which involves extrapolating from previous trends, are not suited to e-science because it is fluid and fast changing. The problem is not the lack of data; there exists a deluge of data from sources such as bibliometric databases, e-repositories and the Web. It is the techniques that would enable this abundant data to be transformed into evidence for impact assessments that are not equal to the task.

Measuring impact exemplifies the kinds of challenge that e-science was devised to address. In this sense, the solution to creating an evidence base for the e-(social) science roadmap lies in its own hands: the use of network analysis, data and text mining to extract and analyze information from extensive sources, within a research program that will foster the necessary interdisciplinary collaborations. The recently announced NSF Science of Science and Innovation Policy program represents a very interesting and timely step towards this.[13]

CONCLUSIONS

A feature of the current state of e-social science is that, despite the substantial investment by the ESRC, its adoption remains piecemeal. Although bids for Nodes and Small Grant projects obviously had to attend to the strategic direction set out in the specification of the calls if they were to be successful, nevertheless the proposals reflected the interests of the groups who authored them, as they slotted their e-social science projects into their ongoing, wider research programs. The upshot is that the outcome of a large-scale e-infrastructure program like NCeSS cannot be guaranteed through top down strategic planning. Instead, much of the Hub's coordinating activities, and especially the e-infrastructure for the Social Sciences Project, aim to harness bottom up innovations that are driven by experimentation by the Nodes and Small Grant Projects as they respond to requirements proposed by their local, substantive social science driver projects. A future 'Whig history' of the emergence of e-infrastructure will no doubt identify a clear line of development but the reality along the way is of uncertainty and risk-taking, only some of which will issue in what are later recognized as successes.

In this environment, user capability becomes central, and this requires striving to provide e-social science tools and services that enable social scientists to improve their research practices and generate results that would not otherwise have been possible. NCeSS must therefore continue to work very closely with social science researchers to seek out their requirements and it must be catholic in the selection of technologies to meet them, broadening out from the original emphasis on Grid computing. At the same time, it must be remembered that the technical and the social are inextricable, requiring attention to awareness-raising, training, support and other activities designed to reduce the cost of adoption.

NOTES

1. http://www.esrcsocietytoday.ac.uk/ESRCInfoCentre/about/strategicplan/
2. http://www.epsrc.ac.uk/ResearchFunding/Programmes/RII/e-Science/default.htm
3. http://www.esds.ac.uk
4. http://www.iceage-eu.org/v2/index.cfm
5. http://www.ncess.ac.uk/events/conference/past_conferences/
6. http://www.euasiagrid.org/
7. http://www2.warwick.ac.uk/fac/soc/nds/
8. http://www.esrcsocietytoday.ac.uk/ESRCInfoCentre/about/delivery_plan/priorities_and_funding/index.aspx?ComponentId=9508&SourcePageId=13007
9. For example, 'Myexperiment' (http://www.myexperiment.org) and nature network (http://network.nature.com/).
10. http://www.jisc.ac.uk/whatwedo/programmes/programme_einfrastructure/eius.aspx
11. http://www.jisc.ac.uk/whatwedo/programmes/programme_einfrastructure/euptake.aspx
12. A recent example is the decision by the UK Arts and Humanities Research Council to discontinue funding of the Arts and Humanities Data Service from April 2008.
13. www.nsf.gov/pubs/2008/nsf08520/nsf08520.htm

REFERENCES

Anderson, A. (2003). *Human-centred design and Grid technologies.* Swindon: ESRC.

Axelson, A-S., & Schroeder, R. (2007). Making it open and keeping it safe: e-Enabled data sharing in Sweden and related issues. Paper, International Conference on e-Social Science, Ann Arbor, MI. Available at: http://ess.si.umich.edu/papers/paper139.pdf

Barjak, F., Weigand, G., Lane, J., Kertcher, Z., Poschen, M., Procter, R., & Robinson, S. (2007). Accelerating transition to virtual research organization in social science (AVROSS): First results from a survey of e-infrastructure adopters. Paper, International Conference on e-Social Science, Ann Arbor, MI. Available at: http://ess.si.umich.edu/papers/paper141.pdf

Batty, M., Steadman, P., & Xie, Y. (2006). Visualization in spatial modeling. In J. Portugali (Ed.), *Complex artificial environments*, pp. 49–70. Berlin: Springer.

Birkin, M., Clarke, M., Rees, P., Chen, H., Keen, J., & Xu, J. (2005). MoSeS: Modelling and Simulation for e-Social Science. In Proc 1st Int. Conf. on e-Social Science, Manchester, UK.

Birkin, M., Townhend, P., Turner, A., Wu, B., & Xu, J. (2007). An architecture for social simulation models to support spatial planning. Paper, International Conference on e-Social Science, Ann Arbor, MI. Available at: http://ess.si.umich.edu/papers/paper214.pdf

Carusi, A-M., & Jirotka, M. (2007). From data archive to ethical labyrinth. Paper, International Conference on e-Social Science, Ann Arbor, MI. Available at: http://ess.si.umich.edu/papers/paper171.pdf

Chorley, A., Edwards, P., & Preece, A. (2007). Tools for tracing evidence in social science. Paper, International Conference on e-Social Science, Ann Arbor, MI. Available at: http://ess.si.umich.edu/papers/paper124.pdf

Cole, K., Schurer, K., Beedham, H., & Hewitt, T. (2003). *Grid enabling quantitative social science datasets—A scoping study*. Swindon: ESRC.

Crabtree, A. French, A., Greenhalgh, C., Rodden, T., & Benford, S. (2006). Working with digital records: developing tool support. Paper, International Conference on e-Social Science, Manchester, UK. Available at: http://www.mrl.nott.ac.uk/~axc/DReSS_Outputs/ICeSS_1_2006.pdf

Crabtree, A., French, A., Greenhalgh, C., Benford, S., Cheverst, K., Fitton, D., Rouncefield, M., & Graham, C. (2006). Developing digital records: Early experiences of record and replay. *Journal of Computer Supported Cooperative Work, 15*(4): 281–319.

Crouchley, R., van Ark, T., Pritchard, J., Grose, D., Kewley, J., Allan, R., Hayes, M., & Morris, L. (2005). Putting social science applications on the Grid. Paper, International Conference on e-Social Science, Manchester, UK. Available at: http://www.ncess.ac.uk/events/conference/2005/papers/papers/ncess2005_paper_Crouchley.pdf

Daw, M., Procter, R., Lin, Y-W., Hewitt, T., Jie, W., Voss, A., Baird, K., Turner, A., Birkin, M., Miller, K., Dutton, W., Jirotka, M., Schroeder, R., de la Flor, G., Edwards, P., Allan, R., Yang, X., & Crouchley, R. (2007). Developing an e-infrastructure for social science. Paper, International Conference on e-Social Science, Ann Arbor, MI. Available at: http://ess.si.umich.edu/papers/paper127.pdf

Dutton, W. (2007). Reconfiguring access to information and expertise in the social sciences: The social shaping and implications of cyberinfrastructure. Paper, International Conference on e-Social Science, Ann Arbor, MI. Available at: http://ess.si.umich.edu/papers/paper127.pdf

Edwards, P.N., Jackson, S.J., Bowker, G.C., & Knobel, C.P. (2007). Understanding infrastructures: Dynamics, tensions, and design. Final report of the workshop "History & Theory of Infrastructure: Lessons for New Scientific Cyberinfrastructures". National Science Foundation. Available at: http://deepblue.lib.umich.edu/handle/2027.42/49353

Fielding, N. (2003). *Qualitative research and e-social science: Appraising the potential*. Swindon: ESRC.

Fraser, M., Hindmarsh, J., Best, K., Heath, C., Biegel, G., Greenhalgh, C., & Reeves, S. (2006). Remote collaboration over video data: Towards real-time e-social science. *Journal of Computer Supported Cooperative Work, 15*(4): 257–279.

Greenhalgh, C., French, A., Tennent, P., Humble, J., & Crabtree, A. (2007). From ReplayTool to digital replay system. Paper, International Conference on e-Social Science, Ann Arbor, MI. Available at: http://ess.si.umich.edu/papers/paper161.pdf

Grose, D., Crouchley, R., van Ark, T., Allan, R., Kewley, J., Braimah, A., & Hayes, M. (2006). sabreR: Grid-enabling the analysis of multi-process random effect response data. Paper, International Conference on e-Social Science, Manchester, UK. Available at: http://redress.lancs.ac.uk/resources/Grose_Daniel/Grid-Enabling_Analysis_Multi-Process_Random_Effect_Response_Data_R/NCeSS06.pdf

Hey, T., & Trefethen, A. (2004). UK e-Science Programme: Next generation Grid applications. *International Journal of High Performance Computing Applications, 18*(3): 285–291.

Heilkema, F., Edwards, P., Mellish, C., & Farrington, J. (2007). A flexible interface to community-driven metadata. Paper, International Conference on e-Social Science, Ann Arbor, MI. Available at: http://ess.si.umich.edu/papers/paper144.pdf

Knight, D., Bayoumi, S., Mills, S., Crabtree, A., Adolphs, S., Pridmore, T., & Carter, R. (2006). Beyond the text: Construction and analysis of multi-modal linguistic corpora. Paper, International Conference on e-Social Science, Manchester, UK. Available at: http://www.ncess.ac.uk/research/sgp/headtalk/20060630_knight_BeyondTheText_paper.pdf

Lin, Y.-W., Procter, R., Halfpenny, P., Voss, A., & Baird, K. (2007). An action-oriented ethnography of interdisciplinary social scientific work. Paper, International Conference on e-Social Science, Ann Arbor, MI. Available at: http://ess.si.umich.edu/papers/paper179.pdf

Milton, R., & Steed, A. (2007). Mapping carbon monoxide using GPS tracked sensors. *Environmental Monitoring and Assessment, 124*(1–3): 1–19.

Molina, A.H. (1997). Insights into the nature of technology diffusion and implementation: The perspective of sociotechnical alignment. *Technovation, 17*(11–12), 601–626.

Peters, S., Clark, K., Ekin, P., Le Blanc, A., & Pickles, S. (2007). Grid enabling empirical economics: A microdata application. *Computational Economics, 30*(4): 349–370.

Pignotti, E., Edwards, P., & Preece, A. (2007). Semantic workflow management for e-social science. Paper, International Conference on e-Social Science, Ann Arbor, MI. Available at: http://ess.si.umich.edu/papers/paper174.pdf

Rogers, E. M. (1995). *Diffusion of innovations.* 4th ed. New York: Free Press.

Shaukat, M., & Fraser, M. (2007). A security framework for data distribution in qualitative analysis tools: Digital rights management in MiMeG. Paper, International Conference on e-Social Science, Ann Arbor, MI. Available at: http://ess.si.umich.edu/papers/paper137.pdf

Townhend, P., Xu, J., Birkin, M., Turner, A., & Wu, B. (2007). Modelling and simulation for e-social science: Current progress. Paper, e-Science All Hands Meeting, Nottingham, UK. Available at: http://www.allhands.org.uk/2007/proceedings/papers/889.pdf

Tutt, D., Hindmarsh, J., Shaukat, M., Fraser, M., & McCarthy, M. (2007). Can you see what I see? Developing coherent support for distributed collaborative video analysis with MiMeG. Paper, International Conference on e-Social Science, Ann Arbor, MI. Available at: http://ess.si.umich.edu/papers/paper168.pdf

Voss, A., Procter, R., Budweg, S., & Prinz, W. (2007a). Collaboration in and for e-research: making the 'O' in virtual organisation work. Paper, German e-Science Conference, Baden-Baden. Available at: http://www.cwe-projects.eu/pub/bscw.cgi/d1248208/Collaboration%20in%20and%20for%20e-Research.pdf

Voss, A., Mascord, M., Arguello Castelleiro, M., Asgari-Targhi, M., Procter, R., Fraser, M., Jirotka, M., Halfpenny, P., Fergusson, D., Atkinson, M., Dunn, S., Blanke, T., Hughes, L., & Anderson, S. (2007b). e-Infrastructure development and community engagement. Paper, International Conference on e-Social Science, Ann Arbor, MI. Available at: http://ess.si.umich.edu/papers/paper170.pdf

Waldrop, M. M. (2008). Science 2.0: Great new tool, or great risk? *Scientific American.* Retrieved 13 June 2008 from http://www.sciam.com/article.cfm?id=science-2-point-0-great-new-tool-or-great-risk

Woolgar, S. (2003). *Social shaping perspectives on e-science and e-social science.* Swindon: ESRC.

5 e-Research and Scholarly Community in the Humanities

Paul Genoni, Helen Merrick and Michele Willson

The terms 'e-research' and 'e-science' are emerging as the favored descriptors to signal both the shift in the practice and business of scholarly work, and an increasingly common direction for national funding and research priorities. As researchers begin to examine this phenomenon, it is becoming clear that disciplinary differences are crucial markers of success and uptake, with much work remaining to be done in areas outside the natural sciences (e.g., Lloyd & Sun, 2005; Jankowski, 2007; Wouters & Beaulieu, 2007). Closer attention needs to be paid to the ways in which diverse disciplines can use and benefit from e-research-enabling technologies such as cyberinfrastructure or Grid computing. Not surprisingly, most research to date has tended to focus on the natural sciences (Costa & Meadows, 2000: 255) with some interesting work emerging around the notion of collaboratories (Finholt, 2003; Bos et al., 2007). There have, however, been considerably fewer investigations of the changing practices, cultures, and communities of scholars in the humanities as they engage with an e-research environment.

The concept of 'scholarly community' has for some time been central to the understanding of scholarship and research, and the types of community (and communication) that are characteristic of different disciplines (Crane, 1972; Meadows, 1974). What *exactly* constitutes or defines scholarly community is, however, an open question, and one which is complicated as modes of communication and research practice are transformed. For the purposes of this paper scholarly community is defined as the multiple relationships that result from the pursuit of shared scholarly interest and endeavour. These may be formal relationships—those that are mediated by professional associations or constructed collectives of scholars; or they may be informal relationships—those that are constituted spontaneously between two or more scholars. In either case it is not necessary that individuals know each other personally in order to belong to the same scholarly community. 'Belonging' may simply result from being part of the extended discourse of scholarship that attaches to any discipline or subject area.

Recent work on the structuring, diffusion and use of scholarship and research emphasizes the complicated and interdependent relations between disciplinary cultures, formal and informal communication, and scholarly communities (Hargens, 2000; Fry, 2004). In this chapter we consider the impact of e-research models on the informal communication practices of humanities scholars, and the extent to which their own perception of 'scholarly community' may have been altered. The broad aim of our research is to investigate the relationship between changing research and communication practices and notions of scholarly groupings and, in particular, differences in e-research practice between the sciences and humanities. Underlying this aim are important questions concerning how (and why) we conceptualize and categorize such practices. That is, the possibilities and the imperatives of an ICT-driven environment invite reflection not only about how to conduct e-research or what it means, but also about the very notion of scholarly community itself.

This chapter reflects on an ongoing research project investigating e-research practices in the humanities, and particularly the impact of the Internet on the informal communicative practices that support and inform research. Our discussion is based on a survey of academics' use of the Internet, conducted at Curtin University of Technology, and initial investigations of academics involved in the Australian-based Network for Early European Research (NEER). Following a brief literature overview contextualizing this research we draw on a small-scale survey of NEER participants as a means of speculating about the evolution of informal communication and related notions of scholarly community as humanities scholars increasingly engage with e-research. We conclude that further investigation of the underlying cultural practices and research needs of humanities scholars is required in order to understand and enact a closer match between their research practices and productive technological relationships.

BACKGROUND

Our focus on informal scholarly communication, and the role it plays in supporting and generating community or the 'invisible college' in a networked environment has necessitated the review of a large and diverse body of literature. This has ranged from older studies of patterns of scholarly communication (Meadows, 1974) and the invisible college (Crane, 1972) to research on the impact of ICTs on traditional research and communication practices (Bruce, 1996; Appleby, Clayton & Pascoe, 1997; Houghton, Steele & Henty, 2003). There is a related body of research that focuses specifically on changes in informal scholarly communication practice; that is, the wide range of written and verbal information exchanges other than those which constitute publication (Hert, 1997; Costa & Meadows, 1999; Koku, Nazer & Wellman, 2001; Henry, 2002; Barjak, 2005).

One of the few studies to date explicitly addressing the humanities argues that 'e-science' is not the most appropriate term to cover humanities-type research (Wouters & Beaulieu, 2007). The term e-science carries connotations regarding the use of high-end computational facilities and Grid computer networks as tools for research in ways that may not be appropriate to humanities research methodologies and practices (Jankowski, 2007, 551). Indeed, as Wouters and Beaulieu (2007) note, "the dominant use of the term e-science in discussions of new information infrastructures for the humanities and social sciences carries with it an emphasis on data-oriented computational or quantitative analysis" (p. 584).

Thus far the Australian approach reflects that of European initiatives rather than the U.S. and U.K. in preferring the umbrella term of 'e-research'. As Jankowski notes, in the Netherlands "the term e-science is avoided and preference given to 'e-research', which is seen as more reflective of the work of both social scientists and scholars in the humanities" (Jankowski, 2007). The Australian government's definition of e-research stresses ICT-enhanced collaboration and enabled research practices rather than focusing on Grid computing per se, noting the supplementary nature of many e-research practices. It also notes the development of completely new research and methods as a result of technological capabilities.[1]

Bodies with an investment in the humanities have also started using the term 'e-humanities' to distinguish the particular needs of their discipline. One manifestation of this trend in Australia is the establishment of the Australian e-Humanities Network, operating under the auspices of the Australian Academy of the Humanities.[2]

In this chapter, e-research is our preferred term for several reasons. Firstly, it can most easily encompass the sorts of informal communication and community-related practices particularly suited to those disciplines within the humanities that have not traditionally relied on large datasets or extensive computational facilities; secondly, because e-research better reflects and encompasses the range of collaborative possibilities of networked research in the humanities; and finally, as the research reported here focuses on experiences in Australian universities and on an Australian Research Council (ARC) nationally funded project it makes sense to use local terminology.[3]

The humanities encapsulate a range of research objectives, methods, and resources that render any undifferentiated coupling with the 'traditional' or natural sciences problematic. Indeed, it has been suggested that the term humanities itself covers too broad and diverse a collection of research and scholarly communication practices to be able to be considered as a cohesive research object (Fry, 2006). This diversity affects the ways in which digital resources are employed in scholarly communication practices and research production.

On the one hand, there is validity in Fry's claim that:

> intellectual fields within a single discipline vary to such an extent in their knowledge creation practices and work organization as to render comparison of computer-mediated communication practices based on broad disciplinary groupings such as the natural sciences and humanities misleading. (Fry, 2006: 302)

On the other hand, the intellectual fields incorporated under the banner of humanities tend to exhibit differences from the sciences (and often social sciences) in a number of ways: predominance of independent scholarship and the lone author (Cronin, 2003; American Council of Learned Societies, 2006; Wouters & Beaulieu, 2007), focus on qualitative rather than quantitative focused methods, and a trend of interpretative and speculative outcomes. That is, intellectual fields in the humanities are more likely to exhibit "a low degree of 'mutual dependence' coupled with a high degree of 'task uncertainty'", which as Fry argues are "less successful in commanding control over channels of communication and are less concerned with co-producing field-based digital resources" (Fry, 2006: 299).[4]

In discussing the importance of variations in formal and informal scholarly communication for the uptake of e-research processes and resources, Fry points particularly to the difficulties in utilizing digital infrastructures to enable collaborative work in "those fields that are non-hierarchical, loosely organized, intellectually pluralistic, with local variation in work organization" (Fry, 2006: 312). Despite her caution about basing comparisons on disciplines, this description would apply to many fields in the humanities. Thus Fry's conclusion about the fate of such fields in an e-research environment is, we would argue, crucial in considering humanities' applications and uptake of e-research initiatives. She notes:

> the lack of centralized coordination and control in these fields will make it difficult for the scholarly community to systematically appropriate and develop digital infrastructures and resources in response to specific cultural needs. Often such fields have to work within externally imposed and developed digital infrastructures and resources. (Fry, 2006: 312)

Thus, central to our investigation has been the work on the transformation of university information resources and scholarly practices at an institutional level (Gibbons et al., 1994; Hawkins & Battin, 1998). In Australia, there has been increasing focus on collaborative and cross-institutional research. The Australian Government's proposed introduction of the Research Quality Framework (RQF) in 2007/8 emphasized national and international output and performance. Similarly, in 2005, the Australian Research Council (ARC) special research initiatives focused on e-research.[5] The centrality of Grid computing in funding models and as impetus for collaboration is hard to avoid. For example, a recent survey conducted under the aegis of the Australian Academy of the Humanities was heavily focused on the use or potential of ICTs and networked computing for research practice (Australian Academy of the Humanities, 2007). Broader questions about cultural and communication practices were not addressed or considered as part of the survey's purview.

Given such systemic encouragement, it is likely that there will be an escalation in the formation of humanities research groupings that are less organic, spontaneous, and instinctive than they may have been in the past. These groupings, it can be hypothesized, are likely to also be more structured, administratively facilitated and grant purposive. In this sense, they may be seen to mirror some of the processes and practices already embedded within the production of knowledge in the sciences. In Australia, "[i]ncreasingly the dominant research model is derived from the sciences rather than the humanities, with some of the benefits, and most of the complexities and difficulties that arise from such models of research teams" (Trigg, 2006: 329). This is an important point if we are to recognize that the difficulties of attaining a 'fit' between humanities research and e-research/cyber infrastructure is not just due to a (potentially determinist) notion of causal changes initiated by a changing technological environment. In many ways these difficulties emerge from, and indeed are exacerbated by, traditional differences between the cultures of humanities and science scholars. Such differences may leave humanities scholars even more disadvantaged as funding incentives for collaborative work become bound up in designing and implementing the technical and economic infrastructures for future e-research.

Our initial research focused on the perceived changes to academic communication and community brought about by the increasing adoption of ICTs (Genoni, Merrick, & Willson, 2005a; 2005b; 2006). Through a mixture of surveys and focus group studies, we examined scholarly communication practices and their relation to ICT usage at Curtin University of Technology in Western Australia. Our study of 107 academic staff and 139 postgraduate research students (246 respondents in total) across a range of disciplinary areas flagged a number of areas for investigation around the possible transformation of disciplinary research cultures and the perception of the impact of ICT usage. Also of interest was the fact that while Curtin's humanities scholars appeared not to be as e-research focused as some of the other disciplines, they still perceived ICT as impacting on their experience of scholarly communication and collaboration (although to a lesser degree than scholars in the sciences and social sciences). The Curtin study also pointed to a need to investigate a clearly identified electronic network of humanities researchers as a means of reaching a better understanding of humanities e-research practices.

NETWORK OF EARLY EUROPEAN RESEARCH

As a result of the evolving nature of e-research formations it is difficult to identify the appropriate unit for analysis in terms of investigating the changing dynamics of different research cultures. Whereas many of the classic studies referred to above have been conducted at the discipline level, it may be more productive to investigate research practices of sub-disciplines, networks, or even projects. We had some difficulty in locating an Australian humanities e-research grouping that was more than simply an electronic list of affiliates before eventually selecting the Network of Early European Research (NEER) as a subject for more detailed exploration. We acknowledge, however, that research conducted on differently sized units of humanities e-research might achieve different outcomes.

Preliminary interviews and questionnaires with NEER members were conducted, and responses were used to reflect on existing literature and the previous Curtin University survey in order to pose questions concerning the methodology and research objectives most suitable for investigation of humanities e-research.

NEER is funded by the ARC as a 'network of excellence'; and is also supported by a number of other institutional bodies. Established in 2004, NEER had approximately 200 members at the time of our survey in 2006 (membership in 2007 was closer to 300) drawn from across most of the Australian universities. These members are comprised of a mix of research and teaching, research-only academics, and postgraduates. NEER has been granted ARC funding until 2009, at which point the management committee will seek other funding sources in order to ensure the network's continuation.

The stated aim of the network is:

> to implement a formal framework for supporting and enhancing current Australian research into the culture and history of Europe between the fifth and early nineteenth centuries. It also aims to foster new research and new connections between researchers, and to develop and nurture the next generation of researchers in the field. (NEER, 2006)

NEER offers an administrative framework to afford and facilitate collaborative information sharing, mentoring and research output across national and international locales. As such it is a grouping that intends some longevity rather than one constituted as a more ephemeral gathering around a particular project or research problem.[6]

As well as providing a Web site (http://www.neer.arts.uwa.edu.au/) and electronic list, NEER offers access to commercial databases, is establishing a digital research repository, PioNEER, and an electronic Australian collections service. Funded activities to date include symposia and conferences; sponsorship for other research-related events; collaborative research programs; and postgraduate training seminars. NEER also supports Confluence, a Wiki space designed to support member interaction and joint research and grant writing. Confluence was activated in February 2007 and thus is still in its early stages with regards to researchers' familiarity with the software.

A further feature of NEER is the research clusters, groups of 3–10 individuals from more than one institution and more than one discipline, collaborating in particular research areas. NEER has to date 14 research clusters, each of which has their own space in Confluence to coordinate and manage their collaborations. Although the NEER Web site notes, "Research clusters are expected to use (Confluence) as the primary means of tracking and recording their communications and collaborative activities",[7] to date there has been a slow uptake of the software's collaborative possibilities with most researchers resorting to email, or to email style attachments within the software (Burrows, 2007). This slow uptake may be related to the members' lack of familiarity with the technology's possibilities (Burrows, 2007), and also possibly because these possibilities require changes to take place in members' research practices.

NEER was approached to participate in this study after the network had been operating for two years. The first stage involved the electronic distribution of a short open-ended questionnaire to the list of members. In order to provide contextual information, participants were asked how they had become involved in NEER, what range of activities they participated in, and whether they were involved in any e-research projects—defined as collaborative work fully or partially conducted through online means. We were interested in foregrounding questions concerning the human or social elements underpinning these initiatives. A total of 38 responses were returned. Given the small number of responses and the limited range of the survey questions, the following discussion is necessarily exploratory in nature, intended to open up and identify areas for further empirical investigation and theoretical development.

INVOLVEMENT IN NEER

When asked about how they had become involved in NEER, most respondents indicated that they had been, in one way or another, invited to participate. Participants were either known of through personal networks, through a shared association with a professional organization or by reputation within the field. From the outset then, NEER could be said to have been built upon a selective use of the scholarly community or invisible college as it related to a particular area of expertise. According to Stephanie Trigg (2006), NEER started with a small core of 50 established researchers and successful grant applicants and then built outwards to include early career researchers, postgraduates and other scholars. She notes the application for funding, "had no difficulty in proving that funding would consolidate networks and groups already in existence, rather than suddenly producing relationships among scholars who had never worked together before (a weakness of many other applications)" (Trigg, 2006: 322).

Therefore, at least in these initial stages, while NEER can be identified as a constructed or contrived network, there were underpinning relationships and an existing community within the group. However, it is also noteworthy that an e-research network of the scale of NEER had not arisen spontaneously out of these relationships but rather needed to be consciously constructed and administered. This is understandable given the institutional imperative of seeking external, large scale funding; a broader issue for academic research networks that will be touched on later. Yet, the consequences of a broader gathering, enabled in no small part because of ICT capacities, opens up a range of issues and possibilities for humanities research to address.

Respondents' reasons for agreeing to become involved in NEER fell into three broad categories: those relating to expansion of contacts or academic networks, those relating to access to information and knowledge, and those that were primarily resource driven. For example, many respondents noted the importance of broadening their connections to other areas and scholars and improving access to academic knowledge. Comments[8] indicative of these sentiments included:

- Reconnected me with my initial academic field;
- Good opportunity to get to know what academics are doing in this area;
- To gain contacts with other early modern researchers;
- Establish a sense of community;
- Share research and teaching ideas . . . share resources and the expertise of personnel.

NEER was also seen as offering concrete benefits. These included opportunities to attend conferences and seminars; funding of projects using sources outside the mainstream funding bodies; and access to resources provided by NEER.

Another key reason mentioned by a number of respondents was the potential for NEER to strengthen the profile of Early Modern and Medieval Studies in Australia and internationally, and to counter the isolation of researchers in the field:

- I believed NEER would be a great way to . . . strengthen the academic position of European studies in Australia, (leading to) even more success and security for the field;
- I care about developing Medieval and Renaissance art history in Australia;
- To overcome the problems of isolation and fragmentation in Australian medieval early modern studies.

Such sentiments indicate the importance of belonging, and a shared sense of identity: key 'aspects' in many understandings of community, and by extension scholarly community.

As noted earlier, the culture of humanities research typically privileges the sole author/investigator research project—although the research itself may be engaged in a discussion with other researchers' work, past and present. In these circumstances a broader scholarly community is necessary in order to expand the development and dissemination of ideas and activities. However, while collaborative research projects are not unknown in the humanities, they have not been the norm. In Australia collaborative cross-institutional research has been considerably constrained by issues of geographic dispersion and the small numbers of specialist researchers located in the same institution. The possibilities of using communication technologies to facilitate broader collective projects (less restricted by geographic constraints and costs) has engendered greater interest in these endeavors, potentially introducing new research practices, and impacting upon the research culture of humanities scholars in the process.

Thus, respondents were asked whether they had been involved in any collaborative research projects online. Of those who responded to this question, 21 had not been involved in any e-research projects; 4 had been involved in projects with other NEER members; 8 in projects with non-NEER members, and 2 in projects both with and without NEER members. Those who had not been involved in any e-research collaborations were more likely to be junior academics or postgraduates rather than longer-term academics: all of those answering 'no' had been employed as academics for 20 years or less, whereas all of the respondents who had been academics for more than 20 years were involved in some type of e-research project. This suggests that the impact of new technology on older academics plays a lesser role than strength of long-term participation in scholarly networks: longer-term academics were more likely to have been in projects with those outside NEER, or both, than with NEER members alone. This accords with previous research that has shown it is established scholars who have access to, and communicate with, the invisible college or network of researchers (Barjak, 2006: 1352).

PERCEPTIONS OF NEER

In considering questions relating to the social aspects of e-research practices and scholarly communication, we wanted to ascertain how people identified their involvement in NEER and how they perceived the grouping. This was important for a number of reasons. Not only might it lead to insight into the types of research taking place, it might also be useful for understanding the success and/or longevity of these types of groupings. Issues such as trust, instrumental motivation, reciprocity and prestige can then be investigated within this broader contextual understanding. Also related are questions to do with degrees of innovation and exposure to new ideas as has been discussed, for example, in social network analysis of weak and strong ties (Granovetter, 1973). Similarly, organizational management literature hypothesizing about different types of innovation and change practiced within networks and communities, when posited as extreme ends of a continuum, is of interest (Dal Fiore, 2007). While NEER is obviously not able to act as representative of all e-research humanities groupings, it does afford a place to explore such issues and their appropriate methods of investigation.

The main focus of the questionnaire was on participant perceptions of NEER, and whether (and if so, how) it had impacted on their understandings of networks, communities, and possible research outcomes. Despite its self-identification as a network, we asked participants to indicate which term they thought best described NEER: either network, team, collaboratory, community, or other. Network was chosen by 30 respondents, with 6 indicating collaboratory; 4 community; and 2 each for team and 'other' (some participants provided two responses). Given that NEER is named as a network, it is perhaps not surprising that this was the most common choice.

In order to gain a clearer understanding of their choice, understanding and application of these terms, participants were asked to elaborate on their response. Network was justified by a number as best describing what they saw as, "a loose association," one with "too many participants with diverse interests to constitute a single community or team;" and a grouping that was "too diffuse, at this point, to be a community." These responses accord with understandings of networks and changing practices of community noted by social network enthusiasts. Koku, Nazer, and Wellman suggest that there is "a movement from tightly-bounded, highly structured bureaucracies to social networks with amorphous boundaries and shifting sets of work relationships" (2001: 1772).

A deeper examination of the responses, however, reveals a more complex picture than this easy delineation would at first suggest. Many of those who chose 'network' revealed a more fluid understanding of the distinctions between each category, and made explicit links between networks, community and collaboration:

- Network does describe NEER well . . . much of it is team work and collaboration between teams and/or individuals is really the goal;
- Network provides the foundation for establishing a community among scholars and across disciplines, enabling collaborative work amongst teams of scholars.

For others, the term network was not seen as encompassing enough of the sense of community that they felt NEER represented:

- I think collaboratory incorporates all the words . . . NEER is a network community in which people collaborate together;
- I was going to tick network here, but then I realized that NEER was much more than that. Through its symposiums, I've been able to meet the people behind the emails and in this way, NEER has established a real sense of community.

These conceptual linkages and fluidity indicate a more complex working understanding of these terms than is often allowed for in the literature. Both the instrumental and strategic affordances of networked relations are viewed as valuable, but responses also evidenced a perception of stronger interpersonal connections linked to community, which might enable a deeper level of trust. Interestingly, for many respondents, networks were seen as preceding community, or as a formative stage that enabled stronger ties to be developed. Given the lack of shared protocols for collaborative research in the humanities, it is interesting to speculate about the extent to which communal relations provide a foundation from which to embark on collaborative information sharing and research. What is apparently important is that NEER provides a means of engaging and communicating with fellow researchers in a manner that performs and may even enhance the benefits of a more traditional scholarly community, in that it can support both 'weak' and 'strong' ties, or in other terms, both 'thick' and 'thin' relationships. In so doing, it serves for some participants the function of a community and for others the function of a network.

EXPANDING SCHOLARLY COMMUNITY

The earlier survey of academics at Curtin University supported the idea that ICTs have expanded the possibilities for networked connections and relational communities. Some three-fourths of the respondents indicated they were now more likely to initiate contact with scholars they did not know, with about the same number agreeing the Internet had made it easier to approach senior scholars (Genoni et al., 2005b). However, some noticeable differences between disciplines emerged when scholars were asked to indicate the frequency they "use the Internet to initiate contact with scholars and research students unknown to you". Only 19% of humanities academics answered 'frequently', as opposed to 30% of those in sciences and 36% in social sciences. Also noticeable was the number of humanities scholars who indicated they 'never' use the Internet to contact unknown scholars (28%), compared to social sciences (4%) and sciences (9%).[9]

In the case of NEER, which was explicitly established to connect humanities academics and researchers, respondents were asked whether they believed their participation in NEER had expanded their scholarly networks/communication. Of the 38 respondents, 27 were in agreement, and 8 disagreed, with a further 3 indicating 'maybe'.

A number of respondents attributed this expansion to NEER's facilitation of more traditional functions such as face-to-face workshops and seminars, which allowed them to network with other scholars. Others identified a combination of traditional and online activities as contributing to their expanded sense of network. Facilities such as the mailing list heightened awareness of more traditional activities such as conferences—and the potential for NEER to serve as a focal point for dissemination of news and events. In addition, as one respondent notes, the very act of establishing NEER infers a sense of community or network that crosses both disciplinary and geographic boundaries. That is, constituting a formal network and naming it as such has immediate implications for individuals' understandings of what sorts of networks or scholarly communities they 'belong' to:

- It has also made me think more consciously of the community of early European researchers in Australia and to think of informing them and involving them in activities than would otherwise be the case.

A number of participants point to the research clusters as important:

- I have recently joined a NEER research 'cluster' in an area that is tangential to my main research area. I would not have committed to doing research in this area if it had not been for the cluster. Moving into that new research area would have been impossible if I was working on my own;
- [NEER], I think, encourages a significant degree of dialogue between different 'formations' of Medieval studies and this has already produced initiatives that are new in the disciplinary sense.

Indeed many respondents commented on the importance of contact with scholars outside their own immediate area of research. Thus, NEER is seen as impacting on scholarly communities not just by providing better access to a pre-existing community of interest, but also by creating *new* networks or relational communities by deliberately crossing disciplinary and institutional boundaries, as well as geographic and hierarchical boundaries. This resonates with the literature addressing the usefulness of weak ties (Granovetter, 1973; Haythornthwaite, 2002) and with Dal Fiore's (2007) hypothesis about the potential of networks to encourage radical innovation.

Impact on Research Outcomes

Central to our investigation of the impact of ICTs on scholarly community is how informal and less tangible practices and communication influence the production, development and dissemination of scholarly knowledge. Participants were therefore asked whether NEER had enabled research outcomes that would not be possible in a more traditional research environment. In this case 25 respondents agreed that NEER had acted in this way; 7 indicated 'possibly', and 5 disagreed (one response was missing). While this question relies on a participant's self perception as to the degree of change or opportunity, this perception is important both in terms of the actual likelihood NEER has increased research opportunities, and also because such responses indicate a favorable attitude towards the technology and e-research practices, thus inferring a stronger possibility of uptake.

Some of the reasons given for impact related to improved funding opportunities and assistance to attend conferences / symposia. Also cited as significant was broader and faster access to information relating to events, and to academic positions. Indeed, a number of respondents pointed to the way NEER enabled certain formations which in some ways ameliorated institutional constraints and pressures: in particular it was suggested that NEER gave their area of research a 'profile' not possible when working as isolated individuals.

One of the interesting outcomes of NEER has been the ways in which it has served to provide a more cohesive framework and sense of identity for participants. This has helped to heighten the awareness of levels of dependency and mutual benefit that may have been previously less apparent. Such frameworks and heightened mutual dependencies may work to counter some of Fry's observations as to the difficulties of the single author culture and lack of collaborative tradition in the humanities

The collaborative cultural practices enacted in laboratories with shared protocols, procedures and expectations are mostly absent in the humanities. If e-research practices are to be successfully undertaken in the humanities, researchers need to develop cultures that value and support collaboration. Groupings such as NEER enable the collaborative, multi-disciplinary and multi-institutional research common in sciences, which is alien to the way many humanities scholars have traditionally operated:

- collaborative projects are not, in my experience, the 'norm' in traditional contexts which tend to produce privatized, individuated projects.

Importantly, a shift towards collaborative research models could be seen as positioning the humanities more favorably for funding and thus successful research outcomes:

- It allows teams to be formed, and team research is understood by the scientific disciplines that control the criteria for research grants and outcomes.

Therefore it is important to emphasize that it is as much the institutional and organizational effects of an e-research funding culture that are impacting on communication practices, particularly in the humanities, as the technologies themselves. However, while NEER's institutional arrangements and technological infrastructure in some ways ameliorate the difficulties of coordination, the importance of the very human relationships established between researchers cannot be ignored.

Impact on concept of scholarly community

Finally, respondents were asked whether participation in NEER had impacted on their understanding or concept of scholarly community. Ten agreed that being a member of NEER had produced this effect, with a further 3 reporting they were 'unsure'. However of the 25 who reported that NEER hadn't changed their understanding, a number qualified their answer to indicate some degree of impact (i.e. in all only half gave a definite negative response). Some comments qualifying the negative responses included:

- No. But it has given much greater definition, and focus to the existing (and previously far more ad-hoc) scholarly networks in the field in Australia;
- My understanding of 'scholarly community' has not changed but the possibilities of accessing such a community have certainly been opened up by NEER;
- My understanding of the concept hasn't changed a great deal, but I think NEER offers the opportunity for more involvement and greater lines of communication in a scholarly community;
- Not changed, but made particular and actual. Many so-called research groupings /networks are really just an e-list. NEER has, for me, a sense of 'real people engaging with one another' about it;
- In theory no: in practice yes.

The last comment is a useful way of framing this apparently ambivalent response: for many, rather than changing their notion of the invisible college, NEER has 'actualised' on a personal level an ideal of scholarly community.

For others, the experience of NEER has had a direct impact on their understanding or perception of scholarly community:

- It encourages scholars to think of bigger projects, and to think outside traditional disciplinary/ institutional boundaries;
- Yes; I've never seen this kind of nation-wide community that isn't defined by its subject matter;
- Yes, I can see the collaborative model as far more productive than the within-university funding model which seems to me to discourage the sharing of ideas;
- It has made my idea of across-institutional academic community more real!

When asked what benefits they thought might emerge from their involvement with NEER, participants emphasized the possibilities for collaboration and increased access to information and networks. Some 16 respondents mentioned the development of collaborative projects (or the potential for collaboration to develop), with 15 citing better access to information, expanded contact with other academics and disciplines and better access to information. Surprisingly, funding was only cited by 3 respondents as a primary benefit—this despite the high number of responses citing funding as a key element in their reasons for joining NEER. This suggests that whilst initial reasons for joining were understood in terms of individual interest, the real benefits are viewed in terms of the 'community'. A number (4 respondents) also referred to visibility as a key benefit—visibility of Australian research in this area, and of the discipline as a whole. Indeed, several participants were explicit in describing the 'benefits' in terms of their scholarly community, rather than the individual: "I don't see it as a way to advance my career . . . so much as the discipline."

CONCLUSION

This preliminary study of NEER has highlighted a number of key issues that need to be investigated in more detail: both reinforcing and challenging assumptions emerging from the literature. Our previous studies (Genoni, et al., 2005a, 2005b, 2006) tried to assess the academic's sense of belonging to the rather amorphous invisible college which in individual cases would be constituted more by differing memberships delineated by discipline, or region (for example, Australian academics; medieval scholars). In approaching NEER there was an expectation on the part of the researchers that the enactment of scholarly community in a more tangible and particularized form (as deliberately constituted and managed to meet certain economic and institutional imperatives) might mean it was viewed as a more instrumental, individuated 'tool', rather than a relational, reciprocal environment 'owned' by its membership. Certainly for some members, 'community' remained only a possibility, needing more time for interpersonal relations and connections to emerge and be nurtured. For others, however, NEER was already viewed as a more relational 'community' than instrumental network, and indeed was considered by many as a welcome alternative to institutionally-driven formations. Indeed such findings raise the possibility that as research funding increasingly shifts to cross-institutional formations, these 'networks' may rival institutions as the primary point of self-identification for individuals.[10]

Another area of interest arising from the study concerns the social-technological relations of network and/or community. In seeking to examine the impact of ICTs on scholarly community and informal communication, there is recognition that many of the changes in an e-research environment are not simply technologically driven but result from and intersect with broader political and institutional developments. That is, the availability of networked technologies themselves are not the sole influence on emergent or changing research and scholarly practices—just as important are the institutional, social and economic imperatives to adopt and use these technologies.

Yet, particularly for humanities scholars, these same institutions do not necessarily provide the appropriate environments to meet these expectations, in the form of increased team-work or connectivity, for example. Few Australian universities can now sustain humanities departments of a sufficient size to provide a localized community of scholars. In this context, the traditional invisible college does not serve such isolated institutionally-located scholars as well as a self-identified and constituted grouping such as NEER. This is particularly important in countries such as Australia where institutions are often geographically isolated from one another, and where the numbers of area-specialist researchers are thinly dispersed.

It appears that the very establishment of NEER is already helping to constitute a community of 'Early European researchers' in Australia in addition to (and separate from) the traditional markers such as published output in journals or papers presented at conferences. Thus it is not the actual transactions, technologies, forms or directions of information flows that distinguish this network but the *perceptions* of its significance and location that make it distinctive—and will, perhaps, assist its ongoing growth and success. The challenge for developers of humanities e-research groupings is to ensure they move beyond the use of the technology as a means of enabling the sharing of data and information—an 'information commons'—and become a forum that enables, supports and sustains collaborative, distributed scholarship—a 'research commons'.

NOTES

1. See, e.g., http://www.dest.gov.au/sectors/research_sector/policies_issues_reviews/key_issues/e_research_consult/
2. See http://www.ehum.edu.au/
3. Choosing to study a 'national' research grouping raises questions about the tensions between the strategic priorities and infrastructural responsibilities of national funding bodies, and the need for many researchers to create international affiliations.
4. Fry's paper builds on Whitley's (2000) theory, which argues "the major differences between disciplines can be characterized in terms of the degree of *mutual dependence* between researchers in making competent and significant contributions to the research front and the degree of *task uncertainty* in producing and evaluating knowledge claims" (Fry, 2006: 300).
5. See: http://www.arc.gov.au/ncgp/previous/e-research.htm.
6. The relationship between these types of ephemeral associations and other more institutionalized or stable gatherings for e-research output is another area outside of this chapter, but one worth consideration for further research.
7. See: http://www.neer.arts.uwa.edu.au/neer_research_clusters
8. Here and elsewhere in this chapter series of comments from respondents are listed as unordered bulleted items.
9. A large proportion of all academics had been involved in a collaborative project using the Net (54% from humanities, 53% in social sciences, and 63% of sciences). The disciplinary differences in the extent of collaboration were, however, interesting. Of these collaborations, only 18% of humanities were international (41% were national and 35%, were local). In contrast, 71% of social scientists and 70% of scientists' collaborative projects were international (with only 21% and 10%, respectively, being local).

10. Thanks to Anne Beaulieu for drawing our attention to this point.

BIBLIOGRAPHY

American Council of Learned Societies (2006). *Our cultural commonwealth: The report of the American Council of Learned Societies Commission on cyberinfrastructure for the humanities and social sciences*. Retrieved February 22, 2008, from http://www.acls.org/cyberinfrastructure/OurCulturalCommonwealth.pdf

Appleby, A., Clayton, P., & Pascoe, C. (1997). Australian academic use of the Internet. *Internet Research, 7*(2): 85–94.

Australian Academy of the Humanities (2007). *Human technologies: Research methods and ICT use in Australian humanities research*. Retrieved February 22, 2008, from http://www.humanities.org.au/Policy/HumTech/

Barjak, F. (2006). The role of the Internet in informal scholarly communication. *Journal of the American Society for Information Science and Technology, 57*(10): 1350–1367.

Bos, N., Zimmerman, A., Olson, J., Yew, J., Yerkie, J., Dahl, E., & Olson, G. (2007). From shared databases to communities of practice: Taxonomies of collaboratories. *Journal of Computer-Mediated Communication, 12*(2). Retrieved December 26, 2007, from http://jcmc.indiana.edu/vol12/issue2/bos.html

Bruce, H. (1996). *Internet, AARNet and academic work: A longitudinal study*. Canberra: Australian Government Printing Service.

Burrows, T. (2007). Personal interview, Perth, 15 April.

Costa, S., & Meadows, J. (2000). The impact of computer usage on scholarly communication among social scientists. *Journal of Information Science, 26*(4): 255–62.

Crane, D. (1972). *Invisible colleges: Diffusion of knowledge in scientific communities*. Chicago: University of Chicago Press.

Cronin, B. (2003). Scholarly communication and epistemic cultures. Paper presented at, Scholarly tribes and tribulations: How tradition and technology are driving disciplinary change. Association of Research Libraries, October 17, 2003, Washington, D.C. Retrieved February 22, 2008, from http://www.arl.org/bm~doc/cronin.pdf

Dal Fiore, F. (2007). Communities versus networks: The implications on innovation and social change. *American Behavioral Scientist, 50*(7): 857–66.

Finholt, T. A. (2003). Collaboratories as a new form of scientific organization. *Economics of Innovation and New Technology, 12*(1): 5–25.

Fry, J. (2006). Scholarly research and information practices: A domain analytic approach. *Information Processing and Management, 42*(1): 299–316.

Genoni, P., Merrick, H., & Willson, M. (2005a). Community, communication, collaboration: Scholarly practice in transformation. Paper presented at, The Next Wave of Collaboration: Educause Australasia, Auckland, April 5–8.

Genoni, P., Merrick, H., & Willson, M. (2005b). The use of the Internet to activate latent ties in scholarly communities. *First Monday, 10*(12). Retrieved February 22, 2008, from http://firstmonday.org/issues/issue10_12/genoni/index.html

Genoni, P., Merrick, H., & Willson, M. (2006). Scholarly communication, e-research literacy and the academic librarian. *The Electronic Library, 24*(7): 734–46.

Gibbons, M., Nowotny, H., Limoges, C., Schwartzman, S., Scott, P., & Trow, M. (1994). *The new production of knowledge: The dynamics of science and research in contemporary societies*. London: Sage.

Granovetter, M. S. (1973). The strength of weak ties. *The American Journal of Sociology, 78*(6): 1360–1380.

Hargens, l. (2000). Using the literature: Reference networks, reference contexts and the social structure of scholarship. *American Sociological Review, 65*(6), 846–65.

Hawkins, B. L., & Battin, P. (1998). *The mirage of continuity: Reconfiguring academic information resources for the 21ˢᵗ century.* Washington: Council on Library and Information Resources.

Haythornthwaite, C. (2002). Strong, weak, and latent ties and the impact of new media. *The Information Society, 18*(5): 385–401

Henry, P. D. (2002). Scholarly use of the Internet by faculty members: Factors and outcomes of change. *Journal of Research on Technology in Education, 35*(1): 49–58.

Hert, P. (1997). Social dynamics of an on-line scholarly debate. *The Information Society, 13*(4): 329–60.

Houghton, J. W., Steele, C., & Henty, M. (2003). *Changing research practices in the digital information and communication environment.* Canberra: Department of Education.

Jankowski, N. W. (2007). Exploring e-science: An introduction. *Journal of Computer-Mediated Communication, 12*(2). Retrieved December 26, 2007, from http://jcmc.indiana.edu/vol12/issue2/jankowski.html

Koku, E., Nazer, N., & Wellman, B. (2001). Netting scholars: Online and offline. *American Behavioral Scientist, 44*(10): 1752–1774.

Lloyd, A. & Sun, Y. (2005). Linking e-science capabilities for e-social science communities: extending the UK-Australia INWA project to the Chinese Academy of Sciences. In *First International Conference on e-Social Science*, Manchester, UK, June 22. ESRC National Centre for e-Social Science, Manchester, UK.

Meadows, A. J. (1974). *Communicating in science.* London: Butterworth.

Network of Early European Researchers (2006). *Aims and objectives.* Retrieved February 22, 2008, from http://www.neer.arts.uwa.edu.au/about/aims_and_objectives

Trigg, S. (2006). 'Medieval literature' or 'early Europe'? How to win grants and change the course of scholarship. *Literature Compass, 3*(3): 318–30.

Wouters, P., & Beaulieu, A. (2007). Critical accountability: Dilemmas for interventionist studies of e-science. *Journal of Computer-Mediated Communication 12*(2). Retrieved December 26, 2007, from http://jcmc.indiana.edu/vol12/issue2/wouters.html

6 The Rise of e-Science in Asia

Dreams and Realities for Social Science Research: Case Studies of Singapore and South Korea

Carol Soon and Han Woo Park

INTRODUCTION

In spite of the growing interest in e-science and e-research among scholars as well as policy-makers, most of the existing published works concentrate on the developments in the Western countries, such as in the U.S. and U.K. To address the research gap in existing literature, this chapter focuses primarily on issues related to scholarly practice in e-research within the context of Asian countries. Amongst countries in Asia-Pacific, both South Korea and Singapore have acquired internationally-recognized status for their strong Internet networks. Technological discourse dominates the education and digital media scenes in Singapore with technology perceived as an indispensable tool in ensuring that the small nation-state stay ahead of its competition, and South Korea functions as an important node in both international and regional research networks. In spite of the clear emergence of e-science as a new way to conduct research and development, little is known about the practices of e-social science research and if, and how these tools facilitate Asian scholars in conducting better research and collaboration in the digital age. Through the insights gained from policy reviews, in-depth interviews with policymakers and social scientists from diversified research backgrounds, this chapter elucidates the general imperatives behind e-science programs in Asia and the state of e-science application in the fields of social sciences. We also identify the key challenges that inhibit the transformation of the e-science dream into a reality for social science scholars and propose recommendations on how some of these barriers may be overcome.

The Relevance of e-Science in Two Tiger Economies

The emergence of the networked economy has brought about significant changes in how information communication technologies (ICTs) are used and adopted in the political, economical and social realms. The application of science and technology in these areas is nothing new, as for decades, scholars have studied the use and effects of ICTs in various aspects of our lives. However, as nations compete against one another to stay ahead in the game of technological innovation and creation, our attention is drawn to the emergence of e-science as a new and dramatically different approach in re-conceptualizing and conducting research. e-Science has been defined as "uses of information and communication technology (ICT) infrastructures for storing scientific data, performing analyzes and carrying out collaborative work, often known in the U.S. as cyberinfrastructures and in the U.K. as e-science" (Hine, 2006: viii). It is evident that even the West where the concept of e-science originates from, the development of ICT networks and infrastructures for purposes of research and development is clearly dominated by data-intensive disciplines such as particle physics, astronomy, biology and genetics (Hey, 2006; Hine, 2006; Wouters & Beaulieu, 2006). Most of the existing literature concentrates on developments in Western countries, such as in the U.S. and U.K. To address this lacuna in scholarly knowledge of e-science in the East, we have selected Singapore and South Korea (hereafter Korea) as two case studies to examine the development of e-science and the emerging issues related to scholarly practice in e-research within the context of Asian countries.

Together with Taiwan and Hong Kong, Singapore and Korea were known as the four successful Tiger economies (Koh & Poh, 2005). In their analysis of the critical role science and technology policies plays in an economy's transition from an industrial economy to an innovation-based economy, Koh and Poh (2005) draw from the cases of Korea and Singapore to demonstrate how developing nations make tremendous progress in their economy by focusing on delivering strategic technology and innovation policies to advance the technological sophistication of their industries. Both the Singaporean and Korean governments increased their funding of research and development activities to further enhance the countries' science and technological prowess. Announced in February 2006, the Singapore Ministry of Trade and Industry (MTI) committed a total of US$7.5billion to drive economic-oriented research and development to sustain innovation-driven growth especially in growing industry sectors such as the life sciences and digital media in the next five years (Ministry of Trade and Industry Singapore, Science & Technology Plan 2010, 2006). The Korean government publicized that it will increase its funding of research and development by more than 15%, from US$8 billion in 2005 to US$9.2 billion in 2006 to create technology-driven small and medium-sized enterprises (SMEs), foster collaboration between businesses and universities, research institutions, as well as boost its biotechnology industry.

In view of the early stages of technology adoption and paucity of innovation creation in many Asian nations, Singapore and Korea have been selected as the case studies for this chapter. These two countries have won international accolades for the dramatic progress made in technology development and their ability to leverage on science and technology to advance the economy. As the following sections will illustrate, although the governments in both countries play an enabling role in launching e-science developments, the current emphasis and the rationale for e-science programs in the two countries are different.

ICT DEVELOPMENTS AS THE ECONOMY DRIVER IN SINGAPORE

When it achieved its independence in 1965, Singapore as a newborn nation-state had to grapple with geo-political challenges and the scarcity of natural resources in its fight for survival. In a short span of about 40 years, the growth pace of the small nation-state has been phenomenal, averaging 8% per annum, an achievement that has been attributed to the government's sound economic planning and focused efforts to attract foreign investments in various industrial sectors (Koh & Poh, 2005). One of the factors that accounts for Singapore's rapid advancement from a Third World to First World status is attributed to the leap-frogging of the economy from the manufacturing stage to the innovation-based stage. The 1990s witnessed a slight shift in the policymakers' priority as they embarked on a strategy to transform the island with a four-million-plus population into an information hub, trading in ideas rather than commodities. Information technology (IT) initiatives, such as the Singapore IT2000 "A Vision of an Intelligent Island" Masterplan and Infocomm 21 Strategy, that were rolled out by the Singapore government in several phases were critical to the nation's economic transformation. Under the Singapore IT2000 "A Vision of an Intelligent Island" Masterplan and Infocomm 21 Strategy, the government aimed to create a digital future for Singapore, a future where innovation, entrepreneurship and e-lifestyle are the norm. Early success was evident and by 2006, home computer penetration among surveyed households reached 78%, with 38% of the households having access to two or more computers, and 71% of households have Internet access (Infocomm Development Authority of Singapore, Annual Survey on Infocomm Usage in Households and by Individuals for 2006, 2007). The success of the IT programs was attributed to the government's efforts to promote infocomm usage in the workforce and among the general public, and emphasizing infocomm usage in the school curriculum.

While this approach has enabled the small nation-state to move from Third World to First World status, it soon became clear to the government that a new strategy which emphasizes innovation and technology creation, as opposed to merely engaging in technology adoption and application, is needed to advance the economy further at the increasingly competitive global technological frontier (Koh and Poh, 2005). The current strategy, the Infocomm Technology Roadmap, will drive the creation of user-driven innovations comprising hardware, software and systems in the next ten years (Infocomm Development Authority of Singapore, Technology

Roadmap, 2007). In the next section, we will examine how e-science serves as a platform for the government to propel the efficiency of resource use in key industries in Singapore to a higher level.

e-Science Application Driven By Economic Imperatives

Established in 2003, the National Grid Office (NGO) is part of the Infrastructure Development division in the Infocomm Development Authority (IDA). The NGO views the next-generation cyberinfrastructure as playing a vital role in increasing Singapore's economic and technological competitiveness in the long run, with networked collaborations facilitating the sharing of resources for the purposes of research and development, commerce, entertainment and national security. By formulating the Grid framework and policies, developing a secure platform and encouraging the adoption of Grid computing, the NGO's ultimate goal is to aid the transformation of the Singapore economy using Grid. Other than the stated mission, the economic slant of the applications of the Grid infrastructure is reflected in the overall organizational structure of the National Grid Steering Committee (NGSC) within which it sits (see Figure 6.1).

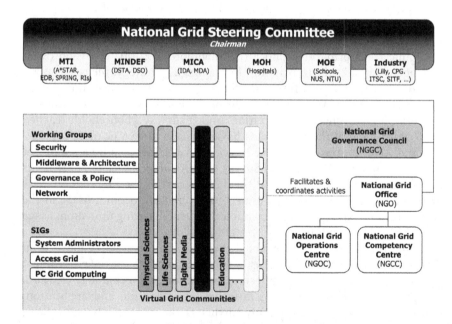

Figure 6.1 Organization structure of the national Grid. *Source:* National Grid Office (2006). Courtesy of the National Grid Office; First appeared in Notes of Global Grid Forum–13 Meeting, 13–16 March 2006, Lotte Hotel, Seoul, Korea, pages 365–375.

Established in late 2002, the primary objective of the NGSC was to bring together diverse stakeholders in a collaborative manner to identify key areas to which the scarce resources for the National Grid should be deployed. Other than the government bodies (e.g. Infocomm Development Authority of Singapore, Economic Development Board and Ministry of Health), universities, research institutes and the industry, representatives from key target industry sectors identified to be the launch pads and test beds of the Grid infrastructure (e.g., physical sciences, life sciences, digital media, manufacturing, education and financial services) also sit in the NGSC to provide greater insights from the end-user and Grid application perspectives. They include MediaCorp Technologies, Lilly Systems Biology and Philips Electronics.

A pilot project launched in 2003, the National Grid Pilot Platform (NGPP) is a multi-agency pilot project set out to increase awareness of Grid computing, promote collaboration among different resource owners and potential Grid users, and interconnect compute resources. The latest phase seeks to extend high productivity computing, storage and software facilities to all businesses, especially the SMEs. The Call-For-Collaboration launched by the IDA on 23 November 2007 aims to bring together keen Grid service providers and independent software-as-a-service (SaaS) vendors to provide related infocomm resources on a pay-per-use basis. For instance, to complement the government's S$500million strategy launched in 2006 to drive research and development in the Interactive & Digital Media (IDM) sector, the NGSC launched a project that promotes access to the large amount of compute resources on the NGPP with the aim of enabling digital media SMEs to undertake higher-quality and larger sized projects farmed out by overseas studios and production houses. One critical outcome is SMEs no longer have to make heavy investments in hardware and software as they only need to pay for resource usage when on a need-basis. Moreover, SMEs do not have to contend with the problem of non-usage of resources when hardware and software are not used in between projects.

It is evident that in the case of Singapore, top-level support by the government and the funding provided for the many initiatives and programs, complemented by strong user support from key industrial sectors, has been crucial in pushing the Grid initiative. In June 2007, the IDA formed the National Grid Advisory Council (NGAC) which is tasked with increasing industry adoption of Grid computing in key economic sectors such as digital media, life sciences, finance and banking, and manufacturing services, some sectors that were previously not part of the e-science vision for Singapore. Such a commitment clearly articulates the government's focus and persistent efforts to promote resource optimization and increase cost savings by businesses in various sectors through leveraging on the Grid environment. Singapore's ability to deploy Grid technology to fulfill its economic agenda is recognized at the international level. As part of the

Asia-Pacific Economic Cooperation (APEC), Singapore will be leading member economies to collaborate on Grid projects that will drive common areas of interest and benefit APEC economies.

THE DOMINANCE OF TECHNOLOGICAL DISCOURSE IN KOREA

It has been widely observed among scholars (Na, 2001; Park, 2002; Park & Biddix, 2008; Rose, 2003) that the consumption of ICTs has become part of the discourse of globalization in the Korean media and has been portrayed as a key facilitator for entry into a global or information society. This recurring theme was manifested more strongly after the financial crisis of 1997 when the government focused on promoting the IT industry and launched a series of policies, such as 'Cyber Korea 21' in 1999 and 'Ubiquitous Korea Vision 2006' (Yoon, 2006). As of December 2006, about 74.8% of the entire Korean population used the Internet (NIDA, 2007). The dramatic expansion of the high-speed Internet service system attracted much international attention and Korea was ranked by the International Telecommunication Union (ITU) as second in the world in terms of diffusion of high-speed Internet service systems (ITU, 2006). The Korean government has played a vital role in spearheading initiatives and implementing policies to engender an Internet-literate population and exploit the benefits of ICTs to guarantee its entrance to the global economy (Yoon, 2006). The following section provides a brief overview of how the Korean government attempts to strengthen its foothold on the global technological frontier by leveraging on e-science to advance research and development.

e-Science Bolstering Scientific Advancements Locally and Internationally

The main focus of Korea's national e-science programs is on enhancing scientific research through the application of high-performance computing coupled with high bandwidth networks in natural sciences and engineering sciences. Since the year 2005, the Ministry of Science and Technology (MOST) and its subordinate organization, the Korean Institute for Science Technology Information (KISTI), have been largely responsible for national cyber-research-infrastructure. MOST has implemented important policies on the development of e-science, for example, shared access to supercomputers and advanced research platforms. As the Grid is being perceived as a key infrastructure for e-science activities that will propel adopting nations into a higher level of research and development, Korea joined the emerging global trend through the introduction of its nationwide Grid program known as K*Grid in 2002 which saw the construction of Grid testbeds and provision of basic Grid services to computing centers and university laboratories (Cho, 2007). The birth of e-science programs in Korea stemmed from the government's mission to integrate and apply cyberinfrastructures for scientific advancements in the country.

In parallel with the K*Grid project, the Access Grid (AG) program was implemented in 2002 and it serves as a collaborative working space where scientists are able to make use of a variety of research resources, presentation applications, and audio/visual facilities for distance collaboration. More recently, the key e-science policy goals laid out for MOST during the period of 2005 and 2007 center on building a testbed for a preliminary e-science research environment. In the course of the next four years from 2008 to 2011, MOST will focus on building an applied research environment for e-science and establishing a technology-assisted center. Table 6.1 summarizes the expenditure for three categories from 2005 to 2007. The largest portion of government budget was spent on developing and improving basic and common softwares as part of developing an integrated system for integrated collaboration in the various research fields (NIA, 2007).

Advanced Research Networks Spurring Collaboration

The Advanced Research Network (ARN), which is Korea's recent e-science program, is another testimony of the clarity of the Korean government's vision in creating and delivering a series of research environments linking scientists and engineers from diverse disciplines in different research institutions together. In Korea, ARNs exist at both the international and domestic levels, and are available for those who conduct distance research collaborations. The international network comprises GLORIAD (GLObal Ring Network for Advanced Application Development), APII (Asia Pacific Information Infrastructure Testbed), and TEIN (Trans-Eurasia Information

Table 6.1   Expenditure of National e-Science Budget (unit: 100,000,000 won)

Items	2005	2006	2007	Total
Common software development and improvement	13	13	67	93
Applied environment construction	11	8	20	39
Outcome diffusion and public relations	1	1	1	3
Total	25	22	88	135

Source: Byun (2007).

Network). Six member countries of the Asia-Pacific Economic Community have taken part in APII since 1996 and it is often used for information technology-related research. GLORIAD, on the other hand, is a global network that includes Asia, Europe, and North America, and it provides the first high-performance networks for the global audience and serves as international connections for e-science and Grid applications. On the domestic front, the Korea Research Environment Open Network (KREONET) is the first national ARN which was launched in 1988. The significance of the KREONET is that it avails collaborative services such as the communal use of a sophisticated research facility and massive storage to about 200 major national research institutions and 100,000 users within a Daeduck research park.

The focus of e-science initiatives in Korea up to this point, which are channeled towards facilitating and furthering research in natural sciences, engineering sciences and information technology development, is different from the approach adopted in Singapore where the development and application of e-science technologies such as Grid networks are geared towards optimizing resource utilization and maximize cost savings. Set against the context of heavy government involvement in e-science in both Singapore and Korea, the next section provides an overview of what we perceive to be the relevance of e-science to the field of social sciences. From in-depth interviews conducted with scholars who are engaged in studying social phenomena that are emerging on the World Wide Web, we provide insights into the potential role of e-science in these two technologically advanced Asian countries and the implications of harnessing e-science in social science research on policy and researchers' attitudes towards e-science as a method of data collection and analysis.

POTENTIAL OF E-SCIENCE IN SOCIAL SCIENCE RESEARCH IN SINGAPORE AND KOREA

As the development of enormous computing power and the capacity to process and store huge amounts of data poses a promising future beyond natural and engineering fields, social scientists are quite aware of and want to leverage the affordances of cyberinfrastructures. In spite of this realization, the adoption and application of e-science in the social sciences has been slower than in the other scientific fields. For instance, across the social sciences and humanities in Korea, researchers have not found themselves wanting to use the new collaborative and research tools that have arisen with e-science technology (Jeong, 2007; NIA, 2007). In this section, we share critical insights gained from interviewing scholars from three research projects. These projects were selected because they reflect the rich diversity in social science research (web archiving, cultural analytics of content sharing and the analysis of political Web spheres) as well as the different challenges encountered. Interviews were conducted with the primary investigators of these projects to find out if and how their work leverages on any form of e-science, their vision on how e-science applications such as the Grid infrastructure can be utilized to meet their research goals, as well as to elicit their views on the main challenges that social scientists and humanities scholars encounter in e-science.

Asian Tsunami Web Archive

In the aftermath of the tsunami that hit Southern Asia on 26 December 2004 which created ripples of catastrophic effects across the globe, researchers from different parts of the world converged and created the Asian Tsunami Web Archive (http://tsunami.archive.org/). The researchers behind this project observed how the global reach and easy access afforded by the medium of the World Wide Web made it possible for individuals from all over the world to obtain information on the Asian Tsunami and set up Web sites to share information at a rapid speed. A project that crossed geographical boundaries and involves international collaborators, the Asian Tsunami Web Archives was a project spearheaded by the Singapore Internet Research Centre (SIRC), part of the Wee Kim Wee School of Communication and Information in Nanyang Technological University. Together with the Internet Archives and Webarchive.org which are based in the U.S., the collection of relevant web materials commenced within a week after the calamity occurred. The investigators set out to collect data from the web to find out how citizens, informal web publishers and official agencies made use of the Internet in response to the tsunami; the information flow among different publishers; and the type of web archiving technology development which may engender a quicker response to events of such a large scale. The data that was collected over a period of six months spanned over 40 countries and within the first four weeks after the tsunami occurred, a total of about 1,599 sites in multiple languages were collected, with the total data size running into terabytes. The data which was collected came in different forms and included email archives, hyperlink structures and snapshots of the Web sites as well as the social networking patterns of the collaborative parties.

In our interview with Senior Fellow Paul Wu, one of the primary investigators from the SIRC, he identified three main factors that are crucial to the success of such collaboration and the collection of massive data on the World Wide Web—technology, manpower and resources in terms of finances and expertise. The expertise and knowledge required for the development of technological applications, such as a comprehensive archival system that does not just collect but aid in the analysis of data are currently lacking in the local context. In the case of the Asian Tsunami Web Archive, Internet Archives supplied the technology in the form of the actual crawling machine and Webarchive.org supplied and aided in the application of the web sphere methodology. Identifying a prevalent issue that is not unique to Singapore, Wu identifies the lack of knowledge and expertise among social scientists as the main impediment to the use of e-science for data collection and analysis purposes. Due to the intricate and specialized knowledge that is needed at both developmental and usage purposes, there is a tendency for social scientists to shy away from using e-science applications. This problem is further compounded by the nature and type of data typically collected in social science research which insufficiently justifies the investments in both time and money to embrace e-science applications like Grid infrastructure. However, the World Wide Web is fast growing as a rich site where social phenomena of myriad forms can be observed (Wu & Heok, 2005). As such, the need to innovate and explore the adoption of e-science techniques may soon become a prerequisite for studies of social phenomena unconstrained by geographical boundaries. From the collaborative Asian Tsunami Web Archive project, Wu and Heok observed that "more countries are beginning to realize that it is mutually beneficial to collaborate as the web is ever changing, growing and connecting beyond the convenient demarcation of a nation's web boundary" (Wu & Heok, 2006: 10). In addition, other than the need for greater collaboration among social scientists to leverage on one another's expertise and resources, there is also a need for cross-disciplinary cooperation between scholars and researchers from social sciences and information science backgrounds.

The Creative Commons project

In the age of the Internet where users of the technology are no longer just consumers of media content, but have also assumed the role of content producers, the use of Creative Commons licenses is becoming an increasingly popular approach to license creative work among authors who want to promote the sharing and use of their work. In one of their most recent work, Cheliotis, Chik Guglani and Tayi (2007) analyzed the worldwide use of Creative Commons licenses, in particularly the popularity of different license types and the various legal, economic and geopolitical factors which may account for their popularity. In their study, commercial search engines like Google and Yahoo! were deployed to collect data. The back-link and specialized Creative Commons search functions, as well as dictionary searches were used to answer broad questions that provided a macro view of the Creative Commons, such as the number of people using the different licenses and how they used the licenses in various parts of the world. However, there exist severe limitations to such a method as such techniques did not allow researchers to embark on a micro analysis of the emerging trends in Creative Commons to understand the specific and different types of users who use Creative Commons licenses, how Creative Commons licenses are used for different media types, the communication exchanges between content users and re-users, and the motivations behind the use of these licenses. This is because in order to provide a more microscopic and qualitative analysis of the Creative Commons, data has to be collected from specific web communities. What this means is that data sizes are potentially massive, depending on the data source. Currently, only snapshots of web communities are collected and the vision for Creative Commons researchers is to collect huge amounts of data in real time, a task which will require large computational resources that are networked to facilitate cooperation and teamwork among geographically-dispersed researchers. In our interview with Cheliotis, he highlighted the significance of e-science:

> There is a strong need for some form of e-science and we need to address the issue of obtaining funding to create a network that will connect researchers who are physically disconnected from one another. If not, we can only work with limited case studies and make observations in snapshots. We aspire to generate real-time data and visualizations that will be updated continuously. To achieve that, we need to work with many researchers and a lot of computational power. (G. Cheliotis, interview, January 4, 2008)

As media literacy skills evolve, we are seeing an increasing number of people going online to consume, produce, distribute and share media content. Like Wu, Cheliotis envisages the World Wide Web to be a growing site of rich data that is waiting to be mined and studied, where existing data can be used to provide extensive insights into cultural flows that are taking place in the cyberspace. Although more social scientists are realizing that much more could be done with the vast data available online, Cheliotis identifies finding the right manpower resources and expertise to manage such projects and bring them to fruition as the main challenge. In addition, getting people to invest in exporting their current research applications to the Grid environment is another barrier that may inhibit the adoption of e-science applications. In order for social science researchers to leverage on the Grid infrastructure which will afford them greater computation power to conduct data collection and analysis on an unprecedented scale, they will have to adapt their existing programs and systems to the Grid environment, a task that may appear insurmountable to many, given the lack of necessary knowledge and expertise to do so within the social sciences.

Korea's Political Web Sphere Study

The second author of this chapter has been a principal investigator in a research project supported by the Korean Research Foundation Grant from December 2004 to November 2007. This project is composed of three main areas—the comparison of Korea's electoral Web sphere with those of other countries (Jankowski, 2007); the analysis of the structure of online relational networking amongst official political Web sites, personal blogs of elected politicians and citizen blogs (Park, Thelwall, & Kluver, 2005; Park & Jankowski, 2008; Park & Kluver, 2009); and a cross-national comparison of Web sites produced by Japanese and Korean politicians (Tkach-Kawasaki & Park, 2007). Through this research project, the second author had to collaborate with several oversea scholars in the areas of brainstorming, writing together, data-collecting/sharing, and conferencing. However, most of these activities were done through commercial softwares (e.g., Skype, MS Office and Webdex). These proprietary programs were neither safe nor confidential enough to conduct scientific communication. However, public e-science communication tools in the social sciences such as instantaneous Q&A information sharing systems and mutual writing/proof-reading documentary softwares are rare in many nations with strong Internet infrastructure, including Korea. Therefore, the development of public e-science tools for scholarly communication particularly among social scientists needs to be perceived as an important policy issue. Given the differences in the socio-cultural work systems of research across different disciplines, the set of e-science technologies targeted for hard sciences may not be applicable to the scientific activity of social scientists. The AG in Korean could have been used to carry out some of these tasks in social science and humanities research but, to the best of our knowledge, there are no social scientists among current users (Moon, 2006; Uram, 2007).

In addition, access to virtual collaboration with massive data storage capacity and advanced research network would have greatly enhanced the quality of a cross-national research project that examined the different styles and practices of politician Web sites between Korea and Japan. This project entailed the downloading and storage of entire Web sites of individual politicians using the Offline Explorer, a paid program that allows one to download certain Web site and navigate the site offline. Due to the limited bandwidth capacity of ordinary Internet network, it was not possible to share archived Web sites with the Japanese collaborator. Only screen-shots were exchanged via email. As evident from Table 6.2 which lists the breakdown of Korean politician Web sites in terms of Web site size, number of folders, and number of files, the data collected in this project was immense and the researchers would have much to benefit from leveraging on a Grid network for purposes of collecting, sharing, storing and visualizing the data.

Table 6.2 Web site Sizes of Korean Politician Homepages

Item	Web site size (byte)	No. of folders	No. of files
Median	269,590,955	84	1,728
Minimum	292,202	7	11
Maximum	4,177,982,280	2,088	11,500

N = 277

WHAT E-SCIENCE HOLD FOR THE
SOCIAL SCIENCES IN ASIA

Each of the three research projects presented in this chapter elucidated the potential effects e-science can unleash in the field of social science research. By recounting the difficulties and challenges pertaining to data collection and analysis of large datasets, they highlight some of the pertinent issues prevalent in the process of engaging in this new advanced form of scientific research. With the World Wide Web expanding by the day as a site that houses immense data which promises to enrich our knowledge of life on and off the web, there is an increasing need among social scientists and humanities scholars to explore and harness new technologies for research work and collaboration. However, the uptake of e-science in the social sciences has been slower than in the other scientific fields. As highlighted in the interviews, some of the prevalent issues that dominate the discourse of harnessing e-science in the social sciences and humanities are the lack of expertise and knowledge, research budgets, available facilities, and research practices for scientific inquiry. Koh and Poh (2005) suggest that governments play four different roles in structuring the science and technology policy and in fostering technology creation and adoption: nurturing a productive research and development culture that is linked to higher education, acting as the principal investor either directly or indirectly through its agencies in areas of research, lowering the cost of risks by encouraging strong university-industry interactions, and facilitating the commercialization of publicly financed research. In cognizance of this framework, there are several possible directions to boost the adoption and application of e-science in the social sciences in Asia.

One of the main obstacles that stand in the way of social scientists and humanities is the lack of technical knowledge and skills which prevent them from approaching and embracing new technologies to conduct research work. There are perhaps several ways to help overcome this barrier, one of which is for more government funding and training programs to be dedicated to training social scientists and humanities scholars in the use of e-science applications. Since 2004, the NGO in Singapore has conducted more than 20 Grid computing courses to over 400 people from the research and development, and academic communities through the National Grid Competency Centre (Agency for Science, Technology and Research, 2005). This training program was aimed at improving the competency and proficiency of ICT professionals in Singapore, particularly in terms of building their expertise in Grid computing. Similar programs tailored to the needs of social science and humanities scholars can be considered. One area of training that may enhance social scientists' knowledge and skills in data collection lies in the field of link analysis, often referred to as the most promising area where Internet studies and e-science can meet (Ackland et al., 2006; Park & Thelwall, 2003). Currently, none of the non-commercial crawlers is superior to major commercial search engines in terms of the coverage of World Wide Web. In order to conduct more effective link analysis in the e-science age, researchers should be armed with new skills, and the roles for scholars and librarians redefined (Nentwich, 2003).

Another way to help overcome researchers' inhibitions about e-science applications is to study specific demands from the social sciences and the humanities during early stages of conceptualization and design of these technologies. This echoes Wouters and Beaulieu's observation that the development of e-science infrastructure is mainly informed by computationally-oriented research, and "input from humanities has so far been virtually nonexistent and input from the social sciences scarce" (Wouters & Beaulieu, 2006, p.57). So far, user studies have typically examined the number/types of information sources, new requests for scholarly databases/repositories, and library interface improvements. For instance, The Ministry of Education in Korea, through the Korea Research Foundation, has broadly drafted policy programs for the social sciences and humanities. The e-research programs they initiated include electronic indexing (e.g., Korean Citation Index), Web sites of academic organizations, and a publicly accessible article repository. Electronic information systems and repositories specialized for science and technology researchers are being developed by the National Technical Information Service. However, such user research does not properly capture a 'revolutionary' transformation of the scientific enterprise which is witnessed to be underway. One possible measure to consider on the level of policy-making is to elicit specific demands and feedback from scholars who have a strong desire and need to adopt e-science technologies in their projects on the role e-science can play in their research processes can be taken. In Singapore, the government is spearheading e-science initiatives such as SG@School and Web Archive Singapore which are realms beyond the 'hard sciences'. In these instances, social scientists may be more involved at the early stages of program conceptualization to ideate the requirements and specifications for infrastructure and program design to enhance the feasibility of application and adoption among social scientists. In addition, such involvement has the potential to make significant advancements in developing a middle-ware that can be used easily by researchers in the social sciences.

Perhaps, one of the most crucial changes that need to take place is the mindset shift among social scientists and humanities scholars. The current impediments to embracing e-science such as investments in both manpower and funding notwithstanding, scholars and researchers in the soft sciences need to recognize and acknowledge the opportunities that avail from leveraging on e-science technologies, such as access to vast data and new modes of data collection and analysis. The emerging era of networked research leads to two possible scenarios that must exist to realize the dreams of e-science. Education and training programs have to be put in place to produce a new breed of social scientists with combined expertise and knowledge of computational science and social sciences. Perhaps, what is more action-able in the shorter term is to engender and promote collaborative efforts between these fields. In an interview with Mr Lee Hyung-Jin, an associate researcher in KISTI, he affirmed the lack of e-social-science research in Korea. There appears to be a lack of desire for either distance international collaboration through the Grid or the use of high performance computing facilities among social scientists (H.J. Lee, interview, March 17 & 18, 2008). Although possibilities in funding research projects that leverage on e-science technologies by government bodies such as KISTI exist, demand is in the present lacking, as social scientists' current choices for their research practices are still predominantly shaped by offline facilities rather than online technology capabilities.

Echoing the need to engender a change in mindset among target users of e-science technologies, Lee Hing-Yan, the Program Director of the NGO mentioned that "the primary concern to the NGSC was not technological issues, which they believed would be addressed, but social ones, such as whether the resource owners would share idle CPUs and storage, and whether users would collaborate over the Grid" (H.Y. Lee, interview, December 10, 2007). In sharing the NGPP experience, Lee Hing-Yan commented that the initiative was an important milestone in the Grid initiative as social and mindset issues were addressed and resolved. The success of this pilot effort is evident from the impressive expansion of a humble and limited base of 200 central processing units (CPUs) in 2003 to more than 1000 CPUs. What is notable in the case of NGPP's success is that the accumulation of computing resources was made possible only through voluntary contribution from organizations which housed spare idle compute-resources. The NGPP provided an opportunity to break down the barriers between different resource owners and promote the sharing of idle and spare resources. H.Y. Lee aptly summed it up when he said, "Until the researchers are prepared to work together, the hoped-for distributed collaboration to address a large science problem will not happen" (H.Y. Lee, interview, December 10, 2007). As we call for policy-makers and technology developers to involve social scientists and humanities scholars during the early stages of technology conceptualization and design, there is also a need for a transformation at another level—researchers in the social sciences have to perceive and acknowledge the value and the significance of their involvement. This is because the benefits and advantages of e-science technologies can only be realized within the social sciences with perceptual and attitudinal shifts amongst policy-makers and users.

ACKNOWLEDGMENTS

The authors would like to express their gratitude to Lee Hing Yan, Giorgos Cheliotis and Paul Wu for contributing to this chapter with their time and invaluable insights. Special thanks to Lonce Wyse and Lee Hyung-Jin for their comments and suggestions.

REFERENCES

Ackland, R., O'Neil, M., Standish, R., & Buchhorn, M. (2006). VOSON: A web services approach for facilitating research into online networks. Paper presented at Second International e-Social Science Conference, Manchester, U.K., 28–30 June.

Agency for Science, Technology & Research (2005). *Official launch of Grid computing competency certification and appointment of Singapore Polytechnic as training service.* Retrieved January 18, 2008, from: http://www.a-star.edu.sg/astar/sciengr/action/pressrelease_details.do?id=0e8b90b2daoc

Byun, O. W. (2007). Main outcome in national e-science project. Presented at the conference of national e-science project results and exhibition, Seoul, 24 August.

Cheliotis, G., Chik, W., Guglani, A., & Tayi. G.K. (2007). Taking stock of the Creative Commons experiment: Monitoring the use of Creative Commons licenses and evaluating its implications for the future of Creative Commons and for copyright law. Paper presented at 35th Research Conference on Communication, Information and Internet Policy (TPRC), Arlington VA, 28–30 September.

Cho, K. (2007). Cyberinfrastructure in Korea. *Computer Physics Communications, 177*: 247–248.

Hey, T. (2006). Foreword. In C. M. Hine (Ed.), *New infrastructures for knowledge production: Understanding e-science,* pp.vii–vii. Hershey, PA: Information Science Publishing.

Hine, C. (2006). Preface. In C. M. Hine (Ed.), *New infrastructures for knowledge production: Understanding e-science,* pp.viii–xvii. Hershey, PA: Information Science Publishing.

Infocomm Development Authority of Singapore (2007). *Annual survey on Infocomm Usage in households and by individuals for 2006.* Retrieved June 1, 2007, from: http://www.ida.gov.sg/doc/Publications/Publications_Level2/20061205092557/hh06_public_v4.4.pdf

Infocomm Development Authority of Singapore (2007). *Technology roadmap.* Retrieved December 12, 2007, from: http://www.ida.gov.sg/Technology/20060417212727.aspx

International Telecommunication Union (ITU) (2006). *ITU Internet report 2006: Digital life.* Retrieved October 20, 2007, from: http://www.itu.int/osg/spu/publications/digitalife/docs/digital-life-web.pdf

Jankowski, N. W. (2007). Exploring e-science: An introduction. *Journal of Computer-Mediated Communication, 12(2).* Retrieved September 13, 2006, from: http://jcmc.indiana.edu/vol12/issue2/jankowski.html

Jeong, G.-J. (2007). National and overseas e-science trends and implications. Presentation at the discussion workshop for national e-science development strategy. Seoul. Also available at http://vod.yeskiti.net/adfile/semdata/16528_0824_05.pdf

Koh, W.T.H. & Poh, K.W. (2005). Competing at the frontier: The changing role of technology policy in Singapore's economic strategy. *Technological Forecasting & Social Change, 72:* 255–285.

Ministry of Trade and Industry Singapore (2006). *Sustaining innovation-driven growth—Science & Technology 2010 Plan.* Retrieved December 18, 2007, from: http://app.mti.gov.sg/data/article/2461/doc/S&T%20Plan%202010%20Report%20(Final%20as%20of%2010%20Mar%2006).pdf

Moon, J. (2006). Construction and usage of Access Grid. Presented at the 2006 AG-Kr Workshop. Daejoen: KISTI. Korean.

Na, M. (2001). The Home Computer in Korea: Gender, Technology, and the Family. *Feminist Media Studies, 1(3)*: 291–306.

National Internet Development Agency of Korea (NIDA) (2007). Survey on the computer and Internet usage. Report about the second half of the year 2006. Seoul: NIDA.

National Informatization Society Agency of Korea (2007). Trends of e-science in major nations and implications for South Korea. Seoul: NIA. Korean.

Nentwich, M. (2003). *Cyberscience: Research in the age of the Internet.* Vienna: Austrian Academy of Sciences Press.

Park, H. W., & Kluver, R. (2009). Affiliation in political blogs in South Korea: Comparing online and offline social networks. In G. Goggin & M. McLelland (Eds.), *Internationalizing Internet studies* (pp. 252–263). London: Routledge.

Park, H.W. & Biddix, J.P. (2008). Digital media education for Korean youth. *The International Information and Library Review, 40(2)*: 104–111.

Park, H. W., & Jankowski, N. (2008). A hyperlink network analysis of citizen blogs in South Korean politics. *Javnost—The Public, 15*(2): 57–74. Also available at: http://www.javnost-thepublic.org/article/2008/2/4/

Park, H. W., Thelwall, M., & Kluver, R. (2005). Political hyperlinking in South Korea: Technical indicators of ideology and content. *Sociological Research Online, 10*(3). Retrieved August 14, 2006, from: http://www.socresonline.org.uk/10/3/park.html

Park, H. W. & Thelwall, M. (2003). Hyperlink analyses of the World Wide Web: A review. *Journal of Computer-Mediated Communication, 8*(4). Retrieved July 29, 2006, from: http://jcmc.indiana.edu/vol8/issue4/park.html

Park, H.W. (2002). The digital divide in South Korea: Closing and widening divides in the 1990s. *Electronic Journal of Communication, 12*(1/2). Available at: http://www.cios.org/getfile/Park_v12n102

Rose, E. (2003) *User error: Resisting computer culture.* Toronto: Between the Lines.

Tkach-Kawasaki, L. & Park, H. W. (2007). South Korean and Japanese politicians online: Comparing political cultures through political Web sites. Paper presented at Association of Internet Researchers, Vancouver, Canada, 17–20 October.

Uram, T.D. (2007). State of the Access Grid. Paper presented at 2007 Access Grid Retreat Chicago, May 14–16.

Wouters, P. & Beaulieu, A. (2006). Imagining e-science beyond computation. In C. M. Hine (Ed.), *New infrastructures for knowledge production: Understanding e-science*, pp.48–70. Hershey, PA: Information Science Publishing.

Wu, H.J. P., & Heok, K.H.A. (2005). Documenting online collaboration between researchers and information professionals: The case of the Asian Tsunami Web Archive. *Singapore Journal of Library and Information Management, 34*: 75–90

Wu, H.J.P., & Heok K.H.A. (2006). A case study of web archiving: Asian Tsunami Web Archives. Accepted by Conference of the Congress of Southeast Asian Librarians (CONSAL) XIII, March, 2006. Manila , The Philippines .

Yoon, K. (2006). The making of neo-Confucian cyberkids: representations of young mobile phone users in South Korea. *New Media & Society, 8*(5): 753–771.

Part IV
Collaboration

7 Creating Shared Understanding across Distance
Distance Collaboration across Cultures In R&D

Petra Sonderegger

As globalization and the impact of worldwide communications networks expand, scholars are increasingly debating the role of physical place in the world. Predictions have ranged from utopian (the 'death of distance,' 'anytime, anyplace communications') to dystopian (rampant global capitalism and the disintegration of societies and traditions). This chapter discusses the role of shared space in innovation, specifically in corporate research and development (R&D). In particular, it explores the role of intangible factors, such as tacit knowledge, shared language, trust and conventions for researchers who are separated by large distances and several time zones as they collaborate on projects.

Collaborative innovation and creativity arise from interactions between people. New ideas are developed by grappling with and rethinking existing ones. Once the ideas are developed, their implementation may be partially achievable through existing technologies, processes or heuristics. In the initial stages, however, innovation requires a willingness to engage with new perspectives, hunches and seemingly absurd suggestions. These are only partly evaluated through rational decision-making. Judging the potential of a new idea relies as much on experience and intuition as it does on logical analysis. While a variety of different perspectives, backgrounds and life experiences is helpful for a group in generating new ideas, expressing and evaluating those ideas collaboratively presumes a shared language, a shared understanding of the problem at hand and a shared set of experiences. These are developed through close and rich personal interactions between group members. They are particularly hard to develop across distance.

This chapter discusses researchers' and managers' everyday experiences and strategies as they engage in collaboration across thousands of kilometers and multiple time zones. It is based on a series of interviews with researchers based in one of the world's new R&D 'hotspots,' Bangalore, India. The analysis of daily, individual interactions reveals the limits of innovating across distance. Barriers to collaboration and innovation can lie in the simplest effects of distance: differing time zones or strange accents. They are also found in a simple lack of physical presence: not having shared a meal or a drink together, or missing facial and physical feedback that cannot be verbalized. Most importantly, they are found in the uncertainty that people have about someone they have never met, never looked in the eye, shaken hands with, or answered in the affirmative: "Can I trust this person?"

WHY LOCATION (STILL) MATTERS

Studies of regional innovation systems (Freeman, 1991) highlight the importance of collocation for innovation. Many recent studies stress the importance of intangible factors for successful collaboration in innovation. Saxenian (1994) describes the role of personal and professional networks in fostering the flow of tacit knowledge and the generation of trust. Storper (1997) argues that innovation centers on processing uncodified information that cannot be understood outside the context of the agents transmitting it. This information can be scientific, social or political. For successful innovative collaboration, "dense and multiple understandings of what is being transacted are required, that is, ways of reading between the lines, of verifying in multiple ways the possible meanings of what is inherently uncertain formal content" (Storper, 1997: 37). This understanding can be achieved in two different ways: it can be facilitated by a long-standing personal relationship based on trust between the collaborating individuals, or it can be based on less idiosyncratic relational assets. These last are defined as "taken-for-granted mutually coherent expectations, routines, and practices, which are sometimes manifested as formal institutions and rules, but often not" (Storper, 1997: 38).

Trust

All collaboration for innovation involves risks. Collaborators must work through repeated phases of uncertainty, surprise and failure before they reach a solution. They must be open to new ideas, but also willing to give and accept criticism. And, they must have faith that all team members are contributing their share and will receive adequate recognition if the solution is successful. Legal instruments such as employment and alliance contracts or patent laws can provide some reassurances. However, successful collaboration requires a much more personal form of trust, a minimum level of goodwill between collaborators. Fear of being ridiculed or taken advantage of inhibits the flow of new ideas.

Traditionally, this kind of trust has been based on shared membership in the same social group. It relies on repeated shared experiences (Child, 2001). Collaborators working across large distances are unlikely to be members of the same social group and will have a very limited basis for sharing experiences. Nevertheless, trust can be established between collaborators located far apart from each other who rely on various forms of technology to communicate. Jarvenpaa and Leidner (1998) demonstrated "swift trust" in dispersed teams that worked together on a project temporarily. These group members assumed the trustworthiness of their collaborators (for the duration of the project) because this was in the group's interest of achieving its project goals. Swift trust works best in situations where collaborators rally around a clear set of goals and tasks.

Unfortunately, innovative collaboration precludes a set of clear objectives, much less a task list that can be handed out and crossed off. However, creating a higher-level awareness among group members about the purpose and importance of their collaboration can contribute to fostering a basic sense of trust. Repeated collaborations can then lead to predictability and firmer forms of trust over time (Davenport, Davies, & Grimes, 1998; Dodgson, 1993). Video and audio conferencing are generally seen to be better suited to establishing trust than text-based communication. But even with the use of these richer media, trust is likely to be slower to fully develop and to be more fragile than between collocated group members (Bos, Olson, Gergle, Olson, & Wright, 2002).

Mistrust can also arise because technology-mediated communication gives a very limited insight into the events at a distant location. An audio conference participant has no way of knowing whether other conference participants who are sitting in a room together are quietly signaling each other. Once mediated communication ends, participants to a conversation have no recourse to observations or chance encounters that might help them gage the sincerity of the other participants. Collocated subgroups can severely impair the overall functioning of a dispersed group, an effect that is exacerbated when each subgroup is composed of members of the same nationality (Polzer, Crisp, Jarvenpaa, & Kim, 2006).

Access to tacit knowledge

Sharing tacit knowledge and passing on knowledge through socialization or learning-by-doing are important aspects of innovation (Nonaka & Takeuchi, 1995; Von Krogh, Ichijo, & Nonaka, 2000; Nonaka & Teece, 2001). Tacit knowledge is not wholly specifiable: the sum of the parts does not fully describe the whole; an observer must refine his understanding of the whole through experience and intuition.[1] As a result, we "can know more than we can tell" (Polanyi, 1961: 30). Tacit knowledge is knowledge that has not been expressed in language or symbols (codified), either because it cannot be fully codified or because it has not been necessary or expedient to codify it. It includes the beliefs and assumptions that people hold without being aware of them; it is available and in use, but difficult to share; and it is often a source of technological and competitive advantage. Nonaka (1998) describes knowledge creation as the process of making tacit knowledge explicit: creating explicit models of previously tacit know-how, assumptions and beliefs. This process requires intense commitment, challenges, discussions, brainstorming and even distractions. It is very difficult for a group to achieve without sharing space and experiences.

The flow of tacit knowledge is particularly important for activities that cannot be uniformly structured, such as innovation and creative work, or work that requires the interpretation of physical or social cues (the two are obviously not mutually exclusive). In research and other innovative work, problems and solutions emerge as hunches or fragments of ideas long before they can be fully and unambiguously expressed. Passing on this kind of knowledge requires, for the most part, face-to-face interactions.

Shared understanding

Shared understanding represents a "collective way of organizing relevant information" (Hinds & Weisband, 2003: 21) and lets a group collaborate more effectively. It encompasses ideas about group goals, the task itself, social aspects of the group (such as roles, interdependencies and communication patterns) and the characteristics and activities of individual group members (Hinds & Weisband, 2003). These ideas are "understood" within a group and therefore information about them does not need to be transmitted with every interaction. They can help group members to anticipate the reactions of other members and allow them to coordinate their actions implicitly.

Shared understanding is "developed through a history of communication, past coordinated action, and/or other common experience (such as professional socialization)" (Dickey, Wasko, Chudoba, & Thatcher, 2006, introduction). It is easy to see how it might be created through frequent, media-rich, face-to-face communication (Daft & Lengel, 1986). According to Hinds and Weisband (2003), physical presence increases collaborators' unintentional, informal and social information exchanges and their awareness of each others' work. It also provides a shared context for the interpretation of new information.

Nevertheless, it is sometimes possible to achieve shared understanding through archived text-based communication (e.g., an on-line bulletin board) since, unlike most face-to-face communication, a central text repository can stabilize meanings across space and time (e.g., Dickey, Wasko, Chudoba, & Thatcher, 2006). Many complex, distributed, collaborative projects have been carried out through technology-mediated communication. The French aviation company Dassault designed an entire business jet in a purely virtual environment, including a database of 40,000 parts and 200,000 fasteners that was shared between workers at some 30 different firms. (*The Economist*, 2005, 16 June) Even pure text-based collaboration has been successful despite its lack of media richness, for example, in developing open source software. Dickey and colleagues (Dickey, Wakso, Chudoba, & Thatcher, 2006) propose that it is not the technological characteristic of the medium, but rather the shared understanding (or lack thereof) in a group that determines its ability to deal with complex, ambiguous tasks across distance.

Despite these advances, face-to-face meetings remain extremely important in establishing shared understanding as the basis for subsequent collaboration. Salter and Gann (2003) found that engineers preferred face-to-face communication for gathering ideas during the initial and most ambiguous stage of their projects. Kaufmann, Lehner and Todtling (2003) find evidence that technology-mediated communication is more suited to maintaining and managing existing relationships than to creating new relationships. In their review of the literature on proximity in work groups, Kiesler and Cummings (2002) find that face-to-face discussion increases cooperation by strengthening bonds, social contracts and group identity. In addition, they find that a high frequency of spontaneous, informal communications plays an important role in creating strong social and work ties between group members and thereby facilitates the exchange of complex knowledge. Tools such as instant messaging facilitate spontaneous communication for distributed groups, but may not suffice.

Cultural differences

As the distance between collaborators increases, it becomes more likely that they will be working in different regional or national cultures. Cultural differences complicate the picture because of *a priori* dissimilar norms and identities. Collaborators who work in different cultural settings are also more likely to be demographically diverse and to have different educational backgrounds. Their perspectives diverge more, and they have a narrower base of shared understanding on which to build. They are more likely to face language difficulties, which in turn inhibit participation in technology-mediated collaboration (Kim & Bonk, 2002; Sarker, 2005). On the other hand, there is some evidence that shared national, ethnic or organizational culture can enhance collaboration across distance: Agrawal, Kapur and McHale (2006) found that shared ethnicity can partially substitute for collocation in facilitating the flow of tacit knowledge.

In summary, shared understanding and the flow of tacit knowledge are key elements of innovative collaboration; and trust, shared context, and frequent interactions (both formal and informal) are central to establishing these elements. Despite proclamations of the "death of distance" (Cairncross, 1997), physical presence and shared space are still important in today's world, especially for people who are highly interdependent and faced with ambiguous situations. This study was designed to explore the potential and the limitations of distance collaboration in R&D, given the communication tools available.

METHODOLOGY

The study is based on a series of individual interviews conducted in 2005 and 2006 in R&D centers in Bangalore, India. It is also informed by several additional interviews and countless informal discussions that took place during that time. Interviews were chosen over a written survey to elicit richer and more open-ended responses. Also, several academics in India discouraged me from conducting written surveys as they had found response rates to be extremely low, and questionnaires were more often than not filled out by a secretary, rather than by members of the target audience.

Interview method and limitations

The format of the interviews was a guided conversation, conducted in a meeting space at the respondents' workplaces. The interviewer guided the discussion to include most or all of a pre-determined set of topics, but allowed the respondents to concentrate on or add topics relevant to interest or expertise.[2]

Respondents were asked to describe the geographical distribution and internal organization of their teams, their use of and experience with different communication technologies (incl. travel/face-to-face[3]) within their teams, the role of cultural and educational differences between team members, and their collaborative networks outside of their team. As often as possible, they were asked to describe specific instances, using current or recent projects as examples. All respondents remained anonymous, and any respondent could refuse to answer a question. Even so, some topics were automatically excluded from the interviews. For example, due to concerns over protection of intellectual property, respondents could not share details about the content of their research. Some managers agreed to be interviewed on the condition that I not ask them about investment numbers. These restrictions were not a direct concern, since the goal of the interviews was to uncover personal work experiences. However, it does render the discussion of work practices very abstract. Many statements would be easier to understand with more specific technical context.

Respondents

Thirty-one qualitative interviews were conducted in 17 R&D centers (all engaged in some form of international research collaboration). All centers were focused on information technology or telecommunications research, although some belonged to parent companies in other industries. Seventeen respondents were researchers and team leaders in these labs; fourteen were senior R&D managers. Ten additional expert interviews were conducted to gain context and background knowledge. The experts also served as sounding boards for some initial, rough conclusions.

Respondents were identified through the interviewer's personal contacts and through references by other respondents. This approach had two advantages: personal references greatly facilitated access to respondents, and the (indirect) personal connection allowed for a more frank and open discussion. For the purposes of this study, these advantages were seen to outweigh the obvious disadvantage that such a sample cannot strictly claim to be representative of the larger population.

The results of all interviews together are presented in the following sections. Direct quotes are from the core set of 31 interviews conducted in R&D centers.

RESPONDENTS' EXPERIENCES OF COLLABORATING ACROSS DISTANCE AND CULTURES

I begin this section by providing a general overview of respondents' experience of R&D collaboration across thousands of kilometers, different national cultures and multiple time zones. The subsequent sections relate to respondents' experience of the issues of tacit knowledge, building trust and creating shared understanding.

Separated in time and space

At first glance, one might think that there is not much to differentiate long-distance and face-to-face collaboration. Respondents repeatedly answered, "No," when asked whether they could recount a specific episode of long-distance collaboration that was particularly difficult or frustrating. A hesitancy to acknowledge problems to the interviewer may play a role here. However, work across distance and the difficulties it presents are also taken for granted by many people who have spent most of their careers in an MNC subsidiary or an outsourcing firm. In this sense, respondents may simply not have striking examples to recount.

As the interviews progressed, respondents' strategies for dealing with or avoiding everyday difficulties of long- distance collaboration became apparent. The use of these strategies suggests the existence of difficulties and indirectly sheds light on the limitations of technology-mediated communication. The prevalence of air travel also belies the "absence of problems" with technology-mediated communication. Almost all respondents had been or were planning to go abroad to meet some of their collaborators.

The most frequently cited problem of work across distance was adjusting for different time zones. Several respondents specifically mentioned that geographical distance was not so much of a problem as time, as reflected in the following remark:

> Being in India can sometimes make work with product units difficult. The distance is not that important, more the time zones. The time zones make it very difficult. We can really only schedule calls at 8:30pm, which is 8am for them. So it's a bad time for us and it's a bad time for them.

For another respondent, time zones were the only major difference between his previous collaboration in the US and his current intercontinental collaboration: "There's not much difference between Texas-Boston collaboration or Texas-Bangalore collaboration. Only that it's night in the US when it's day in India." The difference of 9½ to 12½ hours between India and the U.S. results in very little or no overlap in the official working hours in both places. It also means that there is a limit to the duration of synchronous communication. During regular working hours, each person can only transmit one round of messages per day and has to wait until the following day for an answer. Respondents in this situation missed the immediacy of feedback that they could get from someone working within the same space:

> The main difficulty is if you want to explain something, you can't use the board. It takes more time to write something in an e-mail. If you're working in the same location, you drop by the other person's office, put something up on the board and together you can immediately figure out whether it works or not. This way, you talk on the phone, e-mail a document, and talk on the phone again.[4]

There was a strong tendency in most labs to reduce interdependency with researchers in distant locations as much as company policy would allow. In some cases this meant defining clear boundaries and responsibilities within a project; in other cases it meant conducting entire projects independently of labs in other countries. This approach defeats the R&D strategy of those firms that use distributed teams in order to make optimal use of experts and knowledge located in different areas of the world (Gassmann & Von Zedtwitz, 1998).

Respondents sometimes struggled with language issues when they collaborated with non-native English speakers, or even when both sides were fluent in English. Dialects, the choice of words and technical language caused difficulties or misunderstandings. Accents were another source of confusion. Some language issues, however, were alleviated through the right choice of communication technology. E-mail allows people to take more time to understand or compose a message; both e-mail and instant messaging even out accents and eliminate some cultural markers. Some respondents thought that asynchronous, written communication was the best alternative to face-to-face meetings in these cases because synchronous communication exacerbates language problems and the resulting embarrassment or discomfort on both sides.

Access to tacit knowledge

A few R&D centers were specifically set up in Bangalore to provide their parent companies with a better understanding of the Indian market. However, most labs were still focused on American or world markets. Their researchers lacked a direct, personal connection with end-customers and considered this a severe disadvantage compared to their Western counterparts. As expressed by one respondent, these counterparts "had an advantage in terms of proximity to the customer. They had access to more information, a refined understanding."

Multinational companies increasingly locate their R&D labs close to production facilities. The software research labs in this study benefited somewhat from their proximity to Bangalore's IT industry. However, most had no direct, physical access to factory floors, semi-conductor fabs or sometimes even software engineering and maintenance facilities. In these cases, training one on-site expert is sometimes not enough. It is more difficult for someone who has recently acquired knowledge to pass it on coherently than for an expert to teach it. Teams also take time to discuss new insights in order to relate abstract ideas to their specific tasks and goals: "Now, there are meetings for technical work. Because of the larger team size. It became harder for one person to pass on everything. It takes much longer for people to learn second-hand what they would learn by going out."

Politically sensitive information proved the most difficult to access across distance. Often, the 'real story' isn't available by e-mail because people don't want impolitic statements traced back to them. Even telephone conversations require a basic level of trust that is hard to establish without sitting in the same room:

> I need to understand the evolution. I want to understand why decisions were taken. If I have ideas on how to improve something, I need to know why the decision wasn't taken in the first place. Often the reason was political, so it's not documented and people won't put it on e-mail.

Building trust and personal relationships

A frequent and important experience for many respondents was that collaboration became more 'comfortable' after in-person meetings. A variety of mental barriers to intense and open collaboration were reduced. As the examples below show, what respondents describe as comfort can be interpreted as basic trust in a collaborator's good will. Predictability and knowing how to "read" a person's response are particularly important:

> Meeting someone makes a difference even though science is supposed to be objective. It increases your comfort level; you know how someone responds in a certain situation. It also helps when you have non-technical discussions.

This is an important part of building trust between collaborators. Innovation, by definition, involves taking risks—not just for an organization, but also for the individuals who contribute new, untested ideas: "It makes it easier that I've met them. It's easier to just say things. Without worrying about looking stupid and things like that. To say, 'I wrote this code, what do you think?'" Informal social activities play an important role in increasing the comfort levels. Eating and drinking together or meeting someone's family provided a broader base for the relationship and more insight into the other person's character. Again, this helped to reduce uncertainty and build trust.

Researchers were also aware of the effect that in-person meetings had on relationships with superiors. Through a general conversation, it was possible to establish a personal connection and lay the groundwork for addressing future, more specific issues. The following two comments reflects this:

> Also, it's important for discussions about the future direction of your work. You can discuss with management, get their buy-in. When I am in Bangalore, I don't have any contact with managers in the US. But when I went there, I had meetings with them. That helps when there's a project proposal that needs funding. It's easier to send an e-mail and ask the US for funds.

Several respondents mentioned that in-person meetings were better suited for sensitive issues. General outsourcing fears played a role here. Respondents were highly sensitive to their counterparts' possible fears of losing their jobs to Bangalore-based labs or simply of having to work with people whose qualifications they couldn't judge. More specifically, respondents mentioned that misunderstandings between team members were more easily cleared up at meetings, where it was possible to bring everyone together at the same table.

For collaboration involving language difficulties, face-to-face communication and the increase in comfort levels that results from meeting a collaborator in person have a heightened importance:

> There were problems with the accent in some cases, especially with the technical guys. Also with the language, some of them had difficulty explaining computer terms in English. I met them in India and in the US. Meeting them helped. Now, I can just call them up. There's less frustration about communication difficulties. You can explain the same thing three times and it's ok.

Respondents who collaborate with both the U.S. and East Asia traveled more frequently to meet their Asian than their American counterparts. Physical presence helped them to overcome many language issues and made it easier to pick up the subtle cues that let them ask the right questions to resolve uncertainties.

Creating shared understandings

Shared understanding was an issue at many different levels. The most elementary level concerned communication styles. Did the same sentence mean the same thing in both locations? The next level concerned general work and management practices, e.g., what is the role of hierarchy in an organization? Related to this, the interviews revealed that the practice of corporate research was conceived differently by different groups, leading to misunderstandings, frustration and prejudices. Group identities were an important factor in alleviating the difficulties that respondents faced as they tried to create shared understandings across distance.

National identity

Respondents were asked about the differences and similarities between Indian researchers and their foreign collaborators. Most responses concerned the level of directness in communications and respect for hierarchy: "In the West in general, people are more direct and blunt. In India, people are quieter. It takes more experience for managers to know what is really happening."

In general, the relationship to superiors is a noticeable difference between India and other (Western) countries. A strong top-down, hierarchical organization is still dominant in both the education system and many domestic firms: "The mindset of freshers[5] is: My superior will tell me what to do. So bosses have to tell them that people need to take ownership of their projects, encourage them and lead by example." However, differences between India and the U.S. appear far less significant when placed in the context of world-wide cultural differences. Respondents who worked with colleagues in multiple countries rarely related questions about cultural differences to the U.S. Their initial response in these cases focused on East Asia or Europe. This suggests that differences in the work culture between labs in Bangalore and the U.S.—while present—recede into the background when compared to the differences between Bangalore and other locations around the world.

Organizational and professional identity

Research managers were acutely aware of the problems that could arise from differences in national culture. They consciously tried to reduce differences between their lab and affiliated labs world-wide. The main way of achieving this was to place an emphasis on a shared corporate culture over and above national differences.

The initial struggle of Bangalore-based labs to be perceived as qualitatively equal to Western labs plays a significant role in replicating corporate culture. In trying to prove their worth, employees in these labs orient themselves by the norms and practices of their international peers and their company's headquarters. Building this reputation leads to an emphasis on similarities between labs rather than differences.

It becomes the job of internationally experienced people to teach others how their work and their ideas will be perceived by collaborators outside of India: "There has to be a kind of apprenticeship for people hired in India.

For that you need people who understand the culture on both sides. It's important to put people in touch with our other labs." As suggested by the idea of an apprenticeship, this happens more often through conversations and providing an example rather than by fiat or through formal training (although the latter is also available in some companies). Such socialization happens 'naturally' as long as there are enough people with the relevant experience in the organization.

In addition, travel is generally seen as an important means of replicating a global corporate culture in the Bangalore research unit. About half of the labs in this study have a formal policy of sending new hires abroad when they start or soon thereafter. Researchers are encouraged to visit headquarters or other corporate offices if they are traveling nearby.

Managers also use corporate policies as a way to reinforce the feeling that different labs worldwide work on equal terms. In the case of Google, "Bangalore is a peer to all global labs. The culture, the hiring criteria, everything is similar to the US." In many cases, architecture and interior design were used to highlight the similarities between a Bangalore lab and international labs. Technology campuses were built to replicate the feel of a Silicon Valley technology campus, complete with gyms, cafeterias, and other amenities. Many campuses are gated—as much for security as to create a border between the dust and chaos of Indian roads and the clean, ordered atmosphere on the campus.[6] Smaller labs used simpler touches, e.g., corporate colors or self-serve coffee machines.[7] In addition, newsletters, webcasts of talks and intranets are used to keep people in different labs aware of each other's work—in the hope of encouraging more spontaneous connections.

Even as they pointed out cultural differences, respondents did not mention insurmountable obstacles. They treated difficulties as tactical rather than as fundamental problems. In part, their confidence stemmed from a feeling of equality and connectedness with their international colleagues. As one respondent noted, "Within the company it feels like it's all one set of people." Another suggested "People hired here have a lot of hi-tech exposure. They feel they have the same culture despite being in different places." Corporate efforts are supported by a sense that technology workers already share a similar ethos, regardless of the country where they work.

Shared understanding in the research process

In order to collaborate effectively, researchers need to understand the activity of performing research in fundamentally similar ways. While some respondents thought that research was understood the same way in all cultures they had experience with, others pointed out nuanced differences. Respondents who thought that there was a difference in how research was understood in India and elsewhere often related this to differences in PhD education. There was a sense that (outside a handful of elite universities) doctoral research was not independent enough, too hierarchical.

> A PhD in India or China is not ideal training for research. There is a lot of development talent here. But for research it is more difficult. The PhD here is more hierarchical. It is more about finding a solution— more like a Master's. PhDs from the US know how to do something new, not implementation. In a PhD, you should figure out what the problem is, what are the questions. In pharma, space and physics it might be different. But in computer science we don't get that.

This approach encourages the development of problem-solving skills over problem discovery or problem definition. As a result, internationally experienced researchers found some of their Indian-trained colleagues to be ill-prepared for the fuzzy goals and unstructured work environment of multinational companies' R&D labs.

Overall, the significance of differences in research experience and education is currently fairly limited since many researchers at the R&D labs in this study received some or all of their tertiary education in the U.S. Estimates of the number of people with a foreign degree and/or several years of foreign research experience ranged from 30 percent to 90 percent of a given research group.

In-person communication is most important in the initial stages of the research process: discovering problems, understanding and contextualizing them, and defining goals and priorities. In MNCs' formal processes, defining research goals and setting priorities was highly associated with in-person communication. While some companies have well-defined, IT-supported processes for deciding on a research strategy, the process itself is dependent on physical interaction. Senior managers have meetings with clients to better understand new market needs. (Even those labs most focused on fundamental research placed a high value on input from business units and customers.)

Aside from the in-person meetings required to gather inputs, the management team itself needed to meet face-to-face to evaluate the inputs. It took several days of 'sitting together' to sort out this wide array of inputs and to reach a consensus about the meaning and relative importance of different pieces of information.

The research process itself is considered to be highly dependent on shared space if tacit information and its interpretation are to permeate the research group:

> There is no fixed, standard process despite all the tools. It requires inspiration, and inspiration isn't the outcome of a specific process. Knowing the necessities doesn't lead to the solution. You need to sit

with the information. It's important to make people interact so that osmosis can happen.

Characteristically, face-to-face meetings were used in most labs to kick off a project. After this initial phase, research teams experienced recurrent periods of uncertainty. R&D is iterative: once basic problems are solved, new problems emerge. Therefore, it comes as no surprise that project milestones were also often cited as instances when researchers traveled so that the team could meet in person. The less well-defined a task or goal is, the more important it seems that people can sit around a table or blackboard to figure it out: "This was a difficult problem. We didn't know how to go about it. We had four-hour meetings to figure out the approach. Once the approach is decided, you can use phone and e-mail." For this kind of discussion, immediate—or even simultaneous—feedback is necessary and rarely achievable through mediated communications.

CONCLUSIONS

The difference between technology-mediated and in-person communication is not that some tasks are impossible to carry out across distance, but rather that they are carried out differently: timelines are different and task definitions are revised to accommodate distance and time zones.

While research collaboration without in-person contact is possible, collaborating on R&D across large distances is far from ideal. Embodied and product-specific knowledge tend to be very important, yet hard to transmit. Researchers do not feel they can assume that a distant collaborator means well—especially in view of political debates about outsourcing, offshoring and downsizing. There are important differences in communication behavior and comfort levels between collaborators who have met and those who have not. For the researchers in this study, in-person meetings led to a higher level of comfort in collaboration. They trusted their counterparts more and moved the relationship from a purely professional level to a more personal level; they made fewer negative attributions in situations of uncertainty. An increase in spontaneity and a decrease in formality helped overcome some difficulties in distance communication.[8]

The results also highlight the superiority of in-person communication for researchers while they are trying to develop a common understanding of the research problem and possible approaches to solving it. Coordination of tasks, by contrast, appears to be hindered more by differing time zones than by specific attributes of the communication technology.

In the specific case of high technology firms in Bangalore, a history of business ties with the U.S. and the high presence of internationally experienced employees have fostered a mutual understanding and some degree of convergence of business practices with the U.S.. Given that the R&D

labs in this study are geared towards international markets and many are owned by multinational companies, they must comply with Western standards of quality and professionalism. The efforts of researchers in Bangalore to prove their competence in a global context reinforce Western norms in local labs since the measures of competence are set by the existing labs in the parent or client company. A large part of the research community also shares a common educational background: doctoral or post-doctoral training at US research universities. Difficulties are more pronounced when collaboration involves communities that do not share this common history.

As we have also seen, research managers put a lot of effort into locally replicating a global corporate culture. The efficiency and quality of collaboration increases when people in different locations feel they share a common culture and identity. In some cases researchers felt a connection through a hi-tech identity, in others they drew on membership in a firm. Focusing on company culture can help bridge differences in national culture—perhaps even to the exclusion of local culture. More than one respondent suggested that anyone who had worked for one of the multinational or the larger outsourcing companies in Bangalore would refuse to go back to a traditional domestic firm.

Lester and Piore (2004) posit that innovative work can be divided into analysis (rational problem- solving) and interpretation (figuring things out through conversations). Analysis can be highly process driven and is—to a large extent—a question of coordination. Interpretation, on the other hand, evolves out of conversations and shared experiences. It describes the way a group develops a shared understanding of the environment and how its own work fits into this environment. According to Lester and Piore, interpretation requires shared time and space to develop. As experienced by some of the researchers in this study, one person cannot bring back all of the information gathered on a trip because some of it only makes sense in relation to the people who provided the input.

The interviews support Lester and Piore's model. Respondents used phrases like "thrash things out" and "figure out an approach" to describe what they do in face-to-face communication. These are interpretive processes—a way of discovering what the problem is, rather than analytically solving a given problem with a predetermined method. Deciding on goals, priorities and methods requires judgment, negotiation between collaborators and repeated feedback loops—ideally instantaneous feedback. This work cannot be parceled out, nor can the process by which it is achieved be completely mapped out in advance.

Respondents' descriptions of their use of communication technology provide some additional explanations why mediated communication is ill-suited to interpretation. When using e-mail, phone calls or teleconferencing, respondents felt they had to be more prepared, express things that might otherwise be taken for granted and anticipate difficulties earlier.

They also said that processes took longer. There was less immediate feedback and spontaneous, simultaneous communication was more difficult. Mediated communication forces more structured exchanges (which can be beneficial in some circumstances). However, this is the exact opposite of what is needed for interpretive work.

Further research is needed to better understand the sources of trust and shared understanding in collaborative research. Despite the evidence above, it is not clear how much they depend on physical presence. As communication technologies evolve, they may provide more social and physical context, richer non-verbal feedback and an environment that allows deep, shared experiences. In fact, some new technologies have already improved on these specific factors. Alternatively, collaborators may develop new social forms online to replicate physical ones. Nevertheless, it seems that a handshake, a shared meal or brainstorming together in front of a blackboard will remain important for fuzzy, high-risk tasks, no matter the advances in technology.

NOTES

1. Polanyi (1961:30), who is credited with coining the term "tacit knowledge", provides the following illustration: A doctor, after witnessing an epileptic seizure with his students, says, "Gentlemen, you have seen a true epileptic seizure. I cannot tell you how to recognize it; you will learn this by more extensive experience."
2. The choice of format was validated by the course that many interviews took. Direct questions usually elicited short and comparatively uninformative answers. An invitation to speak freely, such as, "I'm researching long-distance collaboration. Can you tell me about your experiences?" was far more likely to lead to animated discussions and detailed descriptions of work experiences. Once the conversation started to flow, interviewer guidelines were used to steer the exchanges.
3. In-person communication and face-to-face communication are used interchangeably here. Although the term 'face-to-face' is sometimes also used for video communication, this usage is not adopted here.
4. Several respondents had experimented with on-line 'whiteboard' tools, and some used videoconferencing simply so that they could use a blackboard for figurative communication. However, for these persons neither method replaced the interactivity of people simultaneously talking and drawing on the same board.
5. A "fresher" is a recent graduate with a Bachelor's degree and no work experience.
6. On some campuses, entering the gates feels a little like crossing an international border. Not only are the physical environment and social norms inside and outside the campus different; security measures at the gates (including presentation of ID and checks of bags and electronic equipment) are reminiscent of border crossings.
7. Self-serve coffee machines may not seem relevant to a Western reader, but they stand out in the Indian context where most companies, including MNCs, employ peons to deliver tea and coffee to offices. The idea behind providing

self-serve machines is to de-emphasize hierarchies and to provide a location for chance meetings, in other words, to create a water-cooler office environment.

8. This is not to say that face-to-face relationships must perforce result in trust. They can also lead to negative outcomes, e.g., when collaborators discover irreconcilable differences that remained hidden earlier. However, the experience of most respondents was one of increased comfort and trust, and that remains the focus of this analysis.

REFERENCES

Agrawal, A., Kapur, D., & McHale, J. (2006). Birds of a feather—better together? How co-ethnicity and co-location influence knowledge flow patterns. SSRN.

Bos, N., Olson, J., Gergle, D., Olson, G., & Wright, Z. (2002). *Effects of four computer-mediated communications channels on trust development.* SIGCHI conference on Human factors in computing systems: Changing our world, changing ourselves, Minneapolis, MN, ACM Press.

Cairncross, F. (1997). *The death of distance: how the communications revolution will change our lives.* Boston, MA: Harvard Business School Press.

Child, J. (2001). Trust—the fundamental bond in global collaboration. *Organizational Dynamics, 29*(4): 274–288.

Daft, R. L., & Lengel, R. H. (1986). Organizational information requirements, media richness and structural design. *Management Science, 32*(5): 554–571.

Davenport, S., Davies, J., & Grimes, C. (1998). Collaborative research programmes: building trust from difference. *Technovation, 19*(1): 31–40.

Dickey, M. H., Wasko, M. M., Chudoba, K. M., & Thatcher, J. B. (2006). Do you know what I know? A shared understandings perspective on text-based communication. *Journal of Computer-Mediated Communication, 12*(1). Retrieved 4 August 2008, http://jcmc.indiana.edu/vol12/issue1/dickey.html

Dodgson, M. M. D. (1993). Learning, Trust, and Technological Collaboration. *Human Relations, 46*(1): 77–95.

Freeman, C. (1991). Networks of innovators: A synthesis of research issues. *Research Policy, 20*(5): 499–514.

Gassmann, O., & Zedtwitz, M. von (1998). Organization of industrial R&D on a global scale. *R&D Management 28*(3): 147–161.

Hinds, P. J., & Weisband, S. (2003). Knowledge sharing and shared understanding in virtual teams. In C. Gibson & S. Cohen, (Eds.), *Virtual teams that work: Creating conditions for virtual team effectiveness*, pp. 21–36. San Francisco, CA: Jossey-Bass.

Jarvenpaa, S. L., & Leidner, D. E. (1998). Communication and trust in global virtual teams. *Journal of Computer-Mediated Communication, 3*(4). Retrieved 4 August 2008 from: http://jcmc.indiana.edu/vol3/issue4/jarvenpaa.html

Kaufmann, A., Lehner, P., & Todtling, F. (2003). Effects of the Internet on the spatial structure of innovation networks. *Information Economics and Policy, 15*(3): 402–424.

Kiesler, S., & Cummings, J. N. (2002). What do we know about proximity and distance in work groups? A legacy of research. In P. J. Hinds & S. Kiesler (Eds.), *Distributed Work*, pp. 57–80. Cambridge, MA: MIT Press.

Kim, K. J., & Bonk, C. J. (2002). Cross-cultural comparisons of online collaboration. *Journal of Computer-Mediated Communication, 8*(1). Retrieved 4 August 2008 from: http://jcmc.indiana.edu/vol8/issue1/kimandbonk.html

Lester, R. K., & Piore, M. J. (2004). *Innovation—the missing dimension.* Cambridge, MA: Harvard University Press.

Polzer, J. T., Crisp, C. B., Jarvenpaa, S. L., & Kim, J. W. (2006). Extending the faultline model to geographically dispersed teams: How colocated subgroups can impair group functioning. *Academy of Management Journal, 49*(4): 679–692.

Salter, A., & Gann, D. (2003). Sources of ideas for innovation in engineering design. *Research Policy, 32*(8): 1309–1324.

Sarker, S. (2005). Knowledge transfer and collaboration in distributed U.S.-Thai teams *Journal of Computer-Mediated Communication, 10*(4). Retrieved 4 August 2008 from: http://jcmc.indiana.edu/vol10/issue4/sarker.html

Saxenian, A. (1994). *Regional advantage: culture and competition in Silicon Valley and Route 128.* Cambridge, MA: Harvard University Press.

Storper, M. (1997). *The regional world: territorial development in a global economy.* New York: Guilford Press.

8 Moving from Small Science to Big Science
Social and Organizational Impediments to Large Scale Data Sharing

Eric T. Meyer

INTRODUCTION

One of the challenges of building collaborative information systems for scientific and social scientific data is that many new projects are actually extensions of existing projects, often going back decades, which have embedded logic and work practices that are highly resistant to change. This resistance to change cannot, however, simply be attributed to conservatism on the part of individual scientists. On the contrary, many of the scientists that are discussed in this chapter are enthusiastic about the idea of contributing data to larger collaborations in exchange for the additional data that they will, in turn, have available to them. In practice, however, protocols that are the result of years of cumulative decisions at the local level have resulted in information storage systems that are highly idiosyncratic and often resistant to federation. To demonstrate this point, I report on two projects in very different domains which nevertheless share similar barriers to building a collaborative infrastructure.

The issues surrounding moving from small science to big science are not new. Derek de Solla Price (1963) identified some of these issues four decades ago in his work that helped to develop the field of scientometrics. More recently, scholars in computer science have addressed issues of scalability (Simmhan, Plale, & Gannon, 2005; Zheng, Venters, & Cornford, 2007), and any number of papers discussing the implementation of Grid-enabled projects have identified scalability as one of the key issues developers have had to deal with (Pakhira, Fowler, Sastry, & Perring, 2005; Shimojo, Kalia, Nakano, & Vashishta, 2001). Many of these discussions of scalability, however, are focused on large projects such as physics and astronomy Grid-based projects. Smaller e-science and e-social science projects, however, also face issues of scale as they attempt to share data more widely and contribute to larger datasets. One issue to be raised in this chapter is how legacy data can cause significant problems during efforts to standardize and federate datasets. This is not a new issue, as countless scientists are dealing with these issues.[1] Only recently, however, have researchers begun to pay attention to how small scientific projects negotiate the changes required as they move towards becoming large, collaborative scientific projects (Carlson & Anderson, 2006; Walsh & Maloney, 2007) and attempt to sustain these collaborations over time (Bos et al., 2007).

In this chapter, I discuss two case studies that serve to illustrate some of the issues faced when small scientific projects move to large-scale data sharing and collaboration. This text is not intended to be an exhaustive treatment of this topic since it relies on two possibly idiosyncratic cases, but is meant to stimulate discussion on these issues among researchers studying e-science, e-social science and, more generally formulated, e-research projects.

This chapter discusses some of the issues that arise when small scientific projects make the transition to becoming part of larger scientific collaborations, as seen from a social informatics perspective. The data for the paper is drawn from two cases: a systematic study of a humpback whale research project involving federating data about the population and movements of humpbacks in the Pacific Ocean, and observations based on the author's personal experiences as part of a psychiatric genetics collaboration that has recently become involved in contributing data to a large, shared data repository. While these two projects are in very different scientific domains, they share a number of characteristics including decentralized decision-making, limited data management expertise, and long-term collections of legacy data that have contributed to the difficulties the projects have faced in moving from small science to big science. One of the important issues raised by this paper is the tension between the desire for flexibility and innovation in scientific practice as weighed against the need for compatible data standards in large-scale scientific data infrastructures. This tension must be resolved if e-science and e-social science projects are to succeed in the long term.

Marine Mammal Science

Scientists who study whales, dolphins and other marine mammals use a variety of scientific techniques, including acoustics, genetics, and photo-identification to gather data pertaining to marine mammal population characteristics and behavior. In 2006–2007, I studied marine mammal scientists who use photo-identification as a main data collection tool (Meyer, 2007a, 2007b). The study was designed to understand the ways in which the scientists' work had changed when they switched from film-based to digital photography. The research involved 41 interviews with principal investigators, junior researchers, and technicians working at 13 different laboratories in the U.S. and Europe. While the marine mammal scientists are primarily engaged in e-science as opposed to e-social science, their experience trying to build collaborative scientific infrastructures for studying the social behavior of whales and dolphins shares much in common with scientists who study the social behavior of humans. The characteristics of the animal populations under study influences any given marine mammal scientist's desire to share data collaboratively and to spend time, resources and effort building infrastructure for the ongoing sharing of data. For instance, some of the dolphin projects in this research focused on relatively small populations of animals (200–500 dolphins) that did not travel widely. Since the animals were located in a small geographic area and were often only studied by a single group of scientists, there was little incentive to share the data. Quite the reverse was actually true, as some of the scientists studying these small populations had concerns about others using their data without having gone through the trouble of collecting it, as reflected in the following quote:

> Leah Tull:[2] Well, honestly, I'm very protective about it . . . I guess it rather bugs me that I have to do the work and everyone always asks me for a CD . . . it's our scientific study.

Compare this to a large group of scientists studying humpback whales:

> Jacob Tipton: We knew the success of our project we had done in [location], but also its limitations because it largely funded the contribution and analysis of photographs, but not the dedicated gathering of data. So it very much relied on who was already doing work in certain places. So there were these huge gaps and we knew to really to answer the questions about population size, trends, human impacts, stock structure we had to cover some of these new areas.

Humpbacks and other whales can travel thousands of miles during annual migrations. The total population size of humpback whales in the Pacific Ocean is in the range of 15,000–20,000 animals. Scientists hoping to learn more about humpbacks, then, have an incentive to collaborate with other scientists studying humpback whales throughout the Pacific Ocean. By sharing data, they open up the possibility of being able to track individual animals' movements from place to place, rather than just recording their repeated visits to a single location over time. Until quite recently, however, relatively little formal collaboration occurred and most collaborations were formed based on informal relationships. These informal relationships were often based on common attendance at a university or through shared contacts built during professional conferences and meetings. Recently, however, there have been efforts to build much larger databases, including a project called SPLASH (Structure of Populations, Levels of Abundance, and Status of Humpbacks). SPLASH involves over 300 scientists working in 50 research groups working in various areas in the Pacific Ocean (Calambokidis et al., 2007). Several contributing groups of scientists were included in the research study reported here.

In SPLASH, as in other marine mammal photo-identification projects, researchers use photographs taken in the field to identify individual animals and to track the sightings of the animals geographically and over time. The initial efforts to develop the technique of photo-identification go back nearly 30 years. Prior to the early 1970s, much of the dolphin and whale research involved techniques that either disrupted the animals' behavior (such as freeze-branding) or used dead animals (including necropsies on carcasses of animals that had either died naturally or were killed for research purposes). Increasing public interest influenced by the nascent environmental movement in the 1960s and the "Save the Whales" campaign of the 1970s helped draw attention to the need to develop less invasive techniques. More importantly, the passage of the U.S. Marine Mammal Protection Act of 1974 banned most harassment of marine mammals; current research requires special federal permits to be allowed even to approach the animals closely with research vessels to take photographs. Even though there was some initial skepticism about the ability to unambiguously identify individual animals using photographs, the technique is now widely accepted and is practiced by many of the scientists who study these species:

> Dr. Gerald Lemoine: The original seed of the idea . . . came from talking around the campfire . . . It was one of these fun things where ideas come to fruition independently due to synergism and the overall status of the sciences. In the '50s, I don't think anyone would have really come up with that idea . . . I remember telling [a prominent scientist in 1971] about this idea of photo-identifying, and he said, 'Don't do it. It is not worthwhile. You're barking up the wrong tree. You can't do it, you'll be disappointed. The only way to do it is to catch them and brand them.' But, of course, they use photo-identification now very successfully.

Using photo-identification techniques, scientists have amassed large amounts of data on thousands of whales collected in individual catalogs of animal images and databases of related information. The problem as relates to e-science and e-social science, however, is that the data have been collected by dozens of individual scientists who maintain catalogs of humpback whale images, each with their own cataloging schemes, numbering protocols, and databases of associated information. Most catalogs prior to 2003 consist of film photographs in the form of slides, black and white negatives, or black and white prints. Since 2003, many scientists in the field have switched to digital photography, and have designed additional idiosyncratic systems to deal with the digital catalogs which may or may not be consistent even with their own prior catalogs.

> Dr. Marcia Parrett: It's just too complicated—so, right now I have two data bases; one on my older data from 2003 back, which was all of the data collected on film, and now I have a new . . . database that's all

the data collected on digital . . . So, this spring, I'm actually going to [location] . . . and we have a collaborative agreement where we share data back and forth and we'd kept it pretty much in the same format except we need to get more on the same page and we're going to work with their computer guy up there at the end of May and really get our databases uniform. Maybe then, it won't be all . . . the data won't be the same but they'll be the same format.

While there are many in the field who believe strongly in the desirability of sharing these data, considerably fewer currently see a need to make local data collection and storage procedures more consistent within the field. One respondent in this study who had spent time considering these issues was also one of the scientists who, for the time being at least, continued to use film-based photography rather than switch to digital photography:

> Robert Newton: And if you don't have a really good filing system standardized, that doesn't change every time someone thinks it might be better done a different way. So I'm kind of waiting, I guess, to see if it really stabilizes with a naming protocol and a filing protocol that is not going to wander every time someone comes up with a new software for digital pictures. That happens frequently and you'll get, people send us pictures off a camera and they'll be in files maybe a Canon software, or a Nikon one. And you can convert them all to jpegs and fart around with them but, basically, I don't want to be a film processor.

Even among the SPLASH collaborators scientists often continued to work primarily using their established practices, leaving it up to the five SPLASH area coordinators to reformat and rename their contributions to conform to the project's standards.

> Jacob Tipton: . . . We were not as dictatorial [as we might have been]. Because we were working with established researchers in the area and kind of seeking broad collaboration, many of the researchers maybe started incorrectly with the assumption that people had their own ways to do things that worked and weren't necessarily trying to force them to do it one way. But partly because of the rapid start of SPLASH, we weren't fully thought out ourselves. . . . I haven't fully thought out why some of it was as screwy as it was in terms of experienced researchers and the one thing I do think about is that they were dealing with the transition to digital as well and so they had their own system that worked.

This illustrates a key point that is discussed again below: when small scientific projects are faced with sudden and rapid growth by adding numerous non-collocated collaborators, issues of data management and organization often fall to the wayside until problems later surface. This will appear again in the discussion of the GAIN psychiatric genetics project below. For the SPLASH collaboration, the scientists thought first and foremost about getting out into the field, finding humpback whales, recording their identifying features with a digital camera, and recording data such as GPS information and environmental data. The timing of the beginning of the SPLASH collaboration also contributed to the confusion. The first year of the SPLASH collection was 2004, and many of the contributors had either switched from film-based to digital photography either in 2003 or 2004 and were still working through how to adapt their methods and organizational practices to the new technology.

The SPLASH collaboration is just one example of scientists who have struggled as their small disconnected projects are faced with relatively sudden increase in collaboration and in scale. In the case of SPLASH, two forces pushed this change. The first is scientific: the desire of the scientists to better understand the population structure and long-range behaviors of humpback whales. The second force, however, is economic: SPLASH was a funded project, and thus offered scientists the first real chance to begin to respond to the first scientific force. Science costs money, and new funds attract new scientific projects (Carlson & Anderson, 2007). This monetary inducement can make the scientific desire to collaborate come into sharper focus for busy scientists with many demands on their time and attention.

This brief overview of some of the issues facing the SPLASH collaborative should serve to give some impression of how a small scientific project can struggle with information issues as it tries to contribute to larger scientific data infrastructures. Next, I will turn to a scientific project in a completely different domain to understand how some of the specifics of SPLASH are not unique.

Psychiatric Genetics

The second project illustrating the ways in which small scientific projects can struggle when faced with contributing to larger scientific infrastructures involves genomic research into the basis of certain psychiatric disorders, specifically bipolar disorder. Like the humpback research, this is also a long-standing project; over a period of 20 years, researchers have collected blood, genetic data, and phenotypic data on thousands of subjects. Again, while this study at first blush may appear to be primarily an e-science project, the portion which I discuss here is primarily a social science project: collecting interview data on the behaviors and social interactions of individuals with certain mental health disorders, and interviewing their family members. My data for this section of the paper was not collected systematically, but is the result of my personal involvement of this as a central player in the collection and management of phenotypic data for the project over a period of ten years from 1997–2007.[3] During this time, the bipolar (BP) collaboration grew somewhat (expanding from four collaborating institutions to 11), but still was primarily an example of small science. Each contributing university had a small number of staff working on the project, usually from one to five staff members, and the entire collaboration involved fewer than 50 people.

In 2006, the BP project was one of six long-term studies in the U.S. selected to be a contributor to GAIN, the Genetic Association Identification Network. GAIN is a public-private partnership project between the U.S. National Institutes of Health and a number of private sector firms, including Pfizer, Affymetrix, Perlegen, and Broad. There was no funding offered to studies selected to participate in the GAIN project. Instead, the approach of GAIN was to use a carrot to attract scientists to contribute their data in exchange for getting access to extensive genotyping information on their research subjects in the form of genotyping using one million SNP (single nucleotide polymorphism) microarrays. These 1M SNP chips are an order of magnitude larger than many of the previous genotyping projects available to the scientists.

The contribution of the data, however, also has a price: both the phenotypic information contributed by the scientists and the genotypic information generated as part of GAIN were to be made immediately available to researchers worldwide, including to pharmaceutical companies hoping to use the information to help develop new (and presumably potentially profitable) drugs. One major change for the scientists contributing to GAIN has to do with the embargo period. In the past, data collected by the scientists was generally released to other researchers one year after the final collection of data ended and the data had been cleaned for use. This meant that the scientists had exclusive use of the data in its raw format throughout the data collection period, and for at least a year in analyzable, final format. In the case of GAIN, however, the genotypic information is being released to all parties at exactly the same time. The contributing scientists have a 9-month period during which they have exclusive publication rights, but after the 9-month period is up, anyone may publish findings from the data. While the difference between 9 months and a year may seem minor, recall that the previous embargo of a year was for access to the data, which would then require time for analysis. In the case of GAIN, however, there is no embargo at all for access to the data, only for the ability to publish. As a result, the scientists are faced with working on a much tighter schedule and, at the same time, are analyzing datasets that are an order of magnitude larger than those to which they are accustomed. This project is still ongoing at the time of writing and plans are in place to continue to monitor how the scientists deal with this increased pressure to quickly analyze and publish their data.

One hurdle that the BP project had to overcome after being selected as one of the initial six GAIN studies was that the subjects being included in the genotyping had been collected over a period of 20 years using three different versions of the interview instrument, which in turn were encoded into three different phenotypic databases with incompatible variable names and formats. The largest set of items in these phenotypic databases are the answers to over 100 pages of questions, administered as semi-structured interviews performed by trained clinical researchers. Interviews take from 4–6 hours on average to administer, and result in recorded values for approximately 2600 variables. In addition to these data, there are also tables that record each research participant's "final best estimate" which is the clinical diagnosis assigned to that person based on a trained clinician's analysis of his or her interview, family history, medical records, and other information. Each subject has multiple best estimates in the database because at least two clinicians plus the interviewer and an editor each assign a diagnosis, but each has only one final best estimate. These final best estimates are in the form of a hierarchical diagnosis using diagnostic systems that have changed over the years of the study. The earliest diagnoses use a combined DSM-IIIR/RDC system, while the latest subjects are diagnosed with DSM-IV.[4]

Because this interview schedule has gone through several iterations over the 20 years of the project, there are three main versions of the phenotypic database. The first includes data that were collected via paper interviews and entered into an Oracle database designed and maintained by a federal contractor. The second set of interviews were also completed on paper, and then entered into a Paradox database designed by a database designer located at one of the project sites. The third set of interviews were initially done on paper but were then transitioned to direct entry interviewing using laptops and tablet PCs using a proprietary database designed for the study by an external company. All three versions are converted from their native storage formats into SAS files for use and analysis, but their variable names are not consistent. For instance, a similar variable in the first set variables might be "I1120", in the second set "Number_of_manic_episodes", and in the third set "V756". While this seems confusing to outsiders, those familiar with the data have found that having very different names serves as a quick shorthand for being able to see at a glance the source of a variable or set of variables.

The differences in variable names illustrate the difficulty in combining data from several iterations of the same project, let alone trying to combine that data with data from other projects. Because the decisions regarding things like variable naming conventions was left to database designers rather than done in a systematic fashion, trying to later combine these data requires a fairly high degree of understanding of the research project. One of the contributing sites has had several staff members working on a combined dataset that converts variables from all three versions to a standard naming system; this project has taken over two and a half years. Also, because the interview schedule changed between iterations, questions have been rewritten, added and deleted from version to version, so there is no clear mapping from one to another in the majority of cases. When the data were primarily used internally by people very familiar with the research, the analysts were able to informally share knowledge about how best to use the data. When such data needs to be shared more widely, however, these idiosyncrasies can be very confusing. In addition, the group in charge of GAIN data distribution also required well documented data dictionaries for the databases, which had not been kept in a format compatible with the GAIN requirements.

Although considerably more detail could be shared about this study, this short description should illustrate how decisions made by a wide variety of people over a period of many years can have major implications should the scientific data later be re-used in ways that the original designers were unable to foresee. This accumulation of many small decisions, most of which were perfectly sensible decisions at the time, can subsequently result in considerable work trying to reconcile the many differences that are the result of those decisions.

DISCUSSION

As we saw in both the SPLASH and BP collaborations described here, the shift from small to big science can often be fairly rapid and tumultuous. Most of the personnel working on both of these projects are trained in scientific methods and theory; there are few participants with any systematic background in data management and organization. In the case of SPLASH, all of the personnel responsible for designing the database systems and methods of information organization were trained in biology, and none had any formal training in database design or information management. The decision regarding which personnel to assign to these duties relied primarily on identifying staff members with an affinity for and skill with computers. While the databases that were designed as a result were perfectly useable, they did not incorporate fully normalized designs or other features that more trained designers may have included. More importantly, because they were designed by a single user or small group of users, if SPLASH wishes in the future to federate its data even further (possibly by expanding to other regions, or incorporating additional species of whales) it will be faced with trying to integrate incompatible designs.

In the case of the BP project, a small number of people with considerable expertise in data management were part of the decision-making process, but even in this case many of the decisions were not made systematically. For instance, the format for variable names for the third iteration of the phenotypic interview was decided by the company that programmed the database, and had much more to do with the structure of their particular implementation of an EAV (entity-attribute-value) database design than with the needs of the scientific analysts. Even the second iteration of the interview, which was stored in a database designed by a skilled analyst, experienced unexpected variable naming confusion when a number of variable names including the ampersand (&) sign were altered when the data were imported into SAS; SAS does not support the ampersand, so converted both those characters and any spaces to an underscore. Thus, "Total Manic & Depressive Episodes" in Paradox became "total_manic___depressive episodes" in SAS, with three consecutive underscores in the center.

Since much of the analysis in the past had relied on *ad hoc* requests made by investigators to the small number of data experts working in the collaboration for subsets of the data, much of the knowledge about the idiosyncrasies of the datasets was never written down in a systematic fashion. When GAIN required that this data be shared and documented, considerable effort had to be made to translate this knowledge into a written format. Also, the data sent to GAIN was cleaned, but the three versions of the dataset were still separate. The internal effort by one research group to construct a unified dataset was not yet finished at the time the data needed to be provided to GAIN, nor was the group who had spent such time and effort on combining the data willing to release the combined dataset publicly until they had gotten use out of it. The plan was to release the combined dataset to the scientific community after a year of internal use.

Among the striking similarities between these very different scientific domains is the extent to which existing practices are the result of many small decisions made in many small research projects by many individual researchers and technicians over a long period of time. These decisions were often made with little or no discussion of the impact beyond the particulars of the specific local study, often because scientists at the time did not anticipate the future need to share the data with other scientists. As a result, both projects had, over a period of years, adopted highly idiosyncratic methods that hindered an easy transition to sharing data. Because of this, scientists find they have had to spend a great deal of time, effort and money to transform their data into forms that can be used in a larger data-sharing project. In some cases, these barriers may be high enough to dissuade scientists from contributing at all. In other cases, unless the idiosyncratic nature of the data is diminished, users of the collaborative data may find it confusing or misleading. These social realities of scientific practice must be addressed if e-science and e-social science projects are to be successful, particularly when applied to existing scientific protocols.

One of the reasons both the cases described here developed their levels of idiosyncrasy was that both had historically engaged in smaller scale collaboration, but had done so in a very non-centralized fashion. The quote from Jacob Tipton cited earlier in the chapter mentioned that SPLASH didn't "try to force them to do it one way". Likewise, the BP project was always very decentralized, to the extent that individual contributing sites were able to choose to skip portions of the interview schedule and choose to use alternative systems of organization and management locally as long as their final data was provided in the agreed upon formats. Both the SPLASH and BP projects have non-dogmatic leaders who have been flexible in their approach to managing the collaborations. They have, by and large, not attempted to impose decisions, but instead have sought consensus and have allowed considerable individual latitude to their colleagues and contributors. This flexible and decentralized form of leadership is common among scientific and creative teams (Mumford, Scott, Gaddis, & Strange, 2002), and is not inherently problematic. Science relies on the freedom of scientists to innovate (Bush, 1945; Gordon, Marquis, & Anderson, 1962), although some recent work suggests that these patterns are changing in the face of calls for measures of increased accountability and relevance for scientific work (Demeritt, 2000; Harman, 2003). Having collaborative science designed with wide latitude for individual contributors to pursue unique contributions can arguably lead to better, more innovative science. From a data management perspective, however, lack of reliance on standard data structures, naming styles and metadata makes federating data either difficult or impossible.

In addition, data management often is not considered a top priority during the startup phase of scientific research projects. In the cases described here, few of the scientific decision makers had detailed knowledge of the demands of data management, and as a result treated data management as ancillary to the main scientific research design. Also, in both cases the studies were rather hastily implemented, and saw a number of operational changes during the early phases. Encoding these changes into data systems became a case of trying to hit a moving target until the scientific protocol had stabilized. Based on personal observation of these and a number of other scientific projects, however, this initial uncertainty is not uncommon with grant funded research. In the U.S., grants are written, submitted, and revised over a period of years in many cases, and by the time funds are secured there have often been local changes in personnel and wider changes in the state of current scientific knowledge. The grants are also written with some flexibility in terms of specific activities, and the decisions about how to actually concretize the research are often left until the funds have been secured.

The question, of course, is to what extent data management demands should dictate scientific decisions, and conversely to what extent should individual scientists be allowed to ignore issues of compatibility and data availability. This is an important and enormous ongoing issue for scholars interested in working with large, federated datasets. This tension between conformity to standards and freedom to innovate is not resolved, and will arise time and again as e-science and e-social science projects continue to develop and to attract new contributors. It is unlikely that there can be a single answer that will lessen this tension. Collaborative scientific projects will continue to balance the needs of individual scientists for flexibility in their data collection protocols with the demands of federated databases for data to be organized in a consistent and structured manner. However, if e-science, e-social science and, more generally, e-research projects are to succeed in the long term, this tension must be successfully resolved.

ACKNOWLEDGMENTS

An earlier version of this chapter was presented at the 2007 NCeSS conference in Ann Arbor, Michigan, U.S.. Portions of this work have been supported by the Rob Kling Center for Social Informatics, Indiana University, Bloomington, Indiana, U.S.; and by the School of Library and Information Science, Indiana University, Bloomington, Indiana, U.S.; and by the U.K. National Centre for e-Social Science through a grant from the U.K. Economic and Social Research Council (RES-149-25-1022).

NOTES

1. See for instance the ESML Earth Science Markup Language (Ramachandran, Graves, Conover, & Moe, 2004) and the Kepler system for dealing with legacy data in scientific workflows (Altintas et al., 2004).
2. All names are pseudonyms.
3. No data was collected as part of an IRB-approved study, but the author has written permission from the collaboration's lead investigator to discuss the workings of the projects and his own role therein.
4. DSM is the Diagnostic and Statistical Manual of Mental Disorders that lists different categories of mental disorders and gives specific criteria required for a set of symptoms to "meet criteria". These criteria generally include a list of potential symptoms and number of symptoms required, plus the number of days the episode must have lasted to meet criteria. The DSM-IIIR was published in 1987 as a revised version of the 1980 DSM-III, and DSM-IV was published in 1994. The RDC (Research Diagnostic Criteria) is a similar, older system developed in the 1970s.

REFERENCES

Altintas, I., Berkley, C., Jaeger, E., Jones, M., Ludascher, B., & Mock, S. (2004). *Kepler: An extensible system for design and execution of scientific workflows.* Paper presented at the 16th International Conference on Scientific and Statistical Database Management, Santorini Island, Greece, June 21–23.

Bos, N., Zimmerman, A., Olson, J., Yew, J., Yerkie, J., Dahl, E., & Olson, G. (2007). From shared databases to communities of practice: A taxonomy of collaboratories. *Journal of Computer-Mediated Communication, 12*(2), article 16. Retrieved 8 August 2008 from: http://jcmc.indiana.edu/vol12/issue2/bos.html

Bush, V. (1945). Science: The endless frontier. *Transactions of the Kansas Academy of Science, 48*(3): 231–264.

Calambokidis, J., Barlow, J., Burdin, A. M., Clapham, P., Ford, J. K. B., Gabriele, C. M., et al. (2007). *New insights on migrations and movements of North Pacific humpback whales from the SPLASH project.* Paper presented at the

Biennial Conference on the Biology of Marine Mammals, Cape Town, South Africa.

Carlson, S., & Anderson, B. (2006). *e-Nabling Data: Potential impacts on data, methods and expertise.* Paper presented at the Second International Conference on e-Social Science, Manchester, UK, June 28–30.

Carlson, S., & Anderson, B. (2007). What are data? The many kinds of data and their implications for data re-use. *Journal of Computer-Mediated Communication, 12*(2). Retrieved 8 August 2008 from: http://jcmc.indiana.edu/vol12/issue2/carlson.html

de Solla Price, D. J. (1963). *Little science, big science.* New York: Columbia University Press.

Demeritt, D. (2000). The new social contract for science: Accountability, relevance, and value in US and UK science and research policy. *Antipode, 32*(3): 308–329.

Gordon, G., Marquis, S., & Anderson, O. W. (1962). Freedom and Control in Four Types of Scientific Settings. *American Behavioral Scientist, 6*(4): 39–43.

Harman, J. R. (2003). Whither Geography? *The Professional Geographer, 55*(4): 415–421.

Meyer, E. T. (2007a). *Socio-technical perspectives on digital photography: Scientific digital photography use by marine mammal researchers.* PhD dissertation, Indiana University, Bloomington, IN. ProQuest Digital Dissertations database Publication No. AAT 3278467.

Meyer, E. T. (2007b). Technological change and the form of science research teams: Dealing with the digitals. *Prometheus, 25*(4): 345—361.

Mumford, M. D., Scott, G. M., Gaddis, B., & Strange, J. M. (2002). Leading creative people: Orchestrating expertise and relationships. *The Leadership Quarterly, 13*(6): 705–750.

Pakhira, A., Fowler, R., Sastry, L., & Perring, T. (2005). *Grid enabling legacy applications for scalability—Experiences of a production application on the UK NGS.* Paper presented at the UK e-science All Hands Meeting (AHM'05), Nottingham, UK.

Ramachandran, R., Graves, S., Conover, H., & Moe, K. (2004). Earth Science Markup Language (ESML): A solution for scientific data-application interoperability problem. *Computers & Geosciences, 30*(1): 117–124.

Shimojo, F., Kalia, R. K., Nakano, A., & Vashishta, P. (2001). Linear-scaling density-functional-theory calculations of electronic structure based on real-space grids: Design, analysis, and scalability test of parallel algorithms. *Computer Physics Communications, 140*(3): 303–314.

Simmhan, Y. L., Plale, B., & Gannon, D. (2005). A survey of data provenance in e-science. *SIGMOD Record, 34*(5): 31–36.

Walsh, J. P., & Maloney, N. G. (2007). Collaboration structure, communication media, and problems in scientific work teams. *Journal of Computer-Mediated Communication, 12*(2). Retrieved 8 August 2008 from: http://jcmc.indiana.edu/vol12/issue2/walsh.html

Zheng, Y., Venters, W., & Cornford, T. (2007, June). Distributed development and scaled agility: Improvising a grid for particle physics. *Working Paper Series #163.* Retrieved August 30, 2007, from: http://is2.lse.ac.uk/wp/pdf/wp163.pdf

Part V
Visualization

9 Visualization in e-Social Science

Mike Thelwall

INTRODUCTION

Visualizations are a core e-science application: "e-Science means science increasingly undertaken through distributed global collaborations enabled by the Internet, and involving very large or complex data collections, Teras-cale computing resources and high performance visualisation" (Taylor, 2002). Visualization is the primary goal of a significant minority of U.K. funded e-science programs, third in popularity to data tool and middleware development (Wouters & Beaulieu, 2006). Whilst many types of quantitative social science research already routinely use simple visualizations, such as graphs, the recent expansion in computing power has allowed many new and sophisticated types to be created that can shed light on social science data that is difficult to portray effectively with standard graphs. Some areas of social science already routinely employ increasingly complex visualizations (Orford, Harris, & Dorling, 1999), including social network analysis (Wasserman & Faust, 1994), which uses network diagrams as visualizations of network structures. Recent years have seen the development of increasingly powerful, purpose-built visualizations for particular tasks. Moreover, there is now a research field, Information Visualization, which concentrates on the development of new types of visualization and theoretical considerations underlying design choices (Borner, Chen, & Boyack, 2003; Chen, 2004; Spence, 2007; Zhu & Chen, 2005).

From a research perspective, the purpose of visualization is typically to explore "data and information graphically, as a means of gaining understanding and insight" (Earnshaw & Wiseman, 1992: 5). One mantra for software design is to allow the user to "overview [the data] first, zoom and filter, and then [obtain full] details on demand" (Shneiderman, 1996: 337). Visualizations can help mediate between humans and complex datasets: not just to highlight and identify patterns within the entire set but also to help us to select relevant parts of the data to analyze in detail and the most appropriate scales of analysis.

This chapter explores the potential for visualizations in the social sciences with the objective of equipping social scientists with the knowledge to decide how visualizations may help their own research. A secondary objective is to introduce some of the practical issues involved in the decision to adopt a visualization technique. The latter may also be of use to system developers that are not themselves social scientists and also to those seeking to understand factors related to the uptake of computationally intensive visualization in the social sciences. The chapter begins with a discussion of the types of visualization available and some attempts at categorization. A brief history of visualization in the social sciences leads into a set of cases of e-social science visualization initiatives. This is followed by a discussion of the increasing availability of powerful and free online visualization tools and the impact that this may have on future social research.

CLASSIFICATIONS OF VISUALIZATIONS

The classification of visualization types is a difficult task. One Web-based "Periodic Table" of visualizations[1] includes a complex, multifaceted typology and many examples even though it covers only relatively traditional techniques. There are many different types of visualization and different authors have tried to classify them according to almost unrelated criteria, such as application focus, appearance or subject area (Zhu & Chen, 2005). The highly cited classification below (Shneiderman, 1996), in contrast, focuses on the data types to be visualized. The categories overlap and are simplifications but they are nevertheless useful as a framework for understanding difference.

It is complicated to classify the appearance of computer visualizations because many are highly imaginative and individual. The list below gives some categories that could be applied to the appearance of visualizations, showing the variety of options available (for a broader overview of types, see Spence, 2007).

- Motion: static/dynamic
- Number of dimensions: 1/2/3/3+time/more
- Interaction: interactive/passive
- Color: monotone/multicolored
- Semiotic type: the visualization or its parts resemble the phenomenon modeled (iconic) / the representation is completely abstract (symbolic).

In addition to the above, there are also categorizations of the characteristics of the individual elements that make up diagrams, for example: size, color, texture, orientation and shape (Bertin, 1983: 29–92; Spence, 2007). One more categorization of visualization types is also relevant in practice. This concerns the extent to which a method is (a) general purpose and hence may be relatively easy to access and use or (b) is specific to an application or data collection, in which case it may need to be created for a research project, and this may be expensive and time consuming:

Table 9.1 Classification of Visualizations

Data Type	Examples and notes
1-dimensional	In Google toolbar, "PageRank" line length is proportional to the perceived importance of a document.
2-dimensional	Geographic data is commonly spatially organized, lending it to map-like representations
3-dimensional	Data about real world objects is 3-dimensional, such as the environments developed by architects
Multidimensional	Much social statistics data has more than three mathematical dimensions, such as the set of quantitative responses to long questionnaires. Factor analysis is a typical technique used to analyze such data and multidimensional scaling is an example of a statistical technique for representing high-dimensional data in fewer dimensions.
Trees or hierarchical data	Examples include organization diagrams and ontology structures. A common statistical application to represent hierarchical data is a cluster dendogram, although the Treemap below is an alternative mapping technique
Networks	In Webometrics, networks are formed by Web pages connected hyperlinks between them. Various social networks are also well-researched (Freeman, 2000).
Time	Temporal information is often an aspect of other data, and represented in conjunction with it. For example, data concerning the shrinking of a glacier due to global warming would combine 3-dimensional measurements with the dates of those measurements. A visualization of this might take the form of a video of a 3-dimensional representation of the shrinking glacier.

Source: Shneiderman, 1996: 337-339

- Standard: a general-purpose visualization designed for a wide variety of similar applications or data collections. Standard visualizations are often available through free software[2].
- Bespoke: a visualization created specifically for, and tied to, one application or data collection.

RECENT HISTORY OF SOCIAL SCIENCE VISUALIZATIONS

It is useful to seek insights from where visualizations have been successfully employed in the past:

The general consensus in the scientific visualization field is that a broad commonality exists among the visual needs of all numerically intensive sciences. [...] we are keenly awaiting its applications to fields with a shorter history in numerical computing, such as econometrics and the social sciences. Will users from these fields find this environment appropriate to their needs? (Upson et al., 1989, quoted in Orford, Dorling, & Harris, 1998: 7)

As the above quote illustrates, the advent of widely available computing facilities in the 1980s raised the possibility that the use of visualizations might expand in the social sciences. A survey a decade later of visualizations in a range of social sciences found that there had been significant progress, albeit of an uneven nature (Orford, Harris, & Dorling, 1998). In geography and planning, the use of visualizations was widespread in the 1980s. With hindsight, this seems almost inevitable due to the importance of maps and spatially arranged data in geography, and two-dimensional diagrams and three-dimensional models in planning (supported by Computer Aided Design). This trend seems to have continued into the Internet age, for example the Mapping Cyberspace project[3] produced a large number of innovative, colorful and interesting visualizations of different types of data derived from the Internet (Dodge & Kitchin, 2001). Visualizations were also deployed in social statistics in the 1980s to explore large datasets, to aid filtering out unwanted parts of the data to help identify significant relationships.

In psychology visualizations were increasingly used, but this seems to be less natural and more related to the scientists involved: psychology is one of the more numerate social sciences and close to a hard science in terms of scientific culture. Perhaps psychologists had relatively easy access to computers and were eager or willing to experiment. In contrast, visualizations did not seem to have generated new applications in politics, economics and sociology, although there were impressive exceptions, such as a map illustrating visitors' routes through Duisburg Zoo in Germany (Orford et al., 1998: 30), and a network diagram of trade flows (Orford et al., 1998: 29). The field of Social Network Analysis (SNA), which grew in the 1980s, is another important exception (Freeman, 2004). SNA researchers have employed network diagrams and have also measured many aspects of network structures. SNA techniques have been applied to many different types of social data.

If the trends above identified by Orford, Harris and Dorling (1998) have continued and perhaps expanded into the era of e-science, then it would be reasonable to expect that geography, planning and possibly social statistics would continue to lead the way in the development of relatively widely-used visualizations to support core research. In contrast, psychology might experiment with a range of different state-of-the-art visualizations and the other social sciences might lag significantly behind, although with islands of excellence, perhaps starting to deploy some standard visualizations developed for other purposes. This hypothesis is probably flawed to some extent because a feature of modern research is an increasing level of interdisciplinarity (Gibbons et al., 1994), so that researchers from a range of disciplines can expect to be exposed to e-science and its many visualizations. In addition to e-science initiatives involving social scientists, there has been a social science funding program promoting the use of high performance computing for U.K. social scientists, including for the development or employment of visualizations. This has focused around the National Centre for e-Social Science (NCeSS); see Chapter 4 for further details of this initiative.

E-SOCIAL SCIENCE VISUALIZATIONS

The rise of e-social science has overseen renewed efforts to develop and promote high powered visualizations for the social sciences (Wouters & Beaulieu, 2006). The U.K. National Centre for e-Social Science (NCeSS) held a workshop in June 2006 entitled: "Geographic Visualization Across the Social Sciences: State of the Art Review",[4] which showcased 18 separate projects and suggested that, unsurprisingly, visualization is particularly well developed within geography and related fields. Nevertheless, there is no systematic survey of applications from which an overview of the success of these initiatives can be evaluated.

For the prospective user with a large dataset the easiest choice is probably to select a standard graphical representation (see Figure 9.1). For example a free software package may be obtained, learned, and used by a social science researcher. The more difficult choice is to create a new type, a bespoke visualization for the dataset. Since the creation of software for visualizations is a non-trivial computer science engineering endeavor, this would probably require the employment of a specialist programmer and, unless the project operated on a very large scale, the visualization itself or the visualization software are likely to be a significant aspect of the project. The third and fourth choices, intended for researchers without data, are to create or adopt a visual simulation of their theory to show how complex interrelated ideas could coexist or develop in practice. Note that some researchers fall between the 'data' and 'no data' options because they do not have data but are able to indirectly access others' data through interfaces that allow visualizations but not direct data access.[5]

In the following sub-sections, several cases of different types of visualization that aid social sciences research are described. No attempt is made to provide an overall analysis or typology of the use of visualizations in e-social science research. Most previous typologies have been constructed from the perspective of inherent properties of the visualizations rather than from that of the user.

The first case described below is a bespoke visualization created specifically for a given type of data. Some situations seem to be inherently too

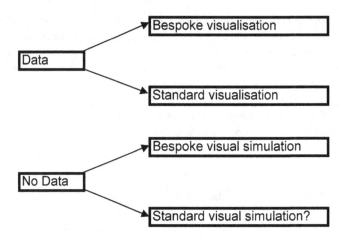

Figure 9.1   Basic visualization choices for researchers.

complex to meaningfully be represented through any standard tool, but special-purpose visualizations can ensure that patterns in the data could be illustrated and visually identified. The second case is a visual simulation designed to graphically illustrate the running of an artificial simple social environment. As the example shows, coupling a simulation to an intuitive visual display allows it to convey useful information to the researcher. The third case is of a new type of standard graphical representation, Treemap, for the representation of hierarchical structures. This illustrates how increasingly complex graphical representations may grow to partially replace those that are currently in use, such as line graphs, histograms and scatter graphs.

Case 1: Wikipedia History Flow Visualizations

IBM's History Flow project[6] provides an interesting example of (a) the use of significant computing resources to create visualizations, and (b) visualizations of a social Internet phenomenon: Wikipedia. Wikipedia (see Chapter 16 for further details on Wikipedia) is a popular collaboratively-authored free online encyclopedia. It is easy to edit pages because they contain an edit button and allow unrestricted access to the reader, which make contributions vulnerable to vandalism. The Wiki software contains many features designed to allow it to operate effectively as a collaborative authoring environment, such as the preservation of version histories for each page. Hence a vandalized page can be quickly reverted to a pre-vandalism state. In addition the page histories form a complete record of all changes and the time of the changes. These histories form the raw data for the History Flow system. The rationale for visualizing the version histories is that they can be quite extensive with hundreds of edits by many different authors for individual pages, and it is time-consuming to identify editing patterns, even for a single page.

History Flow is a software environment for collecting data about changes to a group-edited document and turning that data into a visualization that can reveal editing patterns across time. Applied to individual Wikipedia pages, it summarizes their edit histories. Comparing the visualizations for a set of pages allows editing patterns to emerge, shedding light on the social forces that make Wikipedia. Thus the end result is knowledge about social processes, making it of interest to social scientists, particularly Internet and communication researchers. An analysis of Wikipedia used History Flow visualizations to explore Wikipedia page editing histories in conjunction with tabular and textually represented data (e.g., the average time needed for malicious mass deletions to be undone) to test the hypotheses formed (Viégas, Wattenberg, & Dave, 2004).

The History Flow tool tracks and graphs the content of each page on a sentence-by-sentence level, using a simple graphical representation to allow many different sentences to be simultaneously presented over time. As shown in Figure 9.2, each sentence is represented by a colored line. The line first appears when the sentence is created and disappears when the sentence is deleted. The line angles upwards in the diagram if sentences above it have been deleted and downwards if sentences have been added above it. The total height of the flow (reading from the top of the graph) corresponds to the number of sentences in the current version. The graph should be read left-to-right. At the left of the graph are the sentences in the original version of the page and moving rightwards corresponds to progressing through the page history. An interesting feature of the graph shown is that the zig-zag pattern reflects an 'edit war' between two contributors who repeatedly added and deleted a controversial paragraph. Eventually this argument was resolved. The study showed Wikipedia to be particularly interesting as a collaborative authoring environment that benefits from conflicts being resolved: unlike some other online environments that thrive on discussion, long term arguments distract energy from the task of high quality content creation.

Case 2: Evolino Visual Simulations

Evolino[7] is a research project, with origins in both physics and sociology, to develop visual simulations of the dynamics of group interactions (Scharnhorst & Ebeling, 2005). In contrast to the other cases, Evolino produces a dynamic, evolving display. Each simulation is a computer program that incorporates a mathematical model of social interaction with variable user-defined parameters. The program then runs the simulation, displaying a visual representation of the results. Although it does not need significant computing power or use Internet data, this project is an interesting type of

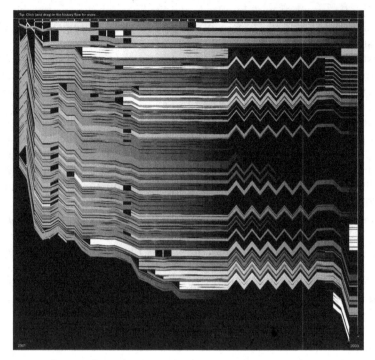

Figure 9.2   A history flow visualization of the Wikipedia chocolate page.

visualization created for research into social systems. It is also noteworthy that the project was run by sociologists and physicists who employed a computer programmer to create an engaging display.

The main Evolino simulation illustrates the process of natural selection and can be used to experiment with different selection processes. As shown in Figure 9.3, it is based upon a group of individuals existing in a 'landscape' in which the darker colors represent more desirable parts. The individuals move within the landscape by a combination of mutation, selection and imitation, with the user selecting the frequency of each of these three operations. A mutating individual moves at random to an adjacent square. For an imitation, two randomly selected individuals are compared and the one in the most densely occupied square attracts the other to move into its square. For a selection operation, two randomly selected individuals are compared, and the one on the lower-valued square moves to the other square. Notice that only the selection step involves the value of the landscape and so the speed at which the 'crowd' moves towards the better quality land partly depends upon the frequency with which the selection mechanism is used. Clearly the model is very simple but can give insights into the dynamics of the situation. For example, in the illustration below, the researcher can deduce from repeated experiments that if the selection frequency is too high and the group starts at the lower of the two peaks, then it is difficult for it to find and occupy the higher peak because the people tend not to risk the lower-lying areas and hence cannot find the more distant better place.

Case 3: Usenet Conversation Analyses with Treemap

The third case derives from Microsoft's Netscan project,[8] an initiative to monitor Usenet newsgroups and to analyze the pattern of postings and discussion. A core strategy of this project is to continually collect newsgroup postings and use Treemap diagrams (Shneiderman, 1992) to simultaneously represent the volume of postings in each newsgroup (the area of each rectangle) and the change in volume of postings (the color of the rectangle: green for increasing volume, red for decreasing volume). Since Usenet is hierarchical and organized by topic, monitoring posting volumes in this way can give useful insights into which newsgroups are hosting more active discussion (Turner, Smith, Fisher, & Welser, 2005).

The Netscan research addresses a set of social science goals, for example understanding leadership and participation profiles in group discussions.

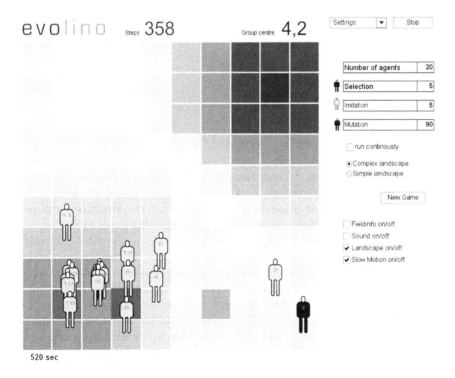

Figure 9.3 A screen-shot of an Evolino simulation.

In addition, it uses significant computing power to process large volumes of Internet data. The investigators use a range of visualizations specially designed to highlight different aspects of the data. For example network diagrams illustrate connections between posters and AuthorLine diagrams illustrate the pattern of posts and replies for individuals. Amongst the range of findings, the diagrams showed different patterns of conversation for different newsgroups: some engaged in lengthy conversations whereas others were more oriented towards questions and answers (Turner et al., 2005). The information has commercial value as well as intrinsic interest: perhaps of most importance to Microsoft are the 'answer people' who are shown to regularly allocate time to answering others' questions on technical subjects without any financial reward. If Microsoft can harness this apparently willing and free help then it may be able to cut down on its paid helpdesk employees. Answer person behavior is made visible by using a combination of visualizations (author line and network view).

Online Examples of Visualizations

The above cases only scratch the surface of the range of types of visualization that can be produced. Monographs about visualization (Chen, 2004; Spence, 2007; Tufte, 2001) and the Internet contain many additional attractive and useful visualizations of large datasets. The following are popular online galleries:

- Places & Spaces: Mapping Science,[9]
- The Atlas of Cyberspace,[10]
- Gallery of Data Visualization.[11]

FAST, FREE 'BORN DIGITAL' VISUALIZATIONS

Having examined a few diverse cases of visualizations, the focus in this section presents a different type of radical innovation: convenience. It is now possible to call upon or create powerful visualizations online with relatively little effort. In contrast, the cases above are examples of research that took years of effort to produce and consequently can only be used as part of research that is able to devote significant resources to produce visualizations. An innovation may be considered radical if it is possible for social scientists to easily create visualizations so that they can be incorporated into their research without focusing on their creation. Perhaps the most radical innovation would be if researchers could casually call upon powerful illustrations to help them form opinions and hypotheses in the initial stages of research, rather than as part of reporting the research findings. In some cases this is now possible, as the examples below illustrate.

Figure 9.4 is a graph created quickly from a large volume of data: it took 20 seconds to build using the free Web site blogpulse.com. Blog-Pulse monitors millions of individual blogs daily and uses a Google-like interface to allow visitors to search them. It also allows users to submit multiple simultaneous queries and plot the results over time in a graph, allowing the detection of trends. Figure 9.4 suggests that the discussion of visualization (for both U.K. and U.S. spellings) increased slightly in blogspace during the start of 2008. This is a traditional type of visualization, a line graph, but the massive online data source used makes it relevant to e-social science. Moreover, the ease with which it can be produced means that researchers can casually create such graphs as part of understanding recent public interest in any topic. Google Trends[12] offers a similar service for search terms: it can produce graphs showing the volume of searching for any given phrase. The advantage of this Google service is that it covers a longer time period (years rather than months) but its disadvantage is that it is not possible to get context from the searches. In contrast, the blog graphs have embedded context in terms of the original blog postings, which can be viewed by clicking on the relevant part of the graph.

TouchGraph[13] is another example of a convenient free online visualization. The TouchGraph Google Browser allows the user to enter a term or phrase of interest and then instantly produces a map (based upon Google searches) illustrating the most important sites for that term and the

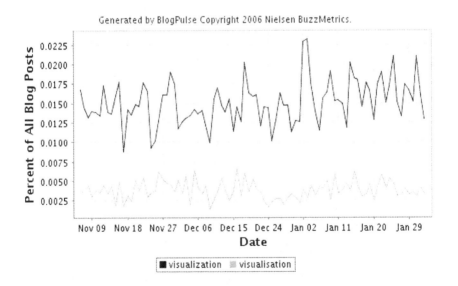

Figure 9.4   Blog posts alluding to visualization during 2007–2008.

relationship between the sites (Hine, 2007). This is a very quick way of getting an overview of the online reflection of a topic. Figure 9.5 illustrates part of a TouchGraph for the term 'cyberinfrastructure'. TouchGraph is an interactive visualization: the nodes in the graph can be clicked for more information, and it is possible to zoom in and out for differing levels of detail. TouchGraph offers a similar facility for the social network site Facebook, allowing users to create a picture of their friends and the friendships between them (see also Heer & boyd, 2005). The issue crawler software at issuecrawler.net (Rogers, 2004) produces similar kinds of diagrams to the TouchGraph Google Browser but more targeted at the social science research community. Similarly, SocSciBot[14] and LexiURL[15] offer the ability for social scientists to collect data for Web link-based network diagrams from the Web (Thelwall, 2004), but using their own or Pajek's[16] visualizations of the subsequent networks.

The above examples are powerful but restricted to particular data sources, although the data sources are enormous and very flexible in terms of the research topics for which they might be relevant. In contrast, the IBM ManyEyes project[17] is a free online environment with many visualization tools that are open to social annotation and commentary. Researchers can upload their own data and try it out in any of the visualization programs. This kind of service takes significantly longer than using TouchGraph

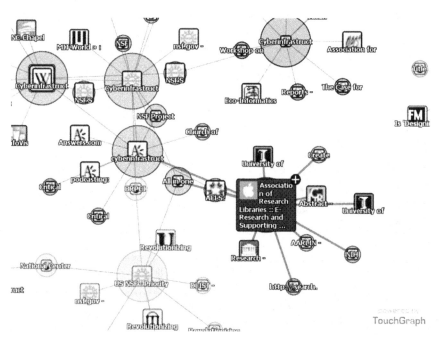

Figure 9.5   A Google TouchGraph of 'Cyberinfrastructure'.

or BlogPulse but could be very useful for researchers needing a complex visualization to help them to make sense of their data.

Mashups and Geographic Visualizations

A 'mashup' is a computer program that combines data from more than one source to deliver an integrated product online. Many of the major Web companies, including Microsoft and Google, have made some of their data available online for use in mashups. Visualizations are sometimes incorporated into these mashups. Mashups are relatively easy and fast to create, although a researcher would have to be a programmer or enlist the help of a programmer to create one. Mashup applications can also be extremely powerful because they can draw upon complex data and powerful programs.

Figure 9.6 is a Google mashup from Tobias Escher (2007) illustrating the geographic diversity of one person's MySpace friends by plotting them on a map of North America. The data used was the set of MySpace home pages of one person and his friends. These pages were scanned to extract the home town of each person, and the home town converted to geographic coordinates. In the form of just a list of town names or geographic coordinates, it would be difficult to identify patterns. The additional geographic information on the mashup map (Figure 9.7) is an effective way to illustrate the distribution of this person's online friends. This map is interactive, inheriting this property from the Google map component of the mashup. Figure 9.7 shows the same mashup and data after a few mouse clicks to zoom in on the data; it is even possible to zoom in to a street-level map. A single mouse click will convert the map into a satellite image showing the terrain of the area.

CONCLUSION

For e-social scientists, the potential for using visualizations is greater now than ever before, but it is important to select carefully the right type of visualization for any type of problem or dataset. This is particularly true because of the human labor required to create a single visualization, in terms of identifying or creating appropriate software and/or achieving enough familiarity with the software and techniques to produce meaningful results. The main advice is simple: look at a range of different types of visualization to get ideas about what is possible, and then engage in dialog with an information visualization expert to arrive at a final decision about the best type to choose and the best strategy to adopt in order to create it. As discussed above, one of the key choices is whether to adopt a standard visualization or to create a bespoke type. In addition, for researchers in fields such as geography and social network analysis, familiarity is needed with field-specific standard practice for the creation and use of visualizations, including any widely used software.

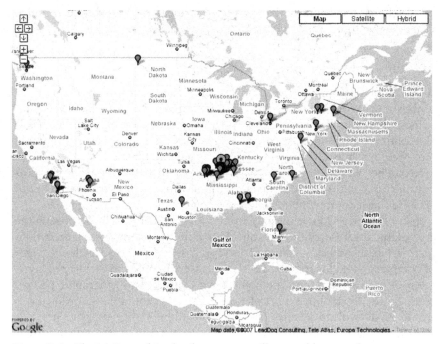

Figure 9.6   The MySpace friends of one person, illustrated by a mashup.

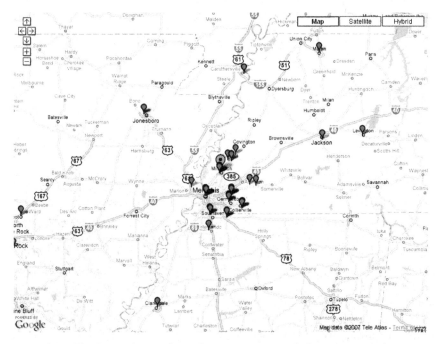

Figure 9.7   The Figure 9.6 mashup after zooming in with four mouse clicks.

The cases above illustrate different ways in which large quantities of data can be tied together with significant computing resources to produce informative visualizations that may be used to illustrate interesting social phenomena. All of the cases appear to be driven by technologists in the sense that the driving force behind each one appears to be the creation of the visualization software by people who are not primarily social scientists, for example computer scientists or physicists. Nevertheless, such people are engaging with social science problems and are able to support social science research goals without a theoretical base in the social sciences.

The ease with which powerful visualizations can be accessed or created is a radical development. If the ability to find relevant visualizations online and use them as a part of the research process becomes part of the armory of many social scientists, then this will increase their research ability. Currently, it seems that the most relevant areas are data with a key geographic component (especially for mashups) and data about public perceptions and public interest in topics.

Since visualizations, including graphs and network diagrams, have been in use for a long time, what kind of evolutions are likely to be seen as e-social science evolves? The following list of developments seem likely outcomes of the increased availability of computing power and network bandwidth, although it is more difficult to speculate about the affects of social shaping (MacKenzie & Wajcman, 1985).

- More complex visualizations—because richer graphics are possible with more computing power (Schirski et al., 2003);
- Quicker production, perhaps leading to more visualizations being used;
- More distributed—because the digital resources can be stored online and ever larger visualizations can be transferred, given increasing bandwidth (Brodlie, Duce, Gallop, Walton, & Wood, 2004);
- More permanence—due to systematic and ad-hoc digital archiving (Hodge, 2000);
- New applications and types of visualizations—e.g., 'opportunist' use of visualizations created for science or industry to be adapted for social science research (Thelwall, 2007);
- More data (Hey & Trefethen, 2003)—for example, Internet data recording Internet users, such as blog postings, and hyperlinks

In the future it seems likely that the ubiquity of computing power will lead to increasing use of powerful visualizations, perhaps giving new insights into complex multi-dimensional social phenomena, such as those primarily investigated through qualitative methods. Parallel to this, however, the Internet is likely to continuously produce ever-increasing quantities of data, challenging social scientists to effectively analyze it to understand the social uses of new technology.

FUTURE RESEARCH AGENDA

In terms of a research agenda for those interested in the phenomenon of visualization rather than using it to support a research goal, at the moment it is not clear how far visualizations have been adopted and what the main obstacles are to their adoption. Obstacles to the adoption of visualizations may be difficult to research because the human behavior element is varied and difficult to generalize but some Computer-Human Interaction research has already tackled relevant issues (e.g., González & Kobsa, 2003). A third important research agenda is more reflexive: to evaluate the effectiveness of visualizations where they are used. The following three broad research agendas form a starting point for future research.

The first broad area is to evaluate the spread of visualizations in e-science. This could be assessed in terms of its overall use throughout the social sciences, in terms of its assimilation into new specialist fields (e.g., Author Co-citation Analysis within bibliometrics) or in terms of the development of new multidisciplinary e-social science fields based around IV or incorporating a significant component of IV (e.g., Knowledge Domain Visualization (KDViz); Geographic information systems). In addition, it would be useful to assess the upgrading of Information Visualization (IV) techniques in existing fields (i.e., the replacement of existing techniques with more sophisticated ones, as has happened in geography) and the impact of individual initiatives, such as the Information Visualization Cyberinfrastrucure project.

A second broad direction for future research is to identify, assess and develop strategies to ameliorate obstacles to the use of visualizations within the social sciences, perhaps drawing a theoretical framework from more general research into the adoption of computing within the social sciences. The following seem to be particularly relevant issues for this: lack of use within a field increasing the opportunity cost of adopting visualizations (e.g., lack of software, lack of acceptance, lack of knowledge about what is possible); the Not Invented Here syndrome creating a barrier to the adoption of standard solutions (Katz & Allen, 1982); and lack of transparency about how visualizations 'work' (e.g., lack of transparency about key aspects of visualizations, perhaps because they use complex algorithms, leading to mistrust).

Finally, it would be useful to evaluate e-social science visualizations through a cost-benefit analysis. This could perhaps be achieved through independent, individual case studies, leading to meta-evaluations and general findings across the social sciences.

ACKNOWLEDGMENTS

Warm thanks to Nick Jankowski, Marc Smith and Eric Gleave for helpful comments on earlier drafts.

NOTES

1. http://www.visual-literacy.org/periodic_table/periodic_table.html
2. For instance, the InfoViz Toolkit (http://ivtk.sourceforge.net) is a general-purpose tool for creating visualizations, Pajek is a well-used program for creating network diagrams (http://vlado.fmf.uni-lj.si/pub/networks/pajek/) and Treemap (http://treemap.sourceforge.net) is also available.
3. http://www.mappingcyberspace.com
4. http://www.ncess.ac.uk/events/ASW/visualisation/
5. An example of this is Blogpulse.com, which can draw time series graphs of word frequencies in blogs (e.g., how many blogs contain the word 'Bush' every day for six months), but BlogPulse will not normally deliver the raw data wholesale to the researchers (Thelwall, 2007).
6. http://www.research.ibm.com/visual/projects/history_flow/
7. http://www.virtualknowledgestudio.nl/projects/evolino/
8. http://netscan.research.microsoft.com, see Chapter 10 for illustrations and more information.
9. http://www.scimaps.org
10. http://cybergeography.planetmirror.com
11. http://www.math.yorku.ca/SCS/Gallery/
12. http://www.google.com/trends
13. http://touchgraph.com
14. http://socscibot.wlv.ac.uk
15. http://lexiurl.wlv.ac.uk
16. http://vlado.fmf.uni-lj.si/pub/networks/pajek/
17. http://services.alphaworks.ibm.com/ManyEyes/

REFERENCES

Bertin, J. (1983). *Semiotics of graphics*. Wisconsin: University of Wisconsin Press.

Borner, K., Chen, C. M., & Boyack, K. W. (2003). Visualizing knowledge domains. *Annual Review of Information Science and Technology, 37*, 179–255.

Brodlie, K. W., Duce, D. A., Gallop, J. R., Walton, J. P. R. B., & Wood, J. D. (2004). Distributed and collaborative visualization. *Computer Graphics Forum, 23*(2), 223–251.

Chen, C. (2004). *Information visualization: Beyond the horizon, 2nd ed.* New York: Springer.

Dodge, M., & Kitchin, D. R. (2001). *Mapping cyberspace*. London: Routledge.

Earnshaw, R. A., & Wiseman, N. (Eds.). (1992). *An introductory guide to scientific visualization*. Berlin: Springer-Verlag.

Escher, T. (2007). The geography of (online) social networks. *Web 2.0, York University*, Retrieved September 18, 2007 from: http://people.oii.ox.ac.uk/escher/wp-content/uploads/2007/2009/Escher_York_presentation.pdf.

Freeman, L. C. (2000). Visualizing social networks. *Journal of Social Structure* (1), Retrieved June 21, 2007 from: http://www.cmu.edu/joss/content/articles/volume2001/Freeman.html

Freeman, L. C. (2004). The development of social network analysis: A study in the sociology of science. Vancouver, Canada: Booksurge Publishing.

Gibbons, M., Limoges, C., Nowotny, H., Schwartzman, S., Scott, P., & Trow, M. (1994). *The new production of knowledge*. London, UK: Sage.

González, V. and Kobsa, A. (2003). A workplace study of the adoption of Information Visualization systems. Proceedings of I-KNOW'03: 3rd International Conference on Knowledge Management, Graz, Austria, 92–102.

Heer, J., & boyd, d. (2005). Vizster: Visualizing online social networks. In *Information visualization 2005*, pp. 32–39. New York: IEEE.

Hey, A., & Trefethen, A. (2003). The data deluge: An e-science perspective. In F. Berman, G. C. Fox & A. Hey (Eds.), *Grid computing: Making the global infrastructure a reality*, pp. 809–824. Chichester: John Wiley.

Hine, C. (2007). Connective ethnography for the exploration of e-science. *Journal of Computer-Mediated Communication, 12*(2), Retrieved February 1, 2008 from: http://jcmc.indiana.edu/vol2012/issue2002/hine.html

Hodge, G. M. (2000). Best practices for digital archiving: An information life cycle approach. *D-Lib Magazine, 6*(1), Retrieved July 21, 2007 from: http://www.dlib.org/dlib/january2000/2001hodge.html

Katz, R., & Allen, T. J. (1982). Investigating the Not Invented Here (NIH) syndrome: A look at the performance, tenure and communication patterns of 50 R&D project groups. *R&D Management, 12*(1), 7–19.

MacKenzie, D., & Wajcman, J. (Eds.). (1985). *The social shaping of technology: How the refrigerator got its hum*. Philadelphia, PA: Open University Press.

Orford, S., Dorling, D., & Harris, R. (1998). Review of visualization in the social sciences: Overview report. Retrieved May 10, 2007 from: http://www.agocg.ac.uk/train/review/review.pdf.

Orford, S., Harris, R., & Dorling, D. (1999). Information visualization in the social sciences-A state-of-the-art review. *Social Science Computer Review, 17*, 289–304.

Rogers, R. (2004). *Information politics on the Web*. Massachusetts: MIT Press.

Scharnhorst, A., & Ebeling, W. (2005). Evolutionary search agents in complex landscapes. A new model for the role of competence and meta-competence (EVOLINO and other simulation tools). *arXiv.org*, Retrieved February 6, 2007 from: http://www.virtualknowledgestudio.nl/staff/andrea-scharnhorst/documents/arxiv_final.pdf.

Schirski, M., Gerndt, A., Reimersdahl, T. v., Kuhlen, T., Adomeit, P., Lang, O., et al. (2003). ViSTA FlowLib—framework for interactive visualization and exploration of unsteady flows in virtual environments. *Proceedings of the workshop on Virtual environments 2003*, 77–85.

Shneiderman, B. (1992). Tree visualization with tree-maps: 2-d space-filling approach. *ACM Transactions on Graphics, 11*(1), 92–99.

Shneiderman, B. (1996). The eyes have it: A task by data type taxonomy for information visualizations. *Proceedings of IEEE Visual Languages*, 336–343.

Spence, R. (2007). *Information visualization* (2nd ed.). Harlow, Essex: Pearson Education Ltd.

Taylor, J. (2002). Call for proposals: Establishment of e-Science Core Programme Centres of Excellence. *Research Councils UK*, Retrieved January 31, 2008 from: http://www.rcuk.ac.uk/escience/calls/callexcell.htm.

Thelwall, M. (2004). *Link analysis: An information science approach*. San Diego: Academic Press.

Thelwall, M. (2007). Blog searching: The first general-purpose source of retrospective public opinion in the social sciences? *Online Information Review, 31*(3), 277–289.

Tufte, E. (2001). *The visual display of quantitative information, 2nd Ed*. Cheshire, Connecticut: Graphics Press.

Turner, T. C., Smith, M. A., Fisher, D., & Welser, H. T. (2005). Picturing Usenet: Mapping computer-mediated collective action. *Journal of Computer-Mediated Communication, 10*(4), Retrieved February 6, 2007 from: http://jcmc.indiana.edu/vol2010/issue2004/turner.html

Upson, C., Faulhaber, T., Kamins, D., Laidlaw, D., Schlegel, D., Vroom, J., et al. (1989). The application visualization system; a computational environment for scientific visualization. *IEEE Computer Graphics and Applications, 9*(4), 30–42.

Viégas, F. B., Wattenberg, M., & Dave, K. (2004). Studying cooperation and conflict between authors with history flow visualizations. In *Proceedings of the SIGCHI conference on human factors in computing systems,* pp. 575–582. New York: ACM.

Wasserman, S., & Faust, K. (1994). *Social network analysis: Methods and applications.* Cambridge, NY: Cambridge University Press.

Wouters, P., & Beaulieu, A. (2006). Imagining e-science beyond computation. In C. Hine (Ed.), *New infrastructures for knowledge production,* pp. 48–70.

Zhu, B., & Chen, H. (2005). Information Visualization. *Annual Review of Information Science and Technology, 39,* 139–177.

10 A Picture is Worth a Thousand Questions

Visualization Techniques for Social Science Discovery in Computational Spaces

Howard T. Welser, Thomas M. Lento, Marc A. Smith, Eric Gleave, and Itai Himelboim

INTRODUCTION

Visualization has frequently been used in the sciences to illustrate findings of quantitative analysis or succinctly summarize those findings to non-technical audiences. In this chapter, we focus on the use of visualization to reveal new relationships, develop hypotheses, refine classification systems, or otherwise discover new insights about the online social world. We advocate the use of visualization primarily as a strategy of discovery and exploration. To this end, we have developed systems for the graphical exploration of datasets and have drawn on existing tools that enable the mass production of visualizations for comparing patterns across wide ranges of cases and contexts. This approach has often led us to seek other types and sources of data or to generate and adapt additional types of visualizations. The result is a varied toolbox for visualizing dimensions of online social worlds, leading to a faceted set of interlinked images, each capturing a different dimension of the authors, conversation threads, and discussion spaces we have studied.

Social life increasingly takes place through computer mediated interaction systems, and these systems are growing in terms of diversity of affordances for action (Gaver, 1991). It is now commonplace for many people to use tools like email, newsgroups, discussion boards, web forums, blog comments, wiki talk pages, instant message conversations, short message services (SMS), Social Networking Services, and several other mechanisms for moving messages. These systems allow the exchange of a rich collection of digital objects. When people gather and interact in computer-mediated spaces, they often leave behind traces that can be processed so that patterns of association and individual patterns of difference become visible. These patterns tell a story about an ecosystem and its inhabitants, a story about variation and the emergence of stable types of social spaces and the roles participants play within them. Because they can summarize large amounts of data and be rapidly compared, images are especially appropriate for the many dimensions we find in online social worlds. Throughout the chapter, we consider how the affordances of computer-mediated interaction affect the behavior recorded in those settings and reveal insights across a range of social contexts.

We review a number of visualization strategies and advocate investigating social media spaces at various scales and levels of detail. We hope to illustrate several aspects of the use of information visualization for exploration and analysis of social media, in particular *faceted exploration* at *multiple scales*. By faceted, we mean that there is a need for integration of multiple visualizations that cut across different dimensions of interaction in the social media space. The term multiple scales refers to the many levels of analysis embedded in online systems. An example of this approach is the 'Community Views' tool kit, which integrates multiple information visualizations and populates them with data produced by a stream of multiple years of Usenet message traffic (Smith & Fiore, 2001). We further describe a series of descriptive tasks that can be applied to any source of online data and which draw from freely available stand-alone visualization packages and standard database and statistical packages.

ATTRIBUTES & ANALYSIS OF COMPUTER-MEDIATED SOCIAL WORLDS

The explosion of social media services marks a shift towards increasingly rich self documenting social systems. Alternatively referred to as the 'read/write' web, these systems build on online tools while adding critical abilities that broaden the population able to use them and further expand the ways and media in which people interact. Each form of social media system broadly enables people to create and share digital objects. Most social media systems share a set of features that support common data structures like threaded conversations and file collections. Social media systems differ in the ways they integrate additional data structures or enable the sharing of new classes of digital objects. For example, while threaded message conversations are a basic affordance of most social media systems, more advanced systems integrate threaded data structures with an access control system based on social network data, allowing messages to be selectively viewed by a list of 'friends' instead of a public group.

For researchers, the defining challenges of research into the social structures of Web 2.0 systems result from the complexity of the social space in terms of relationships, contexts, and temporal flow. In the following, we discuss several key types of online spaces where researchers are analyzing behaviour, contrasting the limited affordances of the Usenet with more contemporary systems. We consider the relationship between affordances for interaction and the dynamics of social action that results from their collective use. In the next section, we categorize several major types of online spaces, including systems for threaded discussion, distributed collaboration, social networking, and virtual worlds; these are reflected in Table 10.1.

Attributes of Online Social Systems

Interface

Interfaces for accessing online spaces increasingly include a wide range of media (text, images, sound) and provide rich details about social networks and the history of interactions. In contrast, early newsgroup reading software lacked records of social context beyond a collection of conversation threads. Subsequent threaded discussion systems embed threads in a larger, enduring context which makes the history of interaction on the site more directly accessible to users, where it can be of significant relevance to social actions like selecting content and choosing to initiate message threads or reply to existing messages. Many contemporary online communities (collaborative systems and social networks) are accessible through commonly available web browsers and integrate threaded interaction with other activities and data found on the World Wide Web. These can include either public pages (like Wikipedia), or member only access pages (like fatsecret). Other types of social media systems introduce proprietary interfaces that can include both specialized client software (i.e., World of Warcraft, Second Life) and hardware restrictions (the Xbox Live computer-mediated interaction system requires the Xbox 360 console). The nature of the interface affects patterns of participation and retention, especially in the presence of competing systems.

Boundaries

Online social spaces give rise to boundaries that shape the structure of interaction and allow subpopulations to develop distinctive norms and practices. Many computer-mediated interaction systems enable the creation of collections of digital objects. In Usenet, newsgroups act as collections around sets of threaded discussions. Each collection marks the boundary of a social population, each of which attempts to define a set of topics and standards of interaction to attract and socialize others to the goals of the participants. The Usenet is composed of newsgroups focused on a range of topics and interests and interconnected with other newsgroups through shared messages. Other systems, like the Slashdot web community, provide a fixed set of general topical classifications.

People and groups have preferences for topics and standards of behavior. Given preference variation, collisions and conflicts are common. The types of boundaries enabled by newer services are even more fine-grained, allowing content to be shared with collections of selected others rather than being made public. Collaborative document editing systems like Wikipedia provide a range of page types with specialized functions: articles, discussion pages, community, and infrastructure pages are clearly distinguished. Within each of these categories are different content areas. Wikipedia participants are themselves clustered into classes based on common behaviors and structural connections. Some participants, for example, might specialize by topic or activity; contributing content on just a narrow set of topics or posting content across topics but in a narrow set of sections (for example, only adjusting the technical formatting of the document). The multiple types of boundaries suggest that a major goal for research into the structure of online spaces is to explore the relationship between boundary types and the structure of social relationships that emerge within them.

Threads

A thread is any structured collection of digital objects that refer to one another in a hierarchy. A thread is created when one object can have one or more 'replies' that themselves may have objects linked to them in reply. Often, these objects are composed of textual messages, but they could be composed of a combination of video, audio, or other digital media. Affordances for threaded conversation systems vary widely. Some, like email lists or Usenet newsgroups, organize threaded content within particular named groups, while web based systems like Slashdot use search and tagging mechanisms to create more dynamic (and short-lived) collections of threaded messages. Further, reputation systems, like the Slashdot Karma social rating system, allow sophisticated systems to filter and group content more flexibly. An important methodological challenge for researchers is to establish general guidelines for how thread length, substantive and temporal proximity of messages, thread structure, and modifications like filtering thresholds shape the thread as a record of social interaction.

Network of relationships

A social network is the pattern of relationships in a population (see Nadel, 1964; Freeman, 2000; Scott, 2000). Those relationships can be defined both from directed actions like sending messages or through joint membership, like when people are part of the same group or participate in the same event. Some systems allow people to explicitly name friends or foes (see Slashdot), while in all systems a variety of implicit network structures can be inferred from interaction records. Network data are used both to visualize local and global social structures and to calculate local and global structural metrics like the centrality of a particular actor or the density of relationships.

History of participation

All users of online spaces develop reputational signals from their history of participation. Systems vary in terms of the range of available behaviors

Table 10.1　Dimensions of Social Spaces that Alter Social Action

	Threaded discussion		Distributed collaborative system	Social Networking	Virtual World
	Usenet	Slashdot	Wikipedia	Wallop	Halo3 Live
Boundaries	Newsgroups	Subject areas	Articles, projects	Affiliation and interaction	Types of missions
Threads	Message Threads	Comment threads	Article talk pages, subsection headings.	Blog entry, responses to entries	Missions
Implicit social networks	Reply structure, co-participation	Comment structure	Multi-context; Comment structure, co-participation	Comment, invites, gifts, etc.	Co-participation,
Explicit social networks	NA	Friends and foes list	Informal on user-pages	Formal, interface visualization	Friends for shared missions
Implicit history of participation	Messages	Messages, submissions	Contributions and messages	Record blogs, comments, uploads,	Co-presence, shared missions, actions
Explicit history	NA (sig files, links off system)	Karma, ID number, connections to others	User contribution record, awards, admin status	Archive of content, start date, connections to others	Skill level, achievement insignias, scores
Identity representation	Email, name, (off system, Netscan)	Name, user-page	Login name, signature, Personal user page	Name, current blog, recent activity, social network	Name, Avatar
Dimensions of data	Text, urls	Text, links, tags	Text, images, sound files	Text, images, links, video, sound	Live actions, voice, web cam

and how records are made salient to other users. A history of participation includes the content, amount, timing and distribution of messages, files, and other communications in the system. Analysis of such histories are leveraged by participants and researchers to characterize contributors to the online space.

Representation of identity

While email based conversations provide limited affordances for representing the identity of the participant, Web 2.0 has revealed increasing dimensions for expressive presentation of self. These can range from distinctive names, signature files, avatars, and personal pages, which can include tags, biographical statements, affiliations, journals, images and other files uploaded or linked to the personal pages.

Dimensions of data contributed

Depending on the purpose of the community, Web 2.0 is providing increasing types of data that can be contributed to the system, both in terms of self presentation and in terms of contribution to the interactive process. While YouTube supports video and Flickr is primarily dedicated to sharing and tagging images, systems like MySpace, FaceBook and Wikipedia are more general purpose, affording display of many types of files.

Analysis: General Considerations

A systemic study of computer-mediated social interaction spaces must consider the dimensions of behavior they contain. Typically, behavioral variables measured as counts, like number of comments or relationships, for instance, show strongly skewed distributions. Correspondingly, wherever appropriate, these measures should be considered in terms of rates of activity, or be standardized or displayed on a log scale. Another consideration is that the boundaries of social action may or may not correspond to boundaries within the online space and may often spread across multiple spaces (Baym, 2007). Once those boundaries of that population can be described, exploratory researchers will want to document the range of typical behaviors and of social roles in those settings. Systematic differences in how participants contribute can be conceptualized as social roles (Welser, Smith, Gleave, Fisher, 2007) and mapping the distribution of these social roles across community boundaries will suggest the appropriate theoretical framework for modeling the social action that occurs within them (Monge & Contractor, 2003). Visualization methods can contribute to all stages of this analysis process, but perhaps are best used to describe the contours of the social system in a way that facilitates comparison across different computer-mediated social spaces.

The many affordances for interaction in online social spaces make data collection and interpretation challenging. However, that complexity also offers a novel opportunity: developing measures of relationships, roles and behaviours that reflect the nuanced variety of social interaction. Consider the general challenge of measuring relationship from records of contributions on online social spaces. Many systems have threaded discussion spaces, and often reply structure is explicitly encoded, where each message is a reply to an earlier post. Such reply structures can imply the presence of a relationship between sender and recipient, and is generally a good indication of such a tie. Other systems allow for interaction that is less direct. For instance, in Wikipedia talk pages, the message recording system does not automatically indicate a recipient. Messages or 'edits' are simply posted under a given topic, even when the author has a specific recipient in mind. The target of these comments must be inferred from indirect information like context, position, timing, and content. Even more nebulous ties can be inferred from co-membership, either in groups, or as relatively concurrent action in some context (e.g., editing of articles in Wikipedia, tagging of photos in Flickr). On the other hand, other systems generate ties in more explicit and visible ways, like in Facebook or Slashdot through the act of naming friends. There are two measurement challenges here. First, what temporal and behavioural bounds should we place on the definition of tie in a given study? Second, and more conceptually, which modes of interaction represent meaningful social relationships within the focal population? The second difficulty stems from the presence of multiple contexts and methods for interaction in these social spaces, the answer to which will depend on efforts to combine different measures and relate them to meaningful social actions, like social influence (Backstrom, Huttenlocher, Klienberg, & Lan, 2006) and the presence of pre-existing relationships (Lento, Welser, Gu, & Smith, 2006). As researchers leverage the nuance and diversity of relationship data from online settings the resulting network measures have the potential to reflect the true complexity of social life, an encouraging prospect.

Finally, we remark that all people have histories, and online spaces provide different levels of access to those histories. An important way that social contexts differ is in the affordances for recording these histories and how they are made available. As social spaces make available more details about actors' prior participation, researchers and participants are increasingly in position to leverage that information. To the extent that the information shapes participants' actions researchers will need to model it's availability in their analysis.

Agenda for Visualization in Social Scientific Discovery

Purposes of applying information visualization to social media

Social media are a rich *potential* source of information about users, their behaviour, and their relationships. However, a simple list of 100 million edits to Wikipedia is not inherently meaningful. Visualization plays a key step in a larger process of identifying meaningful dimensions of interaction, aggregating actions, and visualizing distributions and relationships in the population. Researchers can use this information to understand the social dynamics of these computer-mediated interaction spaces and develop hypotheses for further investigation. The descriptive and exploratory findings are relevant to site owners and hosts of these social spaces as they seek to monitor their investments in community infrastructure and services.

Social media are both a rich and challenging source of data. User activity is recorded in detail, but at a microscopic level: [user_id, thread_id, time stamp]. These detailed records must be scrubbed and then assembled into larger units and variables, like edits per month for a given user. Given the number and fine grained detail of logged events, processing aggregations and making descriptions is a critical methodological and theoretical task (see Welser, Smith, Gleave, & Fisher, 2008). As systems become more sophisticated, they offer a growing range of modes of interaction which contribute more event details, and more complexity to the data management stage.

Even relatively simple computer-mediated interaction services like blogs can generate complex data. A typical blogging service allows users to create a collection of messages that appear in reverse chronological order on a web page. A blog post might contain textual content or a link to outside sources of information, like other web pages, blogs or bloggers. Blog users can set up 'trackbacks', mechanisms that log when other users link to their content. Many blogging services also store profile information about each blogger. These events unfold over time, adding an additional layer of complexity.

Within such a data space, multidimensional visualizations are an effective means of presenting this complexity in an intelligible way. With effort, these illustrate changes over time, differences and similarities among participants, and common population patterns. Choosing the appropriate visualization can highlight particular features that might otherwise be obscured, while inappropriate visualizations might obscure the data or lead to incorrect conclusions.

Challenges of applying information visualization to social media

Effective visualization of any complex data is fraught with challenges, and social media is no different. Examining trends in aggregate data is straightforward when there are only a few variables. Researchers must distil multiple dimensions of social media data into the constraints of the handful of attributes that can be meaningfully represented in two or three dimensions. Social media data have a high number of dimensions; a complete dataset might include dozens of distinct measurements for a number of entities at various scales. Usefully rendering these in a chart or graph relies on several common strategies for illustrating relationships on a Cartesian plane or space.

Making use of color, shape, size, and orientation to map different data dimensions expands the density of data captured in a single class of image. For example, in a typical bar chart, the rate of content contribution of a set of users over time might be shown in terms of the height of the bars, while the orientation—typically the positioning of the bars along the x-axis—indicates the time period in which the contributions took place. To embed additional information, selective use of color can indicate different group affiliations, allowing the viewer to compare contribution over time across a variety of groups. The shape or shading of the bars might also vary depending on particular attributes of the contributors or their contributions. The thickness of the bars might represent another variable, such as the average number of connections the contributors have within the system. Although such approaches can present a lot of information in a single visualization, eventually images can become too complex or violate rules of visual perception that obscure information rather than contribute to revealing its real character (Tufte, 1995, 1997). Further considerations are discussed later in the chapter.

Solutions and approaches to effective information visualization

Information visualization is a topic of deep complexity (Tufte, 1995; Donath, 1999; Freeman, 2000). Our intent is mainly to describe the effective use of the basic application of information visualization techniques to the study of social media rather than provide a guide to advanced topics. We start by identifying the basic data structures present in the social media spaces we are exploring. Some cases call for more than one representation of a data structure. We have found that hierarchies, networks, and time series are dominant data structures. We sought to find representations of the structures that facilitate comparison and discovery of important features. Given the multidimensional quality of these datasets, we recognized the need to integrate multiple views to create a faceted composite image. No one image or view will be sufficient in the face of this complexity. One solution is for researchers to explore ways to thoughtfully juxtapose types of images or otherwise allow viewers to connect measures from multiple levels. Online journals or journals that allow for extensive online appendices have the flexibility to allow full use of visualization.

Even frequently used visualizations, like network graphs, may require adaptation to better convey the multidimensionality of online data. As networks grow larger interpretation quickly becomes swamped by overlay and crowding. A recent critique of network visualizations noted that basic tasks like following the links between any two nodes is often impossible (Shneiderman & Aris, 2006). Promising recent work suggests new approaches to network visualization that combine network with other nodal data to create more informative images (Brandes, Raab, & Wagner, 2001; Shneiderman & Aris, 2006). Semantic Substrates (Shneiderman & Aris, 2006) is a method to project network visualizations into meaningful spatial containers. While most networks are drawn hanging in an empty space, the semantic substrates approach plots networks onto other maps that cluster nodes in meaningful ways. An example is an airline route network map where nodes are plotted onto their geographic locations. A semantic substrate could be a non-geographic map like a treemap that clusters nodes by attributes other that their connections to other nodes (Shneiderman, 2004).

VISUALIZATIONS FOR DISCOVERY

Online communities record many details about the content, context, and dimensions of their participants. We advocate analysis that starts with structural data and leads to the content associated with notable structures.

Mapping Boundaries and Hierarchies: Treemaps and Graphs

Visualization can help reveal boundaries between parts of communities as well as distributions of types of activities within communities. Those boundaries can reflect both institutionally imposed structures and the emergent results of participants' interactions and relationships. It is important to consider how boundaries arise in each online context. Here we consider two contrasting examples suggestive of a range of boundary formation processes.

Figure 10.1 depicts a treemap (Shneiderman, 2004; Smith & Fiore, 2001) of posts to Usenet newsgroups under the Microsoft.public hierarchy [Microsoft.public.excel, . . . excel.programming, etc.] for 2001 (see Turner,Smith, Fisher, & Welser, 2005). Tree maps can be used to explore any hierarchical data where the proportion of cases within each nested set is of interest. Here the area of each box is proportional to messages posted within that newsgroup, while change in message volume is indicated with shade, where darker indicates greater change (color figures are available on the Web site that accompanies this book).

Because people participate in news groups through subscription, the newsgroup name reflects both a market for interest in a topic and a population of readers and discussants. While these divisions shape the boundaries of interaction, they do not strictly determine them. Individuals can cross these boundaries by consuming content from multiple collections or even directing messages to multiple collections. Treemaps like Figure 10.1 reveal the general degree of segmentation in this online social system. Further analysis of cross posting patterns, co-membership and network analysis would refine our understanding of community structure in this system.

Treemaps like these can be applied to other content-oriented sites like Slashdot, Wikipedia, and most topic specific web forums. Here we shift our focus to mapping nested invitation relationships in the social network and blogging site Wallop. Figure 10.2 displays invitation relationships both as a hierarchy and as a graph.

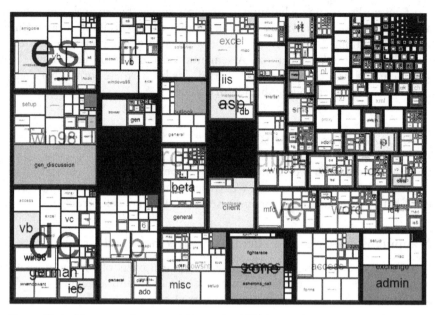

Figure 10.1 Treemap of posts to Microsoft public hierarchy, circa 2001.

In our previous studies of Wallop, we described the rise of different language communities and the contrasts between them (Gu, Johns, Lento, & Smith, 2006; Lento et al., 2006). Entry to Wallop was by invitation only, and thus invitation diffusion highlights the development of community. Here, the Chinese language users quickly grew to become the dominant population in terms of size and activity. Figure 10.3 shows the diffusion of invitations across the English and Chinese language communities. These images illustrate the role of the first gateway invitation, the user identified as 528111 from whom all Chinese language using users trace their descent.

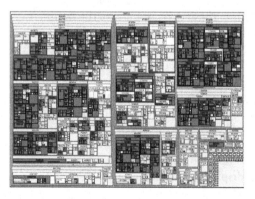 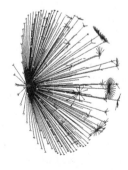

Figure 10.2 Treemap and hyperbolic graph of invitation and language group.

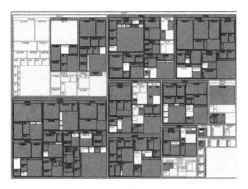 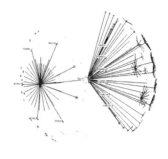

Figure 10.3   Detail tree map of 528111's descendents and Highlight of 528111's lineage.

Each box in the treemap represents a user invited to the Wallop system. The shade of each box indicates that user's most used language. Dark grey boxes indicate that the user made predominant use of the Chinese language character set, light grey boxes indicate users whose messages mostly contain English language characters, and white boxes indicate ambiguous users. Users are depicted as boxes containing smaller boxes representing those who have accepted that User's invitations. As each user joins, they can invite other users, thus, subsequent generations of invited users are nested within the boxes that represent their invitation 'parent'. Both tree maps show that, in compliance with the principle of social homophily, users tended to invite others who were similar in terms of language group. However, this tendency was far from uniform. There are several instances where the invitations were passed from Chinese user to English user and back again.

The hyperbolic network graph is an effective method for exploring a large network that highlights adjacent nodes while downplaying distant ones (Schaffer et al., 1996). This tool is useful for exploration and provides a helpful addition to classic network visualization software like Pajek (De Nooy, Mrvar, Baragelj & Granovetter, 2005). We found that, like the patterns noted in invitation practices, comment interaction in Wallop had occasional language group crossings, but was generally marked by preference to reply to others in the same language (Lento et al., 2006). The absence of sharper segregation of invitation (and interaction) is surprising and may relate to the affordances of the particular space. Wallop allowed users to share images, sound, files, and make a variety of interactions that were not limited to text. The ability of images and audio (at least music) to cross language barriers may contribute to the heterogeneous patterns we observed.

These types of visualizations can provide important stepping stones in research, encouraging the development of further exploration and tests of insights gained through them. The insight that the invitation tree contains more deviations from homophily than one might expect is actually borne out in records of interaction structure (see Lento et al., 2006, Figure 5) which shows comment structure to be integrated into a single core with only a partial tendency towards homophily. An interesting research direction would be to test the notion that numerous affordances for non-text interaction seems to increase cross language interaction compared to otherwise similar social networking systems.

Comparing Patterns of Behaviour across Different Boundaries

To contrast different computer-mediated social interaction spaces requires the creation of a set of common measurements of general attributes. We created measures that enable the comparisons of basic dimensions of individual and population activity in order to characterize differences in types of groups and the people that interact within them.

The scatter plots in Figure 10.4 show the relationship between overall levels of activity (total posts, x-axis) and the size of the community (number of repliers, y-axis) across several different types of newsgroups. Newsgroup classification was based on the name of the newsgroup. For example, newsgroups whose names contained the term "politics" were grouped together. These plots illustrate the power simple metrics can have in distinguishing between different patterns of activity. These images quickly highlight deviations from typical relationships and can indicate classification errors. Consider the highlighted outlier among the computer newsgroups. Similar ratios of posts to repliers in this newsgroup only appear among binary trading groups. In fact, this is a file trading newsgroup masquerading among newsgroups named for discussions of computing topics.

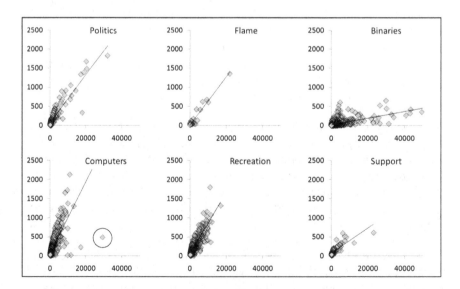

Figure 10.4   Community size compared to number of posts across classes of discussion groups.

Simple scatter plots like these were made using widely available tools like Excel. More customized information visualizations were implemented using the Community Views suite from Microsoft Research. This application reads XML files containing data related to threaded message system participants' behaviors and relationships. The tool facilitates the creation of large batches of related images, enabling the "small multiples" technique (Tufte, 1995).

Figure 10.5 is a set of 'crowd views' generated from data from a range of Usenet newsgroups. The crowd view is a scatter plot with a few additional attributes mapped to the color and size of each glyph. Each crowd view displays a glyph for each author in a newsgroup or other collection of threaded message conversations. The x-axis represents the average number of messages contributed to each thread in which an author participated. The y-axis is the number of days on which an author posted at least one message to the group. The diameter of the glyph is proportional to the author's total contribution in Usenet.

Shade indicates how recently the author was active, the darker the circle, the closer to the end of the dataset the author posted a message. These attributes, when viewed for a given newsgroup or other collection, can

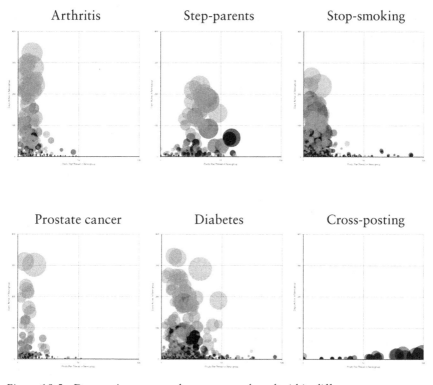

Figure 10.5   Days active compared to posts per thread within different support newsgroups.

tell us about the sorts of conversations that take place in that space. For instance, as the main plume of long-term contributors moves to the right, we generally see a shift from brief contributions to conversations by the regulars, as is typical in Q and A, towards the longer interchanges typical of discussion and social support, and possibly to more argumentative flame war discussions. This general notion suggests that we might see important differences in the nature of conversations when comparing the stepparents and diabetes conversations to those of arthritis, stop-smoking, and prostate cancer. The sixth case is clearly of another type altogether. We can see that contributors to this group tend to be verbose, seldom return to the group, but are otherwise active. Closer examination of posts to the cross-post support group indicates that it is not really a support group, but more of a joke group that gets cross posted to by flame baiters and trolls. The group seems to intentionally play with the idea that people who cross post too much would need support.

Both sets of scatterplots show how these types of visualization can help researchers identify anomalous cases that may result from misclassification or previously unrecognized heterogeneity. Both examples are drawn from discussion groups with relatively few interaction affordances. The same methods can be extended to more complex settings like social networking groups and collaborative systems like Wikipedia or Flickr, but with more dimensions there will be greater need to cut the data along multiple facets to reveal commonalities and key differences.

MAPPING STRUCTURE OF RELATIONSHIPS WITHIN THREADS AND GROUPS

Computer-mediated social systems are rife with ways to infer social ties from interaction records. Systems like Usenet, where threaded discussion automatically entails an explicit sender-receiver relationship, are prevalent, but so are settings where interaction does not automatically encode directed relationships. These include things like chat room records, Wikipedia talk pages, and conversations held in team voice communication systems. Even in these contexts, directed ties are seldom absent, but must be inferred from content and timing cues.

The following network graphs were collected through content analysis of edits to a Wikipedia policy discussion page. These data come from the first archived page of the 'No personal attacks' policy (see Black, Welser, DeGroot, & Cosley, 2008). Each node represents an author who made an edit to the policy discussion page and each directed edge represents a reply, weighted by the number of replies from all interactions of the dyad from threads. The sub graph represents reply relationships in the context of a particular thread and only includes the nodes and replies within that thread. The full graph represents all reply relationships across all of the threads.

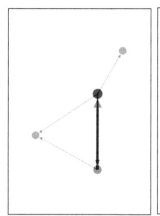 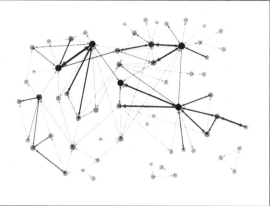

Figure 10.6 Graphs of a thread and the larger group context.

While the subgraph appears isolated, that conversation is actually part of the large component of the full graph because some of the participants in that thread also participated in other threads. We can see from the group level visualization that, except for two exceptions, many of the participants in these threads also participated in other threads, creating the large central component. Within that component, we see a central line of actors who bridge between several different subsections of the graph, have few ties with many messages sent from them, and tend to be connected to others who themselves have intense ties to others.

These network diagrams are from a single discussion page for a particular policy page. They are valuable as initial steps in exploratory network visualization, but should be augmented with other data, like roles or status (Brandes, Raub, & Wagner, 2001). Of course, with the many channels for interaction in Wikipedia a next step in this research would be to overlay some indication of the ties between these actors outside of this discussion, either through their user talk pages or through discussion related to articles, other policies, or Wikipedia projects.

Egocentric network graphs based on comment relationships among Wallop users are shown in Figure 10.7. Here we focus on the structure of relationships among egos neighbors and how that structure was related to ego's longevity in the group. These visualizations are consistent with a general theoretical supposition (McAdam & Paulson, 1993) that participants in a social group's further activity depends on ties to friends who are active in that group. Further, it may be possible that stronger community structure (more dense connections between those friends) may encourage people to continue participating. The dark nodes represent long lived participants while the light nodes were short lived. These local network visualizations are evocative of this possibility, though so far, our research has shown only moderate support for this contention.

Dense community   Sparse

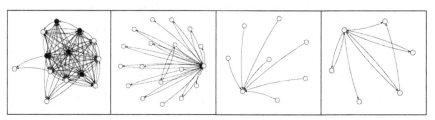

Figure 10.7   Egocentric neighborhood visualizations of social network participants.

Egocentric local network visualizations can represent node attributes with color, size and edge attributes with color, weight, direction and positive and negative valences. These visualizations are a powerful general purpose visualization strategy that can be applied to any interaction system and can, with appropriately chosen attributes, be used to test theoretical arguments about patterned behavior like retention, diffusion, and role development. With more interaction affordances, researchers need to think flexibly about what sorts of interactions should be included to capture theoretical processes of interest.

Characterizing Types of Actors from Histories of Contributions and Relations

Figure 10.8 is a revealing triptych for discerning roles from threaded discussion, especially tailored to distinguish the role of expert (or 'answer person') from that of other common participants. The set includes an 'authorline', a longitudinal characterization of the amount of contributions to particular threads while distinguishing between those initiated by ego and those initiated by others (Viégas & Smith, 2004). Next is a local network visualization documenting directed reply relationships between ego and all degree one alters and all ties among that set. Finally, there is a neighbors' degree histogram, which reports the relative frequencies of ego's neighbors as sorted into increasingly large bins based on degree. This allows us to rapidly assess how many of egos contacts are themselves well connected.

This set of three visualizations allowed us to identify some of the key structural signatures of experts in online discussion spaces (Welser et al., 2007). From these visualizations, we developed metrics from which we were able to predict role behavior with a high degree of accuracy. In this instance, the visualizations were the key step in allowing us to formalize how a particular role manifested in the structure of interaction and subsequently test those insights statistically. Returning to the data to test insights from visualization is a crucial step that distinguishes visualization for discovery from simple illustration.

Authorline of threaded contributions

Local network

Neighbor's degree

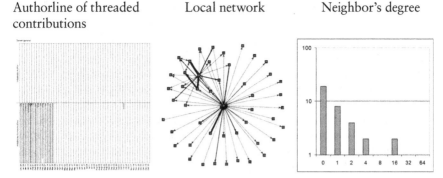

Figure 10.8   Combining types of visualizations to identify roles.

DISCUSSION

As the population of researchers using data from online systems expands, the study of online spaces will increasingly require that findings be understood in light of patterns and observed relations from a range of comparative cases. We sketched some general classes of online contexts and considered how they varied in terms of interaction affordances. The move toward Web 2.0 requires greater awareness of how affordances vary across contexts, what they enable, what they constrain, and how they will impose patterns on interaction processes. Understanding general processes like retention, contribution, coordination, diffusion, conflict, role development, and exchange are basic social science goals. We hope that standardization of general visualization strategies will help researchers focus on these general processes while bracketing the effects of the context-specific constraints, leading to more broadly relevant social scientific findings.

Assessing Visualizations: Building Better Pictures and Better Picture Production Systems

Using visualizations for discovery requires striking a balance between image quality, flexibility of the visualization production system, and the efficiency of image interpretation. Tufte (1995, 1997) and many others have pointed out standards for high quality 'final product' visualizations. While we embrace this spirit, our emphasis is on building tools for mass producing visualizations that are 'good enough' to identify key patterns but afford sufficient flexibility and help streamline the analysis of numerous images. These flexible, rapid, and 'good enough' tools are where we see the most hope for rapid advancement of the field.

Good information visualization can help highlight the range of variation among different entities as well as revealing similarities, patterns and analogies that may have been obscured by other methods. This ability to highlight variation and similarity leverages the power of visual interpretation many people possess. However, visual information processing does not exclude the need for quantitative analysis and, in fact, should be used to stimulate it. Visual analysis does offer non-quantitative analysts the opportunity to grasp and explore a complex data space that would be opaque to them in a quantitative form. Two necessary steps in a discovery research program are testing a statistical model of associations learned from visualization and communicating the results of those tests to a broad audience. Two of our studies (Lento et al., 2006; Welser et al., 2007) illustrate this three stage process: (1) production of visualizations of relationships and behavior to gain insight into patterns and develop hypotheses, (2) operationalize visualization patterns as metrics and variables for use in a statistical model, and (3) communication of model results. Ultimately, the best assessment of exploratory visualizations and systems for producing those visualizations is the predictive power of those models and the theoretical significance of the findings.

Further Challenges in Extending Visualization Techniques to Complex Data

At a certain point, attempting to squeeze more information into a single visualization becomes counterproductive. A common way to contend with this problem is to address it at the data processing stage. By grouping similar measures, eliminating irrelevant information, and recombining different relationships into aggregated measures, it is sometimes possible to effectively represent complex data in a simple visualization. However, such approaches can eliminate the very context which makes the visualization meaningful.

Another approach is to represent complex data through comparison of clearly related images like moving images or presenting multiple representations of different subsets of the data in a single visualization. The key advantage of this approach is that it allows interaction with the data. Each step in the visualization process is clear and easy to interpret, and the viewer can combine the sets to extract meaningful patterns. The strength of this approach—that a series of simple visualizations combines in different ways to present a complex picture of the data—is also its weakness. If the creator of the images is not careful, viewers might combine the visualizations in unexpected ways and arrive at erroneous conclusions. More vexing is the problem of physical and visual memory—most print venues can only allow a few images, and in practice, people cannot retain numerous visualizations in memory. Better strategies for comparing images are needed.

CONCLUSIONS

Although we are enthusiastic about the potential for visualization to aid scientific discovery, there is much room for progress. First, we recognize limitations that stem from the need for additional methods of inquiry, like ethnographic study, statistical testing, and experimental research in order to more fully understand social dynamics. We also recognize a need for greater development of tools for the efficient creation of precisely tuned sets of visualizations. Finally, we hope to see visualization strategies extended across wider ranges of comparable situations. In our recent work, we have sought to find representations of the data structures like hierarchies and network structures that are common in most forms of computer-mediated social spaces. We would like to see much more work that is broadly comparative that might reveal overall patterns in structures and dynamics.

REFERENCES

Backstrom, L., Huttenlocher, D., Kleinberg, J., & Lan, X. (2006). Group formation in large social networks: Membership, growth, and evolution. *Proc. 12th ACM SIGKDD Intl. Conf. on Knowledge Discovery and Data Mining*, August 20—23, (pp. 44-54). New York: ACM.

Baym, N.K. (2007). The new shape of online community: The example of Swedish independent music fandom. *First Monday, 12*(8). Retrieved May 15, 2008, from http://www.firstmonday.org/issues/issue12_8/baym/index.html

Black, L., Welser, H., DeGroot, J., & Cosley, D. (2008). 'Wikipedia is not a democracy': Deliberation and policy making in an online community. Presented at the *Political Communication division of the International Communication Association 2008 annual convention*, May 22-26, Montreal, Quebec (Canada).

Brandes, U., Raab, J., & Wagner, D. (2001). Exploratory network visualization: Simultaneous display of actor status and connections. *Journal of Social Structure, 2*(4): 1-28.

De Nooy, W., Mrvar, A., Baragelj, V., & Granovetter, M. (2005). *Exploratory social network analysis with Pajek*. UK: Cambridge University Press.

Donath, J. S. (1999). Visualizing conversation. *Journal of Computer-Mediated Communication, 4*(4). Retrieved May 22, 2008, from http://jcmc.indiana.edu/vol4/issue4.

Freeman, L. C. (2000). Visualizing social networks. *Journal of Social Structure, 1*(1). Retrieved, May 22, 2008, from http://www.cmu.edu/joss/content/articles/volume1/Freeman.html

Gaver, W. (1991). Technology affordances. In *Proceedings of CHI*, April 28- May 2 (pp. 79-84). New York: ACM.

Gu, L., Johns, P., Lento, T. M., & Smith, M.A. (2006). How do blog gardens grow? Language community correlates with network diffusion and adoption of blogging systems. In N. Nicolov, F. Salvetti, M. Liberman, & J. H. Martin (Eds.), *Computational approaches to analyzing weblogs: Papers from the 2006 spring symposium*, (pp. 24-31). Menlo Park, CA: American Association for Artificial Intelligence.

Lento, T., Welser, H.T., Gu, L., & Smith, M. A. (2006). The ties that blog: Examining the relationship between social ties and continued participation in the WallopWeblogging System. *WWW Third Annual Workshop on the Weblogging Ecosystem*. Ireland: Edinburgh.

McAdam, D., and Paulsen, R. (1993). Specifying the relationship between social ties and activism. *American Journal of Sociology, 99* (3); 640–667.

Monge, P., & Contractor, N. (2003). *Theories of communication networks*. Oxford: Oxford University Press.

Nadel, S. F. (1964). *Theory of social structure*. New York: Macmillan.

Schaffer, D., Zuo, Z., Greenberg, S., Bartram, L., Dill, J., Dubs, S., & Roseman, M. (1996). Navigating hierarchically clustered networks through fisheye and full-zoom methods. *ACM Transactions on Computer-Human Interaction, 3*(2): 162-188.

Scott, J. (2000). *Social network analysis: A handbook* (2nd ed.). London: Thousands Oaks; CA: Sage Publications.

Shneiderman, B. (2008). Treemaps for space-constrained visualization of hierarchies. Retrieved January 17, 2009, from http://www.cs.umd.edu/hcil/treemaphistory/

Shneiderman, B., & Aris A. (2006). Network Visualization by semantic substrates. *IEEE. Transactions on Visualization and Computer Graphics* (Infovis2006), *12*(5): 733-740. Retrieved May 22, 2008, from http://www.cs.umd.edu/hcil/nvss.

Smith, M. A., & Fiore, A. T. (2001). Visualization components for persistent conversations. In *Proceedings of the SIGCHI conference on human factors in computing system*, March 31—April 5 (pp. 136-143). New York: ACM.

Tufte, E. R. (1995). *Envisioning information* (5th printing, August 1995 ed.). Cheshire, CT: Graphics Press.

Tufte, E. R. (1997). *Visual explanations: Images and quantities, evidence and narrative*. Cheshire, CT: Graphics Press.

Turner, T., Smith, M., Fisher, D., & Welser. H.T. (2005). Picturing Usenet: Mapping computer-mediated collective action. *Journal of Computer Mediated-Communication, 10*(4). Retrieved May 2, 2008, from http://jcmc.indiana.edu/vol10/issue4/turner.html

Viégas, F. B., & Smith, M. A. (2004). Newsgroup crowds and authorlines: Visualizing the activity of individuals in conversational cyberspaces. *Proceedings of the 37th Hawai'i nternational Conference on System Sciences*, January 5-8 (p. 40109.2). Los Alamitos: IEEE Press.

Welser, H. T., Gleave, E., Fisher, D., & Smith, M.A. (2007). Visualizing the signatures of social roles in online discussion groups. *The Journal of Social Structure, 8*(2). Retrieved May 2, 2008, from http://www.cmu.edu/joss/content/articles/volume8/Welser/.

Welser, H. T, Smith, M. A. Gleave, E., & Fisher., D. (2008). Distilling digital traces: Computational social science approaches to studying the internet. In N. Fielding, R. L. Lee and G. Grant (Eds.), *Handbook of online research methods*. London: Sage Publications.

Part VI
Data Preservation and Reuse

11 Web Archiving as e-Research

Steven M. Schneider, Kirsten A. Foot and Paul Wouters

WEB ARCHIVING AS A FORM OF INQUIRY IN E-RESEARCH

As the Web emerged since the mid-90s as a distinct media form, scholars have increasingly viewed it as an object of study. To facilitate this work, some scholars have turned to Web archiving as a technique and approach, valuing the potential to complete developmental and retrospective analyses of many kinds of online phenomena. Simultaneously, Web archiving has also emerged as a practice of e-research, in which humanities and social science scholars mediate their work via digital and networked technologies. These developments pose challenges for scholars as they seek to develop methodological approaches permitting robust examination of Web phenomena. Some of these challenges stem from the nature of the Web, while others are associated with institutional structures and traditional patterns of behavior of individuals within different types of institutions.

The Web is a distinctive mixture of the ephemeral and the permanent (Schneider & Foot, 2004). There are two aspects to the ephemerality of Web content. First, Web content is ephemeral in its transience—it can be relied upon to last for only a relatively brief time. From the perspective of the user or visitor (and, especially, the researcher), there is little that can be done without specialized tools or techniques to ensure that content can be viewed again at a later time. Second, Web content is ephemeral in its construction—like television, radio, theater and other "performance media," (Hecht, Corman, & Miller-Rassulo, 1993; Stowkowski, 2002) or performance art. Web content once presented needs to be reconstructed or re-presented in order for others to experience it. Web pages are routinely (and increasingly) constructed by computers without human intervention—servers and browsers request, transmit, receive, and process http requests to create the experience of the HTML page—and the activities are repeated (at least in part) when the page is presented again. In other words, the Web is not easily archived in the way that, for example, printed materials are. Books, film, and sound recordings, for example, can be collected in the form in which they are presented; no affirmative steps are needed to re-create the experience of the original; and indeed, when taken such steps cast doubt on the authenticity of the re-presentation.

At the same time, the Web has a sense of permanence that clearly distinguishes it from performance media and performance art. Unlike theater, or live television, or radio, the objects or components that are assembled and then presented as an HTML page—the images, texts, and HTML code—must exist in a stable form prior to their presentation in order to be experienced. The Web shares this characteristic with other forms of media such as film, print, and sound recordings. The permanence of the Web, however, is somewhat fleeting. The traditional Web site regularly and procedurally destroys its predecessors each time it is updated by its producer (indeed, even the blog-style site, which implies an internal and automatic archive, rarely allows a re-creation of the browsing experience at a point in time, opting instead for a re-presentation of content within an alternative experience). In short, absent specific arrangements to the contrary, each previous edition of a Web site is erased as a new version is produced. By analogy, it would be as if each day's newspaper were printed on the same piece of paper, obliterating yesterday's news to produce today's.

The ephemerality of the Web requires that pro-active steps be taken in order to allow a re-creation of Web experiences for future analysis. The permanence of the Web makes this eminently possible. Although saving Web sites is not as easy as, say, saving editions of a magazine, archiving techniques have been and continue to be developed in such a way to facilitate scholarly research of Web-based phenomena. These techniques allow the Web to be preserved in nearly the same form as it was originally 'performed,' similar to recordings of television and radio performances. At the same time, as Web-based phenomena evolve into ever-more dynamic performance, Web archives begin to share the challenges associated with object-oriented representations of other performance media and art (Rush, 1999).

Concerns over the fragility and ephemerality of digital materials have been expressed for almost twenty-five years. For example, an oft-quoted early statement from a 1985 U.S. government report warned that the "the U.S. is in danger of losing its memory" as governments, businesses and other institutions shifted from paper to electronic records (Nelson, 1987); similar concerns were expressed in Europe at about the same time. With the advent of the Web in the early 1990s, this concern grew significantly as greater numbers of institutions and individuals began producing documents in digital form only, rendering traditional modes of archiving less reliable as instruments to preserve records of social phenomena. By 1995, an opportunity to address this concern emerged with the development of Web harvesting programs. Web harvesters or crawlers are applications that traverse the Web following links to pages, initially from a set of pre-defined seed URLs. Harvesters were initially developed by search engines such as Alta Vista to overcome the increasingly impossible task of indexing the Web through human cataloging techniques. Web harvesting technologies gave life to the notion of archiving Web materials via the Web itself.

Three pioneering efforts to archive the Web appear to have developed nearly simultaneously. In 1995, the National Library of Australia, noting that the growing amount of 'born digital' Australian information required its attention, established a working group to select materials for collection and develop techniques for archiving. Out of this initiative came the project whose name, PANDORA, encapsulates its mission: "Preserving and Accessing Networked Documentary Resources of Australia" (National Library of Australia). The PANDORA project archived its first Web site in October 1996, and by June 1997 the Archive contained 31 titles (Cathro, Webb & Whiting, 2001). In early 1996, American entrepreneur Brewster Kahle founded the Internet Archive, a non-profit, private organization whose similar mission is to provide "permanent access for researchers, historians, and scholars to historical collections that exist in digital format" (Internet Archive, 2008; Kahle, 1997). Internet Archive began crawling in 1996, and made its archive publicly accessible in March 1997, when its database contained about two tetrabytes of Web data (Kahle, 1997). In September, 1996, the Royal Library of Sweden launched the "Kulturarw3 Project" to "test methods of collecting, preserving and providing access to Swedish electronic documents" (Mannerheim, 1998). The project completed its first crawl of Sweden's domain in January 1997.

The impetus behind Web archiving activity was clear: The Web was doubling in size every three to six months from 1993 to 1996, and it appeared that the Web had the potential to become a significant platform on which a wide variety of social, political, scientific, and cultural phenomena would play out. Individuals at different types of institutions, such as libraries and archives, whose mission included the preservation of cultural and historical artifacts and materials, recognized the challenge that digital materials presented. Scholars, on the other hand, were a bit slower to recognize the utility of Web archives. Greene et. al. (2004) published one of the earliest efforts to describe Web archiving to support scholarly research. Other early adopters include Hine (2000). Clearly, the Internet Archive anticipated scholarly uses, and the "Energizing the Electronic Electorate" team at the Annenberg Public Policy Center developed tools and techniques in 1999–2000 that formed the intellectual foundation for WebArchivist.org, a research group supporting scholarly Web archiving founded by two of the co-authors of this chapter (Schneider & Foot, 2000; Schneider, Harnett, & Foot, 2001).

Independent of the development of the Web, but strongly related to the development of new Internet applications for science, a new paradigm of research emerged, initially called e-science. This new model of research practice and funding emerged from the communities of supercomputing and physics (Berman, Fox, & Hey, 2003). The core idea was that it should be possible to use the Internet not only as a medium to distribute information, but also as a medium for powerful computational solutions. The metaphor of the 'Grid' exemplifies this by suggesting that one could plug a particular scientific puzzle into the network and get the solution returned, like one can draw electric power from the power Grid via a socket in the wall. This led to a definition of e-science as the convergence of huge distributed datasets, high-performance computation, and big data pipes for communication, data transfer, and visualization. The first modern Grid was created in the U.S. in the I-Way project in 1995 (Berman, Fox, & Hey, 2003). By 2005, the scope of e-science had spread to the social sciences and humanities and was redefined first as Internet research (Jones, 1999: 1–25), and later as e-research (see Chapters 1 & 3 within). This broader definition of e-research created new connections between scholars involved in the creation of new methodologies in e-science and e-research and the community of researchers who had taken up the Internet as their focused object of study (Brügger, 2005; Schneider & Foot, 2004).

We are only at the beginning of the development of Web archiving as both object and instance of novel research methodologies. Yet, we can delineate the most promising venues for the next few years. Web archiving is in the first instance mainly about Web data: securing access to Web data, long and medium term storage of Web data, and interpretation and annotation of Web data. Data happen to be the single most central concern in e-science and e-research, if we define data in a broad sense—including numerical datasets; complex objects; stored ethnographic observations in the forms of text, audio, and video; traces of individual and collective behavior; and digitized, multi-media historical sources. This confluence will create new possibilities for Web archiving as well as for e-research more generally. As we will see, these will have implications beyond the area of data for research and may redefine defining aspects of public scholarship.

WEB ARCHIVING AND E-RESEARCH PRACTICES

From a social research perspective, the primary reason to archive Web objects is to ensure future access to artifacts that may have analytical value. Web archiving is essential for retrospective analyses of Web objects and developmental analyses of the evolution of Web phenomena over time (Foot & Schneider, 2006). In view of our discussion above of the ephemerality and durability of Web objects, we argue that researchers should archive objects of interest with the assumption that they are potentially dynamic. Assessments of whether, how, and how frequently particular Web objects are actually dynamic may be foundational to other strands of inquiry.

Web archiving is useful for both in-depth studies of a small number of Web objects and broader, large-scale studies as well. For example, scholars interested in the development of one particular site, or of the co-evolution of several sites during a particular timeframe, reap benefits from periodic archiving of their focal site(s) by being able to retrace the emergence of key features, or changes in certain texts or images over time and in relation to other Web objects and offline phenomena. Scholars who pursue research questions that require large datasets also benefit from Web archives, as they enable many forms of structured data mining and correlational analyses of elements such as texts and links.

Web archiving does not by definition privilege qualitative or quantitative methods of analysis. Whether the data corpus generated through Web archiving processes is relatively small or large, either structured or unstructured forms of observation and analysis may be employed in relation to archived materials. Highly structured observations of particular elements within a Web archive enable broader quantitative analyses; more loosely structured or unstructured observations enable richer qualitative analyses. In contrast to data collection practices that entail extracting HTML text from Web pages, or cataloging links that originate anywhere within a site domain without preserving the structure and texts of the site, archiving collections of pages associated by domain or some other heuristic, and including their hyperlinked context, enables many kinds of data collection and analyses. A well-designed Web archive enables researchers to pursue questions regarding the prevalence of particular elements and the rhetorical function of those same elements within a single study.

Many studies of social phenomena on the Web to date have been based on observations conducted at a single point in time, or during a more extended period but without explicit consideration of the possibility of changes during that period. As mentioned above, Web archiving expands the scope of potential research by enabling developmental analyses of a Web phenomenon as it changes over time by tracking changes in Web objects between rounds of capture in the archiving process. It also expands the scope by supporting cross-sectional research, that is, studies of similar phenomena in different geographical/virtual places, or different periods of time. For instance, a comparative study of the Web productions of several scientific institutes within one country or across different countries during a particular period would be greatly enhanced by robust archiving of all the Web pages within those institutes' domains and their outlinked pages. Similarly, Web archiving affords researchers the ability to compare the Web objects produced in relation to routine events such as a national election with those produced during one or more subsequent events (Jirotka, Procter, Rodden, & Bowker, 2006; Teasley & Wolensky, 2001). These kinds of scope expansions, whether pursued through qualitative or quantitative methods, can increase the depth and strength of the research findings and the overall value of the research.

One common observation regarding e-research is that it may enable new forms of collaboration between geographically distributed researchers (Collins, 1992). Although there are many ways that scholars working alone may benefit from archiving Web artifacts, Web archiving enables and/or enhances some forms of collaboration in the study of Web phenomena that might not otherwise be possible or efficient. For example, scholars studying the manifestations of a phenomenon in different languages on the Web may find the possibilities for reciprocal translation and joint analysis greatly enhanced by creating a mutually accessible Web archive. As another example, one reliable way to investigate different cultural and/or governmental influences on Web site content would be for collaborating scholars situated in different countries to archive the same Web pages at the same times, utilizing servers from distinct locations, and to then integrate their collections into a single archive for comparative analysis. In addition to these forms of collaboration, various aspects of the processes of Web archiving may be distributed among geographically disparate teams, thus allowing an increased scale of research beyond what any one researcher or team could manage singly.

In sum, Web archiving has been established in recent scholarship as a promising, and sometimes necessary, approach to e-research concerning social phenomena on the Web. Some forms of inquiry are only possible if scholars anticipate the potential evolution of Web objects and establish a prospective archiving regimen. At the same time, the collection of extant artifacts always results in new artifacts, including the collection itself. Therefore, the creation of Web archives is itself a novel form of knowledge production and representation, as we explain in the next section.

WEB ARCHIVING AS FOUNDATION FOR E-RESEARCH

We suggest that scholarly Web archiving proceeds through a set of distinct series of actions or operations on the path from conceptualizing an archive to making archived objects and associated metadata available to researchers or consumers of research. Considering each process discretely provides the opportunity to examine distinct techniques associated with each process, as well as the challenges posed in implementing each process within a scholarly research project.

The first process, *identification*, includes the steps necessary to make known to an archiving system those Web objects to be considered part of the project. For example, a project examining a set of ten Web sites would fully identify the precise definition of the site, as well as the URL of the page from which archiving activity was to begin. Web objects can be identified for inclusion in a project in a variety of ways, including by experts (researchers) or by processing query results from search engines. Specifying an identification protocol that yields a representative and replicable sample of Web content is a considerable challenge. The dynamic nature of some parts of the Web also poses a challenge to the process of identification.

Having identified a set of objects to be included in an archive, the next process, *curation*, involves creating the set of rules and procedures necessary to collect the desired objects, and to verify that the collected objects match curatorial objectives. These rules might specify, for example, the instructions to be given to the collection process concerning whether to follow or ignore links to other objects, or the disposition of objects inadvertently collected. These rules involve the researcher in ethical dilemmas concerning permissions and notification to producers and distributors of objects to be collected. The process of curation includes the creation of metadata, associated with the identified objects, that is necessary for the collection of those objects, and the verification that collected objects match curatorial objectives.

The process of *collection* encompasses obtaining and storing representations of identified objects. Given a set of identified objects and the rules and procedures to guide the collection, the specific techniques involved with the actual processes of obtaining 'bits on disks' can be determined. The demands of the project and the curatorial objectives will lead an archivist to select from among a variety of collection techniques. For example, an individually-managed collection technique implies that the researcher has assumed the responsibility for the actual collection and storage of archived objects. A system-managed collection relies on software and systems that are administered or managed by individuals or agencies other than the researcher. Consideration of these two collection techniques draw our attention to the locus of control of data collection and suggest potential tradeoffs between robustness and replicability on the one hand, and dynamism, responsiveness, and validity on the other.

Some collection techniques support on-demand collection, suggesting that a researcher can initiate collection of a set of identified objects at any time. On-demand collection has advantages for the research process, as it allows dynamic collection and can be responsive to changes in either the researcher's discovery patterns or to real world events. At the same time, it may short-circuit curation processes (especially object specification) and call into question the systematic nature of the identification processes. One-time collection implies a single crawl or snapshot of identified objects. One-time collection precludes post-crawl or iterative object evaluation or specification. By contrast, periodic collection implies multiple crawls of a set of identified objects at scheduled and defined intervals over a period of time. This approach allows for the comparison over time of archived objects, as well as for refinements of the identification and curation processes over time.

Two processes are associated with generating metadata about collected objects or groups of objects. *Indexing* is the process of generating metadata algorithmically, while *categorization* is the process of generating metadata through observation and analysis. Indexing can involve developing metadata from one of the available sources of information about archived objects, including the object itself, log files from crawling programs, and data developed externally to the archiving project. For example, URLs of crawled objects can be parsed for keywords, to render sites as tree structures, to identify protocols, or to predict MIME types. Log files from crawling applications might be examined to predict object MIME type, assess object change over time through analysis of checksums, reveal the path through which the object was selected by the crawling program, or indicate the date when the object was first discovered or most recently encountered through the identification and collection process. Objects themselves may be interrogated through indexing techniques to estimate the number of words in HTML objects, generate word concordances within and among objects, determine the number of images and outlinks, and prepare lists of images and outlinked pages.

Categorization, which by definition involves researchers observing and analyzing all or a sample of archived objects, includes analyses of object features and content as well as the annotation of objects. Analyzing features is a categorization technique in which researchers evaluate objects, most commonly HTML pages, for the presence, absence or level of either specific technical characteristics or opportunities for site visitor action. There may be a static set of features analyzed or a dynamic list of analyzed features developed during the course of the categorization process. Metadata generated by this process will most often be represented quantitatively with ordinal or interval level data and exhaustive and mutually exclusive categories. Researchers analyzing content of identified or collected objects often but by no means exclusively focus on HTML pages to generate understanding about a set of objects and to illuminate patterns across multiple objects. The categorization process may be applied to all objects or to a subset of objects. The content may be evaluated using a fixed or static set of measures, or a dynamic list of measures may be developed during the course of the categorization process. Metadata generated by this process may be represented quantitatively with ordinal or interval level data and exhaustive and mutually exclusive categories, or it may be represented in an open-ended structure.

The process of *interpretation* provides metadata about collected objects, derived through the processes of categorization and indexing, to support sense-making activities such as discovery and search, and to facilitate selected representation of collected objects. This process may include the design and implementation of an interface to a Web archive allowing users to select archived objects for examination or analysis. Providing full-text search of both metadata and archived objects is an interpretation technique especially well suited to presenting unstructured data generated through annotation of objects, as well as providing access to archived objects containing text matching submitted queries. Structured queries requiring users to select among various permutations of metadata generated about identified and collected objects provides access to archived objects in a fixed setting; this technique is especially well-suited to presenting categorical data generated through categorization of object features and content, and indexing of object content and characteristics. Another technique that robustly presents similar categorical data is open-ended N-way queries using a drill-down approach; in this way, users can graphically construct complex Boolean queries using pre-selected categories and terms associated with object metadata.

Finally, collected objects are made available to archive users through the process of *re-presentation*, in which archived objects are retrieved from a collection and re-presented in a Web browser. Considering this step as a process associated with Web archiving is intended to draw attention to fact that rendering archived objects involves affirmative choices and actions that affect the ways in which the rendering is performed. The techniques associated with this process can be distinguished not only by the technical means of re-presentation but by the approach taken to govern access to the objects, distinguish archived objects from the original objects serviced on the Web, and provide contextual metadata associated with the re-presented objects. For example, presentation of archived objects outside of their hypertextual context—in effect, digitization of born-digital objects—is a technique in which captures of full or partial Web objects are created and presented as images. While this mode of re-presentation preserves some of the information value of the object, the underlying source code and links are not available. Similarly, framing objects within a context that emphasizes its archival context draws explicit attention to the fact that the object is not being served by the original site producer in its original context. Either of these techniques can support the presentation of metadata about the object adjacent to the object itself, thus protecting the original integrity of the object while highlighting the descriptive or analytic metadata associated with the object.

Each of these processes necessarily involves multiple challenges for those constructing Web archives in support of e-research. By highlighting these processes individually, we hope to have identified the multiple types of challenges this undertaking will face. As with any research method, Web archiving is best served when the challenges and techniques are identified and acknowledged in the course of creating and presenting the research it supports.

CHALLENGES AND OPPORTUNITIES FOR WEB ARCHIVING IN E-RESEARCH

Social phenomena are so highly complex and variable, it is difficult if not impossible in terms of external validity (much less desirability) to replicate many studies of social phenomena. When Web archives created and/or employed by scholars are made accessible to others, and research processes are well documented, archive-based scholarship is rendered transparent. It becomes possible for others to attempt to replicate sampling and analysis procedures, or—to formulate it a bit more precisely given the problematic nature of 'replication'—to do a secondary analysis (Lecher, 2006). In the research two of us conducted on the use of the Web by U.S. political campaigns, archival impressions of all of the Web pages referenced in the study we published as a book were provided on a publicly accessible site (http://mitpress.mit.edu/webcampaigning). It is possible that others may observe the same artifacts, with similar analytical techniques, and come to different conclusions. This raises key questions about the importance and role of particular forms of technological and methodological expertise in social research in general and social studies of online phenomena in particular. The possibility of secondary analysis in archive-based studies may also directly or indirectly shape the ways that scholars conduct their research and document their research practices—either to enhance transparency or toward obfuscation—especially as more funding agencies in various countries are mandating the release of social research data along with or shortly after publication of findings.

Another important issue is the relationship between quantitative and qualitative research. Notwithstanding the regular pleas for combining these modes of work, it remains a challenge for many scholars to be able to produce high-quality work in both quantitative and qualitative research traditions. This has partly to do with skills needed (e.g., statistical and formal network analysis on the one hand, close reading and observation on the other hand), but also with basic issues of economy of research. Preparing data collection and fieldwork is already time consuming if one restricts oneself to either quantitative or qualitative research, let alone if one wishes to combine both. Yet, the combination of both can be very rewarding. A weakness of descriptive quantitative research is often that the context of the data is unclear, making the interpretation of the data problematic. Rich qualitative analysis, on the other hand, may suffer from lack of clarity about the extent to which the phenomenon or pattern one finds is relevant outside of the context of the particular case one has studied.

Web archiving does seem to promise novel ways to combine quantitative and qualitative research in one design. First of all, the fact that the datasets can be huge will enable qualitative researchers to check whether a particular phenomenon or pattern they have found in one particular case also seems to be relevant if one looks at a large number of case studies. This could technologically be supported by "pattern matching" software tools (either in the form of Perl or Python scripts, or in NVivo or Atlas.ti type of tools). Second, qualitative data pertaining to a particular case study can be represented as a node in a network, thereby possibly contributing to a better feel for the 'place' of one's case. Third, Web archiving methods enable researchers to collect a variety of quantitative data as harvested metadata. This minimizes the effort on the side of the researcher while still enabling her to couple her own data (whether quantitative or qualitative) to these meta-data. And lastly, quantitative research designs may be enhanced by exploration of concrete instances (e.g., Web pages) of phenomena about which one has quantitative data.

Web archiving employed to support quantitative, qualitative or a blend of these two approaches, can pay off handsomely, in at least two different ways. First, the production of Web archives can create novel datasets to explore research questions in ways that are currently not possible or prohibitively expensive or cumbersome. Second, once these Web archives have been produced, they can be updated, re-analyzed and recombined. This may help to explore additional research questions in the same areas, to open up new areas of research resulting from these recombinations, or to reflexively study the process of research itself. Monitoring the needs of scholars with respect to Web archiving tools and facilities may be part of the latter. The investigation of the U.S. election processes by studying and archiving Web sites of candidates is a good example of substantive implications of Web archiving for social science research (Graubard, 2004). In this study, novel questions about the role of new media in political campaigns could be answered, as well as their implications for the character of political campaigns in the era of the Web. A related study is the Web archive of Dutch political parties maintained at the University of Groningen (Voerman, 2002). In the humanities, the Digital Archive for Chinese Studies (DACHS) focuses on Chinese Web sites in the framework of sinology at the universities of Heidelberg and Leiden (Dougherty, 2007). The latter project is also a good example of the value of sustained small-scale Web archiving. This refers to the main disadvantage of superficial, large-scale Web archives like the Internet Archive or the European Internet Archive for scholarly research. These archives lack the depth and precision in data capture that are usually imperative for scholarly datasets.

A crucial feature of Web archiving as scholarly method is that the annotation of the Web dataset is not delegated to data specialists, but is a joint endeavor in which researchers set the agenda. In its most ambitious form, the results of the analysis of the Web archive become in their turn part of the Web archive. If this is accompanied by metadata describing who uploaded these results, the Web archive can become a crucial tool in a collaboratory or social networking environment by enabling researchers to find each other, comment on each other's results, and set up new projects. This may already add new value, even if the analysis itself would be unaffected by Web archiving as a method. Additionally, it becomes quite feasible to add automatically harvested metadata to the Web archive and include these in, and combine them with, the human produced analysis or interpretation. The analysis itself can of course be supported by specific research software, be it quantitative (e.g., SPSS or UCINET) or qualitative (e.g., NVivo or Atlas.ti). We would like to emphasize again that there are actually no specific methodological or theoretical requirements for the substantive research: both interpretative and formal research designs can be supported by Web archiving, although the technical and organizational requirements would be rather different in each case (for example, the data entry forms need to be adjusted to both the type of questions and the style of the researcher). It will immediately be clear that the more ambitious types of Web archives are actually also datasets about the researchers that have created and used them. In other words, the Web archives can be 'inverted' and analyzed as a dataset about a particular research community and its methodological and communicative way of life or about the historical development of a particular field of science or scholarship. Given the recent emergence of Web archives this has not yet happened, but it is clearly on the horizon.

Lastly, a specific case that bridges the substantive and the reflexive dimensions mentioned above is the opening up of scholarship to the public by enabling non-academic communities to annotate Web archives. According to Dougherty (2007), this is the key implication of Web archiving for scholarly research. Her contention is based on the massive popularity of mundane annotation practices in environments such as email lists, blogs, social tagging, and social network sites. By giving comments and feedback to each other as part of their social life, people nowadays are actually annotating their environment on the basis of their own experiences and expertise. One can see this as additional data that can be incorporated in e-research and Web studies. One can also, however, see non-academic audiences as alternative producers of socially relevant knowledge that sometimes can compete in terms of rigor and increasingly also in terms of available resources, with the most serious scholarship (Hackett 2008). In this sense, Web archiving as method in e-research could then contribute to a crucial turn in the demarcation of scholarly expertise and help develop totally new forms of public scholarship (Massanès, 2006). This supports Dougherty's conclusion that a reevaluation of the notion of expertise must take place before roles for different knowledge brokers in digital culture heritage can be identified (Dougherty, 2007). And last but not least, this also leads to a redefinition of what Web archiving really is about. It is not so much a matter of preserving more or less complete datasets or digital experiences, supervised by designated experts, but rather a strategy for creating multiple paths to artifacts and information that is evidenced by nonhierarchical search tools on the Web (Massanès, 2006), thereby enabling multiple ways of analyzing, understanding and making sense of our world.

TAKING WEB ARCHIVING SERIOUSLY: IMPLICATIONS FOR E-RESEARCH

Taking Web archiving seriously as both a novel research methodology and a data collection suite of tools also means that researchers using Web archiving as (one of) their methodologies will have to be supported with sufficient information expertise and human power. As a consequence, either scholarship in the humanities and social sciences will itself have to become more capital intensive, or scholars will need to have secure access to standardized and personalize-able Web archiving tools in a stable infrastructure, including storage and annotation facilities, provided by the universities or national libraries. We have already indicated that there are good reasons for the development of a combination of two different types of Web archiving: broad and superficial, such as the Internet Archive or the Swedish cultural heritage archive, versus narrow and deep, such as the Digital Archive for Chinese Studies archive. Since we cannot predict which research questions will become pertinent, even in the near future, the production of new Web archives to address particular research questions will keep emerging. This cannot be covered by broad sweeping routine Web archiving, because it is impossible to archive 'the whole Web'. Every Web archive will by necessity always represent a limited sample out of the universe of Web objects. Actually, we do not really know how useful broad, ill-defined Internet archives will be. We do know, however, that social scientists and humanities scholars will for many research questions need focused and well-defined Web archives if they need Web archives at all. Therefore, we would like to offer as our intuition that in the next few years it is most important that scholars across a variety of fields be provided with and/or develop the tools and data infrastructures that enable them to create their own Web archives and to share their experiences in this novel type of research with each other. The development of technical and scholarly standards should go hand in hand with this process. We expect more results from this approach than from the creation of large Web archiving infrastructures that are not driven by research questions and needs.

Complementarily, we urge scholars to initiate Web archiving efforts in collaboration with libraries and archives, or to seek to participate in them. Individual scholars can contribute robustly to institutional Web archives by offering their perspective as would-be or actual users or beta testers of proposed or prototype Web archives. Two of us have had fascinating experiences as the only non-librarians at Web archive planning sessions organized by individual libraries or associations of libraries. There can be significant gaps between what librarians or professional archivists think that scholars-as-archive-users want, and what scholars actually want—dialogue between scholars and librarians/archivists about Web archiving is foundational for redressing these gaps.

We suggest that during the design phase of a research project that will entail Web archiving, investigators identify a library or institutional archive that would be willing to collaborate in the archiving process, or at least be a repository for the Web collection during or at the close of the research project. Terms for long-term preservation and access for other scholars and the public should be negotiated upfront. Scholars may need to supply a collaborating library/archive with forms of metadata beyond those required for the research, but we contend that the long-term benefits of durable, accessible Web archives are worth the effort of coordinating. Through such collaborations, scholars may have opportunities to shape the collection practices, architecture designs, and policy decisions that will have a significant impact on the nature of e-research projects that can be supported, both presently and in the future.

Although Internet researchers still use mainly 'live' Web data that exist in one particular point in time, e-research infrastructures promise to be relevant research environments for scholars using Web archives. This would require the introduction into e-research infrastructures of a flexible Web archiving support structure with considerable scope for the individual scholar and small research group. Even small Web archiving projects tend to produce massive datasets, which can most efficiently be hosted in large data Grids.

So what institutional policies are needed to support and sustain Web archiving as a viable e-research practice? To answer this question, we need to review the current institutional environment of Web archiving, as well as the scope of the implications of Web archiving for social science and humanities scholarship. Most Web archiving projects have been defined in the context of national libraries, pioneered by the libraries of Australia, Sweden, and the U.S. Library of Congress. The Dutch National Library (KB) has recently decided to add a limited experiment in Web archiving to its e-Depot, a pioneering digital facility to preserve digital scholarly publications (Hoorens, Rothenberg, Van Oranje, Van der Mandele, & Levitt, 2007). National libraries tend to focus on the preservation of (digital) cultural heritage and/or the public record of science and scholarship. They are much less oriented towards problems of access to, and sharing of, research data (Arzberger et al., 2004). This means that they also tend to underestimate the complexities of providing researchers with the capabilities to annotate Web archives and to add these annotations to the Web archive. Related to this, as Dougherty (2007) observes in her PhD thesis on Web archiving, "the steps of categorization, interpretation, and representation are overlooked entirely." (Dougherty 2007, p. 42)

The upshot of this is that if national libraries and archives wish to support Web archiving as a research activity, they will need to make a double move. First, the traditional paradigm of archiving, fundamentally based on stable documents, needs to be transformed into a paradigm that enables archiving the permanent/fleeting phenomenon of, as well as phenomena on, the Web. Second, they need to "open up" key elements of the archiving procedures to enable a "natural flow" of research results into the Web archives, both as primary data and as metadata. This requires a rethinking of the responsibilities of archivists and librarians in relation to scholarly research, and vice-versa the integration of key elements of the scholarly production cycle (Borgman & Furner, 2002) into the production of Web archives and their maintenance.

Scientific institutions also need to change, in order to enable researchers to create Web archives as part of their research task and receive the credits for this pioneering work. This is comparable to the need in other fields, like bio-informatics, to recognize the creation of scientific databases as part and parcel of scientific research. This will have to lead to crucial changes in human resource management and personnel policy at universities and research institutes. Presently, the creation of datasets is merely recognized within a particular research project, but not as a research oriented infrastructural task. It will become imperative that funding agencies recognize these new scholarly challenges as critical for new endeavors in the social sciences and humanities.

CONCLUSIONS

Web archiving is a valuable and critical research method for scholars engaged in e-research. As a method, it will likely become increasingly important and relevant to scholars whose research projects rely on data collected from Web resources. As the breadth and depth of such research expands and as analyses of Web-based objects become both more common and more accepted, scholars will find it desirable to develop techniques to capture their datasets in ways that facilitate replication and enhance validation. In addition, external reviewers and funding agencies will expect such research to be conducted using these techniques.

In order to ensure the reliability and validity of Web archives, careful attention to all of the processes and systems involved is required. As in research involving experiments, surveys, content analysis, or any quantitative or qualitative methods, close attention to and documentation of all processes, choices, and decisions is critical to successful social research. We should insist that Web archives deployed in e-research projects embed rich description of these processes. In this way, future users of archives can address the possible impact of choices made in constructing archives on the conclusions drawn by researchers.

As e-research becomes institutionalized around practices supporting digital repositories and data curation, Web archiving will become one of several research methods supported and encouraged. As such, Web archiving presents unique opportunities for scholars to collaborate with institutions such as libraries and archives, and will impose unique challenges on these institutions to collaborate with scholars. At the same time, individual scholars with fewer resources can successfully employ the method. In all cases, the clarity of the research method is more important than the scale of the research effort.

ACKNOWLEDGEMENTS

The authors would like to thank Charles van den Heuvel, Ernst Thoutenhoofd, Sally Wyatt, and the referees for the comments on an earlier draft of this chapter.

REFERENCES

Arzberger, P., Schroeder, P., Beaulieu, A., Bowker, G., Casey, K., & Laaksonen, L. (2004). Science and government: An international framework to promote access to data. *Science, 303*(5665), 1777–1778.

Berman, F., Fox, G., & Hey, T. (2003). The Grid: Past, present, future. In F. Berman, G. Fox & T. Hey (Eds.), *Grid Computing. Making the Global Infrastructure a Reality* (pp. 9–50). Chichester, West-Sussex, UK: John Wiley & Sons.

Borgman, C., & Furner, J. (2002). Scholarly communication and bibliometrics. In B. Cronin (Ed.), *Annual Review of Information Science and Technology* (Vol. 33, pp. 3–72). Medford, NJ: Information Today Inc.

Brügger, N. (2005). Archiving Web sites: General considerations and strategies. Aarhus, Denmark: The Centre for Internet Research.

Cathro, W., Webb, C. and Whiting, J. (2001). Archiving the Web: The PANDORA Archive at the National Library of Australia. 2001. Paper presented at the Preserving the Present for the Future Web Archiving Conference, Copenhagen (June).

Collins, H. (1992). Changing Order: Replication and induction in scientific practice. Chicago: University of Chicago Press.

Dougherty, M. (2007). Archiving the Web: Collection, documentation, display and shifting knowledge production paradigms. Unpublished PhD thesis. University of Washington, Seattle.

Foot, K. A., & Schneider, S. M. (2006). *Web Campaigning*. Cambridge: MIT Press.

Graubard, S. (2004). *Public Scholarship: A New Perspective for the 21st Century* (Report). New York: Carnegie Corporation of New York.

Greene, M. A., Boles, F., Bruemmer, B., & Daniels-Howell, T. J. (2004). The Archivist's New Clothes; or, the Naked Truth about Evidence, Transactions, and Recordness. Ann Arbor: University of Michigan Sawyer Seminar.

Hackett, E. J. (2008). Politics and Publics. In Hackett, E. J., Amsterdamska O., Lynch, M., & Wajcman, J., *The Handbook of Science and Technology Studies Third Edition*, MIT Press, Cambridge, p. 429–432.

Hecht, M. L., Corman, S. R., & Miller-Rassulo, M. (1993). An evaluation of the drug resistance project: A comparison of film versus live performance media. *Health Communication, 5*(2), 75–88.

Hine, C. (2000). *Virtual ethnography.* Thousand Oaks, CA: Sage.

Hoorens, S., Rothenberg, J., Van Oranje, C., Van der Mandele, M., & Levitt, R. (2007). Addressing the uncertain future of preserving the past. Towards a robust strategy for digital archiving and preservation. Arlington, VA: RAND Europe.

Internet Archive. (2008). *About the Internet Archive.* Retrieved May 8, 2008, from http://www.archive.org/about/about.php

Jirotka, M., Procter, R., Rodden, T., & Bowker, G. C. (2006). Special Issue: Collaboration in e-research. *Computer Supported Cooperative Work: The Journal of Collaborative Computing, 15*(4), 251–255.

Jones, S. (Ed.). (1999). *Doing Internet Research: Critical Issues and Methods for Examining the Net.* Thousand Oaks, CA: Sage.

Kahle, B. (1997). Preserving the Internet. *Scientific American, 276*(3), 82–83.

Lecher, H. E. (2006). Small scale academic Web archiving. In J. Masanès (Ed.), *Web Archiving*, pp. 213–226. New York: Springer.

Mannerheim, J. (1998). Problems and Opportunities in Web Archiving, Nordic Conference on Preservation and Access: National Libraries and Research Libraries in a time of change. Stockholm.

Massanès, J. (Ed.). (2006). *Web Archiving*. New York: Springer.

National Library of Australia. *PANDORA: History and Achievements*. Retrieved May 8, 2008, from http://pandora.nla.gov.au/historyachievements.html

Nelson, A. K. (1987). The 1985 Report on the Committee on the Records of Government: An Assessment. *Government Information Quarterly, 4*(2), 143–150.

Rush, M. (1999). A noisy silence. *PAJ: A Journal of Perfomance and Art, 21*(1), 1–10.

Schneider, S. M., & Foot, K. A. (2004). The Web as an object of study. *New Media & Society, 6*(1), 114–122.

Schneider, S. M., & Foot, K. A. (Eds.). (2000). *Annenberg 2000 Election Web Archive*. Philadelphia: Annenberg School of Communication, University of Pennsylvania.

Schneider, S. M., Harnett, B. H., & Foot, K. A. (2001, May 23–28). *Catch and code: A method for mapping and analyzing complex web spheres*. Paper presented at the International Communication Association, Washington, DC.

Stowkowski, P. A. (2002). Languages of place and discourses of power: Constructing new senses of place. *Journal of Leisure Research, 34*(4), 368–382.

Teasley, S., & Wolensky, S. (2001). Scientific collaborations at a distance. *Science, 292*, 2254–2255.

Voerman, G. (2002). Archiving the Web: Political party Web sites in the Netherlands. *European Political Science, 2*(1), 68–75.

12 The Promise of Data in e-Research
Many Challenges, Multiple Solutions, Diverse Outcomes

Ann Zimmerman, Nathan Bos, Judith S. Olson and Gary M. Olson

INTRODUCTION

The need to document, manage, transfer, analyze, and preserve digital data is a significant driver of the development of tools and technologies for e-research. This 'data deluge' is the result of new instruments that collect or log massive amounts of data, the output of large-scale computer simulations, the product of experiments that produce vast quantities of data, and the creation of new databases through the aggregation and integration of distributed and often heterogeneous data (Emmott, 2007; Hey & Trefethen, 2005; 2008; Jankowski, 2007). For instance, in ecology, some types of data that were once collected by hand by ecologists in the field are now being gathered by embedded sensor networks. Small sciences such as ecology, which depend upon fieldwork, often lack the tools, infrastructure, and expertise to manage the growing amounts of data generated by new forms of instrumentation and the digitization and federation of legacy data (Borgman, Wallis, & Enyedy, 2007; see also Chapter 8 by Meyer in this volume). As these fields go from being somewhat data poor to suddenly being data rich, existing methods and tools to manage and analyze data are quickly becoming inadequate. This scenario is increasingly common in many fields, including social sciences and humanities, and even in big sciences such as astronomy and physics (Baru, 2007; Hey & Trefethen, 2008). It is not yet clear how this data deluge will affect research practice and outcomes. The purpose of this chapter is to analyze different approaches to data sharing in order to identify important factors that may lead to success.

Shared access to data and collaboration across disciplines and distance are important to researchers' abilities to access expertise to make sense of new types and/or massive amounts of data and to the goal of e-research to achieve novel discoveries in a shorter amount of time (Hey & Trefethen, 2003; 2005). However, findings from both past and present studies show that efforts to share data face considerable social, organizational, legal, scientific, and technical challenges (e.g., Chapter 15 by Burk and Chapter 8 by Meyer in this volume; National Research Council [NRC], 1997; Piwowar, Day, & Fridsma, 2007). While each of these issues must be dealt with in order for sharing to occur, some authors believe that the most significant obstacle is for individual scientists to "first recognize the benefits and see their way past perceived barriers" (Parr & Cummings, 2005: 362). Researchers' concerns to be recognized and rewarded for their work are major hindrances to data sharing:

> Science is a competitive business. The awards for a scientist are reputation and being the first to make a discovery; their greatest fears are to be misrepresented and being beaten into second place by a competitor. . . . The 'selfish scientist' will participate if it is to their competitive advantage to do so (Goble & De Roure, 2007: 2).

This reality prompted Goble and De Roure (2007) to state that "e-Science is, inherently, me-Science" (p. 2). In other words, the open access vision of e-research will not be realized if researchers do not perceive that sharing their data will benefit them and their work.

Data sharing is more common in some disciplines than in others. Scholars have identified a number or reasons for this, although a comprehensive understanding of this topic remains an open area of research (Arzberger et al., 2004; Birnholtz & Bietz, 2003; Borgman, 2007: 188–192; Chapter 13 by Carlson & Anderson in this volume; Pritchard, Carver, & Anand, 2004). A study by a special committee of the Ecological Society of America (Committee on the Future of Long-Term Ecological Data, 1995) found that fields where data sharing is common are characterized by a mixture of:

- technical capabilities, such as free and easy software for data transfer,
- scientifically motivated needs, especially the questions that researchers want to answer, and
- socially influenced demands and incentives.

Among the latter are those that emerge from the scientific community, such as leadership from key individuals and community acknowledgment of the importance of data sharing. Also important are social influences outside the immediate scientific community, including support from high-profile journals and external funding for data management.

The methods used to make research data available outside the context in which they were collected raise a number of questions for those interested in e-research:

- How do different data sharing approaches affect researchers' abilities to reuse data collected by others?
- Why are data sharing methods that achieve positive results in one context not effective in another case?

- Do shared data get used, and if so, how are they used? Is there evidence, for example, that researchers are combining data from multiple disciplines to address questions that would have not been possible without easy access to online databases?

These questions represent important areas of study that scholars in fields such as information science and science and technology studies have begun to seriously address (e.g., Borgman, Wallis, & Enyedy, 2007; Cragin & Shankar, 2006; Piwowar, Day, & Fridsma, 2007; Zimmerman, 2007; 2008).

The question we take up in this chapter is one that has, to date, received little direct attention: *How do the origins of digital databases and the context from which they emerge affect research practice, researchers' attitudes toward data sharing, and the relationships between researchers and other actors such as computer scientists, data managers, and information scientists?* To address this question, we analyzed approaches that have been employed to make research data available beyond the project in which they were generated or to make them usable to diverse participants in distributed, interdisciplinary collaborations. The material presented in this chapter is based on findings from our own research and a review of literature on data sharing and reuse. In the section that follows, we describe data we collected that provide the basis for this chapter. Next, we present an analysis of the approaches that have been employed to address particular data sharing challenges and the results of various strategies. We find that the methods employed can be viewed as a continuum with approaches at each endpoint having different implications for the *practice* and *attitudes* of researchers and for the *authority* and *visibility* of the larger set of individuals that play a role in activities related to data sharing. We conclude the chapter with a summary of the results, a discussion of their implications, and needs for future research.

DATA SOURCES AND METHODS

Data are the building blocks on which scientific knowledge depends, serving as representations of the physical world and as evidence to support scientific claims. Data are central to studies that have investigated the work practices of scientists and analyzed whether or not broader access to data alters research work, scholarly communication, and the scientific reward system (e.g., Beaulieu, 2001; Brown, 2003; Hilgartner, 1995). In this chapter, we define data as "scientific or technical measurements, values calculated therefrom, and observations or facts that can be represented by numbers, tables, graphs, models, text, or symbols and that are used as a basis for reasoning or further calculation" (NRC, 1997: 198). In addition, our definition includes information (metadata) relevant to the data that is independent of the data themselves but without which the data would be incomprehensible such as experimental conditions, variable codes, etc. Below we briefly describe our data corpus, which includes a meta-analysis of multiple distributed collaborations and a focused view of data sharing in one discipline. Detailed information on methods is available elsewhere (Bos et al., 2007; Olson, Bos, & Zimmerman, 2008; Zimmerman, 2007; 2008).

Science of Collaboratories

The Science of Collaboratories (SOC) was the name of a five-year project funded by the U.S. National Science Foundation (NSF) to study computer-supported distributed collaborations across many research disciplines; these projects have often been referred to as collaboratories. The overall goals of the SOC project were to: (1) perform a comparative analysis of collaboratory projects, (2) develop theory about this new organizational form, and (3) offer practical advice to collaboratory participants and to funding agencies about how to design and construct successful collaboratories. Through our research, we identified many of the social, organizational, and technological barriers that made these projects difficult. We also assembled a database that contains summaries of information on more than 70 collaboratories. Our methods of data collection included interviews with project principals; reading project papers, annual reports, and other documents; and studying web sites. We also interviewed project managers from U.S. funding agencies such as the NSF and the National Institutes of Health (NIH).

As part of SOC's effort to investigate the broad underlying social and technical elements that contribute to successful collaborations, we studied the ways in which some of these projects addressed the sharing of data either within the distributed and sometimes multidisciplinary projects or with those external to the collaboratory. In this chapter, we draw from findings based on data collected from a subset of the collaboratories that we studied. These projects were primarily in biomedicine and environmental science, which were, and still are, facing complex data sharing challenges (MacMullen & Denn, 2005; Ribes & Bowker, 2008; Zimmerman, 2007; 2008).

The Sharing and Reuse of Ecological Data

The more focused study investigated the experiences of ecologists who had used data that they did not collect themselves. The primary method of data collection was semi-structured interviews with 13 ecologists. Interviews were also conducted with data managers in order to obtain another perspective on the sharing and reuse of ecological data. Ecological data were the focus of study because they present significant obstacles to sharing and reuse. The data are widely dispersed, heterogeneous, and complex, which make them difficult to locate and hard to reuse. These challenges are complicated by social factors that hinder data sharing, such as issues of ownership and a lack of reward for sharing. Most of the ecologists interviewed aggregated together data from multiple sources to create their own databases; the resulting databases were small enough to be managed by Microsoft Excel, a program widely used by ecologists. Data Grid technologies that are often mentioned in the context of large-scale e-research are not yet common in ecology.

The unit of analysis in the SOC project was the collaborative project, whereas individuals were the primary unit of analysis in the study of ecologists. The ability to make comparisons across the two levels helped to illuminate differences and similarities that would otherwise have been difficult to discern. For instance, we found that individuals or small teams of researchers can often conduct their work privately, but large-scale collaborations are subject to increased accountability, greater interdependencies, and intensified needs for standardization. These factors affect the production, organization, and sharing of data and have implications for long-term preservation of research data. We expand on this and other findings in the next section.

DATA SHARING AS A CONTINUUM

The origins of digital databases affect work practices, the reuse potential of data, and the authority and visibility of data producers and other individuals such as computer scientists, data managers, and information specialists. As Hine (2006) noted, changes stemming from e-research capabilities are difficult to assess in advance:

> New technologies, such as databases, may provide occasions for developing new work practices in science, and may lead to the exploration of new areas of knowledge, but consequences do not flow directly or predictably from the technology (p. 291).

Our goals are to contribute to a better understanding of the factors that influence the success of different solutions to data sharing, to spur additional research in this area, and to improve the ability to predict and assess the outcomes of various approaches. We draw on cases from our own research and examples from studies by other scholars to show that the outcomes of data sharing approaches occur along a continuum.

At one end of the continuum are approaches that allow researchers to work as they always have, and the labor necessary to prepare data, make them available, and support their use is conducted by others. In this case, data sharing considerations are not injected into the research process, but are managed by others after the fact. The work of these 'others'—actors such as data curators, data managers, information technologists, and even researchers in the domain—is loosely couple, if it is connected at all, to the generation of data. In contrast, solutions at the other end of the continuum force researchers to consider barriers to sharing, integration, and federation at the outset of data collection and to develop solutions in advance to deal with these issues. In this case, tighter links are formed between the production and the sharing of data. One of the results of this approach is that data are contextualized through the process of creation or integration. Further, researchers' practices, attitudes, and relationships with other actors can be changed. In regard to the latter, others' work becomes more prominent, which alters the balance of authority and visibility among researchers and these other actors. For example, individuals with database skills may become an integral part of the research team.

The easiest cases to assess are those that occur at extremes of the continuum; ones that fall in the middle are currently harder to judge as we show in the sections below. Even so, this broad categorization of data sharing approaches provides a means to explore how and in what manner the origin of digital databases affects the degree to which practices of domain researchers and others are or are not changed and the consequences for the relationships among the various actors.

MANY CHALLENGES, MULTIPLE SOLUTIONS, DIVERSE OUTCOMES

It is hard to share data. There are many reasons for this and numerous approaches have been devised to overcome these challenges. We describe some of the issues that make data sharing hard, and we analyze methods that have been developed to address them. Our results show that the same approach can have different outcomes even when situations appear to be similar. The success of the approach should be measured against the desired results. For example, is the goal to motivate researchers to share unpublished data; is to make widely scattered data available in a centralized database for scientists to use to generate novel hypotheses; or are there multiple aims that individuals and organizations wish to achieve?

Aggregating and Integrating Dispersed Data

Oftentimes, the data that are useful to address particular research questions or that would provide opportunities to mine data for new insights are widely dispersed. Bringing these data together in a centralized database has several potential advantages (Bos, 2008). For one, it can help to avoid duplication of effort. In addition, many research questions benefit from the ability to search and analyze a larger set of data. For instance, more sophisticated and powerful analyses can be done than if the data were kept separately. The aggregation or integration of distributed data, which can be carried out by individuals, small teams of researchers, or a group of individuals with diverse skills, is a common way to create a publicly available data resource. The case studies below illustrate some prototypical strategies designed to bring dispersed data together. We analyze the affects of various approaches on research practice and the relationships between actors as well as their success in motivating researchers to make available unpublished data.

Curating published data

WormBase is a resource for data and information on the genetics, genomics, and biology of *C. elegans*. This database is maintained by the International WormBase Consortium, which employs more than twenty curators whose job is to scan published literature for relevant data (Chen et al., 2005). Once data have been found, they are extracted and integrated into the Wormbase database and made available to any user via the Internet. Besides the aggregation of dispersed data, another advantage of a resource like WormBase is that the data benefit from reuse. One of the data curators that we interviewed as part of the SOC project stated that at least half of the e-mail messages they receive concern corrections to the data. This is an important means by which the quality of the data is improved.

Individual investigators can contribute data directly to WormBase, but only a small portion of the researchers in this community choose to do so. We asked one of the data curators we interviewed why she thought more scientists did not contribute data directly to the resource.

> It's not that they don't want to share. . . . They don't hide data. They're willing to share, and the community is very open-minded. Also, they know that once the paper is published, WormBase will include the data in the database. The majority of the data—90–95%—are published.

Those who develop and maintain WormBase essentially relieve researchers from the responsibilities and effort to make data available for sharing. The work of WormBase curators is made possible by funding from the National Human Genome Research Institute and the British Medical Research Council. These agencies also support the creation and maintenance of other model organism databases. The quote above, along with findings by Borgman (2007: 188–189) suggest that the existence and use of resources like WormBase do not have a significant affect on researchers' data sharing behavior. FlyBase, the primary source for molecular and genetic information about the *Drosophila* (fruit fly) genome, operates and is maintained in a fashion similar to WormBase. The data in FlyBase are also derived almost entirely from the published literature even though the maintainers of FlyBase encourage researchers to submit data that will not be published in a journal (Kling, McKim, & Adam, 2003).

The Ecological Society of America (ESA) used a different approach to create an online data resource. ESA developed a digital archive for appendices and supplements, including raw data, associated with papers published in ESA journals. Contribution is voluntary, and the work of preparing the data for sharing is the responsibility of the authors. The approach has achieved a measure of success in terms of number of contributions (Bain, 2005), but since it relies on voluntary deposits of data it lacks the comprehensiveness of WormBase and FlyBase. In addition, the data in ESA archives are not integrated into a common database. Even if resources were available to support this activity, it would be difficult to accomplish since data associated with papers published in ESA journals are diverse in type, format, and description. WormBase and FlyBase have a more singular focus, which makes it easier to integrate data.

Data deposition as a requirement of publication

Drawing on data collected as part of the SOC project, Bos (2008) identified economic incentives as a possible way to solve the cultural and social barriers that make researchers reluctant to contribute data to shared resources. Economic solutions focus on the external reward system and attempt to make data contribution more attractive or make it less desirable to withhold data. Bos noted that the economic method that has been most successful is the requirement that authors provide proof of data contribution as a prerequisite to publication. This is particularly common in molecular biology. Bos cited GenBank as an example. GenBank started with curators combing the literature for data much as WormBase and FlyBase currently do. This approach became hard to sustain as the amount of genetic data grew.

> This method was slow and error prone, but it worked acceptably well for several years. Still, the rapid acceleration of the field due to new sequencing techniques prompted GenBank to investigate ways to get researchers to submit data directly. In the late 1980s, GenBank began partnering with journals on a policy that required authors to deposit data in GenBank as a precondition of publication. . . . Today, most of the important journals in the field of genetics worldwide comply with this system (Bos, 2008: 260).

Bos stated that the success of this model "does not eliminate the problem of how to motivate contributions to public databases" (p. 260). Like WormBase and FlyBase, GenBank is comprised primarily of data associated with a publication, and it does not appear to have motivated researchers to contribute unpublished data.

There are multiple explanations for why published data comprise the majority of data in many aggregated databases. These reasons include the time and effort required by researchers to fully document unpublished data, their concerns about being 'scooped' by competitors, and fears that their data will be misused. Results from the study of ecologists and a recent paper written by members of the International WormBase Consortium show that there is a demand for unpublished data, however (Bieri et al., 2006; Zimmerman, 2007). As one of the data managers interviewed in the ecology project stated, " . . . published data are a poor substitute for having a complete archive of all the data that have been collected." WormBase and FlyBase are important resources for their research communities, but their value as a research tool has not motivated scientists to contribute their unpublished data to these databases. In the next section, we analyze an approach that other projects have used to motivate researchers to contribute unpublished data.

Contribution has its privileges

In 2005, the NIH began requiring all large grant proposals to have a data sharing plan. This was in addition to an earlier NIH policy that stated that data should be made available as widely and freely as possible (NIH, 2003). Two of the NIH-funded biomedical collaboratories that we studied have attempted to motivate researchers to contribute data, particularly unpublished data, by granting special privileges to those who do so. Scientists funded by the Consortium for Functional Glycomics (CFG) produce resources, including physical samples that are valuable experimental materials for other researchers. In return for CFG's sharing of these resources, non-CFG scientists agree to deposit data into the CFG database at least once every ninety days. This 'give in order to get' strategy is also used by the Biomedical Informatics Research Network (BIRN). Scientists in BIRN had expressed hesitation about releasing data before they had time to use them. In response to this concern, BIRN developed a 'rollout' scheme and timeline in which data would first be available only to the producer, then to specified others, then to other members of the BIRN consortium, and lastly to the general public (Olson et al., 2008).

Data as a publication

Peer-reviewed publications, particularly journal articles, are the centerpiece of the formal scholarly communication and reward system (Garvey, 1979). Some projects and publications have sought to make more data available by treating the compilation and synthesis of published and unpublished data as publications. A high-profile example of this approach was the partnership between the influential journal *Nature* and the Alliance for Cellular Signaling's (AfCS) Signaling Gateway.[1] Molecule Pages, a collation of existing information on proteins involved in cell signaling presented in a standardized database, is one aspect of the Signaling Gateway. One type of Molecule Page is expert-authored and peer-reviewed data based on published literature (Saunders et al., 2008: D700). Alfred Gilman, the Nobel-prize winning scientist who initiated the AfCS, described the rationale for Molecule Pages to a writer for the journal *Nature*:

> Being an author of one of the Molecule Pages, which will be updated annually, will be time-consuming. So Gilman says it is essential that the effort should be recognized by faculty committees and granting bodies, in much the same way that they consider the value of authoring a widely cited review article. "If large-scale collaborations in biology are going to work, the community will have to change its ways of evaluating effort," he says (Abbott, 2002: 601).

There are other examples of treating data compilations as publications. For example, in 2000, ESA developed a new form of peer-reviewed publication called Data Papers, which are compilations and syntheses of mostly unpublished datasets (Bain, 2005). Since Data Papers were introduced, less than 20 have been published, and the number per year has not grown over time, so the long-term success of this publication remains to be determined.[2] The Cochrane Collaboration's *Cochrane Reviews* are systematic assessments of evidence of the effects of healthcare interventions that are developed by experts and made available through subscription by John Wiley and Sons. Authors of Cochrane Reviews are encouraged to locate and incorporate unpublished data into the reviews.

It was outside the scope of the SOC project to investigate how or if peer-reviewed compilations of data affect researchers' practices and attitudes toward data sharing and the relationships between those who develop and maintain the databases and those who author the publications. These are rich and important topics for future research.

Overcoming Semantic and Methodological Differences

Above, we analyzed situations in which dispersed data were aggregated in a common space or integrated in a centralized data resource. Here we discuss two challenges that render it difficult to integrate data. First, each discipline and sub-discipline has its own terminology and jargon. In addition, sometimes the same word can have a different meaning in two fields of study. These semantic variations present significant challenges to data sharing. Second some fields, such as ecology, do not have widely standardized methods of data collection (Zimmerman, 2008). Even in fields where standard methods exist, replication is hard to achieve (Collins, 1992[1985]).

Several approaches to semantic differences have been attempted such as linking together existing controlled vocabularies and dictionaries, creating ontologies, using keyword mapping, and employing other mechanisms to provide concept-based searching and semantic interoperability (Adams, 2002; Cortez, 1999; Pundt & Bishr, 2002). An ontology, which has been defined as a specification of a conceptualization, helps users locate information or data about a single concept that can be described using various terms (Adams, 2002; Pundt & Bishr, 2002).

The Geosciences Network (GEON) is a collaboration between geoscientists and computer scientists. The main goal of GEON is to enable researchers to access, synthesize, and model geoscience data from a wide variety of sources. This is a major challenge due to technical issues such as the extreme heterogeneity of data formats and computing systems and because of scientific barriers related to the conventions, terminologies, and ontological frameworks found in the fields that comprise the earth sciences (Ribes & Bowker, 2008). For example, U.S. state geological surveys use a variety of classification systems, and so it is labor intensive and time-consuming to find all the data on the same topic. To address this problem, GEON developed an ontology-based search for geological maps that allows users to integrate maps from nine state geologic surveys in the Rocky Mountain region. In the process of working together on this and other GEON objectives, the relationship between geoscientists and computer scientists was altered. A geoscientist in the project, who we interviewed as part of the SOC project, described the change in attitudes on both sides:

> We need them. We know that. We understand their expertise. At least they can bring something on the table. And we do the same thing for them. We bring some domain [knowledge], and they can come in and really help contribute something to the domain.

The geoscientists perceived that the expertise of computer scientists helped to increase their productivity by reducing the time required to search for dispersed data. The interviewee noted that mutual appreciation between the parties took time to achieve and is an ongoing process.

Changes in the relationships between actors in a collaboration does not necessarily translate to the wider communities outside the borders of the project. When two people develop respect and trust, these do not necessarily generalize to other outsiders. Additional strategies and effort are required to bring about larger scale changes:

> But of course, we want GEON to be bigger and better and more external, and that's still a big challenge for us. And to make sure the community understands that this is the way, this is the future, this is how it should be done—not the old ways that you've been keeping your data on your desktop and not giving anybody any access to it.

This challenge is shared by many of the projects and cases profiled in this chapter. It raises questions about how the experiences and attitudes of a subset of people can be diffused more broadly to their respective communities.

Standardizing in advance

So far, all the approaches we have analyzed in this chapter occur after data have been collected. Another type of solution to the difficulties of sharing data considers impediments in advance of data collection. For example, researchers in one of the multi-institutional, medical collaborations we studied spent almost a year to develop standardized data collection and management protocols for aggregating data produced by the distributed collaboration. No data were produced at any of the sites until these common methods were in place. Another SOC interviewee—a principal investigator associated with a large-scale biomedical collaboration—commented that "the ramp-up time is extraordinary." He explained the reasons for this, relevant to the part of the project that generated mass spectrometry data, which had to be managed and made accessible.

> The bioinformatics core is something that we didn't appreciate at the start and was something that was mandated by NIH. They didn't understand; nobody knew what bioinformatics was, and we spent a long time arguing about it, and we made some false steps there. Now we understand it much more. And the bioinformatics guy plays an integral role . . . He's set the entire infrastructure up for how to organize the data. . . . We're also putting together a knowledge base, which has molecules and functions and other things. . . . He's dealing with information handling, software needs, that kind of thing. It's not like the other stuff where we're trying to develop state of the art reagents for the fields. However, having said that, the program that he has developed for mass spectrometry data is going to be published and made publicly available. It's very, very innovative.

The above quote illustrates appreciation by the principal investigator (PI) for the work of the bioinformatician. What is less clear, however, is the degree to which the authority of the bioinformatics lead was changed from the norm and how visible he is to the project as a whole. The PI's awareness, however, may signal a shift in the role of bioinformaticians and others in the research process. This is hard to predict, but findings by Karasti, Baker, and Halkola (2006) in regard to cross-site collaboration between data managers and researchers in the U.S. Long Term Ecological Research (LTER) Network are worth noting.

> Though the LTER community approach has not produced immediate or generic "solutions" to data management and federation, the networking of sites has generated broad ranging dialogue, much needed problem definition, valuable working solutions and technology arrangements, and new engagements with scientists. These arrangement [sic] have created a general "information management preparedness" and a "data stewardship awareness" (p. 351).

Karasti and her co-authors identify signs such as dialog among stakeholders that may be visible in advance of more dramatic changes in practices and attitudes related to data.

Like the project mentioned at the start of this section, another of the large-scale, biomedical collaboratories we studied did not collect data until the participating labs, which were using the same methods, were able to replicate their results consistently. The PI explained the advantages of this approach:

> Having two labs doing the same thing has been useful in illuminating tacit knowledge, and thus making it easier to accurately standardize procedures—the standardization of procedures is crucial to the success of this collaborative effort. Heightened awareness of tacit knowledge of yourself and others is crucial to the success of a collaboratory in which formalized protocols and standardization are needed. Furthermore, this process of standardization requires much more detail.

This collaboratory made the data publicly available immediately after they were produced and checked for quality.[3] The process of agreeing on standards and replicating results improved the quality of the documentation about the data, and arguably, made them easier for others to reuse. The leaders of the project and the researchers who generated the data considered barriers to sharing, integration, and federation at the outset of data collection and developed solutions in advance to deal with these issues. Again, while this may not change broad practice in the field, it clearly affected the attitudes and experiences of the project members.

The consideration of methods and documentation in advance of data collection is not limited to the life sciences. Carlson and Anderson (Chapter 13 in this volume) studied the SurveyProject resource center, which provides access to the results of a large survey conducted annually of 10,000 U.K. households. Their findings provide an opportunity to compare SurveyProject with the biomedical projects described above. The results were similar across the projects, even though the subject areas were different. Carlson and Anderson observed that one of the factors that supports reuse of SurveyProject data is the attention given to the need to be explicit about the way in which the data were produced and the context of their production.

Cyberinfrastructure is an important component in efforts to share large amounts of data. There is evidence in the cases presented here that there are some instances in which authority resides in a larger set of actors, such as computer scientists and data managers, and is not dictated primarily by researchers. This appears to be the situation in GEON. It also has the potential to become the case in other realms and with other actors. For example, Davis and Vickery (2007) noted that librarians can proceed proactively to build data collections by working directly with researchers to collect, organize, and host datasets generated at their institutions. "In doing so, librarians have the potential to have influence over the emerging datasets market rather than waiting for commercial vendors to harvest and package the data for later re-sale" (Davis & Vickery, 2007: 30).

DISCUSSION

Visions of e-research emphasize large-scale databases that require massive storage capabilities, robust infrastructure for data management and transfer, and sophisticated tools for visualization and analysis. The way in which these databases are created and the contexts from which they emerge will determine if the promise of data in e-research will be fulfilled. In this chapter, we have presented several cases to illustrate some of the factors that play a role and to show the continuum of outcomes that can result. In reality, there are many more complex situations and factors to be examined. For example, anthropology differs significantly in terms of culture, methods, and data from other fields we discussed in this chapter. Funding agencies increasingly encourage anthropologists to share their data. However, this mandate conflicts with anthropologists' views of the meaning of data. Carlson and Anderson (Chapter 13 in this volume) observed that anthropologists see themselves as describing the specificities of particular contexts. Requests for anthropologists to generalize their data to make them more usable by others are difficult to reconcile with the epistemology of that discipline.

Similarly, other authors have shown that researcher views about what count as data, their proper role, and when they are ready for sharing add to the complexity of predicting the outcomes of various approaches to sharing (Collins, 1998; Hilgartner & Brandt-Rauf, 1994). We need to understand more about the complex factors that influence the sharing and reuse of data. Further, it is important to consider the goal when designing approaches to share data. Is the intent to influence the practice of researchers, relieve researchers of the burdens of data sharing, or bring the expertise of other actors more directly into the process of research?

The way in which digital data bases come about affects whether there are shifts in practice for the researcher or for actors such as archivists, information technologists, or librarians. Different types of data sharing approaches place different demands on those who produce and manage data. Some methods depend more on finding ways to motivate and provide researchers with incentives to share than do others. Some strategies delegate the work to specialists whose efforts are loosely coupled with those who generate the data. The origins of the database also affect the reuse potential of research data. When considerations for sharing are injected into the research process, data are more likely to be well-documented, and therefore, they should be more usable to those outside the context in which they were generated.

Small datasets that are created, used, and controlled by single investigators will always be an important part of research, but large databases promise unprecedented levels of replicability and generalizability. Creating, managing, and making these datasets available present challenges that many scientific communities are unready to face. Large-scale collaborations, which are under scrutiny due to the amount of funding they receive, have the potential to set practices and standards that might get picked up by others.

While many fields face the need for large, standardized datasets to tackle system-level problems, it is individual achievements that are often rewarded. The tension between the desire and necessity for collaboration and the need for single accomplishments puts pressure on the 'old' practices of science. Further, as disciplines move toward greater collaboration, changes are usually required to methods of collecting, organizing, and sharing data (Collins, 2003).

Finally, since the efforts devoted to data sharing divert time and resources from other activities it is important to consider several questions. What is the appropriate amount of activity that scientists should invest in sharing? What degree of control should investigators expect to have over data that they share? Do the benefits outweigh the financial and human costs of sharing? Should all data be subject to the same sharing policies? For example, should data gathered by an individual investigator working in a field setting be exchanged under the same guidelines as the large amounts of data gathered by remote instruments? Answers to these and other questions are critical to achieving the promise of data in e-research.

ACKNOWLEDGMENTS

The ideas in this chapter have benefited from comments received at conferences where early versions of this work were presented. These findings are based on work supported by the National Science Foundation under Grant Number IIS 0085981. Any opinions, findings, conclusions, or recommendations are those of the authors and do not necessarily reflect the views of the NSF.

NOTES

1. The AfCS is a large-scale collaborative project funded by the National Institute of General Medical Sciences. AfCS no longer supports the Signaling Gateway, which is now a collaboration between the University of California, San Diego and *Nature* (Saunders et al., 2008).
2. See http://esapubs.org/archive/archive_D.htm.
3. This raises another interesting aspect of such projects that we do not explore here. Projects like WormBase and the biomedical collaboratories

enable PhD-level researchers to participate in research and use their expertise without the pressures of tenure or the long hours that might be required of a laboratory scientist. This provides an alternate career path that may benefit the field.

REFERENCES

Abbott, A. (2002). Alliance for cellular signaling: Into unknown territory. *Nature, 420*(6916): 600–601.

Adams, K. (2002). The Semantic Web: Differentiating between taxonomies and ontologies. *Online, 26*(4): 20–23.

Arzberger, P., Schroeder, P. Beaulieu, A., Bowker, G., Casey, K., Laaksonen, L., Moorman, D., Uhlir, P., & Wouters, P. (2004). An international framework to promote access to data. *Science, 303*(5665): 1777–1778.

Bain, J. L. (2005). An introduction to *Ecological Archives*. *Bulletin of the Ecological Society of America, 86*(2): 86–91.

Baru, C. (2007). Sharing and caring of eScience data. *International Journal on Digital Libraries, 7*(1–2): 113–116.

Beaulieu, A. (2001). Voxels in the brain: Neuroscience, informatics and changing notions of objectivity. *Social Studies of Science, 31*(5): 635–680.

Bieri, T., et al. (2007). WormBase: New content and better access. *Nucleic Acids Research, 35*(Database Issue): D506-D510.

Birnholtz, J., & Bietz, M. (2003). Data at work: Supporting sharing in science and engineering. *Proceedings of the International ACM SIGGROUP Conference on Supporting Group Work, 2003*: 339–343.

Borgman, C. L. (2007). *Scholarship in the digital age: Information, infrastructure, and the Internet*. Cambridge, MA: MIT Press.

Borgman, C. L., Wallis, J. C., & Enyedy, N. (2007). Little science confronts the data deluge: Habitat ecology, embedded sensor networks, and digital libraries. *International Journal on Digital Libraries, 7*(1–2): 17–30.

Bos, N. (2008). Motivation to contribute to collaboratories: A public goods approach. In G. M. Olson, A. Zimmerman, & N. Bos (Eds.) *Scientific collaboration on the Internet*, pp. 251–274. Cambridge, MA: MIT Press

Bos, N., Zimmerman, A., Olson, J., Yew, J., Yerkie, J., Dahl, E., & Olson, G. (2007). From shared databases to communities of practice: A taxonomy of collaboratories. *Journal of Computer-Mediated Communication, 12*(2), article 16. Retrieved July 1, 2008, from http://jcmc.indiana.edu/vol12/issue2/bos.html

Brown, C. (2003). The changing face of scientific discourse: Analysis of genomic and proteomic database usage and acceptance. *Journal of the American Society for Information Science and Technology, 54*(10): 926–938.

Chen, N. et al. (2005). WormBase: A comprehensive data resource for *Caenorhabditis* biology and genomics. *Nucleic Acids Research, 33*(Database Issue): D383-D389.

Collins, H. M. (1992) [1985]. *Changing order: Replication and induction in scientific practice*. Chicago, IL: University of Chicago Press.

Collins, H. M. (1998). The meaning of data: Open and closed evidential cultures in the search for gravitational waves. *American Journal of Sociology, 104*(2): 293–338.

Collins, H. M. (2003). LIGO becomes big science. *Historical Studies in the Physical and Biological Sciences, 33*: 261–297.

Committee on the Future of Long-term Ecological Data. (1995). *Final Report of the Ecological Society of America Committee on the Future of Long-Term*

Ecological Data (FLED) (Vols. 1–2). Washington, DC: Ecological Society of America.

Cortez, E. M. (1999). Use of metadata vocabularies in data retrieval. *Journal of the American Society for Information Science, 50*(13): 1218–1223.

Cragin, M. H., & Shankar, K. (2006). Scientific data collections and distributed collective practice. *Computer Supported Cooperative Work, 15*(2–3): 185–204.

Davis, H. M., & Vickery, J. N. (2007). Datasets, a shift in the currency of scholarly communication: Implications for library collections and acquisitions. *Serials Review, 33*(1): 26–32.

Emmott, S. (2006). *Towards 2020 science*. Redmond, WA: Microsoft Research.

Garvey, W. D. (1979). *Communication: The essence of science: Facilitating the exchange among librarians, scientists, engineers, and students*. Oxford: Pergamon Press.

Goble, C., & De Roure, D. (2007). myExperiment: Social networking for workflow-using e-scientists. *Proceedings of the Workshop on Workflows in Support of Large-Scale Science, 2*: 1–2

Hey, T., & Trefethen, A. E. (2003). The data deluge: An e-science perspective. In F. Berman, G. C. Fox, & T. Hey (Eds.), *Grid computing: Making the global information infrastructure a reality*, pp. 859–906. Chichester, UK: Wiley.

Hey, T., & Trefethen, A. E. (2005). Cyberinfrastructure for e-science. *Science, 308*(5723): 817–821

Hey, T., & Trefethen, A. E. (2008). E-Science, cyberinfrastructure, and scholarly communication. In G. M. Olson, A. Zimmerman, & N. Bos (Eds.), *Scientific collaboration on the Internet*, pp. 15–31. Cambridge, MA: MIT Press.

Hilgartner, S. (1995). Biomolecular databases: New communication regimes for biology? *Science Communication, 17*(2): 240–263.

Hilgartner, S., & Brandt-Rauf, S. I. (1994). Data access, ownership, and control: Toward empirical studies of access practices. *Knowledge: Creation, Diffusion, Utilization, 15*(4): 355–372.

Hine, C. (2006). Databases as scientific instruments and their role in the ordering of scientific work. *Social Studies of Science, 36*(2): 269–298.

Jankowski, N. W. (2007). Exploring e-science: An introduction. *Journal of Computer-Mediated Communication 12*(2), article 10. Retrieved July 1, 2008, from http://jcmc.indiana.edu/vol12/issue2/jankowski.html

Karasti, H. A., Baker, K. S., & Halkola, E. (2006). Enriching the notion of data curation in e-science: Data managing and information infrastructuring in the Long Term Ecological Research (LTER) Network. *Computer Supported Cooperative Work, 15*(2–3): 321–358.

Kling, R., McKim, G., & King, A. (2003). A bit more to it: Scholarly communication forums as socio-technical interaction networks. *Journal of the American Society of Information Science and Technology, 54*(1): 47–67.

MacMullen, W. J., & Denn, S. O. (2005). Information problems in molecular biology and bioinformatics. *Journal of the American Society for Information Science and Technology, 56*(5): 447–456.

National Institutes of Health. (2003). *Final NIH statement on sharing research data*. Retrieved July 1, 2008, from http://grants2.nih.gov/grants/guide/notice-files/NOT-OD-03-032.html

National Research Council. (1997). *Bits of power: Issues in global access to scientific data*. National Academies Press: Washington, DC.

Olson, G. M., Bos, N., & Zimmerman, A. (2008). Introduction. In G. M. Olson, A. Zimmerman, & N. Bos (Eds.), *Scientific collaboration on the Internet*, pp. 1–12. Cambridge, MA: MIT Press.

Olson, J. S., Ellisman, M., James, M., Grethe, J. S., & Puetz, M. (2008). The Biomedical Informatics Research Network. In G. M. Olson, A. Zimmerman, & N.

Bos (Eds.), *Scientific collaboration on the Internet*, pp. 221–232. Cambridge, MA: MIT Press.

Parr, C. S., & Cummings, M. P. (2005). Data sharing in ecology and evolution. *Trends in Ecology and Evolution, 20*(7): 362–363.

Piwowar, H. A., Day, R. S., Fridsma, D. B. (2007). Sharing detailed research data is associated with increased citation rate. *PLoS ONE 2*(3). Retrieved July 1, 2008, from http://www.pubmedcentral.nih.gov/articlerender.fcgi?artid=1817752

Pritchard, S. M., Carver, L., & Anand, S. (2004). *Collaboration for knowledge management and campus informatics*. University of California at Santa Barbara. Retrieved July 1, 2008, from http://www.library.ucsb.edu/informatics/informatics/documents/UCSB_Campus_Informatics_Project_Report.pdf

Pundt, H., & Bishr, Y. (2002). Domain ontologies for data sharing—an example from environmental monitoring using field GIS. *Computers & Geosciences, 28*(1): 95–102.

Ribes, D., & Bowker, G. C. (2008). Organizing for multidisciplinary collaboration: The case of the Geosciences Network. In G. M. Olson, A. Zimmerman, & N. Bos (Eds.), *Scientific collaboration on the Internet*, pp. 311–330. Cambridge, MA: MIT Press.

Saunders, B., Lyon, S., Day, M., Riley, B., Chenette, E., & Subramanian, S. (2008). The Molecule Pages database. *Nucleic Acids Research, 36*(Database Issue): D700-D706.

Zimmerman, A. (2007). Not by metadata alone: The use of diverse forms of knowledge to locate data for reuse. *International Journal on Digital Libraries, 7* (1–2), 5–16.

Zimmerman, A. (2008). New knowledge from old data: The role of standards in the sharing and reuse of ecological data. *Science, Technology, and Human Values, 33*(5), 631–652.

13 Naming, Documenting and Contributing to e-Science

Samuelle Carlson and Ben Anderson

INTRODUCTION

Partly as a result of financial inducement (research funds) but also for sound methodological and substantive reasons, social scientists in the U.K. and elsewhere are beginning to engage with the wider program of 'e-science'. This program is motivated by a multiplicity of factors including the requirement for urgent action to manage the increasingly large quantities of data produced by digital technologies and digitally enabled science. Whilst this 'deluge', 'wave' and 'knowledge overload' may provide novel opportunities for data analysis (Hey & Trefethen, 2003) it brings with it concerns over data mis-use and disclosure. In addition funding bodies are naturally keen to ensure re-use of the results of their investments in data to avoid resources remaining within the disciplines that originally collected them and to achieve a maximum return on their investments (Elias, 2006). Finally there is a stated imperative for groups of social scientists to collaborate on interdisciplinary projects to address large-scale research problems and potentially generate novel and innovative solutions or results (ESRC, 2005).

To be sure, the greater computing capacity and larger sets of data enabled by computing, service and data Grids offer the potential to ask new scientific questions—those questions which can only be addressed through massive analysis, the federation of disparate re-usable datasets and interdisciplinary research. However, although technology makes certain things possible this does not necessarily mean that they will happen. The controversies surrounding the ethics of sharing data (Thompson, 2003) and the methodological reasons for (not) doing so in the social (Fielding, 2003) and natural sciences (Borgman, 2007; Campbell & Clarridge., 2002; Hagstrom, 1974) indicate that how and what to communicate and to whom is more problematic than naïve accounts of scientific collaboration might suppose. To what extent, then, can knowledge easily be disembedded from its producers and original contexts to become explicit data for temporally and geographically distributed re-users? Observations from anthropological research on the diversity and complexity of exchange practices and multiple relationships to objects entangled in wider regional and global systems (Thomas, 1991), together with key recent studies in the field of e-science (Coopmans, 2006; Jirotka & Procter, 2005; Purdam & Elliot, 2005), have underlined how most of the obstacles to data sharing and scientific collaboration are less technological than social, ethical, legal, and institutional, as researchers in fields such as computer supported cooperative work (CSCW) have known for some time (see Bimholtz & Bietz, 2003; Bowers, 1994).

The previously cited studies of scientific practice have also made clear that the large-scale sharing and re-use of data requires the definition of appropriate data standards and description mechanisms collectively termed metadata. Whilst the use of metadata and ontologies will be familiar to most social scientists, it has seen extensive recent attention in the technical sciences through the conception of the semantic Grid:

> in which information and services are given well-defined meaning through machine-processable descriptions which maximize the potential for sharing and reuse . . . with a high degree of easy-to-use and seamless automation enabling flexible collaborations and computations on a global scale (http://www.semanticgrid.org/, accessed 16 Feb. 2008).

This approach is echoed in a review of potential approaches to Grid-enabling quantitative e-social science data suggesting for example that applying such standards at source could ease the design of interoperable systems; that the use of automatic generation of metadata could support better resource and that the collaborative construction of metadata by groups of data users could lead to decentralised methods of quality enhancement following the model of wikipedia (Cole, Schurer, Beedham, & Hewitt, 2003). However, they also note that significant staffing resources would be required to produce effective metadata to Grid-enable existing data in order to render it usable and 'visible' in some future data-space. More problematically as Birholtz and Bietz (2003) note, with the best design and intentions much tacit knowledge can never be captured and even if it were further metadata models may be needed to describe the metadata itself, potentially leading to recursive metadata about metadata (Bowker, 2000). Further, given the constantly shifting nature of human classificatory systems (Schutz, 1962), the requirement to agree to a set of relationships and meanings in a given domain is not a simple task.

More generally it is notable that the overall e-science project, and data-sharing and re-use in particular, can be considered part of recent transformations in universities that impact on the notions of community, authority and accountability amongst academics. As Strathern (2004) observes, collaboration and interdisciplinarity are not new. What is new is the impetus to institutionalise them, often transnationally (Zabusky, 2002). In this context knowledge travels in increasingly varied forms, from stand-alone digitized data, through listserv commentaries to expanding practices of 'knowledge transfer' via patents and commercial ventures. e-Science raises questions about models of knowledge production—of ownership of potentially marketable data, of rights to interpret and exploit, of authorship and collaboration—against a background where similar questions are multiplying across the university system (Hine, 2003). If we set this alongside ongoing transformation in the measurement of outcomes and quality in the U.K. university sector (Strathern, 2000) then it is timely to ask how e-science methods and technologies might interact with these organisational shifts.

Elsewhere we have offered commentary on the nature of the data and implications of disconnecting it from its original collectors and sites based on empirical data gathered through four case studies of science practice undertaken in the U.K. in 2005 and 2006 (Anderson & Carlson, 2006a; Carlson & Anderson, 2007). In contrast, in this chapter we use the same set of case studies to focus on two additional themes that emerged from the case study data. These are the practices surrounding the use of standards and metadata to make data retrievable and comparable and the potential impact of e-science on existing structures of output measurement, authority and expertise.

Fieldsites and methods

The four projects selected for study varied considerably and intentionally in their approaches to data collection, disciplinary backgrounds and use of technologies. As we describe below they were chosen specifically to represent different dimensions of the soft/hard, pure/applied typology introduced by Becher (1987) and developed by Fry (2006); to reflect different levels of maturity of collaboration; to represent both geographical distribution and co-location and to reflect different levels of e-science technology use.

SkyProject is a £10M project initiated in 2001 by a consortium of 11 University departments. Its distributed team composed of scientists, software developers and managers aims at building the infrastructure for a data-Grid for U.K. astronomy, which will form the U.K. contribution to a global virtual observatory. It works closely with similar projects worldwide through an international alliance. The infrastructure developed enables the first beta-users to perform queries across distributed datasets through the SkyProject portal in order to access sequences of observations from a range of telescopes. Demonstrator tools accessed via a PC-based 'workbench' have included the self-assembly of sky-movies and automated filtering and processing of observation data held on a range of distributed databases.

SurveyProject is a resource centre producing a large scale complex survey dataset released every year through the government funded U.K. Data Archive (UKDA). The survey is conducted by a single academic institution although the fieldwork itself is carried out via a sub-contract to an agency. Every year a large number of U.K. households are contacted and interviewed with the resulting data being fed back to the institute for cleaning, processing, checking and packaging. The data are then deposited with the U.K. Data Archive which is responsible for managing access by third parties. The academic institute also has a remit to provide documentation, derived variables and training as well as the maintenance of a user group. Mature computing technologies support every aspect of the production line along which data are collected, processed, released, and analyzed.

CurationProject is an activity which for 20 years has been digitizing records of a collection of more than 750,000 artifacts and 100,000 field photographs collected since 1884 and making them available for study through an online database. With images now being added to the documentation, the project is conceived as an additional 'collection' rather than a catalogue. A curator has also initiated two new projects by which the museum's database is open to a community of researchers, artists and communities' representatives from around the world so that their alternative expertise, taxonomies and meanings can be recorded at the core of the museum.

AnthroProject refers to an anthropologist's undertaking to digitize and distribute all materials so far collected in a range of countries during her academic career, including fieldwork notes, images, maps, texts and videos in order to preserve in a digital medium anthropological materials that were quickly degenerating in their current forms. In addition it is the intention to make these materials available for re-use by other researchers and also available to the descendants of the sources through both an online database and via DVDs. Some of the professor's students opened cultural areas based on sub-sites under the umbrella of the main project. They have developed a wiki, a forum, a proprietary probabilistic search engine designed in partnership with a consultancy firm, and also participate in the Dspace worldwide digital archive.

With respect to Becher's typology, SkyProject represents the 'hard-pure' group of the physical sciences, SurveyProject represents 'soft-applied' group of the applied social sciences whilst CurationProject and AnthroProject represent the 'soft-pure' humanities and pure social sciences. Not represented here is the 'hard-applied' group although several e-science activities from this area have already been studied by others such as Hine (2005) and Fry (2006).

In addition, the case studies enabled the comparison of leading edge e-science projects such as SkyProject, with smaller scale innovative projects such as AnthroProject and with more traditional users of computing technology such as SurveyProject and CurationProject. Finally, the case studies were also distributed across a dimension of maturity. SurveyProject has been in existence for almost 17 years. As such it could not risk any innovation in the use of computing technologies or other processes that might jeopardize the survey itself or the timely processing, documentation and archival of the data. Both CurationProject and AnthroProject have a longer history of the collection of heterogeneous materials even if they have come only more recently to the use of digital technologies for their archival. SkyProject, in contrast, is in its early stages of development. In all cases we felt that scientific practice could potentially be co-evolving with computing technology but that this was more likely to be visible in SkyProject, which was more consciously attempting to re-invent both its scientific practices and its scientific tools, and had perhaps a greater freedom to do so.

For each case study the fieldwork started with interviews of key informants initially recruited through personal contacts. These initial 16 respondents served as sources of further interviewees and acted as sounding boards for early observations. The secondary respondents were selected in part by the key informant's recommendation but also by the individual paths that the 'data' took through each project. This required meeting people involved in data collection, processing, analysis and reuse some of whom were external to the specific case study itself such as staff at the U.K. Data Archive. In addition we analyzed internal and external project documents produced, including project Web sites and observed conference and other face-to-face meetings including a number of U.K. e-social sciences and e-science events. Finally, in the case of SkyProject, we traced email activity and other forms of electronic communication such as through jabber, a wiki, and skype, which were all extensively used.

Making data retrievable and comparable

As we have discussed the implementation of standards for technical and human metadata is considered vital to making data retrievable, reusable, and comparable within research communities. However, our studies have made clear that this task is complicated by the multiplicity of intersecting communities within each project. Thus, even before considering the implementation of metadata, a decision needs to be taken on whom to standardize with amongst the plethora of potential communities. In the case of AnthroProject the collection was split and hosted on various platforms: the university's Dspace archive, a former university library server, a third party university and a consulting company—all of which have specific practices and promote different standards. Even within CurationProject, which belonged to a quite integrated field in which standards had developed, an outreach officer described having the choice of using national capabilities offered by the Joint Information Systems Committee (JISC) in the U.K, by educational officers' online projects, or by initiatives set up between local museums. In the case of SkyProject, on the other hand, a more clearly defined community of practice was thought to exist through membership of the International Virtual Observatory Alliance (IVOA) and participation in subject specific European Grid initiatives. However, as we describe below even here difficulties in standardization became evident.

An organisation can establish collaboration and shared standards from a range of sources be they the subject-matter of research, the methodological approach, administrative status (e.g., archives), institution, discipline, professional specialization or geographical proximity. As no standard could be seen to accommodate all types of research and academic practice, a priority in the case studies often turned out to be determined by the perceived boundary of the community within which standards were negotiated and re-negotiated.

Besides inter-institutional decisions, standards also built up through time, and past practices sometimes took precedence over any potentially more advantageous new approach. At CurationProject, current curators' decisions were highly constrained by their predecessors' choices of what to record. This consideration is all the more important in the case of SurveyProject for whom any change in how the survey is carried out can impact the data it collects.

A second problem with which scientists grapple is at which stage of the research process to adopt standards. Are they to be applied before and in production as Cole and colleagues (Cole et al., 2003) advocate for or at the end of the production process, when data are archived and published? In the case of SurveyProject the respondents suggested that Grid-enabling would have to follow any UKDA standards since it is through them that their data are distributed. Interestingly, however, it was through contribution to a European comparative project that an attempt at multi-country standardization was made. However, SurveyProject respondents reported that bringing changes by establishing standards in data production practices generally produced strong resistance. They discovered that differences between the SurveyProject and the European study—such as differences in samples size, differences in the dates at which waves start, differences in variables, difference in how data are processed—could not be resolved without endangering the longitudinal nature of the U.K. survey. However, because each of the respective country surveys were highly coherent internally and over time, it was noted that differences between them could be bridged by various statistical means before or during the stage of analysis, provided sufficiently rich data was captured in the field.

In the social science case studies it was often at the end of the research cycle that standards were being applied and especially in the ways data are described. As informants pointed out, if standardization takes place at the sole level of terminologies and is done *a posteriori* then this makes data more easily locatable and retrievable. Further, if the original data is sufficiently detailed and well documented then *a priori* standardisation is not necessarily required for many forms of comparative analysis. Inevitably some forms of analysis will be precluded through different approaches to basic measurement, but this is set against the political and practical difficulties of standardisation.

For Whom?

Regarding the more specific question of the implementation of metadata standards within a domain, our studies suggest that the response depends not only on which community an organisation sees itself belonging to but also on which audience the organization wishes to reach. Informants suggested that which standards to implement should depend on who are the main users of the results, but to define this audience is itself an integral part of the problem. SurveyProject and SkyProject were all aware that the ways they present and describe their data determine the audiences that will use it. In turn, audiences that are strongly multi-disciplinary will make it difficult for an institution to adopt a standard descriptive system.

The situation is similarly complex for CurationProject whose audience includes artists, historians, sociologists, chemists, physicists, and anthropologists. Overall, it seemed that the more heterogeneous the audiences of a discipline, the more difficult standards in metadata and common ontologies are to implement. From this perspective, it is not surprising that SkyProject had engaged in the opportunistic definition of a fully-fledged ontology, as its audience was considered more easily defined by the project participants than were those of SurveyProject and CurationProject.

Decided by Whom?

Our interrogation of the SkyProject standards discussion process reveals that ontologies which claim to serve an entire community are often the work of smaller factions within that community. One of the team's member commented in this respect:

> Solar astronomers can't use the metadata we have because it's all 'dark-side' astronomers [astronomers observing at night who also obtain most of the funding] who defined the metadata initially. The 'sunny side' people don't get as much money so their need for metadata hasn't been represented. We have to force the dark-side people to accept the change (SkyProject Manager).

At work here is a tension not only between different user groups with differing levels of power, but also between two approaches to the implementation of data models. One approach aims to establish supposedly 'universal' ontologies within a domain whilst the other promotes ways to articulate or map local perspectives and terminologies. Informants from all projects pointed to further problems associated with aiming at a unified data model within a research community. First-mover advantage and subsequent attempted lock-in was a high priority to avoid lengthy negotiations and frustrations. However, as another SkyProject member noted, even when a data model for sub-specializations can be established, their applicability is often restricted.

An alternative approach illustrated by CurationProject was to promote an opening-up of metadata definitions and documentation processes to a wider range of contributions and to encourage the negotiation of descriptions and annotations (Cole, Schurer, Beedham, & Hewitt, 2003)—the 'wikipedia model'. For the curator, this divergence was due firstly to the fact that disciplines in the humanities simply could not afford the massive investments required to even temporarily maintain a relatively stable ontology. Secondly, reflecting the view of those such as Schutz (1962) and echoing the comments of an earlier respondent, he observed that users always reinterpret and twist categories they are given to serve their specific research interests and strategies. His view was that no ontology could encompass all the potential user-distortions required of it.

CurationProject decided to explore and take advantage of the continual adoption, circulation and redefinition of terms and concepts by users. To do this the team opened access to the museum's database to an initial user group of 50 people representing source communities, artists, curators and experts in other disciplines. These users are able to edit the metadata about objects held in the Museum's database which includes data connecting objects to other objects/information or describing them and their meaning. Access was managed so that groups of users only had access to parts of the database seen as relevant to their specific groupings.

On one view this approach could immediately be seen to undermine the authority of the museum and its curators since the curators' voice will now be just one amongst others. However, the curator(s) did not articulate this fear. Instead they looked forward to the creation of new knowledge to expand the collection and increase its value to users and indeed to its source communities. Beyond the call of Cole and colleagues (2003) for user-generated metadata this curation or archiving project stresses the potential value of allowing not only data users but the data sources themselves to annotate catalogues and resources. This project thus aims to explore and exploit some of the qualities of the folksonomies much described and debated recently (e.g., Macgregor & McCulloch, 2006; Sen et al., 2006; Golder & Huberman, 2006; Millen, Feinberg, & Kerr, 2006). Folksonomies reflect the mental categories of users and not only those of developers; the rich complexity they retain in their expression of many viewpoints not submitted to predetermined hierarchies; their accessibility to a large number is derived from their non-expert character.

Different Approaches to Metadata

The discussion of who decides the content of metadata provided above also indicates different approaches to the choice of which descriptive systems to use and how to relate different systems that may have to ultimately co-exist. On the one hand, CurationProject is actively seeking to undermine hierarchies amongst types of expertise and kinds of information by recording all descriptions provided by a wide range of sources. It thus promotes ways to record multiple ontologies, points of view, and meanings. Although a radical approach within the field, it is generally in line with the museum ethos which aims to record everything that can contextualize its collections. The extent to which this practice is possible for the museum is reflected by the relatively small-scale deployment.

SkyProject on the other hand pursued a different strategy. Although the International Virtual Observatory Alliance (IVOA) of which SkyProject was part had attempted to establish a central ontology to be adopted by the whole community, SkyProject decided to build on the work of a previous data-mining project that had catalogued a wide range of descriptive categories already prepared by Data Centers. These categories were then mapped on to 'Uniform Content Descriptors' (UCDs) and an ontology derived from this overview. This approach allowed SkyProject to quickly incorporate a range of existing catalogues and data:

> If two fields in two tables are described by the same UCD, these fields can be compared because they contain the same quantity. Automated data conversion can then be applied if these fields are expressed in different units. . . . Because UCDs precisely describe the contents of catalogues, they can be used to find similar catalogues. Given a reference catalogue, the list of UCDs which are present in this catalogue is used as criteria to perform a search among all other catalogues: similar catalogues are those that will have many UCDs in common with the reference one (Derriere, Ochsenbein, Boch, & Rixon, 2003: 79).

However, as a developer noted when describing this strategy of translation, even though this approach could accommodate institutional traditions and individual idiosyncrasies, especially when no agreements were made to work on common standards, this was starting to multiply interpretative layers:

> We shouldn't touch the core because people are sensitive; better to put a layer on top. Despite the differences, there will be interoperability [. . .] It's like a grammar transform that can create a common ground out of two ways to describe things—if several common grounds are created, we'll just create another transformer (Developer, SkyProject).

This strategy of interfaces and overarching layers once more implies making explicit the meaning of things in order to define and describe components carefully before translation can take place. Of course it also immediately raises the spectre of meta-metadata as Bowker (2000) has noted.

New forms of measurement

It became clear at a workshop discussing the reuse of qualitative data that by providing information on the context of collection, processing and analysis of data, researchers saw themselves as becoming the subject of data and thus exposed to new forms of evaluation. This was particularly the case where flows of transformations such as a series of codings or re-codings, analyses or other processes was recorded.

Thus, at the same time as being mechanisms for wider access and education, e-science technologies were also viewed as potentially powerful audit tools—"technologies of governance, management and funding" as described by one informant. At CurationProject, for example, one member was working on what he termed "an inbuilt system that automatically traces who does what when" and an associated consulting firm kept precise audit trails of the use made of its retrieval system on the site of AnthroProject as a way to estimate its efficiency and value.

Awareness of the capacity of new technologies to record movement of data and the actions of users in order to derive various performance indexes was also growing. Respondents remarked how the number of users had long been a criteria to attract funding or justify recurrent investment for science support or infrastructure services. In this regard, Corti and Thompson (2004) some years ago suggested that data Grids or even simple online databases may impact these old measurements in new ways. Each of the four projects studied here related to this issue, albeit in different ways. In a SkyProject member's view, for example, "people who own datasets get funding by number of users and will want to publish using SkyProject so that they can precisely establish users" (Developer, SkyProject).

However, the situation was not so straightforward in the case of the UKDA where one respondent noted a long-standing difficulty in getting data users to acknowledge their data source:

> The politics amongst cooperating institutions is often harder than the actual interoperability. . . . The biggest thing they are bickering over? Users. Each user is a tick box for the funding, so how you trace the user has ramifications. Who gets the user in these Grid projects is the stumbling block (Data Manager, UKDA).

In addition, the case studies suggested that as data travel across domains new kinds of measurement are emerging which in turn are generating anxiety. Whilst SkyProject had not (yet) considered how the use made of astronomical data might be quantified and priced, in other domains respondents spoke of real money or tokens paid by institutions so that one can assess how much data are being used by each (Ainsworth, 2005). As an informant noticed, this logic by which "universities are expected to be like commercial enterprises meets a strong resistance amongst academics who are generally terrified by commercial approach to what they produce. . . . They are afraid to find that it might have no value on this scale" (Member, AnthroProject).

Similar suggestions were offered on how one could base academic reputations on the mapping of academics' involvement in various projects as traced by provenance stores so that this, and collaboration itself, becomes a performance index or accounting metric. Given the expected benefits of inter-institutional and interdisciplinarity collaboration, respondents suggested that measuring collaboration would by default be taken as measuring the benefits it can yield with less attention to assessment of actual outcomes.

This process was observed in the recollections of a member of SkyProject regarding the project's initial 'opponents': "We say: 'join us instead; the fact that we can attract you will allow us to request more funding from which you will also benefit'". In this context collaboration, like users support, is primarily motivated by its inscription into funding mechanisms and as Marilyn Strathern has commented this has "all the momentum of a cultural movement, and one which [was] also going to generate resistance" (Strathern, 2000).

Not only did respondents note that e-science shuffled performance indexes, and, by the same token, sometimes redefined the very essence of what was being measured, but there was also some uncertainty about the ways in which e-science projects themselves were to be assessed. In research on the factors of success in e-science, Olson and colleagues (2008) start by asking what defines success in this milieu. In the projects they studied success had many expressions: the use of the collaboratory tools; software technologies (the output of e-science being the technology itself); direct effects on the science done (faster, more efficiently conducted); science careers (the people involved in a project and how they resurface over the years); effects on learning and science education; inspiration for other collaboratories; learning about collaboratories in general; effects on funding, public perception. Similarly, when asked how they felt SkyProject performance was assessed, the project manager revealed highly flexible evaluations of e-science projects:

> For one PI, it's the number of users; for me, it's the numbers of other projects using our bits; for him, we want to see papers out of it (. . .) For the funders, it is quite important that people talk good about the project to them, that is, people of the oversight which includes astronomers, a big IT guy, etc. (Task Manager, SkyProject).

Finally, beyond the spectre of audit respondents noted that another process opened up by e-science challenges academic expertise in its current form, and that is the participative or collective model of creation of knowledge. Under the familiar peer review model, data and its associated interpretation goes through a quality process and starts to be trusted as it passes various stages (Rowland, 2002; Weller, 2001). However, respondents noted that as data starts to be separated from publications and circulated online, more flexible systems of peer-review for data are sought, including evaluations by every user and no longer by a sole group of experts.

Beyond new modes of assessment, e-science was seen as giving visibility to a much wider range of contributions and peer review evaluations than those of consecrated academics.

Giving visibility to knowledge from a variety of sources in turn raises the issue of how this knowledge is to be managed. As we have noted above, opening up the production of knowledge (in the sense of giving it new forms of visibility) implies accepting the delegation of its management and the relaxation of content control. The curator of CurationProject took the example of Wikipedia to illustrate his point: "Wikipedia is open to grassroots. No one manages it centrally: the authors manage. It's not a community, but operates more like a society. No one could manage that. It's the same as with tagging, why should we?" New forms of electronic forums, retrieval systems and archives were seen to invite academics to rethink their identity and participation in such contexts because they grant visibility to the contributions and evaluations of a wider range of actors and sometimes also granted the power to fully act on this knowledge.

Increasing fragmentation

For our informants, apparently regardless of specializations, one of the drivers of e-science was seen to be the ability to "have more things to put together, more to connect, to make more combinations possible." SkyProject, for example, was based on the conception that the technology itself is modular and could be reassembled in different 'architectures'. Thus, various modules, such as MyLab could be deployed by other projects, in a standalone manner, or in combination with other SkyProject modules, such as the Directory module which was the catalogue of all data and services.

The 'segmentation' of knowledge was also reported as a goal in order to make knowledge more manageable. In the case of SurveyProject, the team circulates and manipulates data in batches because data are then easier to clean, with no risk of error running across entire waves of data. One of the strongest impacts of this atomisation on academic practices, however, appeared to lie in the value increasingly granted to small contributions in contrast to highly structured demonstrations or developments resulting from month or year-long research. We have already mentioned how the participation of users might produce changes in review mechanisms. Similarly the disclosure of primary data, methods, codes—and not only the outcomes of research—might also start to be valued. As several respondents suggested, one might look at how developers work in this respect:

> Developers are very interesting because they are familiar with the technology and are generally advanced when it comes to collaboration.

Looking at them would be very useful for scientists because they might well indicate the future. Reputation is built differently amongst developers. There are more small contributions and more flexible ways of assigning reputation, such as shorter laps to peer-review contributions (Developer, SkyProject).

In contrast to the academic values given to long and structured arguments and demonstrations of expertise such as journal articles or books, here value is given to discrete and often small-scale ideas that are contributions to a path or trajectory leading to major outcomes. This shift in the forms and practices of academic knowledge has been described by Osborne who identified a valorisation of discrete ideas; ideas which are "local, strategic and fleeting" or "vehicular, practical, usable, marketable" (2004: 441). He also suggests the threat it represents for experts:

> In today's highly mediated societies there is a huge demand for ideas; ideas which are mobile and "vehicular" rather than oracular. Perhaps this has to do with something like the "democratization" of ideas-work; ideas no longer being the property of the few, such that it becomes almost everyone's responsibility to create ideas. Ideas-work, in other words, is longer confined to an elite of great intellectuals, if it ever was (Osborne, 2004: 435).

Other authors more clearly warned against the negative impacts e-science could have on academic practice in general, Van Alstyne and Brynjolfsson (1996) suggest in this regard a 'balkanization of science'.

Participants' reactions towards what they saw as a 'fragmentation of knowledge' were often ambivalent. In the case of CurationProject we saw that although the curator underlined how CurationProject's site should be conceived as a whole, from the site and its database, an object's 'performances of knowledge' (its image and description) were stored and accessed separately. This was seen as a problem to the extent that a requirement from source communities, curators and donors was often that objects and their interpretative materials should be co-located and co-presented to preserve a context of interpretation. CurationProject appeared to react to this problem by two specific uses of its Web site. First, there are no reproductions of photographs or objects in the database, just information on them. Thus the site provides a commentary on the museum and exhibitions, but does not constitute a virtual museum or exhibition in itself. It refers to lists of publications that one can buy in hard-copies but does not provide the texts themselves. Second, links often send the users to further information existing elsewhere thus providing a way for the museum to create awareness in users whilst still keeping them locked into the museum's Web site. The site therefore displays fragmentary information to be complemented by knowledge located elsewhere.

Conclusions

By drawing on empirical data from four cases studies of scientific practice, this chapter has explored a number of issues that are central to the stated promises of e-science and also highlighted issues that have emerged from some of the innovative practices that have evolved around the use of new technologies. A major issue recognised in e-science is how to bridge differences in the terms and concepts used by researchers across institutions, disciplines and time in order to adequately document data. Different solutions are proposed that range from quasi auto-management by users to the imposition of standard ontologies. We have enumerated some of the implications of these contrasting strategies by showing with whom and where standardisation starts for actors affiliated with a range of fields. We have documented a range of approaches from the top-down of SkyProject to the bottom-up user-driven approach of CurationProject. Such decisions were often related to issues of legacy (SurveyProject) and of the need to move quickly to establish an almost parochial grip on the proposed global standard (SkyProject). In contrast, CurationProject was experimenting with technologies that could allow its archive database to be annotated by the indigenous peoples from whom the materials were originally sourced. Instead of attempting to impose one 'true' (or at least agreed upon) ontology and informed by anthropological views of the mutability of conceptual structures, they were using the technology to capture all possible views and thus all possible ontologies and taxonomies in a manner closely resembling public domain tag-oriented Web sites such as flickr and del.ico.us. Rather than focusing on which of these is 'best' it can be seen that there are merits of each, and experimentation with approaches (and technologies) that can manage the flexible combination of both might prove fruitful in other domains.

A less well recognised issue but of great significance to respondents in the U.K. academic sector was that e-science infrastructures potentially provide powerful audit tools by recording the movement of data, people and the processes of transactional work. Indeed, by compelling researchers to display or at least record their data accesses, processing and methods, experts themselves become subjects of data and are exposed to new kinds of assessments. Here qualitative approaches see their specificity threatened by being forced into quantitative logics and the value given to discrete sets of data and contributions seem to challenge established academic practices. Informants suggested that researchers will be subjected to new modes of evaluation but the specifics of how e-science might impact old measurements of academic productivity in a new way or generate new kinds of measurement remained unclear.

Beyond the spectre of audit, other processes opened up by e-science appear to challenge academic expertise in its current form. Among these are the segmentation and fragmentation of knowledge that e-science infrastructures promote, increasingly granting value to small contributions in contrast to highly structured products resulting from months or even years of research. As a consequence, e-science projects might lend visibility to a much wider range of contributions than is currently the case.

ACKNOWLEDGMENTS

We are indebted to Dr Dawn Nafus for instigating and leading this project in its early stages and for her contributions to the initial fieldwork and preliminary analysis. We hope that the project has developed as she intended and has been of value to her and her colleagues at Intel R&D. This work was supported by ESRC grant no. RES-149–25–1002 (Entangled Data: Knowledge & Community making in E (Social) Science). Sections of this paper are based on the final project report (Anderson & Carlson, 2006b) and have also been published elsewhere (Carlson & Anderson, 2007).

REFERENCES

Ainsworth, J. (2005). Testing for scalability in a Grid record usage service. Paper presented at UK e-Science All Hands Meeting 2005, Nottingham, 19th—22nd September.

Anderson, B., & Carlson, S. (2006a). e-Enabling Data: Potential impacts on methods and expertise. Paper presented at Second International Conference on e-Social Science. Manchester.

Anderson, B., & Carlson, S. (2006b). *Entangled Data: Knowledge & Community making in E (Social) Science—Research Report to the ESRC* (No. 2006–15). Ipswich: Chimera, University of Essex.

Becher, T. (1987). The disciplinary shaping of the profession. In Clark, B. *The academic profession*, pp. 271–301. Berkeley: University of California Press.

Bimholtz, J., & Bietz, M. (2003). Data at work: supporting sharing in science and engineering. Paper present at 2003 International ACM SIGGROUP Conference on Supporting Group Work, Sanibel Island, Florida, USA.

Borgman, C. (2007). *Scholarship in the digital age: Information, infrastructure, and the Internet.* Cambridge, MA: MIT Press.

Bowers, J. (1994). The work to make a network work: studying CSCW in action. Paper presented at 1994 ACM Conference on Computer Supported Cooperative Work, Chapel Hill, North Carolina, United States, ACM.

Bowker, G. (2000). Biodiversity Datadiversity. *Social Studies of Science,* 30(5): 643–683.

Campbell, E. G., & Clarridge, B. R, (2002). Data withholding in academic genetics: Evidence from a national survey. *Journal of the American Medical Association,* 287(4): 473–480.

Carlson, S., & Anderson B. (2007). What are data? The many kinds of data and their implications for data re-use. *Journal of Computer Mediated Communication,* 12(2), article 15. Retrieved 4 August 2008 from: http://jcmc.indiana.edu/vol12/issue2/carlson.html

Cole, K., & Schurer, K., Beedham, H., & Hewitt, T. (2003). *Grid enabling quantitative social science datasets: A scoping study.* Manchester: Manchester Computing, University of Manchester.

Coopmans, C. (2006). Making mammograms mobile. Suggestions for a sociology of data mobility. *Information, Communication & Society, 9*(1): 1–19.

Corti, L., & Thompson, P. (2004). Secondary analysis of archived data. In C. Seale, G. Gobo, J. F. Gubrium, & D. Silverman (Eds.), *Qualitative research practice*, pp. 327–343. London: Sage Publications.

Derriere, S., & Ochsenbein, F., Boch, T., & Rixon, G. T. (2003). Metadata for the VO: The case of UCDs. Astronomical Data Analysis Software and Systems XII. Baltimore, MD, Astronomical Society of the Pacific.

Elias, P. (2006). *The national strategy for data resources for research in the social sciences*. Coventry: University of Warwick.

ESRC (2005). *ESRC Strategic Plan 2005–10*. Swindon, UK: Economic and Social Research Council.

Fielding, N. (2003). *Qualitative research and e-social science: Appraising the potential*. ESRC Scoping Reports on e-Social Science, University of Surrey.

Fry, J. (2006). Coordination and control across scientific fields: implications for a differentiated e-science. In C. Hine *New infrastructures for knowledge production: Understanding e-Science*, pp. 167–187. Hershey PA: IDEA Group.

Golder, S., & Huberman, B. A (2006). Usage patterns of collaborative tagging systems. *Journal of Information Science, 32*(2): 198–208.

Hagstrom, W. (1974). Competition in Science. *American Sociological Review, 39*(1): 1–18.

Hey, A., & Trefethen, A. (2003). The data deluge: An e-science perspective. In F. Berman, G.C. Fox & A. Hey (Eds.), *Grid computing: Making the global infrastructure a reality*, pp. 809–824. Chichester: John Wiley.

Hine, C. (2003). Systematics as cyberscience: The role of ICTs in the working practices of taxonomy. Paper presented at Information, Communication and Society Symposium, Oxford Internet Institute, University of Oxford.

Hine, C. (2005). Material culture and the shaping of e-Science. Paper presented at First International Conference on e-Social Science, Manchester, July 2005.

Jirotka, M., & Procter, R. (2005). Collaboration and trust in healthcare innovation: The eDiaMoND case study. *Computer Supported Cooperative Work (CSCW), 14*(4): 368–398.

Macgregor, G. & McCulloch, E. (2006). Collaborative tagging as a knowledge organisation and resource discovery tool. *Library Review, 55*(5): 291–300.

Millen, D. R., Feinberg, J., & Kerr, B. (2006). Social bookmarking in the enterprise, Proceedings of the SIGCHI conference on Human Factors in computing systems, Montréal, 22–27, April.

Olson, J.S., Hofer, E.C., Bos, N., Zimmerman, A. Olson, G.M., Cooney, D., & Faniel, I. (2008). A theory of remote scientific collaboration (TORSC). In G.M. Olson, A. Zimmerman, & N. Bos (Eds.) *Scientific collaboration on the Internet*, (pp. 73–98). Cambridge, MA: MIT Press.

Osborne, T. (2004). On mediators: intellectuals and the ideas trade in the knowledge society. *Economy and Society, 33*(4): 430–447.

Purdam, K., Elliot, M., Smith, D., & Pickles, S.(2005). Confidential data access, disclosure risk and grid computing. Paper presented at UK e-Science All Hands Meeting, Nottingham, 19–22 September, 2005.

Rowland, F. (2002). The peer-review process. *Learned Publishing, 15*(4), 247–258.

Schutz, A. (1962). *Collected papers I: The problem of social reality*. The Hague: Martinus Nijhoff.

Sen, S. et al. (2006). Tagging, communities, vocabulary, evolution. Paper, Computer Supported Cooperative Work conference, *CSCW 2006*, Banff, Alberta, Canada. Retrieved 8 August 2008 from: http://www-users.cs.umn.edu/~dfrankow/files/sen-cscw2006.pdf

Strathern, M. (2000). *Audit cultures: Anthropological studies in accountability, ethics and the academy*. London: Routledge.

Thomas, N. (1991). *Entangled objects: Exchange, material culture and colonialism in the Pacific*. Cambridge: Harvard University Press.

Thompson, P. (2003). Towards ethical practice in the use of archived transcripted interviews: A response. *International Journal of Social Research Methodology*, 6(4): 357–360.

Van Alstyne, M., & Brynjolfsson, E. (1996). Could the Internet balkanize science? *Science*, 274: 1479–1480

Zabusky, S. (2002). Ethnography in/of transnational processes: Following Gyres in the world of Big Science and European integration. In C. Greenhouse, E. Metz, & K. Warren (Eds.), *Ethnography in unstable places: Everyday lives in contexts of dramatic political change*, pp. 117–145. Durham, NC: Duke University Press.

Part VII

Access and Intellectual Property

14 Open Access to e-Research

Robert Lucas and John Willinsky

In its soaring introduction, the National Science Foundation's (NSF) *Atkins Report* hails the progress made in scientific research since the digital revolution and declares:

> Advances in computational technology continue to transform scientific and engineering research, practice, and allied education. Recently, multiple accelerating trends are converging and crossing thresholds in ways that show extraordinary promise for an even more profound and rapid transformation—indeed a further revolution—in how we create, disseminate, and preserve scientific and engineering knowledge. (Atkins, 2003: 4)

The report has come to be seen as a seminal document of e-science and e-research (and, as it is called in the report and known in the U.S., *cyberinfrastructure*), but the ambition expressed in these sentences has thus far been realized only incompletely. e-Science has done much to advance techniques for knowledge *creation*, such as Grid computing and remote research collaboration, but its engagement with issues of *dissemination* has been more limited. Some admirable strides have been made in the area of data sharing, but less attention has been paid to distributing knowledge within the academy and less still to the public circulation of published research. We hold that the responsibilities of the researcher extend beyond the immediate design, conduct, and supervision of the research. Those additional responsibilities have both epistemological and ethical implications for what it means to do work that goes by the name of research, and those implications have to do with how the research is circulated and shared.

Our theme with this chapter, then, is that the research is not complete until it has been made openly available to others as is currently possible, and how it is made available in this digital age carries with it a new set of epistemological and ethical responsibilities that are the result of changes in how scholarly work is now being published. This is all the more true of those working within the realm of e-research, given that their work has already embraced the advantages which these technologies hold for the advancement of learning. We believe that the case can be made that as e-research represents not just a doing of science using network technologies, but a transformation of how science is conducted, it needs to consider the transformation that has been extended to the publishing processes for research and scholarship that are transforming the nature of access to and use of knowledge.

Research worthy of the name has always had to appear in some publicly accessible form. It may be filed in a university library as a dissertation, submitted to a client as a report, read at the annual meeting of a local society, or published in a journal or book. When it comes to talking about the contribution that research makes to the common stock of knowledge, the way in which the work has been circulated and the way in which it is open to review serve to warrant its claims to be *research*. Just how much of the research is made public is critical to its claims. The research must identify the sources in great detail on which it has drawn; it must justify the design and method deployed; it must share some portion of the data; it must demonstrate how the conclusions were arrived at, while accounting for counterexamples; and finally, it must situate the findings within the larger picture, in ways that speak to immediate implications and future directions.

The critical elements of the well-formed research article have emerged out of a publishing tradition that goes back to the very public scrutiny of Isaac Newton's one and only published article, which was on optics, in the January 3, 1671 edition of the *Philosophical Transactions*, during the first decade of the new genre that has come to be known as the scientific journal (Willinsky, 2006a: 234–44). The critical questions raised by readers of this article in letters to the *Transactions* forced Newton to further clarify his research design and method, as well as the scope of his results. The back and forth of these 'letters' between Newton and his critics in the pages of the *Transactions* until, after four years, Newton said, 'No more,' to the journal's earnest editor, Henry Oldenburg, amounted to the setting of a standard for making research public, a standard that placed the reader in a position not only to replicate the experiment, but to check the sources, scrutinize the analysis, and challenge the conclusions (Kuhn, 1978).

Which is only to say that the researcher's responsibilities for opening a work to the widest possible public scrutiny are no less important to its standing as research than all of the thought and care that she originally invested in the designing and carrying out of the research. In terms of epistemology, we would say that one requisite for believing that a study's conclusions are true, interesting, or useful—and not mistaken or misguided—is that the study has been subject to critical scrutiny on the widest possible basis, among those with relevant knowledge to bring to bear (no matter the library budget of the particular institution at which they are working). Sometimes we make that call ourselves, but more often we leave it up to the editorial and peer-review process, which represents the great contribution of the journal system for scholarly publication. Here, the normally opposed reprobate postmodernist and recalcitrant positivist share a point of common understanding: If you will not allow us (in the broadest possible sense) to see your work, your claims to having done research and have valid findings on a topic is just so much cant. A further aspect of what *open* means in this context of *open access* to research of particular relevance to the e-research perspective is the degree to which, according to the Budapest Open Access Initiative, the resulting work is itself open to data mining, re-analysis, data-mashups and other forms of electronically enabled research on the forms of information and knowledge produced.[1] The giving back to the scholarly community is unrestricted, except in the matter of attribution and the crediting of the authors' original work.

Yet if that is the epistemological side of the coin we would forge in the act of completing the research study, then there is also the ethical side of going public to consider. Most recent treatments of research ethics focus on respecting the rights of individuals who participate in research. They do not, for example, acknowledge a corresponding right among the public to consult the resulting knowledge. Obtaining the *informed consent* of the research subject seems to us only half the story, given the assumption that the research being conducted will constitute a public good held to be of interest to the welfare of the larger society. What then of the researcher's responsibilities, or rather the research community's responsibilities, to establish public norms that support *informed participation* in this democracy not just among the immediate participants, but also among the larger community? That the research must be disclosed to professional scrutiny is a safeguard or check on its quality. To see that it is open to wide circulation and easy access is what ensures that the research falls within a democratically informed public sphere.

A recent instance of the ethics at stake in publishing is found in the tendency of certain corporate sponsors of clinical trials research in the life sciences to leave unpublished or suppress the publication of studies that conclude a given treatment is not helpful, or worse. The situation had become so alarming that the International Committee of Medical Journal Editors declared that it would only publish studies that had been previously registered "at or before the onset of patient enrollment" with that registration taking place at a publicly accessible site, such as Clinicaltrials.gov run by the U.S. National Library of Medicine (De Angelis et al., 2004).[2] This meant that no clinical trial study could escape scrutiny, unless its corporate sponsors wanted to risk not being able to publish the results at all.

The more general ethical principle at stake with the publishing of research has to do with conceptions of public trust and public good. The warrant for conducting research is that such work will contribute to knowledge, which is regarded as a matter of public good. The support of salaries, grants and facilities, especially as these involve public or non-profit institutions, only adds to the weight of public trust at issue in doing research. Thus, the ethical compulsion to do the research well, and to make the resulting knowledge publicly available, ideally through some form of publication that, through its review process, ensures that the work has some initial claim to being research, notwithstanding the further scrutiny it will undergo as a public document.

One might object, at this point, that the importance of publishing research goes without saying. The reason for that, we would counter, is largely because publication is about other things besides epistemology and ethics. Publishing well is a necessary aspect to being recognized as a researcher and a scholar. The very right to continue conducting research depends on the publication of previous work, even as the blind review process ensures that attention is paid to the merits of the current piece of research, rather than judging it on the author's established reputation. Yet the current and intense focus on publishing turns out to have little to do with the open circulation of the work. Getting research into a peer-reviewed journal or an edited book becomes an end in itself for the majority of scholars. There is a small group of academic stars whose work thrives on widespread readership and citation, but for most, publish *and perish* has become the mark of an academic life.

However, a historic moment may well be upon us, one that gives new meaning to the epistemological and ethical issues entailed in the circulation of research. In the course of little more than a decade, the Internet has proven not only a means of transforming how science is conducted under the rubric of e-research, but has proven itself a powerful, global publishing medium for research and scholarship, especially at the level of the article. The researcher has now to reconsider what it takes to do research in a responsible manner, when the public presence of that work has the potential to be—and in many cases has already been—radically expanded. It may look like business as usual within the journal system that dominates scholarly publishing. The vast majority of journals simply moved online without changing how they look or publish (much as Gutenberg's printing of the Bible, with its cursive font and illuminated first letters, created a book that resembled the medieval manuscripts, which the printing press was about to put an end to as a publishing form). Yet the Internet has opened a new world of access to the forms of knowledge that are recorded in journals, if far less so with scholarly books at this point.

You can now walk into a public library or a high school, sit down at a computer station, and tap into a small, but substantial portion of the scholarly work and scientific research that is being currently published; you can explore historical documents and archives, as well as vast sets of data, including the human genome.[3] This work has not just been published within a limited community of subscribing institutions, but has also been made open to readers wherever there is Internet access.

These new forms of access represent a great increase in the ability to tap into the storehouses of knowledge. This public access has been afforded by a new breed of scholarly journal (some having grown out of long-standing print titles, such as the *New England Journal of Medicine*) that makes its contents freely available to readers online, whether immediately on publication or some months after the issue is released (as is the case with *NEJM*, which gives subscribers an incentive to keep subscribing). Yet while journals that offer open access provide one important source of a new global access, a greater part of what Tim Brody (2004) has estimated amounts to 15–20 percent of scholarly work that is now open comes from those authors who, having published in a journal that is restricted to subscribers, have taken advantage of that journal's self-archiving policy to post their published work to an open access institutional repository run by their library or to their own Web site.[4] This is not just a hypothetical increase in access, as there are now a good number of studies that make it clear that studies which are made available through open access journals or institutional repositories are read and cited by more people than those articles that are not freely available (Hitchcock, 2008), with the reasons for greater citation appearing to include not only the free availability but the early release that archiving often achieves and the author's selection of their best works for open access (Davis & Fromerth, 2006).

Suddenly, these developments raise a new set of responsibilities for how that research is allowed to circulate, given that there are a whole new range of options for opening it to critical scrutiny and having it enter the public sphere. When print was the only means of publication, the idea of printing a limited number of copies of a journal—determined by the number of subscribers who covered the costs and to whom it was then exclusively delivered—made perfect sense, with a little photocopying and off-print circulation on the side. This is the time, we are proposing, for reviewing the researcher's epistemological and ethical responsibilities in light of the *open access* option, an option which some journals are actively pursuing, and which most journals not going this way have at least recognized as falling within the rights of their authors (as they permit authors to self-archive the work the journal has published).

As Willinsky has argued elsewhere (2006a), the final step in any research project should be about ensuring the circulation and exchange of knowledge in as wide a fashion as is feasible. We use the word *feasible* because we recognize that there is a whole range of limits to the circulation of knowledge, from economic to educational. However, it also needs to be noted that the possible global and public scope for the circulation of research has recently and rather radically changed with the introduction of new information technologies in relation to the Internet. The overwhelming majority of scientific journals has moved to the Internet over the last ten years. This enables a level of global and public distribution of knowledge that far exceeds what was possible with print technologies. What researchers then need to consider, in the midst of this great migration, is how this new publishing medium can be used to improve both the scientific and public value and impact of research, not just as a source of scientific information, but as a source of public knowledge. The viability of this greater distribution and greater integration of research into public life has been demonstrated by a small but important number of journals that are offering their contents free to the reader.

In our own field of education, for example, there are close to 200 journals that make all or some portion of their content free to read online.[5] This manner of open access publishing is being implemented through a number of different economic models that include charging author fees (largely used in well-funded areas of the sciences, such as biomedical research), relying on subsidies, providing open access after a period of subscription-only access, and offering open access to developing countries. Part of our contribution to these open access developments has been through the Public Knowledge Project (PKP), which Willinsky has directed since 1998 (http://pkp.sfu.ca). In addition to conducting research on various aspects of open access and its impact on both scholarship and the public, PKP developed open source (free) software to facilitate open access by reducing publishing costs. Its most notable offering is Open Journal Systems—for managing scholarly journals and publishing them to the Web—which is currently available in 13 languages and is being used by more than 1,200 journals on six continents to make journals across the disciplines open access.

As a further means of achieving open access to research, a number of the major publishers, such as Elsevier, Springer, Wiley, Sage, Blackwell, and Taylor and Francis, have author self-archiving policies in place that permit authors to post the final drafts of the work published in their journals to a personal Web site or to libraries' institutional repositories.[6] Some funding agencies are now mandating this archiving of work they underwrite, most notably the U.S. National Institutes of Health which, with an annual budget of $28 billion leading to roughly 80,000 articles, now requires any work published as a result of its funding to be made publicly available in PubMed Central 12 months after it appears in a journal (http://publicaccess.nih.gov/index.htm).

A related movement, to which e-science has also contributed, calls for open access to the datasets that underlie published research. Jean-Claude Bradley, who coined the phrase 'Open Notebook Science' to describe this phenomenon, makes the epistemological case, writing, "[I]t is essential that all of the information available to the researchers to make their conclusions is equally available to the rest of the world. Basically, no insider information." (Bradley, 2006) Cambridge chemist Peter Murray-Rust, a participant in e-science and advocate of open data, adds that the data currently being collected is vastly under-analyzed, and "contains huge amounts of undiscovered science" that could be unlocked through coordinated data sharing (2007).

The CODATA committee of the International Council for Science has spent decades advocating for improved data quality and access, but in the past few years, the movement has gathered real momentum. On

December 16, 2007, Science Commons, an offshoot of the copyright reform group Creative Commons, released a legal framework for open data, the 'Protocol for Implementing Open Access Data' (http://science-commons.org/projects/publishing/open-access-data-protocol/). Four days later, Harvard's Dataverse Network Project released version 1.0 of its open source software for archiving and publishing datasets (http://thedata.org/). Here is an initiative that addresses the incentive issue for the open sharing of data by creating a credit system, in which datasets can be properly cited and attributed, and through which the number of times a dataset is cited and used by others can be recorded and credited. As well, the Open Data Commons project released a public domain dedication for data in early 2008 and has declared that the "year of open data" (Hatcher, 2008).

In spite of these successes, however, the road that scholarly publishing had been heading down, prior to this open access movement, and continues to head down in the face of these promising new developments, is one of increasing corporate concentration, with publisher mergers and acquisitions (as well as the corporate acquisition of scholarly society journals). The resulting price increases driven by opportunity as much as anything has been leading over the last two decades to a declining state of access to research, judging by the journal cancellations that have trimmed collections at the best university libraries, while decimating those of less privileged institutions (Kyrillidou 2000). The introduction of open access models through online publishing appears to offer the universities another direction in which to take the circulation of knowledge. Scholarly associations, journal editors and university libraries need to carefully weigh the dissemination of research in terms of this juncture, especially as it bears on the scientific principle of seeking the widest possible circulation, exchange, and scrutiny for knowledge.

Open access publishing serves scholar and public alike, by providing a much wider readership than is afforded by subscription-fee journals (online or on paper). The open access model not only opens the research work to more thorough "professional scrutiny and critique," it also provides greater *accountability* and *visibility* for research. In education, the American Educational Research Association, ERIC, and other organizations have approached this public side of science by providing a form of research digests on selected topics that 'translate' research findings for use by policymakers.[7] While commendable, such initiatives are obviously costly and can provide at best a limited coverage of the literature. They could be greatly extended, we are suggesting, by integrating much more open access to this literature into the very systems for circulating that knowledge.

We have argued that *research* should be understood to include both knowledge creation and dissemination, but to this point, e-science and e-research initiatives have focused on the first of these, particularly through

Grid computing and distributed research teams. The UK's National e-Science Centre defines e-science as "the large scale science that will increasingly be carried out through distributed global collaborations enabled by the Internet" and goes on to describe "very large data collections, very large scale computing resources and high performance visualization," all made possible by the computing architecture of the Grid. (http://www.nesc.ac.uk/nesc/define.html) The British National Centre for e-Social Science defines its charge in nearly identical, Grid-centric terms (http://www.ncess.ac.uk/about_eSS/faq/). Neither makes reference to dissemination of published work.

As mentioned previously, the NSF's *Atkins Report* demonstrates a good deal more vision regarding access and dissemination. "In the future," the report predicts, "we might expect researchers to . . . [a]ccess the entire published record of science online" (10). It recognizes potential applications of access in tertiary science and engineering education (26–27), and includes the following paragraph on public circulation of knowledge:

> *Access by the wider public*—By making access to reports, raw data, and instruments much easier, a far wider audience can be served. Although large teams and major financial investment are required to create comprehensive data repositories and specialized scientific facilities, individuals, even amateurs, working alone or in small groups, given access to such resources, can provide scientific discoveries. A good example is amateur astronomy, which significantly expands the reach of scientific observation. (29)

We applaud the *Atkins Report*'s commitment to expanding access throughout the republic of science. It is worth noting, however, that even here, it is *researchers* who will have access to published work and future researchers and engineers who will benefit from it educationally. Even the report's most ambitious endorsement of wide access, quoted above, is justified solely by the prospect of future knowledge creation by amateur scientists. It fails entirely to address the place of science within the larger republic—the implications of research for democracy.

Now, in invoking the role of research in a democratic culture, we realize that public access to *what is known* through scholarly inquiry, as well as to the debates and controversies that arise through that inquiry, is but one small aspect of what should contribute to the quality of contemporary democracies.[8] It may be a small aspect, but it is precisely the aspect over which researchers have control. It is the very point of their professional contribution, as scholars and educators.

It is also fair enough to raise questions about what this new public presence of research may mean for the integrity of research. Certainly, discomfiting instances are to be found of the political and social corruption of scientific practices. Think of the role that anthropology often played in the service of colonial administrations, or the eugenics movement in the early decades of the twentieth century (Kevles, 1995; Pels, 1997). Today, with the George W. Bush administration in the U.S., issues of political interference in research abound.[9] Yet such abuses, while a source of concern and caution for researchers, hardly argue for isolating or insulating scientific culture from public and democratic culture, especially for the many sciences that hold to the importance, as a first principle, of posing *significant* questions. The open and public discussion of those questions seems a critical element in keeping science a principled enterprise in an ethically responsible sense.

We recognize that disciplines vary in their degree of public orientation, but open access should hold interest even for those that operate at greater remove from the issues of the day. Open access ensures global access for scientists, in an age when even the best institutions cannot subscribe to everything and those in developing countries cannot subscribe to more than a handful without Open Access or programs like HINARI (the Health InterNetwork Access to Research Initiative) or AGORA (Access to Global Online Research in Agriculture). Further, as the *Atkins Report* notes, the public includes dedicated amateurs and teachers in senior high schools and universities, whose participation can only help strengthen the disciplines. And more to the point, the work of many fields *does* hold wide interest. In fact, it is difficult to think of an issue for which science and social science cannot contribute to public discourse. Educational research, for example, has obvious relevance to parents, professionals, policy advocates, and public deliberators from the local level to the international. The public significance should be no less clear for most social and behavioral sciences, the sciences of energy, environment, and agriculture, and the many sciences that bear on medicine, public health, pharmaceuticals, and bioengineering.

Over the past decade, medical research has provided an excellent example of a field making itself part of public culture, with its breakthroughs, controversies, reversals, indeterminate results, and all. The lessons we need to learn from this work concern how the scientific culture of medical research is unmistakably part of the public culture of daily talk and dinner table conversations, of politicians and media pundits.

The expanded coverage of health information in the media, under the rubric of news-you-can-use, is easy to track in newspapers, on television, and the Internet. In the spring of 2003, the *New York Times Magazine* devoted its entire issue to the theme "Half of What Doctors Know is Wrong" (March 16, 2003). It featured articles with titles such as "Medicine's Progress, One Setback at a Time" and those articles thought nothing of describing the details of sample sizes, risk probabilities, and research design flaws of studies published in the *British Medical Journal* and elsewhere. The magazine makes the dynamics of research present: the tentative search for an answer, the challenges and revisions, the study released last week, the reversed position. True, it is the *Times*, which is not everyone's daily newspaper, but this public exposure of medical research's reversals (hormone therapy) and design flaws (mammograms) has appeared, with less detail, on the television nightly news and the tabloid press. And it has not reduced public support for medical research; it has arguably fed support for it, creating a public appetite and expectation of a right to know as a function of the democratic state to support and make available.

This knowledge is now working as part of a public culture, adding to that culture's democratic, and intellectual, quality. That is, this increase in access to health information has changed the relationship of medical research to the public body, changed it in a way that we are tempted to describe as reducing the tyranny of expertise. From the physicians' perspective, having patients and their families arriving at their offices with medical research and other health information in hand has led to a "new method of care," a method which has been encouragingly labeled "shared decision making" (Brownlee, 2003: 54). We hardly need add that *shared decision making* sounds a lot like democracy in action, whether one thinks of a doctor's office, a community school, or a nation. This particular form of sharing has only been made possible by increases in medical research's presence in public culture. As one indication of that, we offer the National Institute of Health's estimate that six million Americans go online each day in search of information about health and disease (NIH, 2003), as well as the NIH's commitment to seeing all of the research that it sponsors publicly available through institutional repositories or open access journals (Suber, 2005). Of course, only a small percentage of those looking for health information may be consulting open access research literature, and those who do may well have trouble applying it.

In an effort to feed this hunger for information, as well as guide this right to know, doctors in the state of Georgia are experimenting with a "health information prescription" (Brownlee 2003: 54). The prescription will guide patients to reliable sources including the National Library of Medicine's MedlinePlus, which includes a layperson's guide to symptoms, diagnosis, and treatment. MedlinePlus, however, also provides patients with direct access to the latest medical research, through the NLM's PubMed database, although most of the 11 million articles in it are not available to the public beyond their abstracts, with the number freely available about to grow substantially through the recent archiving mandate adopted by National Institutes of Health requiring those receiving research funding to deposit their work in the open access PubMed Central.

As the conversation between physician and patient takes on this more informed quality, concerned as it is about both risk and quality of life factors, the educational quality of that exchange goes up for both parties. Clearly, physicians are also beneficiaries of this increased access to research. Doctors speak of having the "newest and best in medical research right at our own desks," if only to discover that "leeches, for example, are now used on some patients to treat the pain of arthritis" (Sanders, 2003: 29). Patients make informed decisions based on their own value systems: "For me, it's a trade-off," as one woman said in deciding to stay with menopause hormone therapy for the mental agility it provided her against the recently established increased health risks of such therapy (Kolata, 2003: A26).

What has changed with medical research, and what needs greater recognition by e-researchers, is how productive this new emphasis on public access to research is for professionals. To go a little farther with the medical research access analogy, the perfect example of this democratic and public engagement with research is ClinicalTrials.gov, a Web site sponsored by the National Institutes of Health, other Federal agencies, and the pharmaceutical industry. The site was launched in February 2000 and as of December 2005 lists 23,500 clinical studies, which are inviting participation from qualified subjects, as well as informing the public about ongoing investigations. The site is global, involving studies in about 120 countries, although most are in the U.S. and Canada, and it receives approximately 20,000 visitors a day.

The ready ability to connect study to study, to compare results and see ideas challenged and discussed, can only add to the quality of scholarly and public discourse. But more than that, our work through the Public Knowledge Project (Siemens, Willinsky, & Blake, 2006) has demonstrated how the Internet can now support systems of "Reading Tools" that can enable readers of a research article to connect the article they are reading not only to related studies, but just as easily to current newspaper articles and government reports on the same topic, to sites with instructional materials for teaching the topic and to online forums where the topic is informally debated.[10] The promise here is of having greater public access to research, combined with greater connectivity among different orders of knowledge (from research to practice and policy), incorporated into the design of scholarly publishing environments in ways that improve the quality of the peer review process (with access to the original datasets) as well as support public accessibility, for example, by providing access to related materials in the media and other public documents.

As scientists since Newton have demonstrated, what makes work scientific is not simply the validity of its claims. What is scientific is far more about open and free inquiry. Technological advances afford us the opportunity to make scientific inquiry freer and more open than ever before, and to expand that culture beyond its previous bounds. In addition to thinking about disclosing research for the purpose of affording sufficient scrutiny from other researchers, e-researchers need to consider these new ways of increasing the circulation of this knowledge. Doing research today means testing the potential of new publishing technologies for opening research to greater scrutiny and impact, as well as to greater integration with other forms of knowing. At this moment, as the research literature moves into this new publishing medium, the researcher has indeed assumed a new responsibility, a new level of accountability, over how public access to the research literature can be improved, as both a scientific and design principle that will only serve to strengthen scientific culture within an informed and democratic public realm.

ACKNOWLEDGMENTS

This chapter builds on work that was originally published in Willinsky (2006b).

NOTES

1. Budapest Open Access Initiative: "By 'open access' to this literature, we mean its free availability on the public Internet, permitting any users to read, download, copy, distribute, print, search, or link to the full texts of these articles, crawl them for indexing, pass them as data to software, or use them for any other lawful purpose, without financial, legal, or technical barriers other than those inseparable from gaining access to the Internet itself" (Chan et al., 2002).
2. From the statement of the medical journal editors: "Irrespective of their scientific interest, trial results that place financial interests at risk are particularly likely to remain unpublished and hidden from public view. The interests of the sponsor or authors notwithstanding, anyone should be able to learn of any trial's existence and its important characteristics" (De Angelis et al., 2004).
3. On open access to research data in the sciences, a recent *Nature* editorial (2005) refers to how researchers can retain credit and rights over the datasets they contribute to the "global academy" by making it freely available online through the use of a Creative Commons license (http://creativecommons.org).
4. See the Sherpa Project (http://www.sherpa.ac.uk/), in which a survey of 127 publishers reveals that 75% grant permission for authors to post some version of their published article in an institutional archive or on a personal Web site.
5. See the American Education Research Association list of open access journals in education maintained by Tirupalavanam Ganesh (http://aera-cr.asu.edu/ejournals/).
6. See Willinsky (2006a) on different types of open access journal publishing, and to check the current self-archiving policies of publishers and journals see the SHERPA project database (http://www.sherpa.ac.uk/romeo.php).
7. See, for example, AERA's *Research Points* (http://www.aera.net/publications/?id=314).
8. The more common philosophical formulation of the relation between science and democracy focuses on the democratic regulation of science, as when Helen Longino asks, "What kind of institutional changes are necessary to sustain the credibility, and hence value, of scientific inquiry while maintaining democratic decision making regarding the cognitive and practical choices the sciences make possible and necessary?" (2002: 213). Also see Philip Kitcher (2001) for a similar approach. Our argument for improved access to research will, of course, bear on the democratic decision making affecting science.

9. See the Union of Concerned Scientists, who documents the degree to which "an unprecedented level of political interference threatens the integrity of government science" (http://www.ucsusa.org/scientific_integrity/).
10. See the Public Knowledge Project Web site for demonstrations of a Reading Tool that is included in the project's journal and conference publishing systems, and is designed to integrate research more fully into other forms of knowledge (http://pkp.sfu.ca/ojs).

REFERENCES

Atkins, D. E., Droegmeier, K. K., Feldman, S. I., Garcia-Molina, H., Klein, M. L., & Messina, P. (2003). *Revolutionizing science and engineering through cyberinfrastructure: Report of the National Science Foundation Blue-Ribbon Advisory Panel on Cyberinfrastructure.* Retrieved December 22, 2007 from http://www.nsf.gov/od/oci/reports/atkins.pdf.

Bradley, J. (2006). *Open notebook science.* Retrieved January 8, 2008, from http://drexel-coas-elearning.blogspot.com/2006/09/open-notebook-science.html

Brody, T. (2004). Citation impact of open access articles vs. articles available only through subscription ("toll-access"). Retrieved March 30, 2008, from http://www.citebase.org/static/isi_study/

Brownlee, S. (2003, March 18). The perils of prevention. *New York Times Magazine,* pp. 52–55.

Chan, Leslie, et al. (2002). Budapest open access initiative. New York: Budapest open access initiative. Retrieved January 8, 2008, from http://www.soros.org/openaccess/read.shtml (accessed October 6, 2003).

Davis, M., P., & Fromerth, M. J. (2006). Does the arXiv lead to higher citations and reduced publisher downloads for mathematics articles? Unpublished paper. Retrieved March 30, 2008, from http://arxiv.org/ftp/cs/papers/0603/0603056.pdf

De Angelis, C., Drazen, J. M., Frizelle, F. A., Haug, C., Hoey, J., Horton, R., Kotzin, S., Laine, C., Marusic, A., John A., Overbeke, P. M., Schroeder, T. V., Sox, H. C., & Van Der Weyden, M. B. (2004). Clinical trial registration: A statement from the International Committee of Medical Journal Editors. *New England Journal of Medicine.* 351 (12): 1250–1251. Retrieved December 12, 2005, from http://content.nejm.org/cgi/content/full/NEJMe048225

Hatcher, J. (2008). *2008—Year of Open Data.* Retrieved January 8, 2008, from http://www.opendatacommons.org/2008/01/03/2008-year-of-open-data/

Hitchcock, S. (2008). The effect of open access and downloads ('hits') on citation impact: a bibliography of studies. Unpublished paper. Retrieved March 30, 2008, from http://opcit.eprints.org/oacitation-biblio.html

Kevles, D. J. (1995). *In the name of eugenics: Genetics and the uses of human heredity.* Cambridge, MA: Harvard University Press.

Kitcher, P. (2001). Science, truth, and democracy. Oxford, UK: Oxford University Press.

Kolata, G. (2003, March 18). Hormone therapy, already found to have risks, is now said to lack benefits. *New York Times,* p. A26.

Kuhn, T. S. (1978). Newton's optical papers. In I. Bernard Cohen (Ed.) *Isaac Newton's papers and letters on natural philosophy and related documents,* pp. 27–45. Cambridge, MA: Harvard University Press.

Kyrillidou, M. (2000). Research library trends: ARL statistics. *The Journal of Academic Librarianship,* 26 (6): 427–436.

Let data speak to data. (2005, December 1). *Nature,* 438 (7068): 531.

Longino, H. (2002). The fate of knowledge. Princeton, NJ: Princeton University Press.

Murray-Rust, P. (2007, April 10). Data-driven science: A scientist's view. Retrieved January 8, 2008, from http://www.sis.pitt.edu/%7Erepwkshop/papers/murray.html

National Institutes of Health (NIH). (2003, March 18). The health information prescription. Washington: National Library of Medicine. Retrieved December 12, 2005, from http://www.nlm.nih.gov/news/press_releases/GAhealthRX03.html

Pels, P. (1997). The anthropology of colonialism: Culture, history, and the emergence of Western governmentality. *Annual Review of Anthropology, 26:* 163–183.

Sanders, L. (2003, March 16). Medicine's progress, one setback at a time. *New York Times Magazine*, pp. 29–31.

Siemens, R., Willinsky, J., & Blake, A. (2006). A study of professional reading tools for computing humanists. Unpublished paper. Electronic Textual Cultures Laboratory, University of Victoria. Retrieved May 24, 2008 from http://etcl-dev.uvic.ca/public/pkp_report.

Suber, P. (2005). Strengthening NIH policy. *SPARC Open Access Newsletter, 92.* Retrieved December 12, 2005, from http://www.earlham.edu/~peters/fos/newsletter/12–02–05.htm.

Willinsky, J. (2006a). *The access principle: The case for open access to research and scholarship.* Cambridge, MA: MIT Press.

Willinsky, J. (2006b): When the research's over, don't turn out the lights. In K. Tobin, & J. L. Kincheloe (Eds.), *Doing educational research: A handbook,* pp. 439–456. Rotterdam: Sense Publishers.

15 Intellectual Property in the Context of e-Science

Dan L. Burk

INTRODUCTION

The advent and proliferation of global computer networks have altered the practice of science, and additional changes seem sure to come. Scientists already routinely collaborate and access informational resources by way of the Internet and associated technologies (Glasner, 1996). Further advances in this direction are contemplated via so-called Grid technologies to enable collaborative sharing of both information and resources on an international scale (Hey & Trfethen, 2003; Newman, Ellisman, & Orcutt, 2003). Such distributed computing architectures promise to make available processing power, data storage, and related large-scale computing resources independent of geographic location. Researchers participating in such technological collaborations are increasingly drawn into distributed communities and far-flung alliances that were previously impossible (Finholt, 2002).

With the promise of such capabilities comes a variety of new challenges and, in particular, new social and cultural challenges to the conduct of research. A variety of non-technical legal and social factors are likely to shape the structure, character, and success of such initiatives (Burk, 2000; David & Spence, 2003). These factors have dual import for on-line social science research: first, as the subject matter of examination using social science methods, and second as determinants to the conduct of such e-research. Crucial aspects of these determinants are centered upon ownership and control of the information and tools associated with e-science. While it is by no means the only legal regime that will affect these aspects of e-science, intellectual property law is expected to play a major role in determining such ownership and control (Eckersley, Egan, & Shun-ichi, 2003).

For example, intellectual property issues were recently identified as a serious concern in the organization and conduct of the eDiaMoND (Digital Mammography National Database) project in the UK (Hinds et al., 2005). This project employs collaborative computing or 'Grid' technologies to allow collection and sharing of digitized mammograms and associated patient data acquired from a nationwide screening program. Anonymized medical radiographic images from the project were digitized and transferred to a computer database accessible for data mining or other algorithmic analysis. Yet ownership and control of the individual images and the collective database remained indeterminate; possible claimants to ownership or control of the images might include the patients, their physicians, radiographic technicians, sponsoring institutions, or even the database engineers.

In previous work, I identified a range of intellectual property issues, primarily arising out of Internet-based legal disputes that seemed likely to become issues for the then-nascent e-science phenomenon (Burk, 2000). Since that time, practices associated with e-science have advanced dramatically, although often along paths that were not entirely anticipated. Early predictions regarding formalized 'collaboratory' research environments have yet to be entirely realized, although experiments in such shared virtual spaces continue. At the same time, the availability of publicly shared research resources, using the readily available medium of the Internet, has grown. New technological architectures for interactive Grid computing resources are under development, but perhaps most surprising has been the mix of cultural and legal influence of open source licensing models to facilitate open access to scientific resources.

In this chapter, I expand and update earlier work to take account of such developments. I begin by reviewing the basic forms of intellectual property most relevant to e-science and their likely application to the tools, methods, and products of e-science. I also discuss the shift in approach towards intellectual property observed in the scientific community over the past two decades. I then turn to the likeliest impediment posed by the confluence of these technological and social factors, which is the jurisdictional inconsistency faced by distributed research collaborations. I discuss contractual solutions to these impediments, especially the spread of open source licensing, not only as a formal legal mechanism to promote e-science but also as a normative statement about the culture and ethos of research practice. I conclude by considering the social and organizational challenges posed by open source licensing itself and the prospects for addressing the transition of this legal mechanism from its original milieu to that of e-science.

INTELLECTUAL PROPERTY

Legal ownership and control over the products of innovative and creative effort have typically been recognized as one or more forms of intellectual property rights. Several of these different forms of intellectual property have become directly relevant to the practice of e-science, as e-science may generate valuable ideas, methodologies, data, databases, texts, software, and even tangible research tools.

Much of the intellectual property related to e-science will fall under the copyright system. Copyright arises spontaneously upon fixation of an original work in a tangible medium of expression, and generally lasts for the lifetime of the author plus 70 years. The rights that attach at fixation include not only the exclusive right to reproduce the work but also some version of the exclusive rights to adapt, distribute, publicly perform, and publicly display the work. Copyright also includes the right to exclude others from reproducing, adapting, distributing, publicly performing, or displaying works that are substantially similar to the protected work. In most countries, these rights are subject to some exceptions or user privileges, such as rights to use short quotations, or to criticize or comment upon the work without permission of the copyright holder.

Restricting uses of the particular expression but allowing ideas to be freely re-used, copyright extends only to the original expression found in the work and not to the idea expressed. Copyright also expressly eschews protection of facts, processes, machines, and functional or utilitarian items. Traditionally, copyright has focused on aesthetic or artistic works, but these categories have come to include texts that 'behave', including software. More traditional texts, such as scientific reports and journals, are also covered by copyright law. Consequently, copyright has become increasingly important to technological innovation as well as to artistic creativity.

Copyright may also offer some degree of protection to databases since it protects the original and creative selection and arrangement of compilations. Frequently, individual data in a database will constitute unprotectable facts, but their selection and arrangement may be covered by copyright. Nonetheless, copyright often offers only relatively weak protection for databases, especially if the selection and arrangement of the data are dictated by the use or structure of the data itself or otherwise dictated by technical or organizational constraints. In such cases, which are frequent, the selection and arrangement may not be considered 'original' and so may fail to meet the criteria for copyright protection.

Patents are a second form of intellectual property that has become increasingly relevant to e-science. Patent law has traditionally been the form of intellectual property directed to functional or utilitarian items: processes, machines, articles of manufacture, and compositions of matter. Patent law excludes from protection products of nature, that is, materials that have not been in some way changed or altered by humans. Patent law also typically excludes from its ambit laws or principles of nature, including pure mathematics, on the theory that these are discoveries inherent in the natural world rather than the products of human ingenuity.

Unlike copyright and trade secrecy, which arise spontaneously based on the nature and use of the protected information, patents entail rights that arise only after the review and approval of a governmental agency. Inventors must apply for a patent, submitting for examination a document demonstrating that the invention meets the statutory criteria of novelty, usefulness, and inventiveness. The application must also disclose how to make and use the invention and must include claims that set forth the characteristics of the technology to be covered by the patent. The examining agency will reject applications that fail to meet these criteria, requiring applicants to either amend their claims to meet the requirements or forgo issuance of a patent.

Because the patent specifies in its claims the limits of the technology it covers, the coverage of a patent may be broad or narrow, depending upon the scope of the claims. Unlike the fairly sharply delineated acts excluded by copyright, the range of infringing acts covered by patent rights is quite broad and expansive. Once approved, the patent confers the exclusive rights to make, use, sell, offer for sale, or import the invention described in the patent claims. Also unlike copyrights, patents typically are subject to very few user privileges or exceptions.

Although patent and copyright are generally directed to different subject matter, the functional and the expressive, they meet in certain technologies that may be considered expressive. While the symbolic indicia of computer code are protected under copyright, functional aspects of software may be subject to patent protection. Most major jurisdictions now recognize software as patentable in some form. In the U.S., this rationale has been taken quite far, first to apply patents to any task or method programmed as a computer process and more recently to apply patents to any process with a useful result. Other jurisdictions, such as those belonging to the European Patent Convention, are more restricted to methods or processes in their application of patents.

In addition to patents and copyrights, considerations of trade secrecy may be important to e-science collaboration. Trade secrecy entails any type of business information that is not generally known but which confers a business advantage. Trade secrecy frequently arises out of contractual obligations; the parties to a business relationship may specify in a contract that certain information is proprietary and will be kept confidential. Trade secrecy sometimes also arises out of other legal duties, such as a duty of loyalty to an employer, or a fiduciary duty to a partner in a business alliance, or from a legal prohibition on improperly profiting from another's efforts.

Finally, the European Union (EU) and some other jurisdictions recognize a form of intellectual property right in collections of information, or databases. Because copyright offers little protection for many types of databases, some nations have sought to foster their domestic database industries with novel forms of database protection. The EU has been the global leader in this trend by way of a database directive requiring the member states to enact a *sui generis*, or novel form of intellectual property protection, prohibiting the unauthorized extraction of information from proprietary collections of information. This directive includes a reciprocity provision, requiring that other nations offer a database protection in their jurisdiction in order for their nationals to gain the benefit of the database right in the EU As a consequence, there is considerable incentive for trading partners of the EU member states to enact reciprocal legislation.

OPEN SCIENCE

Intellectual property rights are typically justified on the utilitarian theory that law should provide an economic incentive in order to foster creativity and innovation. Unlike tangible goods, the intangible subject matter of intellectual property is easily copied and appropriated. Consequently, it is difficult for artists and inventors to exclude others from freely appropriating their creations; this in turn means that it is difficult to charge payment for use of the creation. Intellectual property laws provide legal exclusion to mimic the physical exclusion that inheres naturally in tangible objects or real property. Creators can use legal process to exclude users or to allow access on condition of payment. The opportunity to exclude, and so to charge payment, is thought to provide a monetary incentive for more creation.

The scientific research enterprise, however, has traditionally been viewed as operating on quite a different incentive mechanism, that of open access and reputational reward. This system of open science was classically articulated by Robert Merton in the mid-twentieth century (Merton, 1973). By examining the community of scientific researchers *as* a community, Merton identified a variety of behavioral expectations that scientists claimed to be important to their work and to their interactions. The primary scientific norms that emerged from these studies include:

- *universalism:* the expectation that scientists should judge empirical claims according to impersonal criteria, without regard to the identity of their author;
- *disinterestedness:* the expectation that scientists will subordinate their own biases and interests to the advancement of knowledge;
- *communality:* the expectation that discoveries will be freely shared and dedicated to the community of scientists; and
- *organized skepticism:* the expectation that scientists will subject empirical claims to systematic scrutiny and validation.

Later he added an additional norm of *originality:* the expectation that contributions to the fund of scientific knowledge would be valued for their novelty (Merton, 1957).

As identified by Merton, these norms function together to drive the scientific enterprise, creating community behavior that reputationally rewards contributions to the corpus of scientific information. Scientists are expected to contribute their discoveries freely to the community; such contributed knowledge is vetted through criticism and peer review of published papers or reports. Thus, publication of new scientific discoveries instantiates both the values of communalism and organized skepticism. Contributed knowledge that passes such scrutiny gains for the contributor the recognition and respect of his or her peers. Under the norm of universalism, any contributor to the fund of scientific knowledge can expect to receive such recognition, regardless of social status; the value of disinterestedness ensures that all contributions will be treated on an equal footing.

Merton's analysis has been the subject of subsequent criticism for both alleged theoretical and pragmatic failures—in particular, for accepting at face value the professions of interviewed scientists regarding community norms, rather than tracking scientists' actual practices. Merton's framework nonetheless continues to resonate both with analysts and with the scientific community itself. In particular, the Mertonian framework has provided a useful lens through which to view the collision of open science and proprietary intellectual property. Several analysts have documented and discussed the clash between these two systems of reward (e.g., Eisenberg, 1987; Merges, 1996). The majority of university inventions in fact lack significant commercial value, but the occasional commercial 'blockbuster' university patent fosters a gold-rush mentality toward patents (Rai, 2000). This mentality also attends the prospect for individual scientists to participate financially in significant royalties or to profit from the public offering of small companies built around patented technology, and it creates similar pressure on a personal level towards patenting.

Adherents to the more traditional set of Mertonian norms may view the financial reward system of intellectual property as distorting the research agenda of academic science and improperly commodifying information, techniques, and materials that should be freely accessible to the entire community (Nelson, 2004). On occasion, the community or its formal institutions may mobilize to enforce the traditional normative structure and frustrate the intrusion of financial incentives into the academic research enterprise. For example, in the name of open and communal science, many prominent scientific journals have demanded that as a condition of publication, researchers make openly available materials and data upon which their papers are based. Absent such a requirement for access, researchers might attempt to gain both the financial reward of the intellectual property system and the reputational reward of science, cheating the value of communality by keeping materials and background data proprietary through trade secrecy or patent licensing.

This clash of incentives has been apparent, for example, in the development of the international Human Genome Mapping project, where the sequence information generated under the project became the subject of both public and private attempts at patenting (Boyle, 2003). Early governmental efforts to patent nucleotide sequences generated from the project were vehemently rejected by the genetic sequencing community, primarily on the grounds that such patents would violate Mertonian norms of communality. Interestingly, the justification that patents could be used to keep the sequences publicly available by preempting private efforts to obtain patents was unpersuasive to critics of the governmental patenting effort. In the face of such criticism, the governmental patenting efforts were abandoned (Burk, 2005).

INTERJURISDICTIONAL COLLABORATION

The dispute over disposition of the information generated by the Human Genome Mapping project presages future disputes in e-science collaboration. In many aspects, intellectual property right disputes in e-science will be no different from those in traditional modes of scientific research; the culture clash over norms of openness versus proprietary ownership can occur in the isolated physical laboratory as well as on the distributed computing Grid. Of course, new communicative and computational tools may increase the intellectual property emphasis in e-science. For example, copyright and database protection laws may loom somewhat larger in e-science, given the dependence of e-science on large data collections and on the software necessary to access and process such datasets.

Yet the legal landscape for e-science is likely to differ dramatically from traditional science in at least one aspect. In a global environment of computerized, distributed access and collaboration, application of territorially-based law becomes uncertain. Data located in one jurisdiction may be accessed nearly instantaneously and used in a different jurisdiction; the law governing such use may differ dramatically between such jurisdictions. Scientists located in different jurisdictions may jointly generate new data, techniques, or materials; the laws governing ownership and allocation of such collaborative products may again differ dramatically among jurisdictions.

Determining which jurisdiction's laws should govern is a difficult and often uncertain exercise. Consider, for example, the intellectual property evaluation of the eDiaMoND project mentioned at the beginning of this chapter. The intellectual property concerns studied in relation to this U.K. project were addressed on a relatively parochial scale; data for the project were captured within a single jurisdiction, the UK, and accessibility was considered only within that jurisdiction. Preliminary legal and social analysis for the problem was conducted primarily under U.K. law, and recommendations for resolution of ownership and control were couched in terms of that jurisdiction's institutions. While recognizing the possibility that the data could be made available to researchers in other jurisdictions, the evaluation stayed relatively close to home.

But laws such as those providing intellectual property protection arise under national law. No international or multijurisdictional grant of intellectual property rights exists. Additionally, because the grant of intellectual property rights is unique to each country, the scope and character of such rights varies from country to country. International treaties have harmonized to some extent the characteristics of intellectual property rights around the world. The Berne Convention for the Protection of Literary and Artistic Works has, for well over a century, set minimum standards of copyright protection for signatory nations. Additionally, the treaty on Trade Related aspects of Intellectual Property (TRIPs) sets certain minimum standards for patents, copyrights, and other forms of intellectual property. Accession to TRIPs is a requirement for admission to the World Trade Organization (WTO), membership in which has been sought by the majority of nations (Burk, 1998). Nonetheless, significant idiosyncrasies of national law remain. And, as of this writing, some important jurisdictions, notably Russia, remain outside the WTO, and so outside the TRIPs framework.

In the case of eDiaMoND, preliminary analyses of image ownership assumed that copyright inheres in the images, and the legal analysis proceeded from there. This is arguably the correct legal assumption to make under U.K. copyright law but is far more questionable under U.S. law; copyright is less likely in the U.S. to cover the images because the images constitute facts, which are excluded from copyright. U.S. law certainly recognizes copyright in the artistic arrangement or expression in photographic images, but it is unlikely that mammogram images are arranged so as to be artistic or expressive. Rather, the images were likely captured according to utilitarian criteria. To the extent that the arrangement of the images was dictated by functional considerations, American copyright law is unlikely to protect them.

Additionally, the U.S. lacks the *sui generis* database right found in the U.K. and other E.U. nations, so that the database as a whole could only be protected in the U.S. by copyright. To the extent that the selection and arrangement of images in the database may not be original expression— that is, to the extent that it is dictated by functional or utilitarian considerations—it may fail U.S. copyright requirements. At a minimum, extracting data from the database in such a way so as not to take the selection or arrangement, for example extracting single images, might well avoid any copyright liability in the U.S.

Similarly, under U.S. patent law, a patent or printed publication disclosing an invention anywhere in the world will disprove the novelty of the invention, possibly precluding the inventor from obtaining a patent. However, the novelty of an invention can be disproved by 'knowledge or use' of the invention only in the U.S., its territories, or possessions. Thus, whether online activity is classified as a 'printed publication' or as 'knowledge or use',' and whether the latter type of online activity is deemed to occur in the U.S., may affect the ability to patent an invention in the U.S. (Burk, 1993).

Patents for online collaboration may also be affected by other territorial provisions (Burk, 1993). U.S. law explicitly states that co-inventors need not work in the same physical vicinity in order to be named on a patent. However, U.S. law excludes from consideration for a patent inventive work that is not carried out either in U.S. territory or in a WTO country. Thus, inventive work that occurs in non-WTO jurisdictions, such as Russia, would not qualify for a U.S. patent. In an online collaboration between Russian and American researchers, determining the location of inventive work could be both critical and contested.

Another key patent law provision that is pertinent for open access research is the presence or absence of a research exemption to infringement. Many industrialized nations have enacted statutory experimental use exceptions to their patent law, allowing experimentation with and testing of patented inventions without permission of the patent owner. Canada, lacking such a statutory exception, has developed a strikingly broad common-law exception for experimental patent use. However, the U.S., outside of a very narrow statutory exception for development of regulatory health and safety data, has essentially no experimental use exception for commercial uses of a patented invention.

At the same time, in the copyright area, the U.S. has developed a strikingly broad and flexible fair use exception that is based on common-law and statutory provisions and is unique in the world. The majority of nations follows the statutory approach known in the U.K. and Canada as 'fair dealing',' essentially a list of specific exemptions from copyright liability under specific circumstances. U.S. copyright law, rather than limiting exceptions to a particular list, assesses whether an unauthorized use is permissible or 'fair' on a case-by-case basis, according to broad statutory criteria. Thus, the research use of a copyrighted work may be permissible in one jurisdiction while impermissible in another. This may be a particular problem for software, which may be covered by both patent and copyright law and for which the patent and copyright exemptions may be inconsistent both within and among jurisdictions.

And finally, issues may arise regarding where a legal claim regarding shared data might be adjudicated, that is, which nation's courts might have power to hear the case. Typically, a nation where the data are uploaded or downloaded, or whose nationals have some substantial involvement with the data, would be potential adjudicatory venues (Goldsmith, 1998). A court hearing the case would then have to decide which nation's laws should apply to the claim. Where the legal result in different jurisdictions would be inconsistent, the law includes a set of meta-rules, known as the law of conflicts, to decide which jurisdiction's laws will prevail. Of course, since jurisdictions may apply different legal rules to conflict analysis, meta-meta-rules may be applied to determine which jurisdiction's law of conflicts will prevail.

OPEN SOURCE LICENSING

A legal solution that might be considered to ameliorate such transborder conflicts is the deployment of licenses specifying the law to be applied to a given dataset. This potential legal solution carries with it a host of difficult social science issues. Perhaps the most debated and celebrated developments in collaborative work production has been the emergence of communal software projects facilitated by Internet communications and characterized by a philosophy of open collaboration and sharing. This 'free and open source software' movement has developed as a response to commercial software production that strives to keep software proprietary via intellectual property or technical closure. Commercial firms often distribute only machine-readable versions of programs and keep the human-readable source code restricted. In contrast, the loose confederation of open source software producers holds that software source code should be freely available for others to critique, to tinker with, and to improve.

The role of normative constraints and reputational capital in open source software development suggests that it has much in common with the culture of science (Burk, 2005; de Laat, 2001). The norms of communalism, universalism, and organized skepticism all appear to be operative in the open source and free software community. Just as scientists publish their work to ensure that it remains openly accessible for others to build upon, so open source coders circulate their code, employing 'copyleft' and similar licensing mechanisms to maintain accessibility. In open source, as in Mertonian science, peer review is relied upon to certify additions to the canon of knowledge. In both communities, normative expectations are largely communitarian rather than proprietary, and commercialization of work product is frequently viewed with suspicion. Both communities tend to rely on reputational incentives to prompt contributions to the common fund of knowledge. As scientists insist on freedom to set their research agendas, so open source programmers have insisted on freedom to work on the code that most stimulates their interest.

However, in a collaborative effort where open, normative constraints are the only impediment to deviant behavior, participants could selfishly defect from the community and incorporate the software into proprietary, closed products. Third parties might also obtain the openly available communally produced software and attempt to divert it into a closed form. Even if an open version remained available, the closed version could well become the dominant implementation of the code, crowding out the use and maintenance of the open version. This possibility could be particularly likely if the closed version were attached to or bundled with a dominant, proprietary platform, such as Microsoft Windows. Economic network effects and user 'lock-in' accompanying a dominant product could serve to capture permanently code that began as open source.

This possibility threatens both the structure of the community and the development of its work product. Diversion of collaborative code would not only violate the philosophical tenets of the community but might also disrupt coding collaboration due to the threat of free-riding on work of the community; programmers would be less likely to contribute work to the project if they knew it may be exploited by someone else. Indeed, the threat to the open source project from large corporate software concerns, and most especially from Microsoft, is a dominant theme, and almost a phobia, in open source circles (McGowan, 2001).

Yet over the past decade, the free and open source communities have, in a clever bit of legal jujitsu, adopted the mechanism of standardized form licensing for maintaining open access to their software projects. Open source coders have attached to their products a type of standardized form contract with a particular twist; as a term of copying, adapting, or redistributing the software, the user must agree to maintain open access to the source code. These licenses come in a variety of configurations, with terms that may forbid commercialization of the code, or may allow commercialization, or may allow commercialization on certain specific terms. One particular form of license, known as copyleft licensing, requires any change or improvement of the software to be made available to the public upon the same terms as received; in other words, the license has a 'viral' character, attaching its terms to any products derived from the initially licensed software.

Thus the automatic license, in conjunction with copyright law, becomes an assurance of openness rather than of restriction. This by no means places open source projects in the public domain, at least not as that term is generally employed in discussing intellectual property. Typically, the public domain encompasses those categories of intangible goods not covered by intellectual property, but open source software is unquestionably the subject of intellectual property protection. Copyright protection for these projects has neither been waived nor disclaimed in any fashion; indeed, the currency of intellectual property protection for open source code is the premise upon which copyleft and other open source licenses are based. The threat behind the license is that a copyright suit will ensue if the code is used in any fashion other than the open access under the license.

At the same time, the mystique of open source has given rise to a mythology of 'self-assembling' Internet projects, in which the invisible hand of cooperation coordinates worker output. Undoubtedly, the low-cost communications medium of the Internet does in fact allow open source coders to locate and coordinate projects more easily. Yet both anecdotal and empirical analyses suggest that the practice of open source coding is very tightly controlled by a few project leaders (McGowan, 2001; Tuomi, 2000). Strong normative expectations, backed by social sanctions, are directed at maintaining the focus and trajectory of open source projects. Project participants may vote with their feet; they may exit a project if they wish but typically cannot 'fork' a project to develop code contrary to the direction set by leaders. If a programmer's developmental vision differs from that of the project leaders, her options are to join some different project or to start a project of her own, not to create her own version of software already under development.

Informal sanctions are backed in part by the more formalized threat of legal action for copyright infringement. Attempts to capture open source projects in unapproved proprietary formats are potentially a violation of the license under which permission is granted to copy and adapt the code, and so they are a potential basis for a copyright suit. Such sanctions are of course the major deterrent to unauthorized use of the code by entities outside the open source community, but they also play a role in disciplining activity within the community, particularly where members of the community might be tempted to defect from the goals and values of the community. This function of community discipline potentially complicates attempts to employ copyleft strategies outside the context of software coding.

OPEN SOURCE PATENTING

The vision of open access to copyrighted works has not been limited to the open source community, and copyleft-style licensing, facilitated by the medium of electronic communications, has begun appearing outside the context of open source software. For example, the Creative Commons project provides an online repository of off-the-shelf licenses, conforming to the laws of various nations from which copyright holders can choose to associate with their copyrighted works. A symbol attached to a given work refers the user of the work to a particular standardized license in the Creative Commons repository, where the terms of use for the work can be found. Thus, like open source licensing, Creative Commons licenses rely on the shrink-wrap licensing model, assuming that such standardized licenses form a viable contract and will be enforceable.

To encourage use of Creative Commons licensing for research publications and other copyrighted science materials, Creative Commons has recently turned its attention to scientific research via the Science Commons project (David, 2004). Creative Commons licenses may cover copyrightable aspects of databases, such as the selection and arrangement or output formats. At present they do not extend to uncopyrightable facts, to unoriginal arrangements of data, or to *sui generis* E.U. database rights. Of course, as with mass-market shrink-wrap licenses, Creative Commons or other open source licenses could be extended to cover use or alteration of otherwise uncopyrightable materials, using access to the database as the trigger for the license; access would be granted conditionally upon acceptance of the contract. Off-the-shelf forms for such licenses are not yet available via Creative Commons.

Neither do Creative Commons licenses address, at least at the present writing, the disposition of patent rights. Consequently, the use of such licenses is at best a partial solution to the disposition of intellectual property in electronic collaborations. In theory, there is no reason why the Creative Commons could not include off-the-shelf patent licensing contracts, or that a similar archive of such forms could not be generated.

Some research projects have attempted to generate their own version of open source patent licenses (Cockburn, 2005; Rai, 2005). For example, such licenses govern access to the genomic data assembled in the governmentally funded HapMap Project, which is building an informational haplotype map of human genetic variations. The database is freely available on the conditions that those accessing the data do not file patent applications on information derived from the database and that those accessing the data share information only with others who have agreed to the same terms. Additionally, users of the database agree that any patents they obtain on uses derived from information in the database will be licensed on terms that allow others continued access to the information, limiting commercial use of the communal resource, and also incorporating the viral features of copyleft licensing.

Copyleft-style licensing has also been applied to physical materials, such as the biological materials made available via the Biological Innovation for Open Society (BIOS). The BIOS project is intended to make available biological research tools and techniques. While the project organizers are not adverse to users of these tools filing patents on discoveries made by use of the tools, they intend to preserve public access to the tools themselves. Patenting improvements or modifications that users might make to the basic tools might encumber those tools with proprietary claims, threatening open access. Internet-based electronic resources offer information about the tools and their use and facilitate contact for physical transfer of the tools, but physical access is conditioned on agreement not to patent any improvements or modifications to the tools and to make any such modifications or improvements available on the same terms. No such restrictions are placed on products or discoveries generated by use of the tools; such products or discoveries can be patented without limitation.

However, the transfer of copyleft and related models from the copyright regime to that of patent presents several difficulties in part because the nature of the exclusive rights granted by copyright and by patent are quite different (Boettiger & Burk, 2004; Feldman, 2004). Copyright excludes unauthorized copying and related activities based on access. Access serves as the trigger or activating event for the copyleft license; copying or adapting the open source code opens the copyist or adapters to a lawsuit unless the copying or adapting is done in accordance with the terms of the license. Patent rights exclude all uses of the claimed invention, even those conducted independently, without any access to the invention. In such cases, an infringing act would not serve to channel the infringer into compliance with the terms of the license, as there would be no knowledge of the license.

Additionally, the restrictions on further patenting that are incorporated into some 'open biology' licenses may run afoul of the general public policy of the patent system. In the U.S., federal statutory and constitutional law encourages patenting, and licenses deterring patents might be preempted. Additionally, patents raise competition law considerations that are not necessarily present under copyright law. Certain types of patent licensing arrangements are subject to extra antitrust scrutiny, such as patent 'grant-backs',' which require licensing of technology developed with a patented tool back to the patent owner, and patent 'reach-throughs', which require payment of royalties to a patent owner for products developed with a patented tool. Patenting restrictions in open biology licenses resemble these types of arrangement—for example, requiring products developed with open source biology tools to be licensed back to others on an open source basis—and so may raise antitrust concerns.

But the greatest obstacle to movement of copyleft licenses into e-science may be the social disparity between open source and scientific research settings. Despite their apparent normative similarities, open source coding and academic science have different social profiles. The scientific community is older and more institutionally invested, with an organizational structure not present in open source coding. For example, academic science has an effective hierarchical organization at the level of individual laboratories. Graduate and undergraduate training also contribute a distinct social sub-structure to science. Science is also arguably a more diverse community; the norms of sociology are not necessarily the norms of physics or molecular biology. Academic science is also heavily subsidized by governmental grants, with the result that funding agencies may have interests in the disposition of intellectual property. Other formal institutions, such as institutional ethics review boards and peer review journal publishers, may play roles not contemplated by the open source licensing system.

Consequently, open source licenses used to promote open science may need to consider the role of these organizational structures, rather than blithely adopting licenses from open source programming or other open access projects. As one possibility, open science licenses might need to take into account scientific institutions with behavioral influence that could substitute for the strong informal norms found among open source programmers. For example, in the formulation and enforcement of human genome sequence publication rules discussed above, exclusion of violators from scientific journals played a key role in compliance. This suggests that open science licenses might include as their penalty clauses exclusion from peer review journals, or from peer review funding, or from participation in similar scientific institutions. Such contractual clauses could help match the structure of the license to the structure of the relevant research community.

CONCLUSION

The communal norms of science no longer shield research from the demands of intellectual property, and as a multijurisdictional and collaborative enterprise, e-science is potentially subject to a myriad of conflicting intellectual property regimes. Contractual systems drawn from open source software coding might be deployed to ameliorate some of the effects of conflicting intellectual property systems, but copyleft and related licensing systems were developed to maintain community discipline and demarcate the open source community from outside commercial influences. These licenses may require considerable adaptation before they can perform a similar function for the e-science research community. Further research and understanding of how the e-science community is being and will be structured are essential to assist in drafting licenses that meet the community's needs. Thus, social science research to examine the nature of on-line collaboratives and their adherence to formal and informal norms will help to further the development of e-research including, somewhat recursively, the development of e-social science.

ACKNOWLEDGMENTS

An earlier version of this chapter appeared in the *Journal of Computer-Mediated Communication* (Burk, 2007) and the author wishes to express appreciation for opportunity to revise that work.

REFERENCES

Boettiger, S., & Burk, D. (2004). Open source patenting. *Journal of International Biotechnology Law, 1*(6), 221–231.

Boyle, J. (2003). Enclosing the genome: What squabbles over genetic patents could teach us. In F. S. Keiff (Ed.), *Perspectives on properties of the human genome project*, pp. 97–122. San Diego, CA: Elsevier Academic Press.

Burk, D. (1993). Patents in cyberspace: Territoriality and infringement on global computer networks. *Tulane Law Review, 68*, 1–67.

Burk, D. (1994). Transborder intellectual property issues on the electronic frontier. *Stanford Law and Policy Review, 5*, 9–16.

Burk, D. (1998). Virtual exit in the global information economy. *Chicago-Kent Law Review, 73*, 943–995.

Burk, D. (2000). Intellectual property issues in electronic collaboration. In S. H. Koslow & M. F. Huerta (Eds.), *Electronic collaboration in science: Progress in neuroinformatics, Vol. 2*, pp. 15–44. Mahwah, NJ: Lawrence Erlbaum Associates.

Burk, D. (2005). Bioinformatics lessons from the open source movement. In H. Tavani (Ed.), *Ethics, computing, and genomics: Moral controversies in computational genomics*, pp. 257–254. Sudbury, MA: Jones and Bartlett.

Burk, D. (2007). Intellectual property in the context of e-science. *Journal of Computer-Mediated Communication, 12*(2), article 13. Retrieved September 20, 2007 from http://jcmc.indiana.edu/vol12/issue2/burk.html

Cockburn, I. (2005). State Street meets the human genome project: Intellectual property and bioinformatics. In R.W. Hahn (Ed.), *Intellectual property rights in frontier industries: Software and biotechnology*, pp. 111–130. Washington DC: AEI-Brookings Joint Center.

David, P. A. (2004). Can "open science" be protected from the evolving regime of IPR protections? *Journal of Institutional and Theoretical Economics, 160*(1), 9–34.

David, P., & Spence, M. (2003). Towards institutional infrastructures for e-science: The scope of the challenge. Oxford Internet Institute, Research Report, 2. Oxford: University of Oxford. Retrieved September 20, 2006 from http://129.3.20.41/eps/get/papers/0502/0502028.pdf

de Laat, P. (2001). Open source software: A new Mertonian ethos? In A. Vedder (Ed.), *Ethics and the Internet*, pp. 33–48. Oxford: Intersentia.

Eckersley, P., Egan, G. F., & Shun-ichi, A. (2003). Neuroscience data and tool sharing: A legal and policy framework for neuroinformatics. *Neuroinformatics, 1*(2), 149–66.

Eisenberg, R. (1987). Proprietary rights and the norms of science in biotechnology research. *Yale Law Journal, 97*(2), 177–231.

Feldman, R. (2004). The open source biotechnology movement: Is it patent misuse? *Minnesota Journal of Law, Science and Technology, 6*(1), 117–167.

Finholt, T. (2002). Collaboratories. *Annual Review of Information Science and Technology, 36*, 73–107.

Glasner, P. (1996). From community to "collaboratory?" The human genome mapping project and the changing culture of science. *Science and Public Policy, 23*(2), 109–116.

Goldsmith, J. (1998). Against cyberanarchy. *University of Chicago Law Review, 65*(4), 1199–1250.

Hey, T., & Trefethen, A. (2003). e-science and its implications. *Philosophical Transactions of the Royal Society London, 361*(1809), 1809–1825.

Hinds, C., Jirotka, M., Rahman, M., D'Agostino, G., Meyer, C., Piper, T., et al. (2005, June 22–24). Ownership of intellectual property rights in medical data in collaborative computing environments. National Centre for e-Social Science, First International Conference on e-Social Science. Retrieved September 20, 2006 from http://www.ncess.ac.uk/events/conference/2005/papers/papers/ncess2005_paper_Hinds.pdf

McGowan, D. (2001). Legal implications of open-source software. *University of Illinois Law Review, 2001*(1), 241–304.

Merges, R. P. (1996). Property rights theory and the commons: The case of scientific research. *Social Philosophy and Policy, 13*(2), 145–167.

Merton, R. (1957). Priorities in scientific discovery: A chapter in the sociology of science. *American Sociological Review, 22*, 635–659.

Merton, R. (1973). *The sociology of science: Theoretical and empirical investigations*. Chicago, IL: University of Chicago Press.

Nelson, R. (2004). The market economy and the scientific commons. *Research Policy, 33*(3), 455–471.

Newman, H. B., Ellisman, E. H., & Orcutt, J. A. (2003). Data-intensive e-science frontier research. *Communications of the ACM, 46*(11), 69–75.

Rai, A. K. (2000). Addressing the patent gold rush: The role of deference to PTO patent denials. *Washington University Journal of Law and Policy, 2*, 199–227.

Rai, A. K. (2005). Open and collaborative research: A new model for biomedicine. In R. W. Hahn (Ed.), *Intellectual property rights in frontier industries: Software and biotechnology* (131–158). Washington DC: AEI-Brookings Joint Center.

Toumi, I. (2000). Internet, innovation, and open source: Actors in the network. *First Monday, 6* (1). Retrieved September 20, 2006 from   http://www.first-monday.org/issues/issue6_1/tuomi/index.html

Part VIII
Case Studies

16 Situated Innovations in e-Social Science

Bridgette Wessels and Max Craglia

INTRODUCTION

This chapter explores a user-led approach in the development of e-social science in which an interdisciplinary team integrated technological infrastructure, collaboration, and knowledge in the development of e-social science. e-Social science refers to the "collaboration between computer scientists and social scientists to design and develop middleware in order to address social scientists' substantive research problems in new ways that recognize more fully the complexity of economic and social activities" (NceSS, e-Social Science newsletter Issue 1, Summer 2000, p. 1). In this chapter, 'development' refers to the work done by researchers to adapt Grid technologies (Foster, 2002, Ananthnarayan, et al., 2003) to address an interdisciplinary social research problem.

The e-social science pilot project discussed in this chapter addressed three main dimensions of e-social science: (1) identification of new social research foci, (2) adapting research processes, and (3) developing tools. The way in which these three dimensions of the project were integrated shows that the development of computer-mediated research using the Grid—when grounded in research practice—can develop relevant and innovative tools for the social sciences.

THE PILOT PROJECT

The substantive social science focus of the project "Collaborative Analysis of Offenders' Personal and Area-based Social Exclusion"[1] was to explore the extent to which individual and neighborhood effects are able to account for the geographical variation of crime patterns. This issue has been at the core of environmental criminology since the early work of the Chicago School of Sociology in the 1920s, and the theoretical debate on the relative importance of individual, family, school, social ties, and neighborhood factors on crime patterns continues to the present day (Friedrichs & Balsius, 2003). As evidence regarding the influence of area effects remains unclear and difficult to quantify, the Grid generated an opportunity to undertake large-scale data analysis over distributed information resources. The multi-dimensionality of the research problem suggested the need to take a multi-disciplinary approach, which collaborative e-social science, in principle, has the potential to facilitate. With these considerations in mind, the project had two main objectives:

- To explore, quantify and model the spatial distribution of crime in relation to socio-economic and neighborhood characteristics based on user-driven applications of Grid technology.
- To reflect critically on the evolving relationship among social scientists, technologists, and the Grid for the development of training material and the further deployment of Grid technology in the social sciences.

Three main groups of actors took part in the project: (1) a core team of academic researchers, (2) project partners and data providers from the regional policy-making community, and (3) external private sector data-suppliers who rendered support services, university Grid infrastructure and tools, and Web services developers. The team came together through pre-proposal meetings. Researchers and project partners were picked for their interest in collaborating, sharing resources and their expertise. The consensus for collaboration was the starting point and collaboration evolved through the research process itself, and this flexibility enabled user-led multi-disciplinary development.

The core research team consisted of three urban planners with Geographical Information Systems (GIS) expertise (one of whom was the PI), two criminologists, two sociologists (including the ethnographer), and one computer scientist (Grid Officer). The project partners and data suppliers were the South Yorkshire Police, who provided a unique combination of highly confidential data on the location of known offenders, offences, and victims over a five-year period (1998–2003). The four Local Authorities in the region (Barnsley, Doncaster, Sheffield and Rotherham) provided spatial information (policy boundaries). The government agency, South Yorkshire Connexions, provided data on young people who were not in employment, education, or training.

The support services group included the academic White Rose Grid (WRG) consortium that made infrastructure and development tools available through access Grid services, and the Open Geospatial Consortium (OGC) that supported the development of a platform based on its Web service specifications for sharing the results of the project among the stakeholders. Other data sources included the Census, accessed through MIMAS[2], and the Index of Multiple Deprivation 2004[3]. These three groups of social scientists, data providers/practitioners, and technology providers collaborated in exploring the possibilities of the Grid for use in the social sciences.

Technology and Innovation in the Project

The analytical framework of the project was based on the social shaping definitions of 'technology' and 'innovation'. Technology was defined as a "set of physical objects . . . human activities . . . and knowledge" (MacKenzie & Wajcman, 1985:3). Innovation was seen to be a complex social activity, involving learning processes and the interaction and sharing of expertise among different actors in the project network (Williams & Edge, 1992). The project was a case of 'first practical use' in which inventions are shaped and applied to particular contexts of use (Jewkes, Sawers, & Stillerman, 1958). This phase involves researchers having to learn how to apply an invention in use-contexts—a 'learning by doing' approach (Arrow, 1962). Thus, the researchers, who were used to working tacitly within established social science methodologies had to reflect on their current practice (human activities), re-imagine tools (objects), and interrogate theory and disciplinary boundaries (knowledge) to be able to develop e-social science within pilot demonstrator projects in an interdisciplinary and collaborative way.

Changes to practices and tools were made from action situated in the project (Suchman, 1987) and required researchers to learn new techniques and perspectives in developing e-social science (Williams, Stewart, & Slack, 2005). The researchers worked with existing social science classification systems and had to combine them in new ways; this methodological "articulation" (Bowker & Star, 1999) involved researchers reflecting differences between methods and techniques and making visible some of the ways they juggled these concepts, data, and research tools in developing e-social science. This methodological articulation took place in meetings and workshops that were characterized as "transformational spaces" (Wessels, 2007). The work done in these spaces is situated between established tools and practices and new and untried practices and tools: it is where the social scientists and Grid Officer could experiment with practices and tools and development of knowledge. These spaces enable the 'artful integration' of innovative technology, the Grid, with the social and material worlds of academic perspectives and methods (c.f. Suchman, 1994). This was integral to the co-construction process, both technologically speaking in the use of Grid-related tools in our project, and more holistically in the substantive focus of our e-social science pilot demonstrator project.

Shaping New Computer-Supported Research Tools

The approach of the team was that the knowledge and practices of social science should shape the technological development. The researchers adopted an inductive approach to: (1) explore the different disciplinary approaches in the study of the relationship between young people at risk of crime and the characteristics of their neighborhood, and (2) develop the methodology and relevant tools from the needs of the social science research. The researchers made sense of the research problem through this inductive approach that led to deductive statistical modeling and systematic computer-supported data processing.

The team aligned the above approach with design in use methodologies. Although approaches in participatory design[4] aim to obtain the 'point of view' of users in design processes, they mostly take a design-oriented perspective. Methodologies vary within this tradition, but often a user-needs expert is used to facilitate the participant design process, which can involve scenarios, mock-ups, as well as detailed observations of work practice. Participants are encouraged to feed into the design process usually prior to, and sometimes during, technological development (Crabtree, Rouncefield, O'Brien, Tolmie, & Hughes, 1999; Dittrich, Floyd, & Klischewski, 2002; Jirotka & Goguen, 1994). Co-construction approaches, however, differ by taking the view that user requirements[5] and design are symbiotic, and that the system needs to be constantly refined to develop something relevant to users, organizations, and institutions (Dobson, Blyth, Chudge, & Strens, 1994). A co-construction approach was adapted by having the computer scientists and social scientists work together with an ethnographer in undertaking participatory observation of the project team. This meant that both social and computer scientists were making sense of the research together and learning and developing the Grid from that understanding, which is consistent with Bowker and Star's (1999) notion of articulation discussed above.

The ethnographer was part of the team: she contributed to the sociological aspect of the substantive research and to the research-driven shaping of the Grid as well as undertaking participant observation of the development process. Her role as participant observer was not one of feeding insights to designers, but of aiding the researchers to reflect on their work. The ethnographer's role was overt, and her experience in researching social exclusion as well as user-led technology projects helped her gain acceptance in the team. She participated in all the research meetings and training sessions. She contributed to the social science activity in line with her expertise and as the project progressed she fed back her observations to the team. Through her participation the ethnographer fitted into the dynamics of collaboration allowing other researchers to engage freely in the project in line with their own expertise. However, although the scientists were relaxed about the observation, they nonetheless experienced the classic situation of 'being studied', which made them become highly aware and reflective of their actions, as if they were researching themselves. This distance from the action together with engagement in the action produced a reflexive attitude among the researchers, which is a general feature of ethnographic research (Hammersley & Atkinson, 1989). This ethnographic sensibility adopted by the ethnographer and the researchers resulted in a shared understanding of the research process in ways that enabled them to articulate and contextualize 'user needs' in the design processes that were integral to the project.

Thus the process of design and use was integrated in our pilot project (cf. Suchman, 2002).

The project trajectory was:

1. Development of multi-disciplinary collaborative research and research partnerships.
2. Discussion of theoretical issues to underpin the multi-disciplinary approach.
3. Training for the social scientists and technological development of the Grid.
4. Integration and analysis of the datasets.
5. Further Grid development and sharing outcomes among partners.

Each of these phases in the trajectory is elaborated below.

Phase 1: Developing Multi-Disciplinary Collaborative Research

The fostering of the collaborative approach consisted of a range of meetings and discussions within the core team, and between the core team and the policy and practitioners group, and with the technical expert from the OGC. At the first meeting of the core team, the research-led approach was affirmed by discussions such as: "We don't know what e-social-science is" (urban planner) but "we want to do a good project on the multi-dimensionality of exclusion, neighborhood and young people at risk" (sociologist). In the next eight meetings, each of the researchers discussed their disciplinary approach to the research problem, data sources, and theoretical perspectives.

The criminologists were keen to explore whether neighborhood structure makes it more or less likely that some people will commit offences or become victims of crime. The urban planners were building on a 'needs analysis' project that aggregated small area-level data across a range of education, health, and welfare domains to inform research and planning decisions regarding services for children and teenagers in Sheffield (Signoretta & Craglia, 2002). The sociologists, building on the Communities that Care project (France & Crow, 2005), sought to address the influence of neighborhoods, schools, and family circumstances in relation to risk factors that may propel young people into crime. The Grid Officer, with his computational physics and technology background, wanted to 'listen in and talk' at the meetings so that he could design training and develop the Grid for use by social scientists in an integrated way. The internal dynamics of the project at this stage were those of gaining familiarity with each other's imaginations and languages to improve the discourse within the project.

The core team also had to develop a dialogue and shared understanding with the project-partners. The official 'kick-off meeting' involved the core team meeting with representatives from regional policy makers, service and data providers, and technology providers (OGC and WRG). The Principal

Investigator (PI) brought together the policy makers and service providers through the relationships he had fostered across the region in previous research. The criminologists had established trust with South Yorkshire Police by working with the organization for a number of years, and the sociologists had trusted relationships with agencies from South Yorkshire. The development and maintenance of trust was achieved through the way the researchers had worked with agencies over time. The focus of the kick-off meeting was to outline the project, look at the kind of data needed, and introduce everyone to the Grid. The policy and practitioner community strove to establish links between research agendas and technological tools, and in general the partners saw the project in terms of its social research potential and as an opportunity to support the emerging public policy research alliances in the region. The time and effort spent by the core team at this stage paid off by allowing each partner to see potential value in the project, rather than forcing each of them to subscribe to an assumed single shared objective.

Phase 2: Theoretical Frameworks

In this phase of the project, the core team furthered its discussion of the research problem and conducted literature reviews focusing on environmental criminology, Grid technology, and risk factors for young people. Over the course of eight meetings, the team discussed the ways in which different disciplinary aspects of the project could be integrated, both in relation to the substantive research focusing on the extent to which individual and neighborhood effects account for the geographical variation of crime patterns, and on how the Grid should be utilized to undertake large-scale data analysis over distributed information resources.

The perspectives of the criminologist and urban planners with regard to the relationship between crime and neighborhood contributed to generating hypotheses, but the team, and in particular the sociologists, had to find ways to encompass the area of young people at risk within a crime-neighborhood dynamic. The sociologists were concerned to develop a theoretical framework that would inform the multi-disciplinary research and help to select datasets and research methodologies. They developed research questions to aid the researchers in developing a multi-disciplinary framework. The questions were:

1. Can we construct a reliable set of measures for community-based risk factors that allow us to measure them at ward or neighborhood level?
2. Can we create a 'national norm' with which to compare?
3. If so, what relationship might exist between levels of risk and levels of crime—are neighborhoods in communities with high-risk level young people also areas with high-risk factors?

4. What relationships might exist between levels of risk and levels of crime?

These questions prompted the urban planners and the criminologists to consider their understanding of 'place' and' crime' and ask what data would be needed to address the issues above. The criminologists argued for data that could link the locations of known offenders, offences, and victims. The urban planner wanted data that brought together lifestyles and socio-economic characteristics in clearly identifiable geographic units. The sociologists required data on young people between 16–18 years old—where they lived as well as their socio-economic circumstances. The researchers also felt they needed Census data at Output Area (OA) and Super Output Area (SOA) as well as data from the Index of Multiple Deprivation, to develop a robust model at the national level and to compare regional results with national findings.

The Grid Officer took part in all the meetings so that he could learn to appreciate the social science perspective, but admitted to being "somewhat confused" in trying to understand the rather contested nature of social science and the problems encountered when researching worlds that were "not in the lab." He felt that understanding social science would help him to develop Grid-related tools and training for the social scientists. The Grid Officer knew that the WRG computing cluster provided a reliable service that could be assessed in a variety of ways with varying degrees of interactivity, but he felt that the researchers, who had little experience of UNIX or high-powered computing, would find accessing the computing cluster technologically daunting. He pointed out that access to such systems requires familiarity with client applications and protocols for transferring data and communicating with remote systems, which is further complicated by the introduction of modern protocols for secure communication. Generally, he explained, users are presented with terminals and expected to manage their user account through a command line using UNIX or LINUX, which is a powerful way of operating a system but requires familiarity with these operating systems.

Phase 3: Training for the Social Scientists

The core team took part in three technological and three statistical training workshops, held in the University's computer training rooms. The workshops were led by the Grid Officer who thought it important for researchers to 'get behind the tools' to help them understand how the Grid worked and then to articulate what they needed from the tools. The researchers were given passwords and identifiers to work on the WRG. For the social scientists, UNIX was new, as was the architecture of the Grid. The researchers learned to access the UNIX host Titania, work with files, manage directories, share data using UNIX groups, and access shared data and transfer files, and then progressed to working with scripts to try out the Sun Grid Engine.

A further access issue regarding computer clusters was that researchers are often most familiar with a system such as Microsoft Windows in which the applications generating the Graphic User Interfaces (GUIs) and displaying the GUIs are on the same machine. The problem with a cluster system is that the machine generating the GUI (the application) and the machine displaying the GUI are geographically separated, so the machines have to communicate via the Internet using the X protocol for communicating information about graphical displays. Therefore, to run GUI applications based on clusters meant that the researchers had to install additional applications to which they were not familiar, adding to the sense of distance between methods and tools.

Furthermore, the introduction of secure protocols such as secure shell client (SSH) meant that it was necessary for the researchers to possess a basic grasp of the idea of tunneling of communication—the means by which SSH encrypts communications over a number of different channels. This is the way in which X-windows applications are secured over the Internet, in that the SSH is used to access clusters and enable the tunneling of X traffic used for GUI applications. These procedures were new to many social scientists and required an understanding of the related concepts and practices.

The second half of the workshop series involved the researchers learning the basics of the statistical package, SPlus, and the geographical information system (GIS) ArcView, as well as accessing various datasets in using the Grid. The researchers' training on the Grid enabled them to open ArcView on Titania and to begin to work with the idea of a cluster system. Nonetheless, further research-based learning involved the sociologists and criminologists having to come to terms with the logic of mapping in representing data. The PI, who was an urban planner, stepped in and talked them through what a 'view' was by explaining that: "A view is composed of multiple maps, each with their own table." When the criminologists and sociologists could follow the logic of a thematic map and classification field, they could see how the maps were working as visual representations of data. The Grid Officer also started to work closely with the PI so that the latter could understand how the mapping could work from 'a Grid point of view' and see what tools were needed for mapping with the Grid infrastructure.

The Grid Officer continued to develop ways to facilitate Grid access. The configuration used at Sheffield involved a cluster of 10 Sun computers connected to two other clusters at Leeds and York, forming the WRG (see Figure 16.1). The Grid Officer installed SPlus and ArcView software on the Unix cluster. However, to ensure access to the distributed processing capabilities of the Grid, he had to write bespoke applications (specific applications for particular contexts of use). The first application he developed allowed researchers to retrieve census data from MIMAS and store it locally to perform subsequent analysis. This first application tested the development toolkit of EASA (Enterprise Accessible Software Application),[6] an off-the-shelf application environment, which enables developers to publish an application on a portal for easy access by researchers.

Publishing an application on the EASA portal means that the application has a user interface that is accessible via the Internet and can be used to manage applications running on a remote Grid node or cluster. As such, the portal does not distribute the application, but rather distributes the means by which a user can communicate with that application, i.e., the user interface. The EASA application requires the installation of a client application on the user's machine that enables the EASA client (like the X server) to build an application interface based on instructions that it receives from the EASA portal. This provided two benefits: (1) the researchers were happy because they had a highly usable interface, and (2) in EASA it was much easier to develop user interfaces for applications than using development tools such as X windows, Microsoft foundation classes, or Web applications using technology such as Java swing.

The core team tested the applications by developing a facility for accessing and querying census data via MIMAS. Although this particular application was not used for the project since the 2001 Census became available through another academic service, it provided an important test of the team's ability to develop these types of interfaces.

Phase 4: Integration and Analysis of the Datasets

The analysis of data was divided into two stages: (1) the team analyzed individual variables of the crime and youth datasets, including aggregation at census geography level, calculation of counts, rates, and standardized rates, and identified outliers and extreme values, (2) the researchers analyzed the key variables to identify statistically significant relationships, supported by the review of the literature on environmental criminology. Thus, the criminologists and urban planners worked together on the unique crime

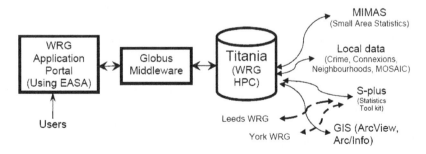

Figure 16.1 The White Rose Grid portal architecture.

dataset provided by South Yorkshire Police (following a written protocol with the University of Sheffield), which included:

1. 371,000 reported victims of crime.
2. 46,800 offenders who have committed 118,000 offences.
3. 17,000 young offenders who have committed 45,000 offences.
4. 70,000 thefts from cars, 63,000 burglaries, 28,000 damage to dwellings.

The data were provided with X, Y coordinates at 10-meter resolution or better (1 meter in some instances) and covered the time period 1998–2003. This collection of data provided the opportunity to link the locations of known offenders, offences, and victims as required for the project. This had not been reported before in the literature because of the difficulty in accessing offender and victim data.

The researchers then downloaded Census data at Output Area (OA) and Super Output Area (SOA) for the whole of England. They drew on 120 variables (based on the review of literature) in the following domains:

1. Ethnicity and age
2. Economic activity and occupation
3. Socio-economic classification and qualifications
4. Household characteristics, including vacancies and overcrowding
5. Tenure
6. Car ownership
7. Migration

This was used in conjunction with the Connexions South Yorkshire data for all 16–18 year olds in South Yorkshire (approximately 30,000 young people) from November 2003 to March 2004, which included unit postcode, age, sex, ethnicity, and whether or not in education, employment, or training. The team also used the 2004 Index of Multiple Deprivation, containing seven domains which relate to: income deprivation, employment deprivation, health deprivation and disability, education, skills and training deprivation, barriers to housing and services, and living environment deprivation and crime at SOA. The researchers decided to focus on a statistical modeling approach which included two stages: (1) stepwise regressions to identify the most significant variables in accounting for the variance of offenders and for reflection on the findings in the light of the literature review, and (2) experimentation with different types of models to see which would yield the best results.

On the basis of the analysis carried out for the county of South Yorkshire, the researchers found that:

1. Over 70% of the variance of victimization was accounted for by the proximity of the residential location of offenders.

2. Offences such as domestic burglary and criminal damage were also strongly related to the location of offenders.
3. The geographic distribution of offenders appeared to have strong correlations with Census data.

Given that very little data linking victims and offenders had previously been available, these are important quantitative findings, which confirm qualitative interviews with young offenders (Wiles and Costello, 2000) and contribute to the theoretical and policy debates in this field. While offences are often correlated to indices of deprivation and their geographical distribution, evidence from this project indicates that the geographical link between offences and deprivation is not direct but 'mediated' by the geographical distribution of offenders. The strong link between census data and offenders, on the one hand, and offenders and victimization, on the other, made a very good case for trying to model the geographical distribution of offenders on a national basis using the census variables and to use the outcome as a relative 'risk' map for potential victimization. The key advantage of such a model would be that it could be done using nationally, and freely available, data (the national census, Index of Multiple Deprivation) without requiring the very sensitive and unique dataset that was available to the researchers for the region of South Yorkshire.

Phase 5: Grid Development and Sharing Outcomes among Partners

After developing a model of the distribution of offenders for South Yorkshire and validating it against the observed results, the model was extended to the whole of England at SOA and then filtered through a 1 hectare-cell Grid based on the residential postcodes provided by the national postal service. The advantage of this procedure was that it reported the results of the model more accurately in relation to where people live. This was considered better than the system of large polygons that integrate sparsely populated areas with more densely populated areas. The final model selected was a General Linear Model of the Poisson family[7] in which the response variable (counts of offenders) was transformed using a logarithmic function. The model was then run for the whole of England at SOA in the following form:

$$\log(\text{observed/expected values}) = \beta0 + \beta1X1 + \beta2X2 + \beta3X3 + \beta4X4 + \beta5X5 + \beta6X6$$

where:

X1 = Percent of economically active unemployed.

X2 = Percent of households renting from other (hostels, secure accommodation, prisons, boarding houses, hotels, and other communal establishments).

X3 = Percent of households with lone parents with dependent children.

X4 = Percent of residential spaces vacant.

X5 = Index of Multiple Deprivation 2004 Health Domain score.
X6 = Index of Multiple Deprivation 2004 Crime Domain score.

To explore the spatial patterns of the model, it became necessary to generalize (smooth) results at different scales. It was at this point in the project that the researchers needed the Grid, which would help them to undertake smoothing at 5 km in an efficient manner. To this end, the Grid Officer developed the second main project application, which enabled smoothing of the model results for England at different scales. This was particularly important for the project, as smoothing the data at 5 km involved calculating the mean value across the neighboring 50 cells for each of the 35 million hectare cells covering England and returning the result for display (see Figure 16.2). Figure 16.3 shows the portal the Grid Officer developed for the researchers to access the application. The researchers, having imported an ASCII file with the data, could then select the number of processors on which to operate. The portal would then schedule the operation via the Globus Middleware, based on the schema showed in Figure 16.1.

It was at this stage that the team saw the advantages of using multiple high-performance computers—smoothing at 10 kilometers took 6¼ hours on a single Pentium 4 processor (3 GHz) but only one hour when performed over 15 parallel processors on the WRG (the Grid infrastructure). This performance was achieved using the specific smoothing algorithm created in the project, because the internal routines of ArcView Spatial Analysis or ArcGIS required too long to compute the necessary calculations. Thus, at this stage of development the team learned that Grid computing is very useful, provided researchers are able to access the Grid infrastructure and parallelize the processing. However, in order to leverage on the infrastructure, researchers have be able to access or write the appropriate algorithms, since most off-the-shelf software on a desktop cannot harness the Grid (Clematis, Mineter, and Marciano, 2003).

Having successfully processed the data through the WRG services, and re-imported the results into a GIS for display purposes, the issue that arose was how to share the results obtained with other partners in the project, including South Yorkshire Police and the four local authorities in the region. In policy terms, the value of this data sharing was to enable the comparison of areas which have a relative higher level of risk (as identified by the statistical model) with areas that are the subject of different policy interventions carried out by agencies operating in the region. In particular the team wanted to identify whether there were any gaps, i.e. areas at high risk not covered by targeted policies.

Two issues needed addressing: firstly, that the entire data analysis and processing had been performed within the secure Sheffield University intranet with access to Grid services controlled via a complex procedure of institutional authorization which then enables the necessary Authenticate, Authorize, and Access services of the WRG. It was necessary to find a

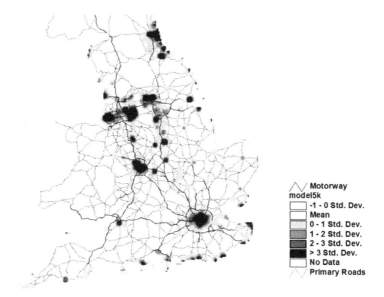

Figure 16.2   Modeled distribution of offenders, England at 5 km.

solution that would allow the controlled publishing of the findings outside of the University firewall as the partner agencies did not have access to the University intranet. Secondly, that such publishing had to allow for the overlay of the policy boundaries defined by the other partners in the framework of their institutional roles. As such boundaries are policy-driven and dynamic, it is necessary that they are regularly maintained by the 'owning'

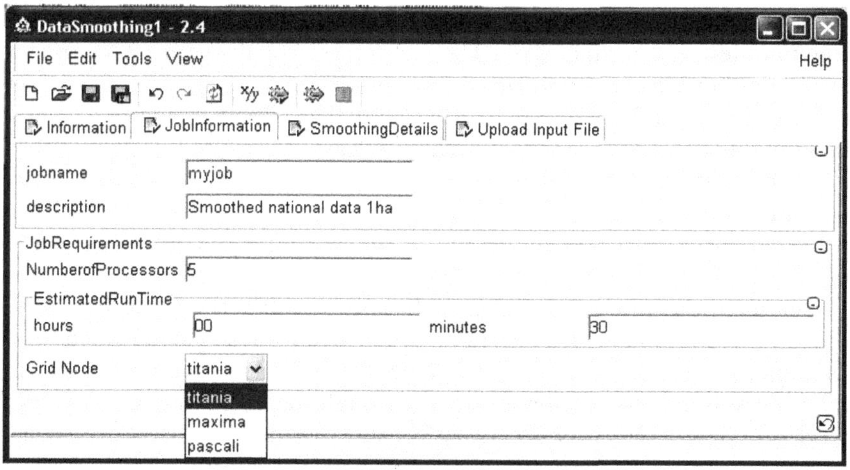

Figure 16.3   Scheduling the job from the White Rose Grid Portal.

organizations and published from their own servers. In other words we did not want to set up a framework for sharing data based on copies of the data transferred to a centralized server, but one that was instead based on distributed servers communicating dynamically. The solution adopted is one that is typical of distributed Spatial Data Infrastructure architectures (Nebert, 2004), and based on the Web Map Service (WMS) specifications of the Open Geospatial Consortium (2001). A WMS provides operations protocols in support of the creation and display of registered and superimposed map-like views of information that come simultaneously from multiple sources that are both remote and heterogeneous. By installing WMS on both the university's and partners' web servers it was possible to overlay the maps of the model results with those of the policy boundaries, and query the overlay to retrieve the attribute information as illustrated in Figure 16.4. This solution allows each partner to retain control of its own data, maintain it easily, and determine the level of detail and attributes to be shared. These are critical characteristics needed to share information and show the value of SDI architectures also in a local context. Moreover, they allow external partners to take advantage of the processing capabilities of the Grid at the results level.

CONCLUSION

The aim of user-driven and research-led development was to appropriate the Grid in ways that were relevant to social science. To explore the relationships between technology, research practice, and knowledge in producing e-social science the project adopted a collaborative approach in developing first practical use. The project shows that the interplay of research practices, on the one hand, and Grid technologies, on the other, is highly situational, and that innovation and first use require the artful integration of different practices, communities, and technologies. The researchers collaborating with others in situated innovations contributed their disciplinary perspective as well as methodological and technological knowledge. They became reflective practitioners, able to listen to other researchers in learning new perspectives, practices, and skills in the articulation of new research practices. The Grid Officer was an important resource and through the co-construction approach he gained an insider's understanding of the project, developed prototypes, provided training and was on hand for any ad hoc development work.

The team demonstrated that not all work requires the Grid, but identifies the context in which the Grid is beneficial for social scientists (for example, smoothing hectare cells). With the help from the Grid Officer, the team was able to develop a bridge (through the EASA portal) to access Grid resources—which is necessary because the desktop software social scientists are familiar with cannot operate in a Grid environment directly—and partition data processing across multiple processors in a distributed

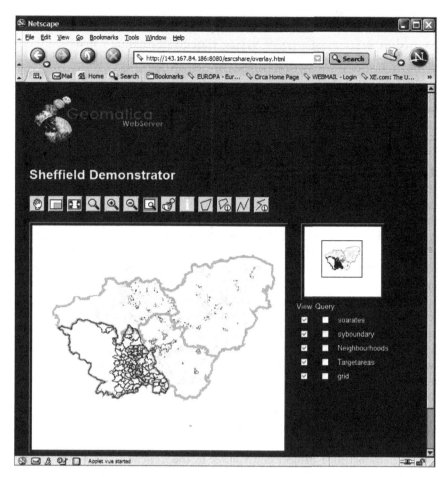

Figure 16.4 OGC-compliant Web Map Service allowing overlay and query of distributed data.

environment. In this sense, the project was truly a pilot, because it operated at a time of transition between desktop and distributed processing environments. Although the technical work in the project is consonant with Open Grid Architecture, further development requires the generation of interoperable catalogues of services and appropriate metadata declaring its service capabilities, provenance, conditions, and so on. Such catalogues and services would need to be easily searchable and accessible across multiple portals of the type experimented with in this project, and be able to interoperate regardless of specific configurations of the Grid deployed in different projects and communities.

Of central importance to the success of the project was the time and effort required to develop a shared understanding of the data. Often the technological debate about the Grid (Woolgar, 2003) and related technologies suggests that because vast quantities of digital data exist, they will be used; it is only a matter of having enough processing capabilities. As this project shows, accessing data is more than a matter of technology—it requires the development and maintenance of a relationship of trust between provider and researcher. Furthermore, the use of data needs to overcome multiple interoperability barriers, including not only the classic categorization into syntactic (data formats), structural (data structures), and semantic (meaning of the data variables) interoperability (e.g., Kuhn, 2005; Shekhar, 2004) but also 'multidisciplinary interoperability', meaning the shared understanding of the analytical approaches, methods, and tools appropriate to the data in the light of different disciplinary discourses in the development of ontologies (Kuhn, 2005). In short, the project required the researchers to work in a co-construction manner, both at the level of technical development and holistically, in the mode of e-social science.

Collaboration needs to move beyond gaining an understanding of a research problem toward integrating and developing a coherent research methodology, analysis, and representation. In developing the Grid for e-social science in this project, the in-depth collaboration of the computer scientist was a key factor in the user-led development of tools. The collaboration among the researchers achieved a robust and secure user-led application. The data were also an important factor, impacting on what information was seen as suitable and how access could be negotiated through trusted networks. The project partners were a key resource in undertaking innovative e-social science, as seen, for example, in the project's access to unique datasets. Finally, the driving factor in the development of the e-social science pilot was the research focus on the relationship between the characteristics of neighborhoods and young people at risk of crime.

The demonstrator project contributes to theoretical debates in environmental criminology and to the development of user-focused training opportunities and facilities that make Grid computing easier for non-experts. The development work produced a technical and social infrastructure for generalizing operational data on crime and youths that can be used by researchers for modeling and (accessible) mapping, allowing local information to be used to address social issues which can inform policy at all levels of government. However, the project also revealed the existence of numerous technical barriers that could only be overcome through ad hoc developments, such as rewriting algorithms normally available in desktop environments to make them accessible for Grid processing.

From a criminological point of view, further research is needed to validate the model developed for the whole country with data provided by police forces other than South Yorkshire. From a socio-technical perspective, further research is needed to explore the ways in which researchers can be supported in identifying the barriers to the use of the Grid, and in learning to identify and utilize particular Grid-related capacities as they arise in research processes. Further research regarding semantic interoperability should explore appropriate methods to analyze data based on the theoretical constructs of different disciplines. This is important as the distributed nature of emerging Grid and spatial data infrastructures means that data is often divorced from the context within which it is collected and used: theoretical models and analytical methods need to be captured and embedded with data so that it is transparent across distributed networks for analysis by humans and by machines in web-based services.

ACKNOWLEDGMENTS

An earlier version of this chapter appeared in the *Journal of Computer-Mediated Communication* (Wessels & Craglia, 2007) and the authors wish to express their appreciation for the opportunity to revise that work.

NOTES

1. The project was carried out at the University of Sheffield in 2003–04 with funding from ESRC award RES-149–25–0027.
2. An information service for the academic sector based at the University of Manchester http://www.mimas.ac.uk/
3. http://www.communities.gov.uk/archived/general-content/communities/indicesofdeprivation/216309/
4. For example, user-centered design processes (Norman & Draper, 1986), participatory design approaches (Schuler & Namioka, 1993), and meta-design (Fischer & Giaccardi, 2004).
5. Computer scientists use the term 'user requirements' to refer to what users of a system need.
6. http://www.easasoftware.com/
7. Poisson models are used in the case of discrete count data that are not normally distributed, for example, in counts of offenders, which have a skewed distribution. The criteria used for the model are: (1) use of nationally available data, (2) good fit of the model, (3) independent variables that are not only statistically significant but also stand up to the literature, (4) with coefficients of the right sign (i.e., the relationship is in the expected direction), (5) and parsimony, i.e., trying to have as few variables as possible to keep the model simple without sacrificing too much in terms of predicting power.

REFERENCES

Arrow, K. (1962). The economic implications of learning by doing. *Review of Economic Studies*, 29, 155–173.
Bowker, G. C., & Star, S. L. (1999). *Sorting things out: Classification and its consequences*. Cambridge, MA: MIT Press.
Clematis, A., Mineter, M., & Marciano, R. (2003). High performance computing with geographical data. *Parallel Computing*, 29 (10), 1275–1279.
Crabtree, A., Rouncefield, M., O'Brien, J., Tolmie, P., & Hughes, J. A. (1999). There's something else missing here: Requirements specification in changing

work and design. Retrieved November 16, 2006 from http://www2.cddc.vt.edu/digitalfordism/fordism_materials/hughs1.htm

Dobson, J. E., Blyth, A. J. C., Chudge, J., & Strens, R. (1994). The ORDIT approach to organizational requirements. In M. Jirotka & J. Goguen (Eds.), *Requirements engineering: Social and technical issues*, pp. 87–106. London: Academic Press.

Dittrich, Y., Floyd, C., & Klischewski, R. (Eds.). (2002). *Social Thinking, Software Practice*. London: MIT Press.

Fischer, G., & Giaccardi, E. (2004). Meta-design: A framework for the future of end-user development. In H. Lieberman, F. Paterno, & V. Wulf (Eds.), *End user development—empowering people to flexibly employ advanced information and communication technology*, pp. 65–87. Dordrecht: Kluwer Academic Publishers.

Foster, I. (2002). The Grid: A new infrastructure for 21st Century Science. *Physics Today*, February, 42–47.

France, A., & Crow, I. (2005). 'Using the risk factor paradigm' in prevention: Lessons from the evaluation of Communities that Care. *Children and Society*. 19, 172–183

Hammersley, M., & Atkinson, P. (1983). *Ethnography: Principles in practice*. London: Routledge.

Jewkes, J., Sawers, D., & Stillerman, R. (1958). *The sources of invention*. London: Macmillan.

Jirotka, M., & Goguen, J. A. (Eds.). (1974). *Requirements engineering: Social and technical issues*. London: Academic Press.

Kuhn, W. (2005). Geospatial semantics: Why, of what, and how? *Journal on Data Semantics* III, Special Issue on Semantic-Based Geographical Information Systems. *Lecture Notes in Computer Science, 3534,* 1–24.

MacKenzie, D., & Wajcman, J. (Eds.). (1985). *The social shaping of technology*. Milton Keynes: Open University Press.

Nebert D. (Ed.) (2004). Developing spatial data infrastructures: The SDI cookbook. Retrieved 6 August 2008 from: http://www.gsdi.org/docs2004/Cookbook/cookbookV2.0.pdf

Norman, D. A., & Draper, S. W. (Eds.). (1986). *User-centred system design: New perspectives on human-computer interaction*. Hillsdale, NJ: Lawrence Erlbaum.

Schuler, D., & Namioka, A. (Eds.). (1993). *Participatory design: Principles and practice*. Hillsdale, NJ: Lawrence Erlbaum Associates.

Shekhar, S. (2004). Spatial data mining and geo-spatial interoperability. Report of the NCGIA Specialist Meeting on Spatial Webs, National Center for Geographic Information and Analysis, University of California, Santa Barbara.

Signoretta, P., & Craglia, M. (2002). Joined-up government in practice: A case study of children's needs in Sheffield. *Local Government Studies, 28*(1): 59–76.

Suchman, L. (1987). *Plans and situated actions. The problem of human-machine communication*. New York: Cambridge University Press.

Suchman, L. (1994). Working relations of technology production and use. *Computer Supported Cooperative Work, 2,* 21–39.

Suchman, L. (2002). Practice-based design of information systems: Notes from the hyperdeveloped world. *The Information Society, 18,* 139–144.

Wessels, B., & Craglie, M. (2007). Situated innovation of e-social science: Integrating infrastructure, collaboration, and knowledge in developing e-social science. *Journal of Computer Mediated Communication, 12*(2), article18. http://jcmc.indiana.edu/vol12/issue2/wessels.htm

Wessels, B. (2007). *Inside the digital revolution: Policing and changing communication with the public*. Aldershot: Ashgate.

Williams, R., & Edge, D. (1992). Social shaping reviewed: Research concepts and findings in the UK. PICT Working Paper No. 41. Edinburgh: Edinburgh University.

Williams, R., Stewart, J., & Slack, R. (2005). *Social learning in technological innovation: Experimenting with information and communication technologies.* Cheltenham, U.K.: Edward Elgar.

Wiles, P., & Costello, A. (2000). *The road to nowhere: The evidence for travelling criminals.* Home Office Research Study 207. London: Home Office.

Woolgar, S. (2003). Social shaping perspectives on e-science and e-social science: The case for research support. A consultative study for the Economic and Social Research Council (ESRC). Retrieved April 29, 2008 from http://www.sbs.ox.ac.uk/NR/rdonlyres/04164366–448C-49B3-B359-FC55CC4A5BD6/879/ESocialScience.pdf

17 Wikipedia As Distributed Knowledge Laboratory
The Case Of Neoliberalism

Clifford Tatum and Michelle LaFrance

INTRODUCTION

In recent years collaborative web applications, such as wikis and blogs, have redefined our understanding of knowledge practice as they have subsequently changed the standard practices of collaborative research. At these sorts of sites, academics, knowledge workers, and enthusiasts contribute to the emergence of new forms of mediated discourse and collaborative knowledge production, exploring the value of shared computational resources and distributed access to datasets under the rubric of cyberscience (Nentwich, 2003: 21–25). Such new forms of technological mediation and collaboration compel the examination of resulting changes in research practice, referred to by some as 'e-research' (Wouters & Beaulieu, 2007).

In the humanities and social sciences collaborative practices have emerged more readily in less formal knowledge exchange environments, such as email lists, academic blogs, and content repositories, where the exchange and negotiation of ideas trumps the often rigid practices of scholarly peer review. While attention has been paid to the use of information and communication technologies (ICTs) in academic knowledge production, scholars have only just begun to realize the potential of these tools to demonstrate how knowledge comes to be accepted as valid and reliable.

Wikipedia is a place where many of these emergent practices and realizations are flourishing. In this chapter, we examine the distributed collaborative processes in a Wikipedia article as a potential model for the practice of academic research. Although Wikipedia contributors are not conducting primary research, the encyclopedic assemblage of knowledge in articles requires intellectual negotiation of new knowledge, particularly with respect to defining what is *in* and what is *out* of an article.[1] Emergent forms of collaborative knowledge production are also apparent in the negotiations of content, structure, and categorization of new articles. As such, Wikipedia exemplifies the tremendous potential of emergent ICT field sites for studies of knowledge practice, realized in both its highly structured, but professionally open environment, and the archival function of the site that records each and every keystroke to provide a detailed account of page content under development. The discussion log accompanying Wikipedia articles provides particular insights into how article content is co-produced among varied and distributed participants.

Simultaneous to the phenomenal success of Wikipedia, there has been considerable diffusion of ICT use in the social sciences and humanities. The openness and inclusiveness of ICT use has created an uncomfortable fit with research-oriented scholarship. A tension of cultural values exists between academic communities of practice and popular usage of these new technologies. ICTs and the Internet cultivate an open—some might say a radically open—ethic that conflicts with protections of intellectual capital embedded in the quality control measures of scholarly knowledge production. Cultural change is slow in the humanities and social sciences, so the changes embedded in increased ICT and Internet usage are more apparent within the contexts of informal scholarly communication, which shares a common set of emerging knowledge practices with popular usage of these technologies. Much of the discourse around the implications of these knowledge practices claims either that knowledge is being diffused to the masses, like in the Wikipedia case, or that we are in the midst of radically new forms of knowledge production (e.g., Arms & Larsen, 2007). Elements of both these claims are likely true, enticing us to ask to what extent on-line mediated knowledge practice will follow established and recognizable processes of knowledge production. To answer this question and to gauge the applicability of ICT-mediated knowledge practice for use in collaborative research, we examine the construction of a single Wikipedia article about the political economy concept, *Neoliberalism*.

In this essay, we use qualitative and content analyses to demonstrate how authors discursively negotiate the content, categories, and structure of Wikipedia's article on neoliberalism. To provide an analytical framework for the Wikipedia process and a baseline definition for knowledge production, we rely upon Latour and Woolgar's (1986) study of the construction of facts in a scientific lab, *Laboratory Life: The Construction of Scientific Facts*. In this text, Latour and Woolgar demonstrate that the production of factual knowledge follows typical patterns and is often reliant upon styles of communication, factors of persuasion, and other non-scientific contexts of practice than truly 'objective' observations or measurements. We couple Latour and Woolgar with the Wikipedia article on neoliberalism, in particular, because the article's archives offer an excellent example of the multiple processes of negotiation authors must undertake for their assertions to be considered 'fact'. This chapter proposes that analysis of Wikipedia's page on neoliberalism enables a rigorous understanding of typical ICT-mediated knowledge practice, as similar processes of 'factual' content construction commonly recur in other collaborative online knowledge production situations.

BACKGROUND: (SOCIAL) CONSTRUCTION

In recent years, scholars in the humanities and social sciences have increasingly argued that knowledge always exists in relationship to social conditions and social norms—this obviously places the individual's ability to know or to produce new knowledge into the context of their social circumstances and surroundings. The traditional positivist account of knowledge, however, holds that what we know is empirically constant and what we wish to know can be revealed or discovered through systematic, rigorous analysis. These two positions bookend a debate about how we arrive at 'knowledge' and what cultural forces or processes of analysis will expose the factual basis of that knowledge. In the 1970s Bruno Latour and Steve Woolgar conducted an ethnographic study of scientists at the Salk Institute for Biological Studies, a neuroendocrinology lab, aiming to determine the role of social factors in the process of fact construction and the scientific reception of new knowledge. The results of their study highlight the numerous non-empirical social factors that invade and mold the sanctuary of knowledge production, the scientific lab.

The overarching argument put forth by Latour and Woolgar (1979) is that social, intellectual, and technical factors, all play a role in establishing—or constructing—facts. Their work touched off an enduring discourse around the nature of factual knowledge. At the height of the social construction debate, numerous scholars suggested that the relationship between 'reality' and the 'constructed' was more complex than social constructionists allowed. Latour and Woolgar did not dismiss issues of realism or objectivity (1986: 176), but admitted their first reports did not account for the existence of an objective reality or recognize that some natural phenomena exhibit repeating, enduring, and often measurable characteristics independent of scientific description and/or evaluation. These arguments reveal an anxiety prevalent in scientific communities around the extent to which factual information or evidence may be molded by the context of its production; the apprehension is that some knowledge must be free from social interference or it loses validity.

Herein lies an important distinction for thinking about the puzzle of Wikipedia as a collection of facts. Latour and Woolgar do not take the position that facts are somehow degraded due to the social conditions of their production—their study reveals the extent to which knowledge production and the production of 'facts' are always collaborative processes situated in an array of encroaching social practices. Facts themselves are still 'indifferent', according to Latour and Woolgar, even if the process by which facts are established entails the sort of collaborative negotiations that would seem to erode their grounding in objectivity. Participants in knowledge production always negotiate the stakes, priorities, and conclusions attached to the acceptance of particular facts. Publication of *Laboratory Life* was a move toward better understanding of social, political, economic, and other contributions to the construction of knowledge in scientific settings (Sismondo, 2004). Whereas other scholars may cling to distinctions between knowledge and reality, particularly to differentiate the constructed and the real, Latour and Woolgar generalize that processes of negotiation are always central to the establishment of facts.

While the Wikipedia phenomenon has introduced new ways of thinking about mediated collaboration, it also provides a baseline account of ICT mediated factual construction. The discursive construction of article content bears a striking resemblance to the process of fact construction in a scientific laboratory as noted by Latour and Woolgar. Wikipedia's article on Neoliberalism emerged over a five-year period; analysis of the article's participant discussions reveals that construction of the article's facts has so far taken place in three distinct, but intermittent cycles over that five year period—we borrow from Latour and Woolgar to name these three cycles and their interrelated processes: *construction* through the *agonistic field* towards *reification*. Though we must note differences in the degree of stability related to social content and the openness of online collaboration, such cycling of the construction of fact process is consistent with Latour and Woolgar's constructionist framework (1986).

The Latour and Woolgar argument is comprised of six interwoven sociological elements. Three of these elements, *construction, agonistic field,* and *reification*, are process-oriented and are the basis for the analytical framework used in this study. The other three elements, credibility, noise, and circumstance, are contextually based criteria. For example, credibility is a result of the various investments made by scientists; credibility facilitates the synthesis and validation of economic and epistemological contributions to the field of research. The element of noise is similar to the concept of a signal-to-noise ratio, whereby wave signals must be distinguished from the surrounding cacophony of irrelevant noises to be 'audible' or valid. The element of circumstance points to the notion that scientific practices exist within an array of specifically localized practices. Contextual elements noted in the Latour and Woolgar study are likely present in Wikipedia, but beyond a brief nod to notions of the prestige or rhetorical muscle of the most persuasively effective Wikipedia contributors, these elements are outside of the scope of this project.

The first of the three process elements identified by Latour and Woolgar, *construction*, refers to the slow process whereby an account or an assertion is simultaneously crafted as it is circulated through the relevant scientific community. Construction is perhaps the most profound of the dimensions mentioned by Latour and Woolgar because it recognizes that even an initial assertion is socially embedded and that the testing of assertions is not separable from their acceptance as fact. *Splitting* and *inversion* are subsequent recursive processes, named by Latour and Woolgar, whereby inscriptions are comprised of discreet data points that congeal into a cohesive statement about the thing (object) of study. Initial acceptance by the scientific community, the building up of supporting data points, and the lack and/ or presence of equally probable explanations contribute to the splitting and inversion of new knowledge. Arguments for or against particular facts exist in a constant state of fluctuation and are stabilized only over time.

Once the statement begins to stabilize, however, an important change takes place. The statement becomes a split entity. On the one hand, it is a set of words, which represents a statement about an object. On the other hand, it corresponds to an object in itself, which takes on a life of its own. It is as if the original statement had projected a virtual image of itself, which exists outside the statement (Latour & Woolgar, 1986: 176).

Whereas *construction* is concerned with data and analysis, the *agonistic field* is concerned with the ways in which the statements are positioned by the researcher and perceived by their community of practice. That is, the agonistic field is where scientists qualify given statements through the interplay of argumentation and persuasion. Persuasive factors may include the unexpectedness of a particular point, the personality and institutional attachments of the author-researchers, the stakes, and/or the style of the paper. Assertions made by authors with inadequate professional reputation or with too many equally probable or alternative explanations will acquire little endorsement from the community. An assertion without sufficient endorsement will require the researcher to persuade and inform their peers such that unequal plausibility can be achieved. Finally, *reification*, the end result of the disorderly negotiations in the agonistic field, refers to the tacit manifestation of a statement; a statement is reified once it has stabilized, that is, it is no longer under dispute by members of the community. Another way of thinking about this is that the intellectual foundations in a research effort are built upon prior facts. Once a fact is generally accepted, it then becomes a part of the intellectual capital within the laboratory and the larger community of practice.

To summarize, if all assertions were perceived as equal among collaborators, they would be deemed inadequate. However, if there is unequal probability among competing assertions, it is the most unexpected, or, more importantly, *the most persuasive assertion* that gains the attention of the scientific community. Perceptions of higher probability are likewise based on a number of factors such as investment or intellectual effort, researchers' abilities to gather evidence, the evidence itself, and, tellingly, the professional reputation and the persuasive abilities of the presenter. When sufficiently convinced, peers stop raising questions; the assertion is no longer held to subjective scrutiny (Latour & Woolgar, 1986: 239–240).

These discursive moves, particularly the negotiation towards and acceptance of some points as more pertinent and effective than others, provide a compelling analogy to the collaborative practice embraced by Wikipedia contributors. To show how contributors employ this framework in an online environment, in the next section, we will present a methods strategy for online analysis and demonstrate how it corresponds to Latour and Woolgar's ethnographic approach.

METHODS STRATEGY

According to the text on the Wikipedia article we examine,

> Neoliberalism refers to [the] historically-specific reemergence of economic liberalism's influence among economic scholars and policy-makers [since] the 1970s . . . the term is used to denote a group of neoclassical-influenced economic theories and libertarian political philosophies which believe that government control over the economy is inefficient, corrupt or otherwise undesirable.

Readers will note that even this rudimentary definition was under (re) negotiation as we drafted this article. Competing definitions on the site tended to reflect the highly charged valence of political terminology in light of the left/right dichotomy of current U.S. politics. As such, the article's primary authors can be seen on the discussion pages explaining, citing, cajoling, and appealing to previously hard-won points of consensus, Wikipedia's standards for content development, and other forms of authority in order to make progress toward common understandings of the term. Our interest in what may or may not constitute neoliberalism ends here; instead, we turn to the site's archival discussions as they demonstrate the negotiation of content, which is our primary interest. As we have stated, discussions among distributed authors demonstrate the very nature of collaborative knowledge production, "[T]he marketplace of ideas that has made Wikipedia a good source when it works well" in the words of the frequent author known as *jncohen*.

Because we are concerned with the negotiations of content that result in the reification of knowledge on Wikipedia, we draw from Computer Mediated Discourse Analysis (CMDA) to qualitatively describe the broad processes of collaboration, contest, and assertion that are active in the creation of the article on neoliberalism. In the broadest sense, our analysis privileges "discourse as social interaction" to understand artifacts produced though online collaboration (Herring, 2004). As the primary analytical means of this study, discourse analysis serves to facilitate qualitative empirical examination of the discussion among contributors of a Wikipedia article. In addition to discourse analysis, we use content analysis to more closely examine and quantify the collaborative activity of the page on neoliberalism. We measure the 'edit' activity in both the article and on the talk page, and we show the frequency, as well as degree, of change in the article itself. By using a single article as our case study, the discourse we examine is internally coherent and contextualized in a bounded sample of interaction (Herring, 2004).

Latour, in his later work on actor-network theory (2005), accounts for a similar intensive interest in practice by noting that the "reason why we went to study the laboratories, active controversies, skills, instrument making, and emerging entities was to encounter unstable states of nature/ society and to document what happens in those extreme and novel situations" (Latour 1991: 287 as cited by Miettinen, 1999). Similarly, Foot and Schneider (2006) orient their work on Web campaigning to a practice-based theorizing. Like in the study of activity systems (Foot, 2001), a focus on practice "suggests that tools—both material and symbolic—are created and transformed within practices" (Foot & Schneider, 2006: 12). Online environments pose some difficulty in examining practice due to the asynchronous mode of activity and the dispersal inherent in ICT mediated work. Wikipedia's precise and exhaustive archive, however, makes it an ideal location to research on-line practices such as collaborative knowledge production.

As the figure below shows, the page on neoliberalism includes a unique URL and is comprised of four tabs along the top of the page (See Figure 17.1). The default tab is the article itself. The other three tabs reveal the talk page, the edit page, and the edit-history of the article. There is also an edit-history page for the discussion text. Interaction among Wikipedia authors occurs simultaneously in two locations: in the article content and in the online discussion of the article's composition. The authors' discussions about the article is the primary dataset for this study. The article itself provides a contextual reference and structural markers for that discussion. The edit history data provides a sense of time-span and frequency for all content edits.

COMPETING DEFINITONS OF NEOLIBERALISM

The Wikipedia article on neoliberalism languished for nearly two years as a small summary article that received little attention; this changed in the beginning of 2004 when the first of three phases of debate and collaboration began to enliven, expand, and reify portions of the article. The first phase was marked by negotiated generation of content; the next was

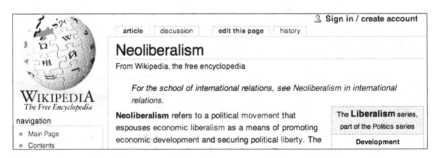

Figure 17.1   Wikipedia page layout.[2]

characterized by a debate around the neutrality of the article's point of view (POV) including challenges to word choice and questions of the political investments/affiliations of the contributors; and the third was a phase notably concerned with the suitability and authority of academic citations included in the latest version of the site. The content generation phase began in earnest when the article grew from less than a thousand words to approximately three thousand words. Contributors then began to refine the content and strengthen the article by working towards a neutral point of view. Whereas the first phase was focused on filling out the content and defining the initial structure of the article, the second and third phases were marked by discussions of perceived bias in the existing content and situating the article in academic literature. Although earlier phases used citations to reference content and basic definitions, this last phase saw considerable effort to specifically align article content and structure with arguments in the domain of political science. As this chapter will show, these three phases correspond with Latour and Woolgar's (1986) construction of facts framework.

Contributors' edit activity reveals the invention and subsequent negotiation of new content, the competition among ideas in the agonistic field, and reification of knowledge into factual object-status—all consistent with the framework described by Latour and Woolgar. However, taking a macro view of the three phases reveals that each phase has a particular focus that also corresponds to steps in the framework. Edit activity in the first phase of content generation is more heavily oriented to article construction. In the second phase, point of view debates are best understood as exercises in resolving the divergence of several points of view. This very clearly represents activity in the agonistic field. And finally, revising the article in line with relevant scholarship through the discussion and application of citations demonstrates the reification of the article as fact. Multiple fact construction processes can be seen to be occurring simultaneously at different phases in the article and at different levels of the article. Moreover, the crucial moment of splitting and inversion also occurs simultaneously and at multiple levels. For the purposes of this study, we provide an analysis at the level of the three phases, rather than inside of each phase.

Content Analysis

The Neoliberalism article is larger and somewhat older than the statistical mean among all articles written in the English version of Wikipedia. For example, Wikipedia users have averaged 17 edits per article out of a total of nearly 200 million edits.[3] By comparison, the article on Neoliberalism was started over five years ago in September 2002 and by December, 2007 had accrued nearly 1200 edits (see Table 17.1) with roughly 515 uniquely identified contributors.[4] Contribution varied among authors, however, and the distribution revealed adherence to the power law associated with networks

(Barabasi, 2003), which predicts that a small minority of users will contribute most to construction of the article. This distribution of author activity is illuminated by Anthony, Smith and Williamson (2005); quality contributions come from both anonymous 'Good Samaritans' who don't contribute very often, and committed 'Zealots' who contribute regularly. While the article itself was 6,500 words in length in December 2007, the talk page with a total of 122 contributors had a cumulative word count of 24,000. That the article had four times as many edits as the talk page, but only a quarter of the word count is characteristic of their respective functions— the article is revised through additions and deletions and the talk page is an on-going discussion. While the article has been in perpetual revision, including large quantities of added and deleted content, the talk page archives the entire background discussion about the article.

Edits to both the content page and talk page are tracked and can be viewed on their respective history pages. Each individual edit can be viewed and compared with any other version of the article or talk page. Figure 17.2 below illustrates edit activity of both the article and the talk page over roughly five years of article construction. The dashed line shows article edit activity of nearly 1200 unique edits over five years. The dash-dot line shows the corresponding edits in the talk page. Three distinct increases in edit activity correlate with the three construction phases. By contrast, the article word count shows construction and revision of the article over the same time period. Variation in word count provides a measure of change in the content in conjunction with frequency of edits. The periodic presence of vertical lines in the article word count curve show instances of mass deletion of text and that very soon after another contributor will typically revert the article to the last version. More recently automated scripts or 'bots' monitor this form of vandalism and automatically revert content back to the previous version. These edits, the simple addition and subtraction of

Table 17.1   Edit Distribution among Contributors to the Neoliberalism Article & Talk Page

	Article		*Discussion*	
Number of Edits	*Number of contributors*	*Percentage of Total*	*Number of contributors*	*Percentage of Total*
1	367	70%	65	53%
2–5	135	26%	43	35%
6–10	8	2%	11	9%
11–50	3	2%	3	2%
>50	2	0.38%	0	0%
Totals	515	100%	122	100%

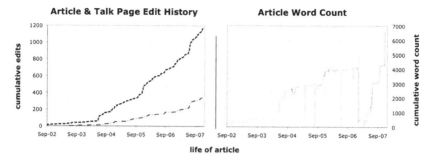

Figure 17.2 Neoliberalism article: Edit activity and word count.

text, are in fact the archival traces of negotiation over final word choice, organization of content, article structure, and ultimately more and more stable meanings upon which to further shared understandings.

Content generation

Two dominant themes run through the early discussion page. Within the first few lines of the first topic thread is the heading, "CALLING ALL WIKI EDITORS HERE!" This heading calls attention to an effort to define the fundamental meaning of neoliberalism. Of course the article itself is dedicated to defining the concept and political affects of neoliberalism; the endeavor to arrive at a basic definition of the word, however, permeates nearly all of the topics of discussion. This attempt at definition fits the criteria of Latour and Woolgar's concept of construction, indicated by the growth of new collaborative content that is accepted and/or uncontested, and thus results in negotiated terminology and a first draft of the article. Splitting and inversion, as defined by Latour and Woolgar, occurs when the words describing neoliberalism become an entity separate from the description. At this point the statement and idea correspond such that the statement represents the idea and established descriptions become conceptual building blocks in further development of the article. By contrast, a single input, although uncontested, would not yet meet the criteria for construction or splitting. This is because it is not yet clear if others have reviewed it. Construction, as such, can be said to occur either as a process of collaboration marked mostly by consensus, where acceptance of the knowledge introduced is implicit due to the lack of contests and challenges to that knowledge, or through explicit approval on the discussion boards about individual or collaborative input.

For example, while discussing possible definitions of neoliberalism, authors used two tactics; they argued about brief definitions and they asserted alternate terms as a measure of similarity and dissimilarity. Numerous alternate terms appeared throughout the discussion threads to explain neoliberalism via synonyms and antonyms; the applicability of alternate terms depended on the author's context and perspective. The term neoconservatism appeared in one case to argue that neoliberalism "is" neoconservatism: "is there any real difference between neoliberalism and neoconservatism?" Another author responded that neoliberalism is the opposite of neoconservatism. Yet another author proposed a merging of the neoliberalism and the neolibertarianism articles. And still another proposed that the term be changed altogether to "economic neoliberalism." Many other terms were debated and considered, such as "monetarism," "mercantilism," "new school of liberalism," and even "religious fundamentalism." The eventually reduced set of definitions showed a congealing of the basic notion of neoliberalism. Instead of open-ended debates, authors began proposing more concise definitions, more often employing terms that had evoked less contentious responses or that elicited little contest at all. Specific ideas emerging from the general discussion indicate a build up of discrete written contributions. While no explicit agreement had been arrived at through discussion of the correct definition, after numerous iterations of the article itself, a stable, less explicitly biased description emerged.

Point of view

The second phase of article construction is characterized by the discussion of a neutral point of view (NPOV)–the cornerstone of Wikipedia's collaborative authoring paradigm. The discussion of NPOV is best understood as activity in the agonistic field because it readily frames the debate about accuracy of the article. Although persuasion and argumentation are present throughout the article, there was a nearly five-month period (29 May 2005—14 October 2005) that the article was deemed to be in a state of disputed neutrality. In the Wikipedia environment, anyone can add a tag to the article indicating that the article's neutrality is in dispute. The article remains active and editable, however, with a neutrality dispute placard in the header (see Figure 17.3). Activity in the agonistic field is operationalized for this study as the argumentative and persuasive assertions among the authors within the discussion area. It is in the agonistic field that authors dispute content, justify edits and deletions, argue factual and theoretical points, and reference authoritative literature. Indications of the agonistic field are found directly in the threaded discussions.

The neutrality of this article is disputed.
Please see the discussion on the talk page. *(December 2007)*
Please do not remove this message until the dispute is resolved.

Figure 17.3   Neutral Point of View (NPOV) Placard.[5]

Two of the initial 25 discussion topic headings specifically addressed neutrality. Titled NPOV and POV, these two sections were small contributions to the overall discussion of neutrality. However, the two entries occurred in or near the period of disputed content. Whereas the construction discourse is comprised of a series of assertions, discourse in the agonistic field is generally more aggressive. This was the case during this first period of the disputed neutrality. Authors' comments included phrases such as, "I really have to disagree with that," "I think the problem here is . . . ," "This is not entirely true," and "You economists are just silly." While the increasing presence of references, the persuasiveness of the debate, and the rather antagonistic nature of dispute over content are all activities characteristic of the agonistic field, it is the dispute over neutrality that most illustrates the occurrence of activity in the agonistic field.

Further, the prolonged nature of the neutrality dispute corresponds with the parsing of article content into categories; the hierarchical organization of content indicates that multiple authors negotiated the relative importance of content elements. Growth of the article's table of contents corroborates this point. In the first phase, the table of contents was brief and focused on theory and practice. By the second phase, as a result of the difficulties during the first phase, a section called "People," about who counted as a neoliberal, was added. In the point of view debate contributors connected theories to theorists to facilitate arguments. The section of the article titled "Who is neoliberal?" initially served as a vehicle to categorize theories in terms of the larger debate. Claims of bias and of contributor point of view were later explicitly reformulated into competing theoretical positions about neoliberalism.

Citation integration

The third phase of the article on Neoliberalism is marked by extensive rewriting of the article to bring it into line within academic literature. This activity once again displays indication of all three steps in the construction of facts but, with reification of facts as the dominant modality. Notably, this phase also marked the emergence of two key authors, both academics, who orchestrated a shift in discursive tone and from what can be characterized as a Wikipedia hobbyist tone to more professional tone with disciplinary standards and practices. This is vividly displayed in the short talk page section titled, "are you kidding me?" In this sarcastic quip, an anonymous writer challenges the article as a "piece of biased shit." In response, a self-identified academic and dominant contributor asks, [instead of complaining in the talk page] "why not actually contribute . . . and add some cited material from intellectuals that you deem fit."

Reification in the laboratory context is the part of the process whereby a position stabilizes from an assertion to emerge as a fact. In the Latour and Woolgar sense, this happens when the assertion is no longer disputed and is integrated into practice. Due to the inherent fluidity in open content environments, indication of reification is somewhat problematic: a Wikipedia article is never actually 'finished,' as edits are made directly on the live article pages. As such, reification in this article is best illustrated by the authors' efforts at rewriting the article in the larger context of published scholarship on political economy. In this way the concepts of neoliberalism are stabilized within the accepted boundaries of established disciplinary arguments. Past versions of the article referenced source material through external links to other online resources. During this time period the word count graph shows a near complete deletion of old content and a stepped rebuilding of the article in chunks (see Figure 17.3). The article shows these chunks added along with relevant academic citations. In the Latour and Woolgar study, assertions and facts are also reified when they emerge in the practices of other laboratories. The analog for Wikipedia articles is that they become reified when they are once again stabilized, but this time within an accepted framework of existing literature. However, this reified state is likely only fleeting, as the notion of neoliberalism itself is still somewhat fluid and thus subject to new interpretations.

DISCUSSION

Even with its potential to devolve into an incoherent mash up of ideas, and in spite of widespread discomfort with an encyclopedia that everyone can edit, the collaborative construction strategies of the Wikipedia article on neoliberalism shows an ordered progression of factual construction over time. In spite of the openness of the Wikipedia platform, collaboration on articles about new social concepts is similar to processes of fact construction, especially the elements of construction and activity in the agonistic field, detailed by Latour and Woolgar in their work on the professional practices of scientific laboratories. Latour and Woolgar's findings stress the interdependence of sociological components in knowledge production and collaboration in order for the construction of facts to occur. This was consistent with our findings as we analyzed the construction of Wikipedia's article on neoliberalism, though reification, or stabilization, of facts in Wikipedia does prove to be a much more fluid concept. In the Wikipedia environment, reification occurs when the article content is no longer in dispute and/or when there is explicit agreement within the discussion. There is, as such, considerable overlap in the indicators of construction and reification. In part, this is a result of adapting the Latour and Woolgar framework to the online environment, though some level of stabilization of content and acceptance in the community characterizes them both.

To tease out the difference between construction and reification in Wikipedia we can look at construction as occurring within parts of content, sections, sub-sections, and particular ideas. Reification, then, would occur with the stabilization of the article as a whole. Acceptance of article construction occurs among the article contributors whereas reification is indicated by an acceptance of the article by the larger community. However, even with these distinctions, the fluidity of content challenges the notion of what it means for an article to be stable. Splitting and inversion occurs where certain statements about neoliberalism survive editing and gain acceptance as building blocks in the explication of the concept. In the agonistic field these textual building blocks serve to either further strengthen cohesive components of the article or are found to be inadequate and therefore deleted. And finally, each phase shows a state of reification where the article itself finds acceptance among the current set of editors. Additionally, when viewed as a group, the three phases exhibit the same sequence of construction. The first phase of content generation is itself representative of construction. The point of view debate in the second phase corresponds with the agonistic activity and the final phase as a whole reifies the content through the work of aligning the article with relevant literature in the field of political science.

Our analysis provokes further thinking around the adoption and adaptation of ICT mediated practices in the process of academic e-research. Whereas the construction of facts appears indifferent to the open content philosophy and the transparency of community practices that are the essence of Wikipedia collaboration, these qualities pose some problems for the academic model of collaborative research. Open content, the ability for anyone to edit Wikipedia, is a common source of fretfulness, but there is much less understanding of the extreme, some might say radical, level of transparency. The qualities of open participation and transparency hold great potential for academic and scientific practice, but they are also at odds with traditional mechanisms for quality control and disciplinary commitments that underpin knowledge claims.

Academic Resistance to Open Content

Academic blogs, academic email lists, open journals, digital repositories, and a variety of ad-hoc collaborative projects on the web point to a tension between the openness of ICT practices generally and the durability of traditional academic knowledge practices. This tension creates a kind of secondary market for knowledge, where ideas are exchanged, both published and unpublished works are presented, and where intellectual debates are enacted in the open and often with a more diverse, a more inclusive set of participants. Broadly speaking there are two ways of orienting this domain of scholarly discourse. On the positive side, contributors can claim the emergence of growing public scholarship where ideas more readily traverse disciplinary boundaries and the discussion is more engaging outside of the academy. On the negative side, opponents can claim that the openness of online scholarly discourse diminishes the role of peer review, disciplinary contributions, and other quality control measures, and thus weakens the value of new knowledge. Ideas flow more freely in an online environment than in traditional media of exchange such as conferences, workshops, and publications. The point here is not that ICTs are subverting peer review, nor that they should. Rather, that the values of transparency and access embedded in the open movement, although philosophically consistent with academic principles, are in conflict with the actual traditions of the academy.

To illustrate this tension, in a recent promotional video[6] Jimmy Wales, the co-founder of Wikipedia asks us to "imagine a world in which every single person on the planet is given free access to the sum of all human knowledge." Two statements of fact are embedded in this statement. First, that not all people have access to knowledge, and second, that accessible knowledge is not all in one place. To accomplish what Jimmy Wales asks us to imagine is virtually impossible given the social and infrastructural complexities of overcoming the twin barriers of access to and containment of all human knowledge. To put this in an academic context: in April 2007, the National Science Foundation and the British Joint Information Systems Committee (NSF/JISC) held a workshop addressing "The Future of Scholarly Communication," about the use of ICTs in the practice of scholarship. The workshop was well attended with broad international representation from academic and governmental institutions as well as industry stakeholders. In their conclusions, the joint NSF/JISC claim that new ICTs, and the availability of digital content, create new and qualitatively different forms of scholarship (Arms & Larsen, 2007). And further that, these new practices are contributing to a 'cyberinfrastructure' that enables 'novel forms of research'. The joint team argues that the biggest challenge to realizing new and innovative research and asking new and innovative research questions is the lack of a standard infrastructure. Crucially, it remains unclear what kinds of novel research practices are possible and the extent to which new mediated research practices can be adapted to academic modes of knowledge production.

That scholarship has changed in concert with ICTs is not in doubt. Wouters and colleagues (Wouters et al., 2007: 337) provide a comprehensive review of Science and Technology Studies literature and conclude that it is "empirically established that mediating technologies are influencing scholarly and scientific methodologies." The combination of forces in open research projects and academic traditions would seem to enable collaboration in ways previously unseen. For example, the combination of a premium on consensus and freely editable content enables a plurality of viewpoints in processes of knowledge production. While the neutrality of Wikipedia content is quintessential to their process and the potential for change is constant, how these factors affect and suspend meaning (Forte, 2003) is particularly problematic for the advancement of new e-research practices. Even stable and reified articles can be changed significantly as new participants enter the discourse and make edits or activate the agonistic field with new arguments. As Emigh and Herring (2005) point out in their study of Wikipedia, a few actors can circumvent the efforts of a larger group while absolutely working within established norms and disciplinary boundaries. Although the platform is stable, the article content cannot be because open content means that anyone can change any article with only a connection to the Internet and a Web browser. This points to a very different function for knowledge and knowledge practices as they emerge from sources such as Wikipedia. Whereas Wikipedia is a repository of knowledge, academic research must be more formally reified in order for it to function within the auspices of the academic disciplines. Nevertheless, an interdisciplinary collaborative project would benefit from all participants having simultaneous access to the real-time status of co-produced content on a wiki-type platform.

The dynamics of open content are already very similar to the culture of academia (Boettiger & Burk, 2004). More specifically, "the general normative expectations in science are largely communitarian rather than proprietary. Scientific submissions to the public body of knowledge are based on reputation incentives and are only indirectly related to a maximization of future profits" (Boettiger & Burk, 2004: 223). This similarity suggests that e-research collaboration and open content practices might be readily compatible. While it is true that hierarchy still exists in Wikipedia, barriers to participation are significantly less than in academic modes of knowledge production. There are significant implications for how we collaborate and what kinds of knowledge can be produced via open content projects.

In his well-known account, Raymond (2001) characterizes the development of open source software as a "babbling bazaar of differing agendas and approaches" (Raymond, 2001: 21) from which an efficient process and stable product emerges. This is as opposed to the more centralized management of software development, which can be viewed as tightly controlled "Cathedral-building". While, Raymond's object of study, the Linux project, did not topple Microsoft's dominant position in the Operating System market, the diffusion of Linux has contributed to structural changes in the industry, as well as in some instances the opening of Microsoft's practices (e.g., Gonsalves, 2007). Moreover, the growing use of blogs and wikis, for example, is providing access to alternative sources of knowledge that challenge authoritative sources (Rogers, 2004); these alternate sources of information are flouting the authority of traditional information and knowledge institutions (Bennett, 2003). To be sure, the very nature of working in a digital environment calls into question all sorts of boundary assumptions. Of particular interest here is the often discussed blurring of boundaries between producers and consumers of media, which is an important characteristic of changing knowledge practices.

Whereas scientific communication that follows the formal practices of conferences, workshops, symposia, and journal publications has been slow to adopt new technologies, it is in the informal modes of scholarly communication where adoption of ICTs is revealing the most visible changes in knowledge practices. The open content movement has contributed to changes in collaborative knowledge practice despite the lag in changes to the dominant structures of academic knowledge production. The opportunity to contribute to collective knowledge resources, such as, but not limited to, Wikipedia, has tapped into a pent up desire to contribute. The aggregate of large-scale contribution to online projects has the continuing potential to pressure dominant structures towards change. So while this emerging space will not topple the academic enterprise, it will likely continue to introduce structural changes in academic practice, and thus continue to give definition to e-research as a practice commensurate with the still evolving infrastructure standard.

NOTES

1. Wikipedia explicitly forbids the inclusion of primary research and regularly polices contributors' practices to maintain standards for article construction.
2. Source: http://en.wikipedia.org/wiki/Neoliberalism; accessed 28 January 2008
3. Source: http://en.wikipedia.org/wiki/Special:Statistics, accessed 7 December 2007.
4. Source: http://en.wikipedia.org/wiki/Neoliberalism, accessed 28 January 2008.
5. Source: http://en.wikipedia.org/wiki/Neoliberalism; accessed 28 January 2008.
6. Source: http://wikimediafoundation.blip.tv/#447562, accessed 28 January 2008.

REFERENCES

Anthony, D., Smith, S., & Williamson, T. (2005). Explaining quality in Internet collective goods: Zealots and Good Samaritans in the case of Wikipedia. Paper presented at the Economic Sociology and Technology Conference, Ithaca, NY, 23—24 September.

Arms, W., & Larsen, R. (2007). The future of scholarly communication: Building the infrastructure for cyberscholarship. Report of the National Science Foundation & British Joint Information Systems Committee. Phoenix, AZ, 17–19 April.

Barabasi, A. (2003). *Linked: How everything is connected to everything else and what it means.* New York: Plume.

Bennett, L. (2003). Communicating global activism: Strengths and vulnerabilities of networked politics. *Information, Communication & Society,* 6(2), 143–168.

Boettiger, S., & Burk, D. L. (2004). Open source patenting. *Journal of International Biotechnology Law,* 1, 221–231.

Emigh, W., & Herring, S. C. (2004). Collaborative authoring on the Web: A genre analysis of online encyclopedias. Proceedings of the *Thirty-Eighth Hawaii International Conference on System Sciences (HICSS-38).* Hawaii: IEEE Press.

Foot, K. (2001). Cultural-historical activity theory as practice theory: Illuminating the development of a conflict-monitoring network. *Communication Theory*, *11*(1): 56–83.

Foot, K., & Schneider, S. M. (2006). *Web Campaigning*. Cambridge, MA: The MIT Press.

Forte, M. (2004). Co-construction and field creation: Web site development as both an instrument and relationship in action research. In E. A. Buchanan (Ed.), *Readings in virtual research ethics: Issues and controversies*, pp. 222–248. Hershey, PA: Idea Group.

Gonsalves , A. (2007). Microsoft's open-source strategy coming into focus. *Information Week* (July 30).

Herring, S. (2004). Computer-mediated discourse analysis: An approach to researching online behavior. In S. A. Barab,, R. Kling, & J. H. Gray, (Eds.), *Designing for virtual communities in the service of learning*, pp. 338–376. New York: Cambridge University Press.

Latour, B. (1991). Technology is Society Made Durable. In J. Law (Ed.), *A Sociology of Monsters: Essays on power, technology and domination*, pp.103–131. London: Routledge.

Latour, B. (2005). *Reassembling the social: An introduction to actor-network-theory*. New York: Oxford University Press.

Latour, B., & Woolgar, S. (1979). *Laboratory Life: The social construction of scientific facts*. Beverly Hills: Sage Publications.

Latour, B., & Woolgar, S. (1986). *Laboratory Life: The construction of scientific facts*. Princeton, NJ: Princeton University Press.

Miettinen, R. (1999). The riddle of things: Activity theory and actor network theory as approaches to studying innovations. *Mind, Culture, and Activity*, 6, 170–195.

Nentwich, M. (2003). *Cyberscience: Research in the Age of the Internet*. Vienna: Austrian Academy of Sciences Press.

Raymond, E. S. (2001). The cathedral & the bazaar: Musings on Linux and open source by an accidental revolutionary (Revised & Expanded ed.). Sebastopol, CA: O'Reilly Media.

Rogers, R. (2004). *Information politics on the Web*. Cambridge, MA: MIT Press.

Sismondo, S. (2004). *An Introduction to science and technology studies*. Oxford: Blackwell Publishing.

Wouters, Vann, K., Scharnhorst, A., Ratto, M., Hellsten, I., Fry, J., et al. (2007). Messy shapes of knowledge—STS explores informatization, new media, and academic work. In E. J. Hackett, O. Amsterdamska, M. Lynch, & J. Wajcman (Eds.), *The handbook of science and technology studies, Third Edition*, pp. 319–362. Cambridge, MA: MIT Press.

Wouters, P., & Beaulieu, A. (2007). Critical accountability: Dilemmas for interventionist studies of e-science. *Journal of Computer Mediated Communication*, *12*(2). http://jcmc.indiana.edu/vol12/issue2/wouters.html

Contributors

Ben Anderson is Director of the Technology and Social Change Research Centre (TaSC) at the University of Essex. He has a BSc in Biology and Computer Science (Southampton University, UK) and a PhD in Computer Studies (Loughborough University, UK) and has used techniques from cognitive psychology, anthropology, sociology and ethnography during his time as an academic and commercial research scientist engaged in user studies, human computer interaction and applied social research. His recent research has focused on e-social science practice, secondary data analysis including the use of time-use diary data to analyze social change and the use of spatial microsimulation to produce small area estimates of ICT usages, household expenditure and income deprivation. Web site: http://chimeraweb.essex.ac.uk/tasc/; email: benander@essex.ac.uk

Anne Beaulieu is deputy program leader and senior research fellow at the Virtual Knowledge Studio for the Humanities and Social Sciences (VKS) in the Netherlands. She also leads the VKS collaboratory on virtual ethnography. She has published extensively on new ethnographic methods, on biomedical digital imaging and databasing technologies, on issues in data-sharing, and on bioinformatics as new infrastructure for the knowledge economy. She is currently investigating new forms of visual knowledge in the context of online databases of images. Web site: http://www.virtualknowledgestudio.nl/; email: anne.beaulieu@vks.knaw.nl.

Nathan Bos is a Senior Staff Researcher in Cognitive Engineering at the Johns Hopkins University Applied Physics Laboratory. His research is in computer-supported cooperative work and long-distance scientific collaborations. He has published recently on partially-distributed collaborations and use of multi-player simulations for learning. Email: Nathan.Bos@jhuapl.edu

Dan L. Burk is Chancellor's Professor of Law and Founding Faculty at the School of Law at the University of California, Irvine. An internationally prominent authority on issues related to high technology, Burk has taught in the courses Patent, Copyright, Electronic Commerce, and in related areas. He is the author of numerous papers on the legal and societal impact of new technologies, including articles on scientific misconduct, on the regulation of biotechnology, and on the intellectual property implications of global computer networks. Web site: http://www.law.uci. edu/profile_d_burk.html; email: dburk@uci.edu

Samuelle Carlson is an anthropologist. She graduated from the School of Le Louvre and the E.H.E.S.S. Paris before studying at Cambridge University where she obtained a PhD. As a researcher at the University of Essex Technology and Social Change Research Centre and a consultant for Arts Council England she developed research interests in the fields of Design, Open Source, and the technologies and materialities of interdisciplinary collaborations. Email: S.Carlson.01@cantab.net

Max Craglia is the research coordinator of the Unit of the Joint Research Centre of the European Commission that has the responsibility for the technical development of the Infrastructure for Spatial Information in Europe (http://inspire.jrc.it). He is one of the founders of the Vespucci Initiative for the advancement of Geographic Information Science (www. vespucci.org) and he is also the editor of the International Journal of Spatial Data Infrastructures Research (http://ijsdir.jrc.it). Prior to joining the JRC in 2005, Max was a Senior Lecturer at the University of Sheffield teaching GIS for urban planners, and researching areas of spatial data infrastructure deployment and use, and data policy. Web site: http://sdi.jrc.it/Members/craglma; email: massimo.craglia@jrc.it

Kirsten Foot is an Associate Professor of Communication and Adjunct Faculty in the Information School at the University of Washington. Her research focuses on the reciprocal relationship between information/communication technologies and society, and as co-director of the WebArchivist.org research group, she develops new methods and tools for studying social and political action on the Web. She is particularly interested in practice-based theories of technology and the dynamics and politics of communication and knowledge production in networked environments. She is the co-author of *Web Campaigning* (MIT Press, 2006), co-editor of *The Internet and National Elections* (Routledge, 2007), and has published articles on Web archiving, Web sphere analysis, practice-based theory, and computer-mediated communication. Email: kfoot@u. washington.edu

Jenny Fry is a lecturer in Information Science at the University of Loughborough. Previously she was a research fellow at the Oxford Internet Institute researching the legal, ethical, and institutional barriers to e-science. She has held postdoctoral fellowships at the Royal Netherlands

Academy of Arts and Sciences, Amsterdam and the School of Information and Library Science at the University of North Carolina, Chapel-Hill. Her research has been concerned with the disciplinary shaping of networked digital resources and information practices. Web site: http://www.lboro.ac.uk/departments/ls/people/jfry.html; email: J.Fry@lboro.ac.uk

Paul Genoni teaches with the School of Media, Culture and Creative Arts at Curtin University of Technology, Perth, Western Australia. His teaching and research areas include scholarly communication, content management in research library collections, and journal impact metrics. He has a PhD in Australian literature from the University of Western Australia and also continues to undertake research in contemporary Australian fiction and travel writing. Web site:http://www.humanities.curtin.edu.au/about/staff/index.cfm/p.genoni; email: p.genoni@curtin.edu.au

Eric Gleave is a sociology graduate student at the University of Washington. His research ranges from historical analysis of high risk collective action and norms of war to social network models of roles. His dissertation applies methods from survival analysis to network dynamics to classify types of social networks based on their generative processes. Email: eric.gleave@gmail.com

Peter Halfpenny is Professor of Sociology at the University of Manchester and Executive Director of the U.K. ESRC National Centre for e-Social Science. He is responsible for the overall strategic management of the Centre's program of research, outreach and capacity-building. His own research interests are in the integration of computing tools and services into a comprehensive support environment for social science researcher practitioners, and the investigation of the adoption and adaptation of e-science tools across the social research community. Web site: http://www.ncess.ac.uk/about_us/people/?centre=&person=1; email:peter.halfpenny@manchester.ac.uk

Itai Himelboim is a Telecommunications Assistant Professor at the Grady College of Journalism and Mass Communication, University of Georgia. His areas of research range from communication technologies and society, media and social networks and media ethics. Itai examines online social networks in political discussions and online news Web sites. He is concerned about the flow of information among individuals and institutions on the Internet.Email: itai@uga.edu

Nicholas W. Jankowski is Visiting Fellow at the Virtual Knowledge Studio for the Humanities and Social Sciences (VKS) in the Netherlands. He has been researching community and new media since the mid-1970s.

During this period, he has co-edited some half-dozen books on community media, research methodology and new media; a recent co-edited collection is *Internet and National Elections: A Comparative Study of Web Campaigning* (Routledge, 2007). Jankowski is initiator and co-editor of the journal *New Media & Society*. He is founding board member of the European Institute of Communication and Culture (Euricom) and editor of the Hampton Press book series *Euricom Monographs: New Media and Democracy*. Web site: http://www.virtualknowledgestudio. nl/; email: nickjan@xs4all.nl

Michelle LaFrance is a Doctoral Candidate in English at the University of Washington. Her interests include the socio-political operations of knowledge production and the rise of disciplinary structures in the modern research university. Her dissertation work considers the impact of recent movements in learning assessment and critical pedagogy, and the organization of knowledges in English departments. When not teaching in the UW English Department, she is a documentary film-maker and Celtic language activist. Email: mlf@u.washington.edu

Thomas M. Lento is a Data Scientist at Facebook and a PhD candidate in the Department of Sociology at Cornell University. His research interests focus on social network topologies, diffusion, contagion, and the spread of rumor in online networks, particularly weblog and threaded discussion networks. His dissertation research uses social relationships as predictors of continued participation and changes in activity levels in both Wikipedia and the Wallop weblogging system. Email: tml5@cornell.edu

Yu-Wei Lin is Research Associate at the ESRC National Centre for e-Social Science (NCeSS). She received her PhD in Sociology in 2005 from the University of York and previously worked at the Free University Amsterdam. She has been investigating socio-technical and organisational dynamics in information and communication technology (ICT) development, particularly on open source software development in a virtual environment. Her recent work at NCeSS focuses on how innovative ICT supports and shapes social scientific research practices and methodologies, and related usability issues involved in the development and uptake. Web site: http://www.ncess.ac.uk/about_us/people/?centre=&person=6; email: Yuwei.lin@manchester.ac.uk

Robert Lucas is a PhD student at the Stanford University School of Education. His research concerns teachers' construction of professional knowledge in the context of Open Educational Resources and Open Access educational research. He holds a B.A. in Social Studies from Harvard University and a M.Ed. in Technology, Innovation, and Education from Harvard's Graduate School of Education. Email: rmlucas@stanford.edu

Helen Merrick teaches in the Department of Internet Studies at Curtin University of Technology, Western Australia. Her research interests are mostly within social studies of science and technology, with a particular interest in science fiction and feminist science studies. Publications include a forthcoming book on feminism and science fiction (2009) and chapters in *The Cambridge Companion to Science Fiction* (2003) and *The Routledge companion to Science Fiction* (2009). Email: h.merrick@curtin.edu.au

Eric T. Meyer is Research Fellow at the Oxford Internet Institute (OII), a department of the University of Oxford. He is one of the researchers on the Oxford e-Social Science (OeSS) project, which is a node of the U.K. National Centre for e-Social Science (NCeSS). OeSS studies the social, legal, institutional, and ethical issues related to e-research. He has written on a variety of topics related to science and technology from a social informatics perspective; his PhD, awarded in 2007 from Indiana University, was one of the first doctoral degrees in this field. He also has extensive experience working with large datasets and scientific collaborations from his 10-year stint as a national data manager in the U.S. Web site: http://people.oii.ox.ac.uk/meyer; email: eric.meyer@oii.ox.ac.uk

Gary M. Olson is Donald Bren Professor of Information and Computer Science at the University of California at Irvine. His research investigates the socio-technical factors involved in geographically-distributed science and engineering. He is a co-editor and co-author of a number of chapters in the forthcoming book *Scientific Collaboration on the Internet,* which includes a theory of remote collaboration and several case examples. Email: gary.olson@uci.edu

Judith Olson is Donald Bren Professor of Information and Computer Science with appointments also in the Merage School of Business and the School of Social Ecology at the University of California at Irvine. Her research interests are in the area of distance work, doing fieldwork, laboratory experiments, and agent-based modeling of collaborations in science, engineering, non-profits, and corporations. She is co-author of a number of chapters in the forthcoming book, *Scientific Collaboration on the Internet,* including the theory of remote scientific collaboration and several case studies. Email: jsolson@umich.edu

Han Woo Park is an Assistant Professor at YeungNam University, Republic of Korea. He obtained his PhD from the State University of New York at Buffalo in the USA. He has worked as a research associate for the Royal Netherlands Academy of Arts & Sciences (NIWI-KNAW). His research focuses hyperlink analysis, social network analysis, e-science/e-research, Internet politics and infometrics. Currently, he is a co-editor with the

Journal of Contemporary Eastern Asia. Web site: http://www.hanpark. net; email: hanpark@ynu.ac.kr

Rob Procter is Professor and Research Director of the U.K. National Centre for e-Social Science (NCeSS), University of Manchester, responsible for coordinating and developing its research program. His research interests are focused on the 'social shaping' of e-science and e-infrastructure and, in particular, the barriers and enablers to their adoption. His broader research interests lie within the field of socio-technical issues in the design, implementation, evaluation and use of interactive computer systems, with a particular emphasis on ethnographic studies of work practices, computer-supported cooperative work and participatory design. Web site: http://www.ncess.ac.uk/about_us/people/?centre=&person=4; email: rob.procter@manchester.ac.uk

Steven M. Schneider is Professor in the Department of Social Sciences and Humanities at State University of New York Institute of Technology. He is also co-Director of WebArchivist.org and co-Editor of PoliticalWeb. info. His research focuses on the use of the Internet for political action. With Kirsten Foot, he has recently published *Web Campaigning* (MIT Press, 2006). Email: steve@sunyit.edu

Ralph Schroeder is a James Martin research fellow at the Oxford Internet Institute at Oxford University. His publications include *Rethinking Science, Technology and Social Change* (Stanford: Stanford University Press, 2007) and *Possible Worlds: The Social Dynamic of Virtual Reality Technology* (Boulder, CO: Westview, 1996). He is an investigator with the Oxford e-Social Science (OeSS) Project. He is currently working on shared virtual environments and on the social implications of e-science. Web site: http://people.oii.ox.ac.uk/schroeder/; email: Ralph. Schroeder@oii.ox.ac.uk

Marc A. Smith is Chief Social Scientist at Telligent Systems, purveyor of fine quality social media platforms and services. His research explores computer-mediated collective action, specializing in the social organization of online communities and computer mediated interaction. Smith's research applies social network theory and methods with collective action dilemma theory and interactionist sociology to study the ways group dynamics change when they take place in and through social cyberspaces. Smith's goal is to visualize social cyberspaces, mapping and measuring their structure, dynamics and life cycles. Web site: http://connectedaction.net; email: marc.smith@telligent.com.

Petra Sonderegger is researching changes in innovative collaboration across large distances as people increasingly use communication technology.

She holds a PhD in communications from Columbia University and an MBA from the University of Bern, Switzerland. Earlier, Petra was a team leader and project manager for the idea factory BrainStore. She has also worked extensively in management training and management development. Email: pcs2002@columbia.edu.

Carol Soon is a research scholar pursuing her doctoral studies with the Communication & New Media Programme at the National University of Singapore. Her research interests involve new media and gender, online social networks, e-science and political communication. For her dissertation, she investigates the phenomenon of political blogging from the perspective of social movement theories. She has also taught courses in ICT theories and the social psychology of new media. Prior to joining academia, Carol's work involved marketing and branding in both profit and non-profit sectors. Email: wtsoon@nus.edu.sg

Clifford Tatum is a PhD student in Communication at the University of Washington. His research is focused on ICT-mediated collaboration and the ways in which new technologies both inspire new collaborative practices and create a vantage point for examination of embedded social structures. Of particular interest is academic interdisciplinary research in collaborative settings and open innovation in commercial sectors. Clifford is a 2008 Huckabay Teaching Fellow at the University of Washington. Web site: www.cliffordtatum.com; email: clifford@u. washington.edu

Mike Thelwall is Professor of Information Science and leader of the Statistical Cybermetrics Research Group at the University of Wolverhampton, U.K. He is also visiting fellow of the Amsterdam Virtual Knowledge Studio, a Docent at Åbo Akademi University Department of Information Studies, and a research associate at the Oxford Internet Institute. He has developed tools for downloading and analysing web sites, blogs and social networking sites, including the research web crawler SocSciBot and software for statistical and topological analyses of site structures (through links) and site content (through text). His publications include over a hundred refereed journal articles, and the book *Link Analysis: An Information Science Approach*, and he sits on nine editorial boards. Web site: http://www.scit.wlv.ac.uk/~cm1993/mycv.html; email: m.thelwall@ wlv.ac.uk

Alex Voss works for the ESRC National Centre for e-Social Science at Manchester University. He studies the uptake and use of advanced information technologies in research practice, focusing on how researchers meaningfully relate practices, technologies and organizational arrangements to each other as they grapple with the practicalities of their day-to-day work. Alex is a computer scientist by training but seeks to combine his technical understanding of e-infrastructures with social scientific research methods to develop new ways to foster uptake of advanced ICTs in a number of research domains. Web site: http://www. ncess.ac.uk/about_us/people/?centre=&person=7; email: alex.voss@ manchester.ac.uk

Howard T. Welser is an Assistant Professor of Sociology at Ohio University. His research investigates how micro-level processes generate collective outcomes, with application to status achievement in avocations, development of institutions and social roles, the emergence of cooperation, and network structure in computer mediated interaction. Currently he is focusing on how network structure and reference groups influence retention, contribution, and diffusion in computer mediated social spaces. Web site: http://www.cas.ohiou.edu/socanth/faculty/welser.html; email: welser@ohio.edu

Bridgette Wessels is Lecturer in Sociology. Her funded research includes: privacy and identity in digital contexts; public participation in e-enabled services; e-social science; e-government; multi agency e-services; social exclusion; ICT in everyday life; mobile telephony; community telematics and policing. Publications include: *Inside the Digital Revolution: Policing and Changing Communication with the Public* (Ashgate, 2007); *Information and Joining up Services: The Case of an Information Guide for Parents of Disabled Children* (Policy Press, 2002); papers in *The Information Society, Journal of Computer Mediated Communication, New Media & Society, European Journal of ePractice,* and *Sociology: Thought and Action*. She has served as an expert consultant for European Union and British ICT research. Web site: http://www.shef. ac.uk/socstudies/staff/staff-profiles/wessels.html; email: b.wessels@shef-field.ac.uk

John Willinsky is Professor of Education at Stanford University School of Education. He is the author of *Empire of Words: The Reign of the OED (Princeton Univ. Press, 1994),* The *Access Principle: The Case for Open Access to Research and Scholarship* (MIT Press, 2006), and is a developer of Open Journals Systems software. Web site: http://ed.stanford. edu/suse/faculty/displayRecord.php?suid=willinsk; email: john.willin-sky@stanford.edu

Michele Willson lectures in Internet Studies with the School of Media, Culture and Creative Arts at Curtin University of Technology, Perth, Western Australia. Her research interests include scholarly communication, community and network theory, and the politics and ethics of technically being-together. Her publications include *Technically Together:*

Rethinking Community within Techno-Society (Peter Lang, 2006). She has a PhD in Politics from Monash University, Victoria. Web site: http://www.humanities.curtin.edu.au/about/staff/index.cfm/m.willson email: m.willson@curtin.edu.au

Paul Wouters is program leader of the Virtual Knowledge Studio for the Humanities and Social Sciences (VKS) in the Netherlands and professor of knowledge dynamics at the Erasmus University Rotterdam. He has published on the history of the Science Citation Index and in the fields of information science and scientometrics. Since 1999, he has focused on the emergence of new informational practices and structures in scholarly research. He is particularly interested in the implications of digital research objects for the dynamics of knowledge generation and translation. Web site: http://www.virtualknowledgestudio.nl/; email: paul.wouters@vks.knaw.nl

Ann Zimmerman is Research Assistant Professor in the School of Information at the University of Michigan. Her research interests include the secondary use of scientific data, the affect of cyberinfrastructure on scientific practice, and the relationship between large-scale collaborations, policy, and research management. Most recently, she has studied researchers' use of high-performance computing. She is co-editor, with Gary Olson and Nathan Bos, of the MIT Press book *Scientific Collaboration on the Internet*. Web site: http://www-personal.si.umich.edu/~asz/; email: asz@umich.edu

Index

A

Abbott, A. 231, 237
Access See open access
Ackland, R. 121, 124
Acord, S. K. 12, 29
Adams, K. 231, 232, 237
Adolphs, S. 90
Adomeit, P. 180
Agrawal, A. 133, 145
Ainsworth, J. 249, 254
Allan, R. 68, 68, 89
Allen, T. J. 178, 180
Altintas, I. 158
American Council of Learned Societies
(ACLS), 6, 28, 94, 107
Amsterdamska, O. 220, 327
Anand, S. 223, 239
Anderson, A. 74, 88
Anderson, B. vi, 22, 148, 152, 157,
159, 223, 234, 235, 240, 242,
254, 329
Anderson, O. W. 157–159
Anderson, S. 74, 90
Anderson, T. 56, 67
Anthony, D. 318, 326
anthropology 22, 26, 46, 235, 240,
243, 246, 249, 253, 256, 267,
272, 329, 330
AnthroProject 22, 243, 244, 249,
Appleby, A. 92, 107
Arguello Castelleiro, M. 90
Aris, A. 190, 202
Armbruster, C. 14, 28
Arms, W. 311, 324, 326
Arrow, K. 293, 307
arXiv 17, 271
Arzberger, P. 218, 220, 223, 237
Asgari-Targhi, M. 90

Association of Internet Researchers
(AoIR) xiii, xiv, 9, 11, 23, 26,
29, 56, 125
Atkins Report 5, 6, 28, 37, 259, 266,
267
Atkins, D. E. 25, 51, 54, 67, 259, 271;
see also Atkins Report
Atkinson, M. 90
Atkinson, P. 294, 308
Australian Academy of the Humanities
93, 94, 107
Australian e-Humanities Network 93
Australian Research Council 93, 94
Australian-based Network for Early
European Research (NEER) 92,
96–106
Austrian Institute of Technology Assess-
ment 4, 30, 52, 125, 327
Axelson, A-S. 76, 88

B

Backstrom, L. 188, 201
Bailey, C. W. 25, 28
Bain, J. L. 229, 231, 237
Baird, K. 83, 89, 90
Baker, K. S. 233, 238
Band, J. 27, 28
Barab, S. A. 327
Barabasi, A. 318, 326
Baragelj, V. 193, 201
Barjak, F. 84, 88,99, 107
Barlow, J. 158
Bartram, L. 202
Baru, C. 222, 237
Battin, P. 94, 108
Batty, M. 76, 88
Baym, N.K. 187, 201
Bayoumi, S. 90

Beaulieu, A. xiv, 7, 18, 53, 54, 55, 56,
        62, 64, 69, 91–94, 107–108,
        110, 122, 125, 163, 167, 181,
        220, 224, 237, 310, 327, 329
Becher, T. 51, 62, 67, 242–243, 254
Beedham, H. 74, 89. 241, 247
Benford, S. 76, 89
Bennett, L. 325, 326
Berkeley Research Impact Initiative
        (BRII) 17
Berkley, C. 158
Berkman Center for Internet & Society
        26
Berman, F. 36, 37, 51, 52, 54, 67, 180,
        207, 208, 220, 238, 255
Bertin, J. 164, 179
Best, K. 68, 89
Biddix, J.P. 125
Biegel, G. 68, 89,
Bieri, T. 230, 237
Bietz, M. 223, 237, 241, 254
Big science vi, 4, 24, 147, 256
Bijker, W. 60, 61, 67
Bimholtz, J. 241, 254
Birkin, M. 58, 67, 76, 88
Birman, J. S. 26
Birnholtz, J. 223, 237
Bishr, Y. 231, 232, 239
Black, L. 196, 201
Blake, A. 269, 272
Blanke, T. 90
Blyth, A. J. C. 294, 308
Boettiger, S. 285, 287, 325, 326
Boles, F. 220
Bonk, C. J. 133, 145
Boonstra, O. 61, 67
Borgman, C. 6, 7, 17, 24, 28, 218, 220,
        222, 223, 224, 228, 237, 240,
        254
Borner, K. 163, 164, 179
born digital See digital.
Bos, N. 21, 91, 107, 131, 145, 148,
        158, 222, 225, 227, 229, 237,
        238, 239, 255, 329, 337
Bowers, J. 241, 254
Bowker, G. C. 25, 28, 45, 46, 52, 53,
        55, 69, 85, 89, 209, 220, 225,
        232, 237, 239, 241, 254, 248,
        293, 294, 307
Boyack, K. W. 163, 164, 179
boyd, d. 174, 180
Boyle, J. 278, 287
Bradley, J. 264, 271
Braimah, A. 89

Brandes, U. 197, 201
Brandt-Rauf, S. I. 235, 238
Breure, L. 61, 67
Brodlie, K. W. 177, 179
Brody, T. 263, 271
Brown, C. 224, 237
Brown, L. 14, 28
Brown, N. 59, 60, 64, 65, 68, 69
Brownlee, S. 268, 271
Bruce, H. 92, 107
Bruemmer, B. 220
Brügger, N. 208, 220
Brynjolfsson, E. 252, 256
Buchanan, E. A. 327
Buchhorn, M. 124
Buckholtz, A. 13, 28
Budapest open access initiative 261,
        270, 271. See also open access.
Budweg, S. 85, 90
Burdin, A. M. 158
Burk, D. L. 22, 222, 273, 274, 278,
        280, 282, 285, 287, 325, 326,
        329
Burrows, T. 97, 107
Bush, V. 157, 158
Buyya, R. 25, 28
Byun, O. W. 115, 124

C
Cairncross, F. 133, 145
Calambokidis, J. 149–158
Caldas, A. xiii, 5, 29
Callon, M. 60, 68
Campbell, E. G. 240, 254
Carlson, S. 22, 148, 152, 159, 223,
        234, 235, 240, 242, 254, 330
Carter, R. 90
Carusi, A-M. 76, 89
Caruso, J. B. 12, 31
Carver, L. 223, 239
Casey, K. 220, 237
Cathro, W. 207, 220
CERN 4. See also Big Science.
Chan, L. 270, 271
Cheliotis, G. 119, 123, 124
Chen, C. M. 163, 164, 172, 179
Chen, H. 88, 181
Chen, N. 228, 237
Chenette, E. 239
Cheverst, K. 89
Chik, W. 118, 124
Child, J. 130, 145
Chilvers, J. 60, 68
Cho, K. 115, 124

Chorley, A. 76,89
Chudge, J. 294, 308
Chudoba, K. M. 132, 145
Clapham, P. 158
Clark, K. 74, 90
Clarke, M. 88
Clarridge, B. R. 240, 254
Clayton, P. 92, 107
Clematis, A. 302, 307
Cockburn, I. 284, 287
Cohen, S. 145
Cole, K. 74, 89, 241, 245, 247. 254
collaboration (distant, distributed,
    global, interdisciplinary
    international, remote, virtual)
    vi, xiii, xiv, 5, 6, 7, 9, 10, 14,
    17, 18, 19, 20, 21, 24, 35,
    37, 39, 42, 43, 44, 50, 55, 59,
    65, 76–82, 85, 87, 93, 94, 95,
    97, 99, 100, 103, 104, 106,
    109, 110, 112, 113, 115, 116,
    118, 120–123, 129–135, 137,
    138, 142, 143, 145, 147–149,
    151–153, 155–158, 163, 183,
    209, 210, 217, 222, 224–226,
    231–233, 236, 240–242, 244,
    250, 251, 259, 266, 273, 274,
    276, 279–282, 284, 291, 292,
    294, 306, 310, 313, 315, 316,
    319, 322–325, 329, 330, 330,
    333–335, 337. See also collabo-
    ratory.
collaboratory 59, 75, 100, 215, 225,
    234, 250, 274, 329
Collins, H. M. 209, 220, 231, 235,
    236, 237
Conover, H. 158, 159
Contractor, N. 6, 28, 187, 201
Cooney, D. 255
Coopmans, C. 45, 51, 53, 59, 68, 241,
    255
Corman, S. R. 205, 220
Cornford, T. 147, 159
Cortez, E. M. 231, 238
Corti, L. 249, 255
Cosley, D. 196, 201
Costa, S. 91, 92, 107
Costello, A. 301, 309
Crabtree, A. 76, 89, 294, 307
Cragin, M. H. 224, 238
Craglia, M. 23, 291, 295, 307, 308,
    330
Crane, D. 91, 92, 107
Crisp, C. B. 131, 146

Cronin, B. 94, 107, 220
Crouchley, R. 58, 68, 75, 89
Crow, I. 295, 308
Cummings, J. N. 133, 145
Cummings, M. P. 223, 239
CurationProject 22, 243, 244, 245,
    246, 247, 249, 251, 252, 253,
cyberinfrastructure ix, 4, 5, 6, 13, 24,
    25, 28, 29, 31, 35–37, 51, 52,
    54–66, 67, 73, 89, 91, 107, 110,
    112, 115, 116, 124, 174, 234,
    238, 259, 271, 324, 337. See
    also infrastructure.
cyberscience 4, 7, 25, 29, 255, 310. See
    also e-science, e-research.

D
D'Agostino, G. 288
Daft, R. L. 132, 145
Dahl, E. 107, 158, 237
Dal Fiore, F. 100, 102, 107
Daniels-Howell, T. J. 220
data
    analysis 7, 9, 10, 58, 74, 77, 81,
        116–122
    collection xiii, 5, 7, 9, 10, 20, 116
        -122, 165
    dataset (database) xiii, 7, 12, 16, 40,
        43, 65, 74, 75, 77, 80, 81, 87,
        93, 96, 120, 122, 132, 147–150,
        153–157, 163, 166, 167, 172,
        175, 182, 183, 190, 207–209,
        214–216, 215, 218–236, 240,
        242, 243, 247, 248, 252, 253,
        264, 265, 268–270, 269, 274–
        276, 279–285, 295, 296–301,
        306, 310, 316
    deluge 80, 87, 222
    metadata 78, 81, 157, 210–218, 224,
        241, 244–248, 305
    mining 77, 81, 209, 227, 248, 261,
        274
    preservation (storage) vi, 9, 18, 21,
        22, 120, 273
    repository (archive) 25, 243, 244,
        266
    sharing vi, 21–22, 24, 40, 46, 55, 81,
        85, 106, 147–151, 156, 157,
        222–231, 235, 236, 240–242,
        241, 264, 281, 285, 297, 298,
        302, 304
    qualitative 73, 81, 214, 248
Dave, K. 169, 181
Davenport, S. 131, 145

David, P. A. 37, 44, 52, 273, 284, 297
Davies, J. 131, 145
Davis, H. M. 234, 235, 238
Davis, M., P. 263, 271
Daw, M. 78, 89
Day, M. 239
Day, R. S. 222, 224, 227
De Angelis, C., 261, 270, 271
de la Flor, G. 89
de Laat, P. 282, 288
De Nooy, W. 193, 201
De Roure, D. 223, 238
De Solla Price, D. J. 24, 31, 147, 149,
    159
DeGroot, J. 196, 201
Demeritt, D. 159
Denn, S. O. 225, 238
Derriere, S. 203, 255
Dickey, M. H. 132, 145
digital (age, archive, data, digitaliza-
    tion, humanities, libraries,
    media, photography, reposi-
    tories, revolution, studies,
    technologies) 6, 7, 13, 14, 15,
    17, 21, 22, 27, 37, 40, 41, 44,
    46, 50, 51, 54, 55, 56, 57, 62,
    65, 73, 76, 81, 93, 94, 96,
    109–111, 113, 148, 150–152,
    172, 177, 182–185, 205–207,
    213–219, 222, 224, 226, 227,
    229, 235, 240, 243, 244, 259,
    273, 306, 323–325, 329, 3313
    336, 337
Dill, J. 202
Dittrich, Y. 294, 308
Dobson, J. E. 294, 308
Dodge, M. 166, 179
Dodgson, M. M. D. 131, 145
Donath, J. S. 190, 201
Doorn, P. 61, 67
Dorling, D. 163, 166, 180
Dougherty, M. 215, 216, 218, 220
Draper, S. W. 307, 308
Droegemeier, K. 67
Dubs, S. 202
Duce, D. A. 177, 179
Dunn, S. 90
Dutton, W. xiii, 76, 89

E

Earl-Novell, S. 12, 29
Earnshaw, R. A. 163, 179
Ebeling, W. 169, 180
Eckersley, P. 273, 288

Economic and Physical Research Coun-
    cil (EPSRC) 35, 40
Economic and Social Research Council
    (ESRC) 50, 73, 158, 240, 255,
    307, 331, 332, 335
Edge, D. 293, 309
eDiaMoND (Digital Mammography
    National Database) 40, 47, 48,
    52, 255, 273, 279, 280
Edublogs 26
Edwards, P. N. 25, 28, 76, 85, 89, 90
Egan, G. F. 273, 288
Eisenberg, R. 278, 288
e-humanities 93. See also humanities,
    e-social science.
e-infrastructure 35, 73–76, 78–80,
    82–87, 334, 336. See also infra-
    structure, cyberinfrstructure.
Ekin, P. 74, 90, 240, 255
Elliot, M. 241, 255
Ellisman, E. H. 273, 288
Ellisman, M. 238
Elsevier 13, 26, 29, 264
Emigh, W. 325 326
Emmott, S. 222, 238
Enyedy, N. 222, 224, 237
e-research v, vi, ix, xi, xiv, xv, 3–5,
    7–11, 15, 18, 19, 21, 22–25,
    35–59, 61, 62, 65–67, 86,
    90–97, 99, 100, 102–107,
    109, 110, 122, 148, 158, 205,
    208–210, 213, 216, 218–220,
    222, 223, 226, 235, 236,
    259–262, 265, 269, 273, 287,
    310, 323–326, 333
Escher, T. 175, 179
e-science v, vi, xi, xiii, xiv, 4, 5, 13,
    18–25, 29, 30, 35–37, 40, 44,
    47, 50–57, 60–64, 67–69, 73,
    74, 78–80, 82, 84, 85, 87,
    90–93, 108–125, 147, 148, 150,
    152, 156–159, 163, 166, 167,
    178, 180, 181, 207, 208, 223,
    238, 240–244, 249–255, 259,
    264, 265, 266, 273, 274–276,
    279, 286–288, 309, 327, 330–
    335. See also e-research, e-social
    science, cyberscience.
e-social science v, vi, vii, xiii, 18, 22, 23,
    37, 41, 43, 46, 47, 50, 51, 54,
    57, 58, 73–76–85, 87, 109, 123,
    147, 148, 150, 156–158, 163,
    164, 167, 173, 177, 178, 241,
    244, 254, 266, 287, 291–293,

295, 304, 306, 329, 336. See also e-research, e-science, cyber-science.

European Association for Studies of Science and Technology 25

European Internet Archive 215

F

Faniel, I. 255
Farrington, J. 76, 90
Faulhaber, T. 166, 180
Faust, K. 163, 181
Feinberg, J. 247, 255
Feldman, R. 285, 288
Feldman, S. 67
Fergusson, D. 90
Fielding, N. 74, 89, 202, 240, 255
Finholt, T. A. 42, 52, 91, 107, 273, 288
Fiore, A. T. 183, 191, 202
Fischer, G. 307, 308
Fisher, D. 171, 180, 187, 189, 191, 202
Fitton, D. 89
Floyd, C. 294, 308
Foot, K. 21, 205, 207, 208, 220, 221, 316, 327, 330, 334
Ford, J. K. B. 158
Forte, M. 324, 327
Foster, I. 291,308
Foster, I. 25, 29
Fowler, R. 147–159
Fox, G. C. 52, 54, 67, 180, 207, 208, 220, 238, 255
France, A. 295, 308
Fraser, M. 58, 68, 75, 76, 89, 90
Freeman, C. 130, 145
Freeman, L. C. 165, 166, 179, 190, 201
French, A. 76, 89
Fridsma, D. B. 222, 224, 227
Fromerth, M. J. 261, 271
Fry, J. 18, 35, 37, 38, 50, 51, 52, 53, 55, 64, 68, 92, 93, 94, 103, 106, 107, 242, 243, 255, 327, 330
Furner, J. 218, 220

G

Gabriele, C. M. 158
Gaddis, B. 157–159
Gallop, J. R. 177, 179
Gann, D. 133, 146
Gannon, D. 147, 159
Garcia-Molina, H. 67
Garvey, W. D. 9, 11, 29, 230, 238
Gassmann, O. 136, 145
Gaver, W. 182, 201

Genoni, P. v, 19, 66, 91, 95, 107
Genoni, P. 19, 66, 91, 95, 101, 105, 107, 331
Gerndt, A. 180
Giaccardi, E. 307, 308
Gibbons, M. 59, 68, 94, 107, 167, 179
Gibson, C. 145
Glasner, P. 273, 288
Gleave, E. xiv, 21, 178, 182, 187, 189, 202, 331
Goble, C. 223, 238
Godlee, F. 15, 29
Goguen, J. 294, 308
Golder, S. 247, 255
Goldsmith, J. 281, 288
Gonsalves, A. 325, 327
González, V. 178, 179
Google ix, 10, 14, 26, 27, 28, 30, 31, 118, 140, 165, 173, 174, 175,
Gordon, G. 157–159
Graham, C. 89
Granovetter, M. S. 99, 102, 107, 193, 201
Graubard, S. 215, 220
Graves, S. 158, 159
Gray, J. H. 327
Greenberg, S. 202
Greene, M. A. 207, 220
Greenhalgh, C. 68, 76, 68, 89
Greenhouse, C. 256
Grethe, J. S. 238
Grid ix, x, 5–9, 23, 25, 28, 30, 41–44, 52, 55–58, 67, 68, 73–81, 86–94, 112–125, 147, 159, 180, 207, 208, 218, 220, 226, 238, 240–245, 249, 254, 255, 259, 266, 273, 274, 279, 291–308
Griffiths, R. 14, 28
Grimes, C. 131, 145
Grose, D. 75, 89
Gu, L. 188, 192, 201
Guglani, A. 118, 124

H

Hackett, E. J. 216, 220, 327
Hagemann, C. 16, 28
Hagstrom, W. 240, 255
Hahan, T. B. 69
Hahn, R. W. 287, 288
Halfpenny, P. v, 19, 46, 73, 83, 90, 331
Halkola, E. 233, 238
Hammersley, M. 294, 308
Hampton, K. 56, 68
Hargens, l. 92, 108

Harley, D. 12, 24, 29
Harman, J. R. 157–159
Harnett, B. H. 207, 221
Harris, R. 163, 166, 180
Hatcher, J. 265, 271
Hawkins, B. L. 94, 108
Hayes, M. 89
Haythornthwaite, C. 102, 108
Heath, C. 68, 89
Hecht, M. L. 205, 220
Heer, J. 174, 180
Heilkema, F. 76, 90
Hellsten, I. xiv, 327
Henry, P. D. 92, 108
Henty, M. 92, 108
Heok, K.H.A. 118, 125
Herring, S. . C. xiii, 315, 325, 326
Hert, P. 92, 108
Hewitt, T. 74, 89
Hewitt, T. 74, 89, 241, 247
Hey, A. See Hey, T.
Hey, T. 52, 54, 55, 57, 67, 68, 73, 90,
        110, 124, 177, 180, 207, 208,
        220, 222, 238, 240, 255, 273,
        288
Hilgartner, S. 224, 235, 238
Himelboim, I. 21, 182, 331
Hindmarsh, J. 68, 75,89, 90
Hinds, C. 273, 288
Hinds, P. J. 132, 145
Hine, C. 4, 6, 23, 24, 29, 44, 46,
        48, 52, 53, 56, 59, 60, 68, 69,
        110, 124, 125, 174, 180, 181,
        207, 220, 226, 238, 242, 243,
        255
History Flow project 21, 168, 169
Hitchcock, S. 263, 271
Hodge, G. M. 177, 180
Hofer, E.C. 255
Hoorens, S. 218, 220
Houghton, J. W. 92, 108
Huberman, B. A. 247, 255
Huerta, M. F. 287
Hughes, J. A. 294, 307
Hughes, L. 90
Hughes, T. 37, 52
Human Genome Project 4, 22, 228,
        278, 279
humanities 3, 6, 7, 11, 16, 19, 20, 23,
        24, 35, 36, 37, 38, 54, 55, 56,
        57, 58, 60, 61, 62, 63, 64, 66,
        67, 69, 65, 91–96, 98–101, 103,
        105–107, 116, 117, 120–123,
        205, 208, 215–219, 222, 243,

247, 310–312, 329. See also
        e-humanities.
Humble, J. 89
Hurd, J. M. 11, 29
Huston , P. 15, 29
Huttenlocher, D. 188, 201

I
Infocomm Development Authority of
        Singapore 111–113, 124
information communication technology
        (ICT) 56, 60, 61, 63, 92, 93–95,
        98, 101, 102, 105, 109, 110,
        111, 114, 121, 310, 311, 313,
        316, 323, 324, 326, 329, 332,
        335, 336
infrastructure 5, 6, 9, 20, 21, 25, 36,
        37, 41–45, 47, 48, 51, 54- 56,
        59, 65, 66, 73–87, 93–95, 103,
        110, 112–120, 122, 147–149,
        152, 184, 189, 217, 218, 222,
        233, 235, 242, 249, 253, 291,
        292, 298, 302, 306, 307, 324,
        326, 329, 330, 334, 336. See
        also cyberinfrstructure, e-infra-
        structure.
International Telecommunication Union
        ITU) 114, 124
Internet xiii, 3–9, 12–15, 18–21, 26,
        35, 37, 44, 46, 55, 56, 92, 101,
        109, 111, 114, 117, 118, 120,
        121, 163, 166, 168, 169, 172,
        177, 207, 208, 217, 218, 228,
        262, 263, 266, 267, 269, 270,
        273, 274, 281, 283, 285, 298,
        299, 311, 325, 331, 333, 334,
        336, . See also Internet Archive,
        Association of Internet Research-
        ers, Oxford Internet Institute.
Internet Archive 42, 45, 117, 207, 215,
        217, See also European Internet
        Archive

J
Jackson, S. J. 25, 28, 85, 89
Jackson, S.J. 89
Jaeger, E. 158
James, M. 238
Jankowski, N. W. v, xv, 5, 9, 29–30, 50,
        56, 68, 91, 93, 108, 119, 120,
        124, 125, 178, 222, 238, 331,
        332
Jarvenpaa, S. L. 131, 145, 146
Jeanneney, J.-N. 26, 30

Jefferson, T. 15, 29
Jeong, G.-J. 116, 124
Jewkes, J. 293, 308
Jie, W. 89
Jirotka, M. 40, 48, 52, 76, 89, 90, 241, 255, 288, 294, 308
Johns, P. 192, 201
Jones, M. 158
Jones, S. xiv, 56, 68, 208, 220

K

Kahle, B. 207, 220
Kalia, R. K. 147, 159
Kamins, D. 166, 180
Kanuka, H. 56, 67
Kanuka, H. 56, 67
Kapur, D. 133, 145
Karasti, H. A. 233, 238
Katz, R. 178, 180
Kaufmann, A. 133, 145
Keen, J. 88
Keiff, F. S. 287
Kerr, B. 247, 255
Kertcher, Z. 88
Kevles, D. J. 267, 271
Kewley, J. 68, 89
Kiesler, S. 133, 145
Kim, J. W. 131, 146
Kim, K. J. 133, 145
King, A. 228, 238
King, C. J. 12, 29
Kircz, J. 61, 68
Kirriemuir, J. 26, 30
Kitcher, P. 267, 271
Kitchin, D. R. 166, 179
Klein, M. 67
Kleinberg, J. 188, 201
Kling, R. 37, 52, 55, 69, 158, 228, 238, 327
Klischewski, R. 294, 308
Kluver, R. 125
KNAW. See Royal Netherlands Academy for Arts and Sciences
Knight, D. 76, 90
Knobel, C. P. 25, 28, 85, 89
Knorr-Cetina, K. 57, 69
Kobsa, A. 178, 179
Koh, W.T.H. 121, 124
Koku, E. 51, 52, 92, 100, 108
Kolata, G. 269, 271
Koslow, S. H. 287
Kuhlen, T. 180
Kuhn, T. S. 260, 271
Kuhn, W. 306, 308

Kyrillidou, M. 265, 271

L

Laaksonen, L. 110, 237
LaFrance, M. vii, 23, 310, 332
Laidlaw, D. 166, 180
Lan, X. 188, 201
Lane, J. 88
Lang, O. 180
Larsen, R. 311, 324, 326
Latour, B. 23, 24, 30, 311–317, 319, 321, 322, 327
Law, J. 327
Lawrence, S. 12, 29
Le Blanc, A. 74, 90
Lecher, H. E. 213, 220
Lehner, P. 133, 145
Leidner, D. E. 130, 145
Lengel, R. H. 132, 145
Lengwiler, M. 60, 68
Lenoir, T. 58, 69
Lento, T. vi, 21, 182, 188, 192, 193, 200, 201, 332
Lester, R. K. 143, 145
Levitt, R. 218, 220
Leydesdorff, L. 10, 30
Liberman, M. 201
Library of Congress 26, 42, 218
Lieberman, H. 308
Lievrouw, L. A. 56, 68
Limoges, C. 59, 68, 107, 179
Lin, N. 9, 29
Lin, Y.-W. v, 19, 73, 83, 89, 90, 332
Lloyd, A. 91, 108
Longino, H. 270, 272
Lucas, R. 22, 259, 332
Ludascher, B. 158
Lynch, M. 327
Lyon, S. 239

M

Macgregor, G. 247, 255
MacKenzie, D. 177, 180, 293, 308
MacMullen, W. J. 225, 238
Maloney, N. G. 148, 159
Mannerheim, J. 207, 220
Marciano, R. 302, 307
Maron, N. L. 12, 30
Marquis, S. 157–159
Martin, J. H. 201
Mascord, M. 90
Massanès, J. 216, 221
McAdam, D. 197, 201
McCarthy, M. 75, 90

McCulloch, E. 247, 255
McGowan, D. 282, 283, 288
McHale, J. 133, 145
McKim, G. 55, 69, 228, 238
Meadows, A. J. 91, 92, 108
Meadows, J. 91, 92, 107
MediaCommons 16
Meier, W. 69
Mellish, C. 76, 90
Merges, R. P. 278, 288
Merrick, H. v, 19, 66, 91, 95, 107, 333
Merton, R. 277, 278, 288
Messerschmidt, D. 67
Messina, P. 67
metadata See data.
Metz, E. 256
Meyer, C. 288
Meyer, E. T. 20, 147, 148, 159, 222, 333
Meyer, J. 52
Michael, M. 59, 68
Microsoft ix, 10, 21, 30, 171, 172, 175, 191, 192, 195, 226, 238, 282, 298, 299, 325, 327
Miettinen, R. 316, 327
Millen, D. R. 247, 255
Miller, K. 89
Miller-Rassulo, M. 205, 220
Mills, S. 90
Milton, R. 76, 90
Mineter, M. 302, 307
Ministry of Science and Technology (MOST) 114
Ministry of Trade and Industry (MTI) 110, 124
Ministry of Trade and Industry Singapore 110, 124
Mock, S. 158
Moe, K. 158, 159
Molina, A.H. 84, 90
Monge, P. 187, 201
Monkman, M. 16, 31
Moon, J. 120, 124
Moorman, D. 220, 237
Morris, L. 68, 89
Mrvar, A. 193, 201
Mumford, M. D. 157–159
Murray-Rust, P. 264, 272

N

Na, M. 125
Nadel, S. F. 185, 201
Nakano, A. 147, 159
Namioka, A. 307, 308

National Academies Press 14
National Centre for e-Social Science (NCeSS) xiii, xiv, 5, 6, 19, 28, 41, 43, 46, 73–88, 108, 158, 167, 266, 288, 331–335
National e-Science Centre (NeSC) 5, 25, 30, 266
National Institute of Health (NIH) 17, 153, 180, 225, 230, 233, 238, 264, 268, 269, 272
National Internet Development Agency of Korea (NIDA) 125
National Research Council (NRC) 222, 238
National Science Foundation (NSF) 5, 6, 28, 35, 42, 51, 67, 79, 89, 225, 236, 259, 271, 324, 326
Nazer, N. 51, 52, 92, 100, 108
Nebert D. 304, 308
Nelson, A. K. 206, 221
Nelson, M. R. 9, 31
Nelson, R. 278, 288
Nentwich, M. 4, 30, 37, 44, 52, 122, 125, 310, 327
Newman, H. B. 273, 288
Neyland, D. 59, 68
Nicolov, N. 201
Nissenbaum, H. 6, 30
Norman, D. A. 307, 308
Nowotny, H. 59, 68, 107, 179

O

O'Brien, J. 294, 307
O'Neil, M. 124
Ochsenbein, F. 203, 255
OeSS Project 5, 30, 50, 76, 77, 78, 333, 334
Office of Science and Technology 5
Olson, G. M. vi, 21, 107, 131, 145, 155, 158, 222, 225, 230, 237, 238, 239, 250, 255, 333, 337
Olson, J. S. vi, 21, 107, 131, 145, 155, 158, 222, 237, 238, 255, 333
Open Access Repositories (Open-DOAR) 18. See also open access, data repository.
open access vi, 16–18, 22, 26–29, 31, 44–46, 223, 259, 261, 263–265, 267, 268, 270–272, 274, 277, 280, 283–286, 332, 336
Orcutt, J. A. 273, 288
Orford, S. 163, 166, 180
Osborne, T. 252, 255
Ostriker, P. P. 67

Oxford Internet Institute (OII) xiii, 25, 29, 52, 255, 287, 330, 333, 334, 335
Oxford e-Social Science 50, 76, 333, 334

P
Pakhira, A. 147, 159
Park, H. W. v, 19, 109, 114, 120, 121, 125, 333
Parr, C. S. 223, 239
Pascoe, C. 92, 107
Paterno, F. 308
Paulsen, R. 197, 201
Pels, P. 267, 272
Peperkamp, B. 61, 67
Perring, T. 147, 159
Peters, S. 74, 90
Pickles, S. 74, 90
Pignotti, E. 76,89
Piore, M. J. 143, 145
Piper, T. 288
Piwowar, H. A. 222, 224, 227
Plale, B. 147, 159
Poh, K.W. 121, 124
Polzer, J. T. 131, 146
Portugali, J. 88
Poschen, M. 88
Preece, A. 76, 89
Price, M. 6, 30
Pridmore, T. 90
Prinz, W. 85, 90
Pritchard, J. 68, 89
Pritchard, S. M. 223, 239
Procter, R. v, 19, 52, 73, 83, 85, 88, 89, 90, 209, 220, 334
Public Library of Science (PLoS) 17
Publishing Research Consortium 16
Puetz, M. 238
Pundt, H. 231, 232, 239
Purdam, K. 241, 255

R
Raab, J. 197, 201
Rabeharisoa, V. 60, 68
Rahman, M. 288
Rai, A. K. 278, 284, 288
Ramachandran, R. 158, 159
Rascoff, M. 14, 28
Ratto, M. 327
Raymond, E. S. 325, 327
Rees, P. 88
Reeves, S. 68, 89
Reimersdahl, T. v. 180

Ribes, D. 225, 232, 239
Riley, B. 239
Rip, A. 59, 69
Robinson, S. 88
Rodden, T. 76, 89, 209, 220
Rogers, E. M. 84, 90
Rogers, R. 174, 180, 325, 327
Rose, E. 125
Roseman, M. 202
Rothenberg, J. 218, 220
Rouncefield, M. 89
Rouncefield, M. 294, 307
Rowland, F. 250, 255
Royal Netherlands Academy for Arts and Sciences (KNAW) xiv, 54, 60, 64, 65, 69, 333

S
Salaway, G. 12, 31
Salter, A. 133,146
Salvetti, F. 201
Sanders, L. 269, 270,
Sarker, S. 133, 146
Sastry, L. 147, 159
Saunders, B. 231, 236, 239
Sawers, D. 293, 308
Saxenian, A. 130, 146
Schaffer, D. 193, 202
Scharnhorst, A. xiv, 169, 180, 327
Schirski, M. 177, 180
Schlegel, D. 166, 180
Schmiede, R. 69
Schneider, S. M. vi, 16, 21, 31, 205, 207, 208, 220, 221, 316, 327, 334
Schroeder, R. xiii, 18, 35, 38, 44, 50, 51, 52, 76, 88, 89, 220, 237, 271, 324, 327, 333
Schuler, D. 307, 308
Schumann, N. 58, 69
Schurer, K. 67, 74, 89, 241, 245, 247, 254
Schutz, A. 247, 255
Schwartzman, S. 107, 179
science and technology 38, 46, 52, 53, 58, 59, 69, 107, 109, 113, 114, 121, 122, 179, 181, 220, 224, 237, 238, 288, 324. See also science and technology studies.
science technology medicine (STM) 13
science and technology studies (STS) 59, 60, 62–65
Scott, G. M. 157, 159
Scott, J. 185, 202

Scott, P. 107, 179
Second Life 11, 26, 30, 184
Sen, S. 247, 255
Shankar, K. 224, 238
Shaukat, M. 75, 90
Shekhar, S. 306, 308
Shepherd, J. 11, 30
Shimojo, F. 147, 159
Shinn, T. 59, 69
Shneiderman, B. 163–165, 171, 180,
    190, 191, 202
Shun-ichi, A. 273, 288
Siemens, R., 269, 272
Signoretta, P. 295, 308
Simmhan, Y. L. 147, 159
Singapore Internet Research Centre
    (SIRC) 117
Sismondo, S. 313, 327
SkyProject 22, 242–244, 246, 248–253
Slack, R. 293, 309
Smith, K. K. 12, 30
Smith, M.A. 21, 171, 178, 180, 182,
    183, 197, 188, 189, 191, 192,
    198, 201, 202, 334
Smith, S. W. 318, 326
Smithsonian 42
social network (networking) x, 6, 7, 11,
    12, 42, 82, 99, 100, 117, 163,
    165, 166, 174, 175, 182–186,
    190, 194, 196, 198, 215, 216,
    331–335
social science v, 3, 5, 6, 7, 11, 16, 18, 19,
    20, 23, 24, 35–39, 42–48, 50,
    54–62, 73–80, 88, 95, 101, 106,
    109, 116–123, 152, 163–167,
    171, 174, 177, 178, 182, 199,
    205, 208, 215, 216, 218, 219,
    222, 243, 245, 267, 273, 281,
    287, 291–294, 297, 304, 310–
    312, 331 See also e-social science.
Sonderegger, P. 20, 129, 334
Soon, C. 19, 109, 335
Spence, M. 44, 52, 273
Spence, R. 172, 180
Standish, R. 124
Star, S. L. 293, 294, 307
Steadman, P. 76, 88
Steed, A. 76, 90
Steele, C. 92, 108
Stewart, J. 293, 309
Stillerman, R. 293, 308
Stirling, A. 60, 69
Storper, M. 130, 146
Stowkowski, P. A. 205, 221

Strange, J. M. 157–159
Strathern, M. 241, 242, 250, 256
Strens, R. 294, 308
Stronks, E. 67
Suber, P. 268, 272
Subramanian, S. 239
Suchman, L. 293, 295, 308
Sun, Y. 91, 108
SurveyProject 22, 234, 242, 243, 245,
    246, 251, 253
Sutherland, I. 58, 69

T

Tatum, C. 23, 310, 335
Tavani, H. 287
Tayi. G.K. 118, 124
Taylor, J. M. 5, 25, 163, 180
Taylor, J. xiii
Teasley, S. 209, 221
Tennent, P. 89
Thatcher, J. B. 132, 145
Thelwall, M. vi, 20, 21, 120, 121, 125,
    163, 174, 177, 179, 180, 335
Thomas, N. 241, 256
Thompson, J. B. 13, 14, 26, 27, 31
Thompson, P. 240, 249, 255, 256
Tkach-Kawasaki, L. 120, 125
Todtling, F. 133, 145
Tolmie, P. 294, 307
Tomita, K. 9, 29
Townhend, P. 76, 89, 90
Townsend, R. B. 13, 14, 31
Trefethen, A. 54, 68, 73, 90, 177, 180,
    222, 232, 238, 240, 255, 288
Trigg, S. 95, 97, 108
Trow, M. 107, 179
Tufte, E. R. 172, 180, 190, 195, 199,
    202
Turner, A. 76, 89
Turner, T. 171, 172, 180, 191, 202
Tutt, D. 75, 90

U

Uhlir, P. 220, 237
University of California, Berkeley (UC
    Berkeley) 12, 17, 24, 26, 28, 29
Upson, C. 166, 180
Uram, T. D. 120, 125
Uszkoreit, H. 67

V

Van Alstyne, M. 252, 256
van Ark, T. 68, 89
Van der Mandele, M. 218, 220

Van Lente, H. 61, 69
Van Oranje, C. 218, 220
Van Selm, M. 9, 29
Vann, K. xiv, 45, 46, 53, 55, 69, 327
Vashishta, P. 147, 159
Vedder, A. 288
Venters, W. 147, 159
Venugopal, S. 25, 28,
Vickery, J. N. 234, 235, 238
Viégas, F. B. 169, 181, 198, 202
virtual
  organization 7, 9
  environment 54 75, 81, 132, 274,
    332, 334
  methods (research) 56, 81
  ethnography 329
  reality (world) 56, 58, 183, 186, 209
Virtual Cell 58
Virtual Knowledge Studio for the
  Humanities and Social Sciences
  (VKS) xiv, 7, 18, 54–55, 60, 63,
  69, 329, 331, 335, 337
visualization vi, ix, x, xi, 5, 7, 9, 10, 16,
  18, 20, 21, 25, 55, 58, 77, 80,
  119, 163–175, 177, 178, 182,
  183, 186–191, 193, 195–201,
  208, 235, 266
Voerman, G. 215, 221
Von Lohmann, F. 14, 31
Voss, A. v, 19, 73, 83–86, 89, 90, 335
Vroom, J. 166, 180

W
Wagner, D. 197, 201
Wajcman, J. 177, 180, 220, 293, 308,
  327
Waldrop, M. M. 16, 31, 85, 90,
Wallis, J. C. 222, 224, 237
Walsh, J. P. 148, 159
Walton, J. P. R. B. 177, 179
Ware, M. 16, 31
Warren, K. 256
Wasko, M. M. 132, 145
Wasserman, S. 163, 181
Wattenberg, M. 169, 181
Webb, C. 207, 220
Webometrics 20, 165
Weigand, G. 88
Weinberg, A. M. 4, 31
Weisband, S. 132, 145
Wellman, B. 51, 52, 92, 100, 108
Welser, H. 21, 171, 180, 182, 187, 188,
  189, 191, 196, 198, 200, 201,
  202, 336

Wesch, M. 26
Wessels, B. 23, 291, 293, 307, 309, 336
Whiting, J. 207, 220
Whitley, R. 62, 69
Wikipedia vii, ix, x, 21, 23, 26,
  168–170, 184, 186–188, 191,
  196, 197, 201, 251, 310–317,
  320–326, 332
Wiles, P. 301, 309
Wiley 264
Williams, R. V. 69
Williams, R. 293, 309
Williamson, T. 318, 326
Willinsky, J. 22, 31, 259, 260, 263,
  264, 269, 270, 272, 336
Willson, M. v, 19, 66, 91, 95, 107, 336
Wiseman, N. 163, 179
Wittenburg, P. 67
Wolensky, S. 209, 221
Wood, J. D. 177, 179
Woolgar, S. 23, 24, 30, 45, 59, 67, 51,
  53, 68, 74, 90, 311, 312, 313,
  314, 317, 319, 321, 322, 327
Wouters, P. xiv, 4, 7, 18, 21, 24, 31,
  53–56, 60, 62, 64, 69, 91–94,
  108, 110, 122, 125, 163, 167,
  181, 205, 237, 310, 324, 327,
  337
Wright, M. H. 67
Wu, B. 76, 89
Wu, H.J. P. 117–119, 123, 125
Wulf, V. 308
Wyatt, S. xiv, 24, 31, 219

X
Xie, Y. 76, 88
Xu, J. 76, 88, 89

Y
Yang, X. 89
Yerkie, J. 107, 158, 237
Yew, J. 107, 158, 237
Yoon, K. 114, 125
YouTube 11, 26, 187

Z
Zabusky, S. 241, 256
Zedtwitz, M. von 136, 145
Zheng, Y. 147, 159
Zhu, B. 163, 164, 181
Zimmerman, A. vi, xiv, 21, 107, 158,
  222, 224, 225, 230, 231, 237,
  238, 239, 255, 337
Zuo, Z. 202